CATHOLIC-JEWISH ENGAGEMENTS ON ISRAEL

JUDAISM AND CATHOLIC THEOLOGY

CATHOLIC-JEWISH ENGAGEMENTS ON ISRAEL

HOLY LAND, POLITICAL TERRITORY, OR THEOLOGICAL PROMISE?

EDITED BY
Gavin D'Costa, Bishop Etienne Vetö, CCN,
AND Thomas Joseph White, OP

CUA
THE CATHOLIC UNIVERSITY OF AMERICA PRESS
WASHINGTON, D.C.

Chapter nine of this book previously appeared in *First Things* (April, 2005).
It is reused with permission.

The paper used in this publication meets the minimum requirements
of American National Standards for Information Science—
Permanence of Paper for Printed Library Materials, ANSI Z39.48-1992.

∞

Cataloging-in-Publication Data is available from the Library of Congress

ISBN (paperback): 978-0-8132-3974-3 | ISBN (ebook): 978-0-8132-3975-0

Book design by Burt&Burt
Interior set with Meta Pro and Good Pro News Compressed

TABLE OF CONTENTS

SECTION 2: THE BIBLE/TANAKH ON THE LAND PROMISED TO THE JEWISH PEOPLE

SECTION 3: THE PEOPLES IN THE LAND: PALESTINIANS AND JEWS AND THE MEANING OF THE PROMISE

SECTION 4: THE THEOLOGY OF THE STATE UNDERLYING CATHOLIC AND JEWISH APPROACHES TO ISRAEL

SECTION 5: CRITIQUE OF THE THEOLOGICAL AFFIRMATION OF THE 'LAND,' 'PEOPLE,' AND 'ISRAEL'

INTRODUCTION: HOLY LAND, POLITICAL TERRITORY, OR THEOLOGICAL PROMISE?

JEWISH-CATHOLIC DIALOGUE ON ISRAEL

Gavin D'Costa, Bishop Etienne Vetö, CCN, and Fr. Thomas Joseph White, OP

This volume arises from a conference in Rome in 2021, sponsored by the Thomistic Institute, Pontifical University of St. Thomas Aquinas, Rome, and the Bea Centre, Pontifical Gregorian University, Rome. Special thanks to Molly Egilsrud and Rev Dr Jackson Johnson for their administrative help. Some contributors were unable to be present due to the Covid crisis, but we have retained their contributions.[1] All writers revised their work in the light of the conference and the courteous and challenging exchanges that took place.

Terminologically in this introduction we use the term 'Jews' to designate both biblical Jews and those Jews today who derive from rabbinical Judaism. We use 'Tanakh' to designate the scripture of the Jewish people. We use 'the land' to designate the biblical land of the Jews, which in the Bible has different territorial boundaries. We use 'Israel' to designate this land today, without prejudice to the disputed territories and claims of Palestinian groups to a state called Palestine. We use 'the State of Israel' to designate the democratic political collective that have power in contemporary Israel. Regarding 'Catholics,' we use the term to designate Roman Catholic Christians.[2] The

1 This explains the slightly uneven number of texts in sections 1–2.

2 Due to circumstances, we replaced one Catholic contribution with an Anglican Palestinian contribution (Yazid Said), but his arguments cut across denominational lines and his essay is

Catholic Bible includes Hebrew Scripture or the 'Old Testament' and the 'New Testament.' Although the Tanakh and Old Testament are a 'shared' scripture, we should recall the Tanakh and the Old Testament contain different books in differing order, and are read by two interpretative traditions that have been characterized by hostility toward each other.

The overall goal of our volume is to address a single question: what, if any, is the theological significance of the emergence of Israel in 1948? Is it political territory or in some sense a holy land or a theological promise that is yet to be realized or one that is taking place? Or none of these? Or perhaps more than one? Since 1967, the majority of religious Jews have slowly become united in affirming a theological significance to the events of 1948—not without substantial differences between them. Since 1965, after the Second Vatican Council, this question has been on the horizon of the Catholic theological agenda but not properly addressed. This volume is a landmark in Catholics addressing the question in the company of Jews who both express their own views about the matter as well as raise questions to their Catholic colleagues.

There are four ways in which we approached our task to provide a volume that would have multiple forms of usage. First, we set out to explore different Catholic views of Israel after Vatican II. Second, we look at different religious Jewish views of Israel. Secular Jewish Zionism does not feature in the discussion. Third, we set these Catholic and Jewish insights out in parallel so that the reader can contrast and compare the different approaches and learn from their overlap, oversights, contrasts, and irreconcilable elements. This format is designed to generate further discussion for Catholics and Jews. We requested a very brief interjection after each main section, by either a Jewish or Catholic scholar, to help the reader begin their own journey of reflection. These reactions are not meant as formal scholarly overviews. The fourth way was to break down the different components of this question, initially looking at the whole (opening section), and then separately as parts that make up the whole (sections 2–5). The component parts, for both Jews and Catholics, are the Bible; traditions of interpretation of the Bible; voices of authority within the tradition; the phenomenon of Israel in 1948 including the tragic situation of the Palestinian people; and what to make of Israel in 1948 in light of the Bible, traditions of interpretation, and voices of authority. This is a schema that does not presume commonality and smothering of otherness, but one that will allow both religions to learn from and sometimes challenge each other.

---

ground breaking in terms of a Palestinian Christian voice.

For Catholics, the plot line leading to the question is asymmetrical to the Jewish plot line. For most of Catholic history the Jewish dispersion from the land has been understood, in the teachings of Catholic theologians, as a punishment for deicide and the Jewish rejection of their own messiah. Augustine and Aquinas are significant—and nuanced and complex—in formulating and passing on this tradition. The Holy See was initially uncomfortable about a Jewish state in the nineteenth and twentieth centuries for a host of reasons. In 1947, the See accepted the UN Partition Plan but campaigned hard for international jurisdiction for Jerusalem and the holy places. It was not until 1993 that Israel was formally acknowledged with the exchange of diplomats and the signing of a Fundamental Agreement, forty-five years after the State of Israel was founded.

The theological plot line goes back to the Second Vatican Council. Two important Catholic Conciliar documents from this Council—*Lumen Gentium* 16 (1964) and *Nostra Aetate* 4 (1965)—have put the Jewish people and their 'irrevocable' (Rom 11:29) covenantal promises center-stage. However, *Nostra Aetate*, the first official Catholic statement on the Jewish people, had to be explicitly unrelated to geopolitical Israel so that the theological concerns of the Council fathers could not be misunderstood. The Catholic Church did not want the statement on the Jews to be construed as support for Israel in the Middle East. It was concerned to address the deicide charge against the Jews that was seen to fan the flames of anti-Jewish sentiment, leading to antisemitism and its political consequences.[3] To achieve this, the Church was keen to emphasize its 'spiritual' concerns, and not any temporal geopolitical advocacy. Otherwise, the declaration would not have been promulgated.[4] *Nostra Aetate* used the term 'spiritual' [*spiritualite*] three times in no. 4 to underline this. This had a theological rationale.

Even so the document faced opposition from many Arab countries and Eastern Christians who viewed it as siding with, or implicitly siding with, Israel in the Middle East. There was also minor opposition from 'traditionalist' Catholic groups who felt the Council was reversing previous magisterial

3 See Norman C. Tobias, *Jewish Conscience of the Church: Jules Isaac and the Second Vatican Council* (Palgrave MacMillan, 2017).

4 See the story of this travail in Giovanni Miccoli, "Two Sensitive Issues: Religious Freedom and the Jews," in *History of Vatican II, vol. 4: Church as Communion: Third Period and Intersession, September 1964–September 1965*, ed. Giuseppe Alberigo and Joseph A. Komonchak (Orbis Books, 2003); John M. Oesterreicher, "Declaration on the Relationship of the Church to Non-Christian Religions," in *Commentary on the Documents of Vatican II, vol. 3: Declaration on the Relationship of the Church to the Non-Christian Religions: Dogmatic Constitution on Divine Revelation: Decree on the Apostolate of the Laity*, ed. Herbert Vorgrimler (Burns and Oates, 1969), 1–136.

teachings.[5] The European and American bishops pushed hard against these currents, although none would probably envisage this political question of the land eventually requiring theological attention. The final vote for the document showed a deep consensus: 2,221 votes in favor, and 88 against. The specially appointed Commission for Religious Relations with the Jews was founded in 1974 to implement the Council's teachings.[6] Relations with the new State of Israel after 1948 was conducted by the Secretary of State, as per all international diplomatic relations with nation-states. However, there was no formal recognition of Israel through the Secretary of State until 1993, under the pontificate of Pope John Paul II.[7]

During Pope John Paul II's pontificate, the relationship with the Jewish people moved forward with vigor, taking up the Council teachings and building upon them.[8] In 1980 the pope noted that there remains, in the eyes of the Catholic Church, a fundamental identity through time of biblical Jews with post-biblical and contemporary rabbinic Jews.[9] In 1993 the Fundamental Agreement between Israel and the Holy See was signed.[10] From 1980, the Church had to take contemporary Jewish self-understanding seriously as a datum that related to Paul's view of the 'irrevocable' gifts and promises made to the Jewish people. Romans 11:29 has been cited in every significant document on the Jewish people since 1964. In 2015, the Commission for Religious Relations with the Jews published a document with this title: "'The Gifts and the Calling of God Are Irrevocable' (Rom 11:29): A Reflection on Theological Questions Pertaining to Catholic-Jewish Relations on the Occasion of the 50th Anniversary of *Nostra Aetate* (no. 4)." The public launch of that document included Rabbi David Rosen, a contributor to this book. Rosen said

5 This is best represented by Marcel Lefebvre, *I Accuse the Council!*, trans. Jaime Pazat de Lys, 2nd ed. (Angelus Press, 1998).

6 See its own self-description at christianunity.va/content/unitacristiani/en/commissione-per-i-rapporti-religiosi-con-l-ebraismo/commissione-per-i-rapporti-religiosi-con-l-ebraismo-crre/en.html.

7 David Rosen, "Israel-Vatican Relations since the Signing of the Fundamental Agreement," in *The Vatican-Israel Accords: Political, Legal, Theological Contexts*, ed. Marshall J. Breger (University of Notre Dame Press, 2004), 167–82. See also Leonard Hammer, "Discerning Israel's Interpretation of the 1993 Holy See-Israel Fundamental Agreement," in Breger, 67–96.

8 See David Dalin and Matthew Levering, eds., *John Paul II and the Jewish People: A Christian-Jewish Dialogue* (Rowman and Littlefield, 2007).

9 John Paul II, "Address to Representatives of the West German Jewish Community," 1980; available at ccjr.us/dialogika-resources/documents-and-statements/roman-catholic/pope-john-paul-ii/jp2-80nov17; and Yehezkel Landau et al., *John Paul II in the Holy Land: In His Own Words. With Christian and Jewish Perspectives* (Paulist Press, 2005).

10 See Breger (ed.), *The Vatican-Israel Accords*, and esp. Leonard Hammer, "The Holy See-PLO Agreement and Its Significance for Israel," in ibid., 150–67.

of the document: "Perhaps then I may be permitted . . . to point out that to fully respect Jewish self-understanding, it is also necessary to appreciate the centrality that the land of Israel plays in the historic and contemporary religious life of the Jewish People, and that appears to be missing [from 'Gifts']."[11] It was the first time that a rabbi shared the stage with Catholics at a Vatican press conference. His question is now being addressed in this volume.

From the Jewish side, the narrative about the land is understandably quite different. The promise of the land starts with Abraham and since, in St. Paul's words, it is irrevocable, the promise will continue forever. This promise is a deeply twinned theme in the shared Bible, whereby the gift of the land is part of God's promise to the people so that they may serve God faithfully and be a light to the nations. After the third exile (*galut*) of the Jewish people from the land, the biblical, rabbinic, and liturgical traditions continued to embed the desire to return and dwell in the land. The return would allow for all *mitzvot* to be fulfilled, although the rabbis had begun to reflect on living outside the land with continued fidelity. There are different voices in the rabbinic tradition regarding how the gift of the land will be given and received.[12] Many of these differences constitute the disagreements between the Jewish contributors.

It is well known that in the eighteenth century, when Jewish Zionism emerged, it was secular Jews and Bible-based Christians that championed the cause of Zionism—while most religious Jews were deeply suspicious.[13] It took the 1967 war to shift that position so that today most religious Jews

11 See Commission for Religious Relations with the Jews, "'The Gifts and the Calling of God Are Irrevocable' (Rom 11:29): A Reflection on Theological Questions Pertaining to Catholic-Jewish Relations on the Occasion of the 50th Anniversary of *Nostra Aetate* (No. 4)," December 10, 2015, available at https://www.christianunity.va/content/unitacristiani/en/commissione-per-i-rapporti-religiosi-con-l-ebraismo/commissione-per-i-rapporti-religiosi-con-l-ebraismo-crre/documenti-della-commissione/en.html (hereafter "Gifts"); and Rosen, "Israel-Vatican Relations." See other Jewish voices on this topic: Walter Würzburger and R. J. Zvi Werblowsky, "Land, People and Nation in Jewish Perspective," in International Catholic-Jewish Liaison Committee, *Fifteen Years of Catholic-Jewish Dialogue 1970–1985: Selected Papers* (Libreria Editrice Vaticana, 1988), 3–8; Rabbi Henry Siegman, "A Decade of Catholic-Jewish Relations—A Reassessment," *Journal of Ecumenical Studies* 15 (1978): 243–60, who after *Guidelines* writes: "the failure of the Vatican Guidelines to deal with the theological dimension of the Jewish relationship to the land of Israel constitutes a grievous omission. Within the context of the document's own declared desire to understand Jews as they understand themselves, it must be faulted for failing to spell out to Catholics that in the year 1975 it is impossible to understand Jews, nor can anyone communicate meaningfully with them about their deepest fears or aspirations, without an appreciation of the role of the State of Israel in Jewish consciousness" (251). All three cited participated as Jewish representatives in the International Liaison Committee with the Catholic Church.

12 See Lawrence A. Hoffman, ed., *The Land of Israel: Jewish Perspectives* (University of Notre Dame Press, 1986).

13 David Novak, *Zionism and Judaism: A New Theory* (Cambridge University Press, 2015), chap. 3.

are Zionists in some form or another. There is a spectrum of opinions on almost any single point—including the view of the Palestinians within religious Zionism. Most of the Jewish contributors to this volume are concerned with gaining justice for the Palestinians and are sensitive to the tragedy of homelessness caused by the formation of Israel in 1948. The question for religious Jews is adapting the traditions to advance a framework to address the contemporary question. Another form of religious Zionism, not found in this volume, seeks to remove all Palestinians from greater Israel and embrace what is seen as the gift to the Jewish people.[14] Two observations should be made. First, even when a Jewish voice was recruited to speak critically of this project, they did so from within a Jewish religious Zionist paradigm. Second, nearly all our participants asked whether this gift, central to the covenant, is understood as revoked in Catholic eyes within a post-supersessionist theology.

The Catholics contributing to this volume believe that the land question needs addressing.[15] The dialogue has reached a certain maturity where controversial topics require attention. All Catholic contributors have one thing in common: they express radically different levels of theological support for Israel, never in the sense of a nation-state, but for the people living in the land—with justice for the Palestinians. Their support for the people and the land promise takes varying forms and different paths: from the principled agnostic (the land promise cannot be denied, it cannot be affirmed—Rastoin); to natural law being invoked to support Israel, recognizing that there might be a slim bridge to a theological rationale (White); to the biblical promises being transformed, but not erasing the promises to the Jewish people (D'Costa, Wright, Anderson). In this process, the Catholics address questions regarding the Bible, tradition, the teachings of the magisterium, the Palestinian people, and differing forms of Jewish Zionism and their complex relationship to Catholic theology.

The Jewish participants in this volume represent a similar broad consensus, with inevitably differently-shaped contours. Ever since the Council, Jewish organizations have been actively involved in dialogue with the Vatican, informally at first, but eventually formally—amidst many continuing personal friendships. Since the Catholic Church works through the organs of the Holy See, it called upon multiple Jewish groups to establish a single

14 See Karma Ben-Johanan, *Jacob's Younger Brother: Christian-Jewish Relations after Vatican II* (Harvard University Press, 2022), 194–229.

15 A previous conference just for Catholic theologians had started this process. See Gavin D'Costa and Faydra Shapiro, eds., *Contemporary Catholic Approaches to the People, Land, and State of Israel* (The Catholic University of America Press, 2021).

Jewish organisation to advance this dialogue. Since 1990 the International Jewish Committee on Interreligious Consultations (IJCIC) is the official Jewish representative to the Holy See's Commission for Religious Relations with the Jews. IJCIC member organizations include the American Jewish Committee, Anti-Defamation League, B'nai B'rith International, Central Conference of American Rabbis, Israel Jewish Council on Interreligious Relations, Rabbinical Assembly, Rabbinical Council of America, Union for Reform Judaism, Union of Orthodox Jewish Congregations of America, United Synagogue of Conservative Judaism, and World Jewish Congress. Dialogue with the Chief Rabbinate of Israel was a later fruit of Pope John Paul II, after he met with both Chief Rabbis in Jerusalem in March 2000. The first meeting of the Chief Rabbinate and the Holy See was organized in 2002 in Jerusalem, and since then such meetings have been conducted annually, alternately taking place in Rome and Jerusalem.

The Jewish writers in this volume are concerned that the Catholic Church had not addressed this question, although all of them are cognizant of the complex reasons for not yet doing so. Some explicitly address what they see as Catholic mixed messages and ask for clarification. All of the main papers set out their case for differing forms of Jewish religious Zionism, ranging from a deep reserve in supporting religious Zionism because of the injustices against the Palestinian peoples (Meyer), to seeing the resources for addressing this very problem within the Jewish religious tradition (Meyer, Ahrens, Novak, Rosen, Korn, Moss), to questioning whether secular Jewish Zionism has a plausible case (Novak, Korn), and in confirming that the Bible and rabbinic tradition stand behind the people, the land—and in very different ways, the state. This is done while registering important demands and restraints on the Jewish people in the land. The nation-state is seen as a contingent but necessary part of upholding the promise. This is a profound difference between Catholics and Jews, but one that generates grey areas which are helpfully explored in different essays. The other significant difference can be found in the handling of the Old Testament and Tanakh texts. Most of the Jewish scholars read these unambiguously, even if differently, but most of the Catholic scholars are confronted with further layers of interpretative questions (the New Testament, tradition, and the magisterium). Same text perhaps, but different hermeneutic and interpretative traditions pertinently raise the question regarding whether 'same' is applicable.

The question about the land promise in this volume is broken into distinct elements so that the analysis and proposals can be far-reaching and make a substantial contribution to scholarship. Below we outline the sections and the chapters to help the reader negotiate the collection. We begin with opening reflections from Archbishop Bruno Forte and a response from the

Jewish scholar, Karma Ben-Johanan. Forte contextualizes the land promise question within the larger whole of the advancing of Jewish-Catholic relations since Vatican II. His choice of a Jewish document to do this is telling. It marks Catholics relating to the 'Other' in their own terms and as they see themselves. Forte pushes this point when it comes to the land question, both, seemingly recognizing and affirming Jewish Zionist forms of theology, while also overwriting these Christologically—in Christians seeing in Israel, the beginnings of a transformation that will reach over the entire earth.

If Forte's position holds these two points in tension, Karma Ben-Johanan's response to him questions the possibility of this balancing act. She raises two haunting questions. Can Catholics really see and affirm the Jewish Other and not colonize Jewish experiences and views? She wonders if this is the asymmetric problematic in the entire conversation: that Christians see Judaism as part of their own identity; whereas Jews view Christianity as genuinely Other. Ben-Johanan pushes Forte to clarify: is his affirmation of the land promise related to the future alone and thus to Christianized Jews when, as Paul hopes, they will once more be included when the full number of gentiles "come in" (Rom 11:25), and then the eschaton begins? And if not, is Forte supporting Jews and Israel per se and the land and people that are a historical reality since 1948? If the former, Jews are once more instrumental to serving Catholic theological ends and not given attention in their own right.

In the first section we begin with overarching positive arguments that lead to forms of Jewish and Catholic affirmations of the land and people of Israel, drawing on the distinct traditions of each community. There is a Jewish theological defense of religious Zionism presented by Rabbi David Novak, and a more textual (biblical, and rabbinic and modern) defense of religious Zionism from Rabbi Jehoschua Ahrens. Novak builds his case from a metaphysical viewpoint: God's election. He views this operating in four stages. God chooses to create the world and the universe. He then freely chooses to create a relationship between Himself and all humans. When humans try and choose their own power and rule, rather than God's, when they try to overthrow genuine human freedom to relate to God, the covenant between God and humans is in trouble. God then elects the Jewish people to restore the covenant, not because of any inherent superiority, nor as a condemnation of other peoples. This choice is the way God chooses in the Torah. This relationship is eventually destined to be enjoyed by all peoples and nations. Finally, for a people to have a coherent polity, rather than fracture into individualism, a land is given by God, so that his people may serve and praise God and be a light to the nations. Novak argues this gift does not preclude others in the land or another nation within the gifted land. Novak proposes that since Christians accept the 'Old Testament' as revelation, they too could and should accept this theology of the land.

Ahrens explores the biblical and rabbinic tradition to show the central place of the land, even after the destruction of the Temple and the dispersal of Jews in the second century. While acknowledging minority rabbinic dissenting voices, the overwhelming weight of the tradition, right up until the present day, affirms in different ways that the land was given to the people as a gift from God. Ahrens is clear that this is a gift that makes demands from the Jewish people to live according to God's commands. He also explores the place for the Palestinian people within this scheme. He shows a large middle ground.

Gavin D'Costa advances a position that he calls minimalist Catholic Zionism which views the creation of Israel in 1948 as part of God's irrevocable promise to His beloved people, the Jews. D'Costa bases his argument on scripture and the recent teachings of the Catholic magisterium. He argues that a fulfillment theology can uphold the irrevocable gift of the land to the people found throughout the Old Testament. This gift, while unconditional, also imposes conditions on the Jewish people. This gift is not annulled or cancelled in the New Testament; rather, it gains a Christological dimension that is of course unacceptable to Jewish worldviews. D'Costa argues that this affirmation of the land and people can be applied to Israel in 1948, but without certainty that this is the beginning of the end days, or a sure eschatological sign. It may be such an event, but on biblical grounds it cannot be ascertained with certainty. D'Costa then addresses some objections to his proposal from a Catholic and Jewish viewpoint.

Each subsequent section looks at one aspect of the multifaceted arguments presented in these opening pieces. In the second section, we turn to what is most important for both traditions: the biblical sources which are shared, but with the New Testament raising questions about the reading of the 'Old.' The post-biblical sources are sometimes fuel to the fire of mistrust and mischaracterization, but for both traditions they are vital. Two Catholic scholars begin the exploration.

William Wright faces the key Catholic biblical hermeneutical question regarding the land promised to the Jewish people in the Old Testament. Is that promise still 'valid' in the light of the New Testament? He faces this question through inspecting the hermeneutical procedure in a 2001 Pontifical Biblical Commission document that addresses the land issue. Wright proposes a new hermeneutical approach, questioning the helpfulness of employing the notion of the *sensus plenior* within a historical critical framework. The fit is uncomfortable. Instead, he suggests employing the metaphysics of *res*, the reality designated in the Old Testament text has signification but that which is signified is still transformed, but not erased or replaced, in the reality of Christ. The resurrection offers a pivotal analogy. The body, like the land in our question, is still retained and intact—and thus continuous, but it is also discontinuous as it is a transformed heavenly body (and thus a transformed land). The gift of the land to the Jewish people need not be denied, but its meaning and significance will be different for Christians as it is Christologically interpreted.

Gary Anderson advances a case for a form of Catholic Zionism. Either Catholics can deal with Israel purely on a geopolitical level, thereby ignoring the theological dimension, or they can recognize that Israel is a theological issue. Anderson maps two forks in the road. The first leads to a supersessionist position like that of Augustine, who viewed the loss of the land as a punishment for rejecting the messiah. Anderson says that option is no longer possible. The other alternative is often viewed as siding with evangelical Christian Zionism: unconditional and politically right-wing support of Israel, all construed within an eschatological scenario that has already begun. Anderson carves out an alternative, one might say a form of minimalist Catholic Zionism (he does not use these terms) that affirms the land of Israel as part of God's love and promise to his people. Anderson allows for the possibility of a messianic dimension but refuses any certainty on this matter. His position is like that of D'Costa's. Finally, Anderson draws on Jewish sources stemming from Genesis 12 and employed by Uriel Simon (a Jewish thinker), to show that the Jewish striving for peace and justice, and thus partitioning and sharing the land, is expected of the Jewish people. Anderson puts the biblical perspective at the center and negotiates complex challenges by using these biblical resources.

Rabbi David Rosen shows how deeply embedded within Jewish identity is God's promise of the land. The Bible, prayer life, and the rabbinic tradition all testify to this. Most helpfully, Rosen, himself a key person involved in negotiations between Israel and the Holy See, outlines the terrain of contemporary Israeli politics and its religious dimensions. This is vital to understanding the transmission, and sometimes perversion, of the biblical tradition. Rosen shows the historical shifts from a middle-ground religious Zionism, which always held a place for the Palestinians—to a more aggressive and militant Zionism in tandem with the rise of the Likud party. Rosen ends with a plea for Christians to address the question of the land, as it is so deeply central to Jewish identity.

In the third section, we face another stumbling block to a theological affirmation of the land and people from either a Catholic or Jewish perspective. To put it starkly: Jewish celebration (Yom Ha'atzmaut, Independence Day) is a Palestinian disaster (*Nakba*—the catastrophe). For Palestinian

Christians, Christian Zionists and Jewish Zionists write out of history the Palestinian people into homelessness and landless wandering. There is an obvious irony and reversal of narratives. This challenge is faced head on.

In Rev. Yazid Said, an Anglican Palestinian priest, we have a unique voice that is ground-breaking in the literature. Said recognizes the Old Testament biblical promises related to Israel and honors them. This is rare in the literature from Palestinian theologians, but Said cannot fully affirm that the promises apply to present-day Israel in the context of the oppression of the Palestinian people. Said is critical of various Palestinian liberation theologies for their methodology and replacement theology; following Archbishop Rowan Williams, he steers a middle course between secular views and nationalist, aggessive religious views. Said carefully shows that his own views are very close to Meyer's, a Jewish contributor in this volume.

Rabbi Eugene Korn faces the issue of the Palestinians from a religious Zionist perspective and explores the considerable biblical and rabbinic resources available to work toward a peaceable settlement with the Palestinians (Muslim and Christian) communities living in the land. He rejects the ultra-nationalist religious Zionists as failing to be resourceful and as freezing the tradition within rabbinic times, thereby delivering a blunt and problematic answer to the complex contemporary political troubles. Korn is tough in stating his criticism of Christian Palestinians, arguing that their position is almost uniformly supersessionist/replacement theology. It is a point agreed with by Said, although Said is critical of Korn. Korn acknowledges the tension between the religious view he advances which strives for peace and the deconstruction of the on-the-ground bitterness and distrust between Jews and Palestinians. We see in Korn what is found in every Jewish contribution to this volume: a desire to resolve the Palestinian question justly, but also recognizing the tragic near impossibility of this hope.

In the fourth section we turn to the theology of state underlying Catholic and Jewish approaches to the land promise. Fr. Thomas Joseph White argues for subtle but enduring support of Israel as a nation-state based on Catholic traditions of natural law. He analyses the Fundamental Agreement of 1993 reached between the Holy See and the State of Israel in terms of natural law principles and shows these to be robust and helpful for affirming Israel's right to exist, for allowing space for theological views on this matter, and for accommodating Palestinian claims to a just and peaceful settlement and for their nationhood. White argues that Catholic theological affirmation of the land gifted to Israel in the Old Testament cannot be a stable solution either theologically or politically: theologically, because it is disputed amongst Catholic theologians and does not have the tradition or the New Testament clearly supporting such a proposal; and politically, because it introduces a factor more likely to inflame some parties and cause complacency in others. White does consider a theological approach, deriving from *Nostra Aetate*, which allows the land to be seen as fitting rather than as necessary. But he argues that the natural law theological affirmation best delivers what is required.

The Jewish contribution is equally subtle and complex. Yonatan Moss's piece begins with reflections of the two essays of the next section—which indicate how the essays in this collection are closely interconnected. Moss then turns to the minority tradition of interpreting the biblical obligations as "you shall love the *gēr*, for you were *gērîm* in the land of Egypt" (Dt 10:19), and "you shall not wrong or oppress the *gēr*, for you were *gērîm* in the land of Egypt" (Ex 22:20). These texts are important as these injunctions can only be fulfilled in a political and demographic situation of majority and minority populations. The state needs to exist in order to have a demographic situation where Jews are a majority living together with a minority population as envisaged by the Bible. Moss then draws on the Egyptian-Iraqi luminary, Rabbi Saadia Gaon (882–942), who as academy head, prolific writer, and community leader, had a long-lasting effect on medieval Judaism. Saadia's interpretation of how these commands are to be fulfilled are applied to the Palestinians by Moss, rendering *gērîm* as minority populations, not strangers. This tradition provides religious justification for a Jewish state to be accountable for the welfare of the Palestinians.

We also wanted to register concerns with the entire project, and included these critiques as part of the debate. Two very nuanced and careful presentations attain this goal in the fifth section. Rabbi David Meyer argues for a halakhic route to sharing the land based on a nuanced reading of Meir Simkha HaCohen of Dvinsk (1843–1926). Meyer uses Meir Simkha's reading regarding the gifting of something that does not properly belong to the receiver, to analogically apply it to negotiating the land to the Palestinians—to seek peace on the land. This halakhic reading undercuts the intrinsic holiness of the land for something higher, the holiness of God's Torah, but without reducing or instrumentalizing the land. Meyer's argument is aimed to make the most ardent religious Jewish Zionist reconsider, not that the land is not part of God's gift to his people, but rather that this gift can and should justifiably be shared. The registering of this halakhic position admittedly sits within a type of Jewish Zionism, but Meyer seeks to reconfigure it on grounds that are deeply traditional and persuasive to fellow Jews. It was perhaps telling that the objections to Jewish religious Zionism were within the parameters of tentatively accepting Jewish religious Zionism.

Catholic Marc Rastoin argues an elegant case, based on both Jewish and Christian sources, on why the settling of the Jewish people on the land in

1948 cannot, with any certainty, be affirmed as the fulfillment of the promise. Neither can it be denied. Rastoin negotiates a path of not knowing and a path of not grasping, that which is finally and theologically a gift. He develops his argument noticing how, in his view, contemporary Jewish Zionists have become like Catholics prior to Vatican II: assuming the right to have worldly power based on religious truth. While Catholics have moved to a position more akin to Jews in their dispersal from Israel, where they recognize their voice to be one amongst many in the public square and must negotiate social power (if they have any at all), many Jews in Israel are moving in the opposite direction. Rastoin suggests that we could learn from each other's histories and be restrained in our theological claims. In this Catholic view, we ironically find not a refusal of the position that the land is gifted from God to the Jewish people, but a problematizing of everything that seems associated with that claim. Thus, we cannot affirm or deny it.

This volume will help Catholics and Jews to theologically reflect on the land promise: political territory, or holy land, or theological promise? Catholics have only begun this process. Jews have done so since Abraham.

1

BETWEEN JERUSALEM AND ROME

SOME REFLECTIONS FROM A CATHOLIC POINT OF VIEW ABOUT THE DECLARATION ADOPTED IN MARCH 2016 BY THE CONFERENCE OF EUROPEAN RABBIS, THE RABBINICAL COUNCIL OF AMERICA, AND THE CHIEF RABBINATE OF ISRAEL

Archbishop Bruno Forte

A STATEMENT OF HISTORICAL SIGNIFICANCE

The declaration "Between Jerusalem and Rome" is an important contemporary Jewish Orthodox reflection on the relationship between Judaism and Christianity, prepared in the context of the fiftieth anniversary of *Nostra Aetate*, the declaration of Vatican II which transformed the attitude of the Roman Catholic Church toward other world religions, and particularly toward Judaism. Dated on Rosh Chodesh Adar I, 5776 (February 10, 2016), this document was adopted in March 2016 by the Conference of European Rabbis and the Executive Committee of the Rabbinical Council of America and presented to Pope Francis on August 31, 2017, by a delegation of the three most relevant rabbinic international institutions, namely the Conference of European Rabbis, the Chief Rabbinate of Israel, and the Rabbinical Council of America.[1]

1 See also the Orthodox Rabbinic Statement on Christianity published by the Center for Jewish-Christian Understanding and Cooperation (CJCUC) in 2015, *To Do the Will of Our Father in Heaven:*

It is with every good reason that the approval of the text and its presentation to the bishop of Rome can be defined as an historical event: for the first time the international Orthodox Rabbinate has provided a unified reflection on the theme of dialogue with the Catholic Church (not only in reference to the conciliar text *Nostra Aetate*, but also to the entire development of relations with the Jewish world, which the text had itself initiated and promoted), and has wanted to present the document to the pope, in the spirit that the declaration itself affirms: "Despite the irreconcilable theological differences, we Jews view Catholics as our partners, close allies, friends and brothers in our mutual quest for a better world blessed with peace, social justice and security."

In welcoming this important delegation, Pope Francis highlighted that in "our shared journey, by the graciousness of the Most High, we are presently experiencing a fruitful moment of dialogue," attested to in a significant way by the document "Between Jerusalem and Rome." The pope observed that the text

> pays particular tribute to the Second Vatican Council's Declaration *Nostra Aetate*, whose fourth chapter represents the 'Magna Carta' of our dialogue with the Jewish world. Indeed, the ongoing implementation of the Council's Declaration has enabled our relations to become increasingly friendly and fraternal. *Nostra Aetate* noted that the origins of the Christian faith are to be found, in accordance with the divine mystery of salvation, in the Patriarchs, in Moses, and in the Prophets. It also stated that, given the great spiritual heritage we hold in common, every effort must be made to foster reciprocal knowledge and respect, above all through biblical studies and fraternal discussions (cf. no. 4).

It is thanks to this new climate that over the last decades Jews and Christians have been able to draw increasingly closer, "in an effective and fruitful dialogue," deepening their mutual understanding and intensifying their "bonds of friendship." While undoubtedly Pope Francis has also recognized that "the Statement *Between Jerusalem and Rome* does not hide the theological differences that exist between our faith traditions," he has nonetheless highlighted that "it expresses a firm resolve to collaborate more closely, now and in the future." In brief, the declaration represents a step forward from which we cannot retreat; rather, we can only go forward with renewed momentum in our shared search and our relations based on mutual

Toward a Partnership between Jews and Christians, initially signed by over twenty-five prominent Orthodox rabbis in Israel, United States, and Europe, and that now has over sixty signatories.

respect and fraternal closeness in obedience to the love of the Eternal One for all his children.

BIBLICAL-THEOLOGICAL CONTENTS OF THE DECLARATION

The declaration comprises a preamble and three parts, which I would like to outline and reflect upon from a theological point of view and from the perspective of Christian-Catholic practice. The *Preamble* recalls the biblical foundations of the particular mission of the Jewish people with respect to humanity. Starting from the biblical narrative of creation, according to which "God fashions a single human being as the progenitor of all humanity," the declaration sustains the fundamental principles underlying all possible forms of encounter and dialogue between individuals and human groups: "The Bible's unmistakable message is that all human beings are members of a single family. And after the deluge of Noah, this message is reinforced when the new phase of history is once again inaugurated by a single family. In the beginning, God's providence is exercised over a universal, undifferentiated humanity."

It is within this universal design of divine providence that we locate the election of the patriarchs Abraham, Isaac, and Jacob, to whom the Eternal One entrusts the mission "to found the nation of Israel that would inherit, settle and establish a model society in the holy, promised land of Israel, all while serving as a source of light for all mankind." Through innumerable trials, the Eternal One always manifested His fidelity to Israel, at the time of the exile as well as throughout the succession of innumerable persecutions, until the darkest moment—defined by John Paul II when referring to Nazism as the "absolute evil"—"when six million of our brethren were viciously murdered and the embers of their bones were smoldering in the shadows of the Nazi crematoria."

Yet, at that very same time, "God's eternal covenant was once again manifest, as the remnants of Israel gathered their strength and enacted a miraculous reawakening of Jewish consciousness. Communities were reestablished throughout the Diaspora, and many Jews responded to the clarion call to return to Eretz Yisrael, where a sovereign Jewish state arose." It is in this very context of rebirth that the two duties of the Jewish people toward humanity have emerged more clearly: "to be a light unto the nations" (Is 49:6) and "to secure its own future despite the world's hatred and violence." As a confirmation of this dual task, the declaration recalls that "the Jewish nation has bequeathed many blessings upon mankind, both in the realms of the sciences, culture, philosophy, literature, technology and commerce, as well as in the realms of faith, spirituality, ethics and morality," recognizing in this "a manifestation of God's eternal covenant with the Jewish people."

The Shoah undoubtedly represents the historical "nadir" of the sufferings of the Jewish people. In this regard, the declaration makes a series of affirmations that come very close to what the Catholic Church sustained in the document *Memory and Reconciliation: The Church and the Faults of the Past*, issued by the International Theological Commission to accompany the request for pardon made by Pope John Paul II on the occasion of the Jubilee of the year 2000, recognizing without hesitation the responsibility of Christians in history. The Shoah, this document states, was certainly the result of the pagan ideology that was Nazism, animated by a merciless antisemitism that not only despised the faith of the Jewish people, but also denied their very human dignity. Nevertheless, "it may be asked whether the Nazi persecution of the Jews was not made easier by the anti-Jewish prejudices imbedded in some Christian minds and hearts . . . Did Christians give every possible assistance to those being persecuted, and in particular to the persecuted Jews?"[2] There is no doubt that there were many Christians who risked their lives to save and to help their Jewish neighbors. It seems, however, also true that "alongside such courageous men and women, the spiritual resistance and concrete action of other Christians was not that which might have been expected from Christ's followers." This fact constitutes a call to the consciences of all Christians today, so as to require "an act of repentance (*teshuva*)," and to be a stimulus to increase efforts to be "transformed by renewal of your mind" (Rom 12:2), as well as to keep a "moral and religious memory" of the injury inflicted on the Jews.[3]

We could mention here how the declaration *Between Jerusalem and Rome* is also the fruit of the courageous act of repentance of John Paul II, who already as a young priest had not hesitated to defy Nazi barbarism by saving the lives of a number of Jewish people, and who throughout the course of his long life had maintained special relationships of friendship and esteem with not merely a few Jewish people. We could discern in all this a providential closeness between Jews and Christians in reacting to the "absolute evil": the sufferings endured during the Shoah were followed not only by the birth of the State of Israel and the new life of the Jewish nation in the territory linked to the history of the patriarchs and the prophets, but

2 See the document by the Commission for Religious Relations with the Jews, *We Remember: A Reflection on the Shoah* (March 16, 1998), no. 5.

3 The document, entitled *Memory and Reconciliation: The Church and the Faults of the Past* was discussed and approved in its definitive form during the session of the Commission held from November 29 to December 3, 1999; available at vatican.va. The cited text is at point 5.4.

also by the growing understanding of the Christian people of the unbearable weight of the "absolute evil" and of the necessary ensuing consequence that emerges in view of a new relationship of respect, love, friendship, and cooperation with the children of Israel.

A "TURNAROUND"

The declaration recognizes *Nostra Aetate* as a genuine "turnaround": "Fifty years ago, twenty years after the Shoah, with its declaration *Nostra Aetate* (no. 4), the Catholic Church began a process of introspection that increasingly led to any hostility toward Jews being expurgated from Church doctrine, enabling trust and confidence to grow between our respective faith communities." In this context "the courageous role" played by Pope John XXIII is acknowledged, not only "in rescuing Jews during the Holocaust," but also in overcoming that "teaching of contempt" that had caused so much harm in the relationship of Christians with their Jewish brothers. The declaration makes a decisive affirmation in this regard of the value of the contribution of the Second Vatican Council: "In its most focused, concrete, and, for the Church, most dramatic assertion, *Nostra Aetate* recognized that any Jew who was not directly and personally involved in the Crucifixion did not bear any responsibility for it."

Rightly, then, and with a refined understanding of the developments in Catholic theology on the matter, the declaration mentions that which for believers in Christ is the foundation of the irrevocable uniqueness of the Jewish people in the history of salvation: "Basing itself on Christian Scriptures, *Nostra Aetate* asserted that the Divine election of Israel, which it calls the gift of God, will not be revoked, stating, God . . . does not repent of the gifts He makes or of the calls He issues." There is then a citation from a text of Pope Francis—a great friend of the Jewish people—in the Apostolic Exhortation *Evangelii Gaudium:* "God continues to work among the people of the Old Covenant and to bring forth treasures of wisdom which flow from their encounter with his word" (249). Thus it follows that the bond that the Church recognizes with Israel on the basis of divine election is unique, and so strong, that the document of the Commission for Religious Relations with the Jews published on the occasion of the fiftieth anniversary of the declaration *Nostra Aetate* (December 10, 2015) does not hesitate to affirm: "The dialogue with Judaism occupies a unique position for Christians; Christianity is by its roots connected with Judaism as with no other religion. Therefore the Jewish-Christian dialogue can only with reservations be termed interreligious dialogue in the true sense of the expression; one could however speak of a kind of intra-religious or intra-familial dialogue *sui generis*."[4]

Thus, "the Catholic Church neither conducts nor supports any specific institutional mission work directed toward Jews,"[5] toward whom instead it is possible and dutiful to seek a *shared path toward full reconciliation,* recognizing that this will pertain to a time that the God of the promise has reserved for us all. This clarification immediately frees us of reckless expectations: leaving aside any possible individual spiritual journeys, which correspond to the particular designs of the Eternal One for each of us, Israel and the Church are called to walk unmingled, even if inseparable, toward the final wholeness to be undertaken by the Lord, in that eschatological 'shalom' which is the object of the messianic hope of both peoples. The idea of "reconciliation along the way" thus definitively overcomes any theory of substitution, according to which the Church had taken the place of Israel in the divine plan of salvation: it is Paul himself who alerts us to the risk of thwarting what he terms the "mystery" (Rom 11:25) upon which basis Israel remains the witness of the election and the promises of God and with its faith constitutes for the Church "the holy root" (see Rom 11:16, 18) upon which it is grafted and from which it will never be possible to be separated.

Therefore, for Christian theology, in the unity of the economy of salvation there is Israel, the people of the covenant that has never been revoked, and there is the Church, the people established by the covenant of Christ's blood: there is a single salvific design, but different covenants, from that with Noah to that with Abraham and the patriarchs, from the Mosaic covenant to that established by the death and resurrection of Lord Jesus. There is a single fundamental structure of the relationship effected through revelation, but different phases and forms of economy. In this light, one well understands the words of the prayer of Pope John Paul II at the Western Wall in Jerusalem, quoted in the declaration *From Jerusalem to Rome*: "God of our fathers, You chose Abraham and his descendants to bring your Name to the Nations. We are deeply saddened by the behavior of those who in the course of history have caused these children of yours to suffer, and asking your forgiveness we wish to commit ourselves to genuine brotherhood with the people of the Covenant." As the declaration observes, "these welcoming attitudes and actions stand in stark contrast with centuries of teachings of contempt and of pervasive hostility, and herald a most encouraging chapter in an epic process of societal transformation."

4 "Gifts," 20.

5 "Gifts," 40.

THE "LAND": A RELEVANT THEME, ONLY HINTED AT

The theme of the "land" is almost absent from the declaration,[6] despite its relevance for the faith and history of Israel, as well as for the Christian faith. The Hebrew term *eretz* (land) is so important that it occupies the fourth place in order of recurrence in the First Testament (2,504 times). Its meanings are many: if the land is in general a gift from the Creator to the creature, the land of Israel is the one promised to Abraham together with his descendants (see Gn 12:1–2, Dt 26:1–3). Marked by the touch of God, the promised land will bear the traces of His passage, as Jacob observes: "Certainly, the Lord is in this place and I did not know it" (Gn 28:6). It is a land where milk and honey flow (Ex 3:8), a land promised to the fathers (Ex 6:41), a condition of free life fully realized in obedience to the Most High: not just a land free from a foreign dominion, but the land on which the chosen people will have to live free from the bonds of sin and firm in fidelity to the covenant that binds them to God.

Symbol of the Lord's generous and free gift, this land is also a constant reminder of a task to be lived: it is inseparably promise, grace, and vocation! Ownership of the land itself will be conditioned on fidelity to the covenant (Dt 4:1–2, 8:9–18), so that Israel may be effectively the people of God (4:20). In this sense, the promised land is an objective to be conquered over and over again, and this will happen if the people are docile to the will of God (Jos 1:6–9). Precisely so, the promised land is kept in the memory and desire of the chosen people, it becomes the symbol and the seal of the covenant with God and represents the deposit of the hope of Israel. *Eretz Israel* is, above all, the object of the yearning of the people chosen from among the peoples, as these beautiful verses by Yehudah Ha-Lewi, Jewish poet of the eleventh century, make clear: "If I had wings, I could fly to you, O Jerusalem, when I grow up distance . . . Your stones give me pleasure, your dust I honor. The air of your country is real life for our soul."[7]

The Holy Land is, then, *the symbol and the seal of Israel's covenant with God*, as André Neher writes: "The Zohar wants *Eretz* to be the *ketubah*, the marriage contract of God and Israel, and we feel how much this image tends to make the presence of the land material and immutable in the Jewish

6 There is a hint in the *Preamble*: "When God chose Abraham, and, subsequently, Isaac and Jacob, he entrusted them with a double mission: to found the nation of Israel which would inherit, settle and establish a model of society in the holy promised land of Israel, and at the same time serve as a source of light for all humanity." At the end of the same *Preamble* it is stated: "After the Shoah, finally, Jewish emancipation in the diaspora, as well as the right of the Jewish people to live as a sovereign nation in their own land, have been accepted as obvious and natural facts."

7 Quoted in Abraham Joshua Heschel, *Moral Grandeur and Spiritual Audacity* (Farrar, Straus and Giroux, 1996), chap. 5.

religious economy."[8] Finally, the promised land is for the people chosen by God the *deposit of their hope*: as Abraham Joshua Heschel writes, "the Jew in whose heart the love of Zion is extinguished is condemned to lose his faith in the God of Abraham, who gave the earth as a pledge for the redemption of all men."[9] Therefore, "for the Jews the land of Israel represents their home, their hope, everything they have. It is not only the memory or our past that bind us to the earth: it is our hope and our future."[10] The faith of Israel considers the Holy Land "the place where the divine plan of history can reveal its original and unique meaning. It was sanctified by the words of the prophets, by the sufferings of an entire people, by the tears and supplications of millennia of history, by the toil and dedication of the pioneers. This holiness is precious in the eyes of God, vital for the people, light for history."[11]

This "theology of the land" is founded in the memory of the wonders accomplished by God in the history of the salvation of His people: thus, for example, as happened when they came out of slavery in Egypt, even the entrance into the promised land is the fruit of the divine initiative and the crossing of the Jordan near Jericho traces the events of the exodus and the crossing of the Red Sea. Once reached and inhabited, then, the promised land will have to be defended by faith: thus, the walls of Jericho will collapse not by the strength of military art, but by a solemn liturgy lasting for seven days, in which the protagonist will be the Ark of the covenant (Jos 3:1). If therefore it was faith that brought down the walls of the city of Jericho (Heb 11:30), it will be the lack of faith that creates an impediment to the conquest and lasting possession of the land. This is why enjoying the promised land will be inseparable from the "new heart" with which the people will inhabit it, and the tragedy of exile will be a consequence of infidelity to the gift received. Moreover, the bitter experience of slavery experienced will push the chosen people to a new and richer understanding of the meaning of the promised land.

The land in which God wants to live will be recognized in the human heart renewed by the breath of the Spirit:

8 André Neher, *Chiavi per l'ebraismo* (Marietti, 1988), 67. On this theme of the "land" according to the Jewish understanding see the valuable work of Alain Marchadour and David Neuhaus, *La Terra, la Bibbia e la storia* (Jaca Book, 2007).

9 See Heschel, *Moral Grandeur and Spiritual Audacity*, chap. 5.

10 Abraham Joshua Heschel, *Israele eco di eternità* (Queriniana, 1977), 61; translated as *Israel: An Echo of Eternity* (Farrar, Straus and Giroux, 1967).

11 Ibid., 111.

> I will give you a new heart, I will put a new spirit within you, I will take away from you the heart of stone and I will give you a heart of flesh. I will put my spirit within you and I will make you live according to my statutes and I will make you observe and put my laws into practice. You shall live in the land that I gave to your fathers; you shall be my people and I will be your God. (Ezek 36:26–28)

In this light, the return to the land of Israel will become a sign and an anticipation of the return to the land that the prophets see taking place in the distant future and which will affect the whole of humanity. From this perspective, the announcement of the beatitudes will move, according to which it will be the meek who "will inherit the earth" (Mt 5:5). Moreover, Jesus will flee from any attempt to reduce the hope of the kingdom to a political and military expectation: those who are sent by him must be witnesses of His resurrection to the ends of the earth (Acts 1:6–8).

The eschatological gathering, predicted by the prophets, is not for Jesus only the gathering of Israel in the land of the fathers, because all the children of God will be gathered in the unity of the Father and the Son through His redemptive death on the cross and new life at Easter. With the ascension into heaven, the Son of Man will abandon the present earth to lead the new people to the definitive land, which will no longer have any differentiation from heaven. Thus, in the perspective of the Christian faith, the journey of human beings together with God in this world will be wedded in the fulfillment of the eschatological promise with the journey of God, who from heaven will descend to earth and from this will return to heaven, opening the way to the final exodus. Also for Christians, therefore, the Holy Land will have a particular value and meaning: the land of the patriarchs and prophets, the land of the chosen people which—according to Paul—is the "holy root" of the Christian tree (Rom 11:16–18), the privileged land where the history of salvation for all has been realized.

It is in the Holy Land that Jesus was born, lived and worked, and it was from there that His disciples left to announce His resurrection to the world. Faith in him is not addressed to an abstract God, far from human events, but to the God who entered history, who spoke to the saints and prophets and became flesh in the fullness of time. Christianity is not the religion of salvation from history, but of the salvation of history, of a salvation, that is, which passes through the intimately connected events and words in which divine self-communication took place. This is why the land where the history of revelation took place is of absolute importance for the faith of Christ's disciples: it is precisely this land that make us understand in the richest and most profound way what God wanted to tell us about himself, helping us to enter His language and to savor in depth the words and events of His revelation. The stones of the Holy Land nourish the faith of the children of God: evoking the similarity that runs in Hebrew between the terms *eben* (stone) and *ben* (son), Jesus will not hesitate to affirm: "I tell you that God is able from these stones to raise up children to Abraham" (Mt 3:9).

TOWARD A NEW FUTURE

It is in the light of these premises that the declaration delineates an "evaluation and reevaluation" of the state of relations between Judaism and Christianity. Acknowledging honestly a certain initial skepticism "due to the long history of Christian anti-Judaism," the text observes that "over time, it has become clear that the transformations in the Church's attitudes and teachings are not only sincere but also increasingly profound." Particular attention is reserved for the work of the Bilateral Commission between the Chief Rabbinate of Israel and the Holy See: over the course of thirteen meetings, with the venue alternating yearly between Rome and Jerusalem, it has been able to effectively highlight shared values while respecting differences.

An evaluation of the journey undertaken is expressed in these terms: "We, both Catholics and Jews, acknowledge that this fraternity cannot sweep away our doctrinal differences; it does, rather, reinforce genuine mutual positive dispositions toward fundamental values that we share, including but not limited to reverence of the Hebrew Bible." The theological differences are stated with honesty, and could be summarized in the formula coined by Shalom Ben Chorin: "The faith of Jesus unites us, but the faith in Jesus separates us." Notwithstanding this profound difference, the declaration observes that "some of Judaism's highest authorities have asserted that Christians maintain a special status because they worship the Creator of Heaven and Earth Who liberated the people of Israel from Egyptian bondage and Who exercises providence over all creation."

The declaration then continues with a decisive affirmation also for the future: "However, doctrinal differences and our inability to truly understand the meaning and mysteries of each other's faiths do not and may not stand in the way of our peaceful collaboration for the betterment of our shared world and the lives of the children of Noah. To further this end, it is crucial that our faith communities continue to encounter, grow acquainted with, and earn each other's trust." The "road forward" is traced thus: the text recognizes that the great mission of the Jewish people "to be a light unto the nations," thus "contributing to humanity's appreciation for holiness, morality and piety," and offering an antidote to rising secularization, often not exempt from forms of ideological secularism.

In this light, one can perceive how Christians and Jews share the task of taking their distance from both secularism and religious extremism: "We therefore—states the Document—seek the partnership of the Catholic community in particular, and other faith communities in general, to assure the future of religious freedom, to foster the moral principles of our faiths, particularly the sanctity of life and the significance of the traditional family, and to cultivate the moral and religious conscience of society." In brief, both Jews and Christians have the common duty to bear witness to the Eternal One before humanity against any negation or false appropriation of His name, which is holy and blessed.

The reference to the violence inspired today by forms of insane religious fundamentalism—"facing many Christians in the Middle East and elsewhere they are persecuted and menaced by violence and death at the hands of those who invoke God's Name in vain through violence and terror"—is translated into an appeal of Orthodox Judaism to the Catholic Church "to join us in deepening our combat against our generation's new barbarism, namely the radical offshoots of Islam, which endanger our global society and does not spare the very numerous moderate Muslims. It threatens world peace in general and the Christian and Jewish communities in particular. We call on all people of good will to join forces to fight this evil."

The patrimony of faith, shared by Catholics and Jews, is well capable of sustaining this common commitment at the service of all humanity: in offering an example of this shared patrimony, the text cites the recognition of the divine origin of the Torah, the idea of final redemption, "the affirmation that religions must use moral behavior and religious education—not war, coercion, or social pressure—to influence and inspire." Purifying consciousness from every form of antisemitism thus offers a contribution to progress in the quality of life of all humanity: and it is precisely here that the declaration makes a profound and significant acknowledgment to the Catholic Church: "We call upon all Christian denominations that have not yet done so to follow the example of the Catholic Church and excise antisemitism from their liturgy and doctrines, to end the active mission to Jews, and to work toward a better world hand-in-hand with us, the Jewish people."

The final aspiration is moreover poignant as it evokes the calls of the biblical prophets, yet no less Jesus's words on the mount:

> We seek to deepen our dialogue and partnership with the Church in order to foster our mutual understanding and to advance the goals outlined above. We seek to find additional ways that will enable us, together, to

> improve the world: to go in God's ways, feed the hungry and dress the naked, give joy to widows and orphans, refuge to the persecuted and the oppressed, and thus merit His blessings.

Obedience to the Eternal One and love for all His creatures are thus the ultimate reason for which the journey in dialogue between Jerusalem and Rome must go ahead, open to the surprises of the Eternal One and nurtured by the sincere yearning for the faithful obedience of Jews and Christians to His will. In this way too, both Jews and Christians will together obey the command of the Eternal One: "Shemà Israel, Adonai Elohenu, Adonai Echad."

2

RESPONSE TO ARCHBISHOP FORTE

Karma Ben-Johanan

I am deeply honored to enter into conversation with Prof. Forte, whose immense contribution to Jewish-Christian dialogue I have been following over many years. I would like to state, from the outset, that though I am Jewish myself, I do not have the pretense to speak here as a representative of the Jewish community. I am participating in this insightful conversation as a scholar with a profound interest in the remarkable transformative strength of the Jewish-Christian relationship, and in the determination of both the Jewish and the Christian communities to better their relations while also maintaining their faithfulness and sense of continuity with their respective traditions.

Archbishop Forte's paper provides a splendid example of the nature of the transformation of Jewish-Christian relations in choosing, as the topic of his lecture, the relatively recent Jewish Orthodox declaration on Jewish-Christian relations, "Between Jerusalem and Rome." This declaration in itself responds to previous Catholic initiatives, and first and foremost to *Nostra Aetate* 4. Yet *Nostra Aetate*, as we know, is itself in correspondence with Jewish interlocutors and experiences, so that we have in front of us a Catholic voice responding to Jewish voices responding to Catholic voices responding to Jewish voices, an evolving tradition of dialogue.

"Between Jerusalem and Rome" testifies to the fact that the Jewish-Orthodox community recognizes the gravity of the shift that had come about in the Catholic Church's approach to Jews and Judaism. At the core of the Jewish Orthodox declaration, one finds a careful balancing between, on the one hand, identifying Christians as central partners to the Jewish mission of amending the world, and, on the other, evoking the unbridgeable doctrinal differences between Judaism and Christianity. Prof. Forte affirms the Jewish Orthodox emphasis on difference in stating that "Israel and the Church are called to walk unmingled, even if inseparable, toward the final wholeness to be undertaken by the Lord, in that eschatological 'shalom' which is the object of the messianic hope of both peoples."

Nevertheless, while respecting difference, Catholics have also often expressed the Church's deeply felt conviction that Judaism is not exactly an external partner to Christianity, but one that is intimately connected to the Church herself. In Prof. Forte's text, this conviction is especially present in the citation he brings from 2015's "Gifts," stating that "the Jewish-Christian dialogue can only with reservations be termed interreligious dialogue in the true sense of the expression; one could however speak of a kind of intra-religious or intra-familial dialogue sui generis." Indeed, the fourth section of *Nostra Aetate* begins with stating that thinking about the Jewish people means, for the Church, "searching its own mystery," and John Paul II affirms that "the Jewish religion is not 'extrinsic' to us, but in a certain way is 'intrinsic' to our own religion."

This, it seems to me, is at the heart of the Jewish-Christian asymmetry; while Jews tend to define Christianity as another religion, Christians tend to define Judaism as a fundamental yet somewhat inchoate form of Christianity. The Christian dialectical perception of Jews and Judaism as both self and Other is rooted, of course, in the Christian identification of the story of Israel as encapsulated in the Hebrew Bible both as the history of the Jews and as the history of the Church, the two belonging, in different ways, to the category of "Israel." The biblical narratives therefore reveal at one and the same time information about God's dealings with the Jewish people, while also pointing beyond the particularity of the Jews to the horizon of a universal faith community. As part of the Church's post-*Nostra* theology, Catholic theologians and Church officials began to see these two components not as either or, not as replacing one another in the progress of history (with the Christ event as the supersession's junction), but rather as complimentary, which means that the Bible speaks to both Jews and Christians and about both Jews and Christians in their "unmingled" status through history. The central concept, invoked by John Paul II, of the "never-revoked" covenant between God and the Jewish people implies that the dawning of Christianity did not make the ways in which contemporary Jews uphold the covenant obsolete.

This dialectic perception of the biblical "Israel"—extended to the present people of Israel through the concept of covenantal irrevocability—seems to be of utmost importance for the question of the theological meaning of the land of Israel, too. Is the doctrinal importance that contemporary Judaism attaches to the land of Israel a locus of "significant doctrinal differences" between Jews and Catholics, or rather, it has an "intrinsic" Catholic theological meaning? Does the affirmation of the irrevocability of the Jewish covenant with God include the land of Israel?

Prof. Forte begins his sensitive engagement with this uneasy question with affirming the special place that the land of Israel occupies in Jewish consciousness in the Hebrew Bible, to eminent Jewish authors such as Yehudah Halevi, the Zohar, as well as to modern thinkers such as Andre Neher and Avraham Yehoshua Heschel.

In the second stage, he ties together the Jewish memory of the biblical past in the land of Israel with the eschatological future: "enjoying the promised land," Prof. Forte says, "will be inseparable from the 'new heart' with which the people will inhabit it, and the tragedy of exile will be a consequence of infidelity to the gift received." Additionally: "the return to the land of Israel will become a sign and an anticipation of the return to the land that the prophets see taking place in the distant future and which will affect the whole of humanity."

The repeated use of the future tense by Prof. Forte raises an important question about the theological status of the present: does the current history of Jews—their gathering in large numbers in the Holy Land / the land of Israel / Palestine (clearly it is not even possible to agree on the place's name), and the foundation and continuous existence of the State of Israel (with all its difficulties), pertain to the covenantal history of the Jewish people, considering the place of the land within the biblical concept of the covenant? If so, would Prof. Forte say that the current history of Jews in the land is a fulfillment, even a partial one, of those prophetic verses which he cites? Or rather, would he say that this history is itself a sign of the eschatological future? If this is the case, does the current reality in the land of Israel anticipate a future conversion of Jews, even if one avoids any attempt to hasten this point in time? To phrase it differently, is the particular relationship between the Jews (after Christ) and the land important only for its future "abandonment" for the sake of a more "definitive land, which will no longer have any differentiation from heaven"? And if Catholic theology cannot affirm a theological meaning to the current history of Jews in the land, would it not entail that Jewish history is merely a parenthesis, a time in which the Jewish branches are broken off from that good olive tree, awaiting their final regrafting?

On the other hand, is it not the case that a non-supersessionist view which affirms the continuous, present particularity of the relationship between the Jews and the land necessarily entails a discriminative attitude toward other non-Jewish inhabitants of the land, and a biased approach to the Israeli-Palestinian conflict?

These questions seem to me impossible to answer, yet impossible not to attend to, precisely due to the growing Catholic conviction that the Judaism which is internal to the Church's identity is not only Old Testament Judaism, but has something to do with the post-Christian Jewish history. This makes the concreteness of the land of Israel, and the particularity of the Jewish interpretation of the Hebrew scriptures, important for Christianity not only in a metaphorical or eschatological way.

On the other hand, an attempt to answer these questions—which are of course far from being consensually answered among Jews—may entail also making judgments and prioritizing certain Jewish perceptions and lifestyles to others. It might even mean entering into the murky waters of evaluating contemporary Jewish behavior in terms of sin and docility to God's will. How would Jews (who see Christians as 'others') feel about such decisive Catholic evaluations of their own history, for better or worse?

The question of the land thus penetrates directly into the heart of the Jewish-Christian complexity. The fact, however, that we can discuss these things together, in the here and now, is already a piece of heaven.

3

BRIEF RESPONSE

Archbishop Bruno Forte

I thank Prof. Karma Ben-Johanan for her cordial response to my presentation. It seems to me that she has grasped in depth the spirit of my intervention and has enriched my contribution with relevant reflections. Prof. Ben-Johanan has also put a central question: "Does the affirmation of the irrevocability of the Jewish covenant with God include the land of Israel?"

My answer to the question is: yes, and no! Yes, because the promised land is a constitutive part of the covenant between the Lord and Israel, and in this sense the return of the Jews to the land of the promise is a true eschatological sign and a witness of God's fidelity to the covenant. No, because Israel has always given witness in history to the fulfillment of the Eternal One's promises, even during the times of the diaspora and the tragedy of the Shoah, when the promised land seemed only to be a dream and an unrealized hope. The conversion of Israel to the Lord, then, is that which every believer—in the Jewish people and in the Christian church—must continually carry out in order to correspond to the covenant of love with the living God and which must be fully fulfilled for all in the time of the eschaton.

Also, in this sense, *Nostra Aetate* has stressed the Jewish roots of Christianity: the fourth section of this declaration helps us to understand that the relationship with Judaism has to be seen as the catalyst for the determination of the relationship with the other world religions. The Jewish faith is not for Christians another religion, but the foundation of their own faith, although clearly the figure of Jesus is the key for the Christian interpretation of the Old Testament.

That is why the dialogue with Judaism occupies a unique position for Christians and can only with reservations be termed interreligious dialogue in the true sense of the expression; one could better speak of a kind of intra-religious or intra-familial dialogue. In his address in the Roman Synagogue on April 13, 1986, Pope John Paul II expressed this situation in these words: "The Jewish religion is not 'extrinsic' to us but in a certain way is 'intrinsic' to our own religion. With Judaism therefore we have a relationship which we do not have with any other religion. You are our dearly beloved brothers and, in a certain way, it could be said that you are our elder brothers."

This special condition is expressed by the apostle Paul by saying that Israel is the holy root of the Christian tree. And the land, where this tree is rooted, is holy for both, Jews and Christians, sign and anticipation of the eschatological land, where God will be all in all.

SECTION 1

THE OVERALL CASE FOR A POSITIVE THEOLOGY OF THE LAND AND PEOPLE OF ISRAEL

4

THE CASE FOR A CATHOLIC THEOLOGICAL AFFIRMATION OF THE LAND AND PEOPLE OF ISRAEL

Gavin D'Costa

I will initially present a brief case for a Catholic theological affirmation of Israel.[1] I will then defend my position from some objections in the form of questions and answers.

THE CASE FOR A CATHOLIC THEOLOGICAL AFFIRMATION OF ISRAEL

At Vatican II, the documents *Lumen Gentium* 16 and *Nostra Aetate* 4 insisted that the Jewish covenant made by God to his people, the Jewish people, is irrevocable—drawing on Romans 11:29. That text refers to biblical Judaism.[2] In 1980, Pope Saint John Paul II took the further step of identifying the biblical Judaism of *Nostra Aetate* not only with the Church's own roots, but also with post-biblical rabbinic Judaism, the basis for modern contemporary Judaisms.[3] Thus, the pope highlighted that contemporary Judaisms are seen

1 A full version of my position is found in Gavin D'Costa, *Catholic Doctrines on the Jewish People after Vatican II* (Oxford University Press, 2019). Minor sections of the material of this paper draw on Gavin D'Costa, "Catholic Zionism," *First Things* (January 2008): 14–19. See also the range of Catholic views on this matter in Gavin D'Costa and Faydra Shapiro, eds., *Contemporary Catholic Approaches to the People, Land, and State of Israel* (The Catholic University of America Press, 2022).

2 I outline the Council and its teachings in Gavin D'Costa, *Vatican II: Catholic Doctrines on Jews and Muslims* (Oxford University Press, 2014), chap. 3.

3 See ccjr.us/dialogika-resources/documents-and-statements/roman-catholic/pope-john-paul-ii/jp2-80nov17.

as in covenant relationship with God for the gifts, promises and callings made by God to the Jews are irrevocable. What does God's irrevocable covenant mean regarding those specific promises and gifts—specifically the 'land promise' to the Jewish nation? Is that particular gift still valid?; and if it is, can it be applied to the re-emergence of Israel in 1948?

Addressing this question in a tense Middle East is very difficult: Muslims and Jews all have a stake in the answer. God's revelation demands justice and peace, and it also has a relation to the land promise. Given the focus of my argument, I cannot attend fully to the importance of the Palestinian claims to the land—which I see as legitimate and compatible with the argument advanced here. I support the Holy See's Fundamental Agreement of 2000 with the Palestinian Liberation Organization and the subsequent recognition of a Palestinian State by the Holy See in 2015. The Holy See draws upon the 1947 UN Partition Plan as its starting point for both 'Israel' and 'Palestine'—and does not draw on revelation but international law for this position.[4]

My argument has three steps. First, what does the Old Testament say about the land promise? Second, what does the New Testament say about the land promise? Third, how do these teachings relate to the founding of Israel, starting in 1948? Each of these steps has different weak points which I will also note.

First Step

The Old Testament is rich with different themes related to the land. When 'covenant' is mentioned, 70 percent of references are linked explicitly to the promise of the land. Amidst this complexity there are three indisputable elements—all established by the Pontifical Biblical Commission's (PBC's) examination of this issue.[5]

The first is God's promise of the land to Abraham and his descendants (Gn 12, 15, 17). The Jewish people are not chosen because of the land, but the land serves their mission before God. Key figures like Moses never enter the land. They are hardly less Jewish for it. The people existed first. The boundaries of the land are drawn differently in the biblical texts. Genesis 15:18–21

4 George Emile Irani, *The Papacy and the Middle East: The Role of the Holy See in the Arab-Israeli Conflict, 1962–1984* (University of Notre Dame Press, 1986). International law, for its validity, must also draw upon the revelation of justice given in Christ, so we cannot avoid a Christological dimension to natural law and international law from a Catholic perspective.

5 See for example the Pontifical Biblical Commission, *The Jewish People and Their Sacred Scriptures in the Christian Bible* (May 24, 2001), 33, 37, 48, 54, 65.

depicts the largest area, while smaller but varying borders are depicted in Deuteronomy 1:7, 7:22, and 11:24, Numbers 34:1–15, Ezekiel 47:13–20, and Exodus 23:29. Scholars dispute whether these are boundaries 'fixed' by God in the narratives or territory related to historical context and existing political conditions to facilitate a home for the people. Within these overlapping narratives, the land promise is still central, even if the geographical boundaries are not clearly and definitively established and accepted.

Second, Israel's gift of the land from God also requires, from His people, a moral and cultic purity (Lv 18:24–28, Dt 28:15–68, Nm 35:34, Jos 24:14–24). One aspect of moral purity requires treating the stranger justly. The biblical narrative shows that the people consistently fall away from this high calling. Becoming the people is a process with a lot of messiness and no easy linear trajectory.

Third, lest the gift and the process of becoming God's people become a cause for complacency, Leviticus 18:28 contains a stark warning: "If you defile the land, it will vomit you out as it vomited out the nations that were before you." This is key for why Catholics cannot see the modern return of the Jewish people as *the* fulfillment of biblical prophecy regarding the end times—because the signs of the end times are clearly not present. Further, this presumes to make a judgment that only God can make.

I want to emphasize that reading all the texts within the entirety of the Old Testament allows us to see the continuity of the tradition of the promise, but also that it has many qualifications and conditions, even while none of these ever finally undermine the irrevocable gift from God. I have not touched upon a wide range of issues, such as the destruction of the inhabitants of the land (the *cherem*), the place of the Temple, or the role of Jerusalem.

My initial conclusion, supported by a range of Catholic exegetes and the PBC, is that the land promise made to Israel in the Old Testament is central to the idea of the promises and gifts made by God to his people. This position is supported by a number of Catholics in the collection who build their case upon the biblical Old Testament texts (Anderson, Wright, and the Anglican contributor, Said). The weak point in this part of the argument is whether the promise of the Old Testament can simply be transferred to a contemporary event in the twentieth century without significant supporting argumentation. Another weakness relates to how the mainstream of Catholic tradition has read this promise. Is it possible to avoid a supersessionist reading of the Old Testament while keeping intact the Church's Christological center in the New Testament? Does the land promise evaporate into a spiritual body once Christ is risen? This has been the main tradition of exegesis, but a tradition that has also been part of a supersessionist reading in negating the promises made to Israel and transferring them, while transforming them, to Christ and his Church.

Second Step

The New Testament: here the church is never called the 'New Israel.' In the eighty usages of 'Israel,' this word usually refers to the Jewish people, to their polity, or to the land directly. There are four New Testament themes that are important in this context.

First, Jesus is entirely committed to the land and the Jewish people. Jesus orients his ministry in relation to the land, both at the beginning and the end of his ministry. The birth narratives enact the people's exile in Egypt followed by the holy family's return to the land from Egypt (see Mt 2:13–23). During Jesus's ministry he rarely leaves the land. He is only concerned with Israel, his people (Mt 15:22–28). Going "to the ends of the earth" is left to the Church gathered around him after the resurrection. This conforms to the expectations regarding the arrival of the Jewish messiah in Jerusalem—who will be a light to the nations. Jesus's messianic ministry will make Israel, the people and the land, a light to the nations so that all will worship Israel's God. This thematic becomes dominant in Jewish messianic groups in the present day, that is, Jews who follow Jesus either in ecclesial separation from or in unity with the gentile followers. Most see the land promises applying to themselves as Jews—and this should make us self-critical about the dominant supersessionist readings in the Catholic tradition stemming from gentile readers (see two paragraphs below re: Kinzer).

Second, many of Jesus's teachings focus on the land. Take for instance: "Blessed are the meek, for they shall inherit the earth" (Mt 5:5). Many biblical scholars argue it is better rendered: "Blessed are the meek, for they shall inherit the *land*." Matthew was drawing on Psalm 37:11. In that psalm the Hebrew *eretz* refers to the land of Israel, not the 'world.' Four other verses in Psalm 37 repeat the phrase "inherit the land" with the land of Israel as the clear referent. This would mean that his Jewish disciples would eventually "inherit" the land in the renewal of all things. Most biblical scholars focus on the "meek," not that they are Jewish and that this is their inheritance.

Third, after the resurrection, in Acts 1:6, Jesus responds affirmatively to the question regarding his restoration of the kingdom to Israel. While he is confident of this, he also warns the disciples that the exact timing of this event is "not for you to know." It is the Father's initiative and in his hands. Any Jewish listener—and all the disciples were Jewish in the narrative—would know that this reference is to the land. Mark Kinzer's book *Jerusalem Crucified: Jerusalem Risen* offers a close exegetical reading of the

New Testament on this theme, showing that Acts and Luke are centrally structured around the importance of the land.[6] Kinzer's is a messianic Jew.

Fourth, the focus on the land is not confined to Jesus alone. St. Paul cites the land gift in Acts 13:19 as part of his recalling God's mighty acts, culminating (but not finishing) in Jesus Christ. It is the same Paul who also in Romans 11:29 says that these gifts are irrevocable. For any Jewish reader it would be clear that one of these gifts is the land. It is, after all, the secondary focus of the covenantal gift, after the primary one: the creation of a people. All these and many other passages point to one thing: the early followers of Jesus knew that the land was central to the Gospel, both in its promise to the Jewish people and its relationship to a messianic restoration.

However, the New Testament is complex as it reconfigures the Old, messianically. The promises are intact, but they are messianically understood. If the land promise is not consigned to "replacement theology" or read in a 'hard' supersessionist manner, we must ask whether the restoration of the land to the people of Israel in 1948 might be considered as an eschatological sign of the return of Jesus. While it is difficult to deny that this might be the case, we cannot know the hour and must, as Jesus tells us, remain diligent discerning the signs. Hence we can navigate a path between saying that geopolitical Israel in 1948 must be understood in purely secular or political terms on the one hand, and, on the other hand, adopting a confident militant Christian Zionism that sees Israel in 1948 as the beginning of the end times. If this navigation is possible, which I think it is, does it not have sufficient biblical warrant? The middle path here is recognizing the gift and the promise as part of God's providential care and love for his people. That much is clear. We must discern the signs of the times in history to say more regarding eschatology. This two-step strategy is important for my Catholic theological affirmation, which distinguishes itself from strong forms of evangelical Christian Zionism that are confident that the eschatological scenario has begun.

Finally, what of the New Testament references that seem to move away from the particularity of the land and universalize the kingdom? The PBC notes this type of tension within the New Testament texts. This universalizing de-territorializing reading has been dominant in Catholic history, although not as the only reading. A typical universalizing trope is found in the claim that, for example, the location of the trans-geographical temple is the risen body of Christ. Jesus says he will rebuild the temple which is his risen body (Jn 2:19). Likewise, the specific promise of the land transmutes into a universal kingdom of God with no location. This universalist movement in the New

6 Mark Kinzer, *Jerusalem Crucified: Jerusalem Risen* (Wipf and Stock, 2018).

Testament, leading to the cosmic Christ, remains grounded in the particular, the historical Jesus of Nazareth. The particular is the gate to the universal. I would suggest that in a post-supersessionist reading, the universal does not dematerialize or destroy the particular. Is it possible to say that the specific gift of the land is precisely there for a universal purpose: to call the nations to worship the one true God? One can exist with the other.

Hence, one might propose that just as Jesus Christ is the scandal of particularity, so are the land and the Jewish people, both of which constitute his material formation. This reading from a Catholic perspective is finally a different reading from any Jewish perspective (other than messianic Jews who follow Yeshua), and necessarily so. This does not dishonor either those Jews who see things differently (secular or religious) or in some way instrumentalize the Jewish history of 1948 for Catholic purposes. It is a simple and necessary recognition that this history is part of God's providence. Catholics cannot say anything on this matter without theological warrant, and since that warrant derives from a trinitarian God, which is revealed in Christ, we cannot and should not imagine the possibility of theological agreement. There may be commonalities and overlaps, but ultimately a soft supersessionism is part of Christianity—for Jesus is Israel's messiah.

When the PBC investigated this question, they acknowledged differing traditions regarding the significance of the land in the New Testament for Christians. This question is genuinely not resolved. However, the section treating the New Testament ends: "It should not be forgotten, however, that a specific land was promised by God to Israel and received as a heritage."[7] This claim is the result of historical critical investigation. How it dovetails with the faith claims of the New Testament is unclear and unresolved in Catholic exegetical circles. In one sense, this is the weak point of this step of the argument because it is against the grain of tradition—and the tradition counts. But it also recognized that tradition contains replacement theological currents and that these need to be rethought. Christology cannot in any way be abandoned or minimized in rereadings but must be constitutive of any rereading. The interpretation that I am advancing does not de-particularize the promise of the land, nor does it slip into a relativist position—that both Judaism and Christianity are true as they stand—which is not possible to hold. The weakness of this section is the requirement to show how the land promise is reconfigured in Christ and applicable to the land.

My conclusions so far are (1) that the promises to the Jewish people regarding the land can be read as intact—and this is in keeping with the intentions of the Council, that the irrevocability of God's promises should

7 Ibid., 57.

not be denied; (2) that those promises are reconfigured in Jesus Christ, but not in a way that dematerializes the land promise to the Jewish people; and (3) that the land promise to the Jewish people may well be related to an eschatological sign, something that is an open question and we cannot determine.

Does any of this apply to Israel in 1948 and thereafter? While all the above may be true and valuable, we cannot simply assume that it applies to modern-day Israel. This is an extra-biblical reality, or better a post-biblical reality, and thus hermeneutics has to do the further step of discerning applicability, even if the theological case that I have made above is convincing.

Third Step: Modern Israel

I use the term "modern Israel" to denote the Jewish people living upon the land, *not* the form of nation-state or any particular political party that may run that state, nor its prudential judgements. Some form of governance is required for the safety and security of the Jewish people in the land, but I take the *form of governance* to be a contingent factor. This echoes most of the main contributors' Jewish essays in this volume. Second, I pragmatically keep with the Catholic Church's affirmation of the 1947 UN boundaries when speaking about "Israel" and "Palestine," recognizing that this is problematic and requires further theological reflection.

Might the biblical promises relate to Israel in 1948 onward in terms of people and land, not in support of any government or particular form of governance? Here the question might be divided into two aspects. First, is there is an ingathering of Jews to the land? This is certainly the case. This may be God's providential action. We cannot dismiss this 'sign.' Second, is it a 'sign' of the end days?

The first question should and can be answered affirmatively, especially given the lead of Pope John Paul II. In his 1991 Pastoral Visit to Brazil, the pope met with Jewish leaders in Brasilia. In his speech to these leaders, he cites from Ezekiel 34:13, employing the Old Testament to read modern history, including a passage central to the land promise: "May our Jewish brothers and sisters, who have been led 'out from among the peoples and gathered from the foreign lands' brought back 'to their own country' to the land of their ancestors, be able to live there in peace and security on the 'mountains of Israel,' guarded by the protection of God, their true shepherd."[8]

8 Available at https://www.vatican.va/content/john-paul-ii/it/speeches/1991/october/documents/hf_jp-ii_spe_19911015_brasile-comunita-ebraica.html. The Ezekiel passage reads: "And I will bring them out from the people, and gather them from the countries, and will bring them to their own land, and feed them upon the mountains of Israel by the rivers, and in all the inhabited places of the country."

If that gathering was the initiative of secular Zionists with the support of evangelical British Christians, it does not seem to matter to the pope. That the pope interprets this ingathering biblically does matter. This is not a text with magisterial authority, but it is an important text for supporting such a possible reading.

However, "God's providential care for his people" is logically different than the question regarding whether modern Israel is *the* beginning of the end days, a sign of *the* final fulfillment of God's actions in salvation history. Attention to Jesus's teachings requires modesty about confidently declaring this to be the case, as we "cannot know the hour" (Mt 24:26).[9] Further, close attention to the biblical promises reinforces reticence: the people may be "vomited" out as we are reminded in Leviticus. It has happened before. We cannot force God's hand or prematurely declare that this event in 1948 is *the* fulfillment of scripture. I am not ruling out that this is the beginning of the end days, but support a considered reticence that is appropriate to the truth of revelation.

Conclusion

The ingathering of the Jewish people and their preservation as a people in the founding of Israel in 1948 is deeply biblical and cannot be ignored. It is a sign of God's providential love and care for his people and part of his irrevocable covenant. I call this minimalist Catholic Zionism for the sake of accurate terminology—and in contrast to Protestant maximalist Zionisms that see Israel in 1948 as the definite beginning of the end times. The weak points of this section include the absence of the Palestinian people and the *Nakba* as having to interrogate this narrative—and I point to Said's remarkable piece in this volume that attempts to do just that, as well as Vetö's insightful question to Said regarding whether a basically secular country can be seen in these religious terms, and whether the main religious elements in this country are aggressively against the type of concerns for the Palestinians that would be central to Catholic minimalist Zionism.

CATHOLIC AND JEWISH OBJECTIONS TO THE CLAIM

There are many Catholic and Jewish objections to the form of minimalist Catholic Zionism that I am proposing. I have indicated just some of these above and in what follows, I try to tentatively address just a small portion of

9 *Catechism of the Catholic Church, English Updated Edition*, 2nd ed. (Libreria Editrice Vaticana / Our Sunday Visitor, 2020), 673, argues the same, citing Acts 1:7; see Mk 13:32.

objections. I have addressed one of the most important objections obliquely: that theologically affirming the land as a gift to the Jewish people is contrary to Palestinian rights and claims to the same land. It is not, and the Holy See in its diplomatic actions shows how both are reconcilable in principle and in practice. That the Holy See still underwrites the UN boundaries, while neither of the two parties formally uphold them, is not a decisive problem to my advocation for this view. This Catholic view maps out a possibility and indicates how that possibility would allow justice for the Palestinians—and for the theological affirmation of the land to coexist side by side. This position has several repercussions which are important to address.

First, it means that the arguments advanced by many (not all) Eastern Christians and Palestinian Christians would have to be addressed and examined as to whether they are still operating in a supersessionist mode.[10] This is not an a priori dismissal of the arguments advanced, but a clear challenge that they are not in conformity with the Church's teachings regarding the irrevocable covenant—here in relation to the specific promise of the land.[11] While many of these authors concede that Jews have a right to exist on the land with Palestinians (both Muslim and Christians and others), they also deny the Jewish people a right to see the land as a gift from God (even if there were a just solution to the Palestinian suffering and dispossession). That solution not only refuses to engage with the biblical promises in scripture, it is also inattentive to the issues of justice and peace and the rights of Jews to have a safe 'national' existence in the Middle East as much as Palestinians. Admittedly, the single-state solution with equal citizenship cannot be dismissed or affirmed on biblical grounds. As long as a geopolitical solution ensured the safety of the Jewish people, their ability to be a light

10 See Naim Stifan Ateek, *Justice and Only Justice: A Palestinian Theology of Liberation* (Orbis Books, 1989); Naim Stifan Ateek, Cedar Duaybis, and Maurine Tobin, eds., *Challenging Christian Zionism: Theology, Politics and the Israel-Palestine Conflict* (Melisende, 2005). Among some Arab Christians one finds bold expression of supersessionism: e.g., Fr. George Makhlour of Ramallah: "The church has inherited the promise of Israel. The church is actually the new Israel. What Abraham has promised, Christians now possess because they are Abraham's true spiritual children just as the New Testament teaches." Cited in Paul Charles Merkley, *Christian Attitudes towards the State of Israel* (McGill-Queen's University Press, 2001). For strong arguments that the New Testament does not underwrite any form of Christian Zionism, see two works by Gary M. Burge: *Jesus and the Land: The New Testament Challenge to 'Holy Land' Theology* (Baker Academic, 2010), and *Whose Land? Whose Promise?* (Pilgrim Press, 2003). For an insightful critical analysis of these texts, see Samuel J. Kuruvilla, *Radical Christianity in Palestine and Israel: Liberation and Theology in the Middle East* (I. B. Tauris, 2013). Said's article in this volume is a ground-breaking move against this type of hermeneutics.

11 Rabbi Eugene Korn in this collection makes this explicit challenge. David Mark Neuhaus argues for a Jewish nation-state's right to exist in "A Catholic Perspective on the People, Land, and State of Israel," in D'Costa and Shapiro, *Contemporary Catholic Approaches*. See Jamal Khader, "Christian-Jewish Relations from a Christian Palestinian Perspective," in ibid.

to the nations, and their freedom of religion, a Catholic should be open to these possibilities. However, a single-state solution is hardly in keeping with the UN mandate, international law, or the long-term prospects for peaceful existence of both groups and the rights of nationhood. These prudential decisions are best kept open with the singular goal of achieving a safe and secure long-term existence for Jews and Palestinians to live on the land.

Second, it means that Catholics should be just and balanced in their criticisms of both groups if and when it is necessary. To make a theological affirmation of the land as part of the promises and gifts to the Jewish people, on the one hand, is not to underwrite the social, political, and juridical decisions made by the government or the law courts of Israel in an uncritical way. Some forms of Christian Zionism have often been configured as an underwriting of a nation-state by God.[12] Christian Zionists like Pat Robertson in effect say: "if you oppose Israel, you oppose God." This is to problematically conflate the people, the land, and the modern State of Israel as indivisible. I am not arguing for such an equation. Equally, there should be critical analysis of Palestinian culture, not only a solidarity with their suffering and oppression—which is also required. Too often, the opposite side of theological affirmation of the land has been the Boycott, Disinvestment, and Sanctions movement within Christian Churches—with its implicit and sometimes explicit questioning of Israel's right to exist.[13] Not all BDS groups share this assumption, but many do.

This leads to another important objection, found most eloquently in Fr. Thomas Joseph White's essay in this collection. He argues persuasively that Catholic support of Israel is best advanced on natural law and human rights arguments on two grounds. The first is that such a support is non-partisan and applies the same types of principles to both groups in the dispute in the Middle East. Second, it achieves the outcome that the theological route is trying to take, but with fewer casualties on the way—and it achieves the goals on more secure grounds. This view is shared by many Catholics involved in Jewish-Christian dialogue.[14]

12 See Samuel Goldman, *God's Country: Christian Zionism in America* (University of Pennsylvania Press, 2018).

13 See Nelson's introductory essay in *Peace and Faith: Christian Churches and the Israeli-Palestinian Conflict*, ed. Cary Nelson and Michael C. Gizzi (Presbyterians for Middle East Peace, 2021).

14 See the essays by Christian M. Rutishauser, "Land and State of Israel: Theological Reflections from a Roman Catholic Perspective," and Dirk Ansorge, "Does a Catholic Theology of Sacraments Help to Achieve an Affirmative Approach to the State of Israel?," in D'Costa and Shapiro, *Contemporary Catholic Approaches*.

In response, I would suggest a both/and approach, whereas Fr. White's position does not actually make clear whether the theological arguments are valid. He implies that they are pragmatically unhelpful at this stage. He may well be right. But if there are valid theological arguments deriving from revelation applied to history, should revelation and its teaching and application be subject to political prudence? For the Catholic Church, matters of revelation must come first, although viewing the same situation from a natural law perspective can help in a dialogue with those from different faiths or none. Of course, revelation should be subject to prudential judgment about its proclamation and the way it is proclaimed, but it is important for the Church that Catholics know what the contents of revelation are, and how these contents apply. There is also a related moral duty to the Jewish people in the light of previous supersessionist theologies that have spelled the extinction of the Jewish land promise—along with the denial of the covenant promise made by God to his people. There is also a related moral duty to the Palestinian people. The both/and approach that I am advocating would join with White's very substantial arguments for natural law and international law approaches in conjunction with a theological affirmation. Logically, the latter is the underwriting of the former as natural law cannot be divorced from its Christological context.[15]

Another objection appears to come from Pope Benedict XVI, which certainly sides with White's position above (in affirming the importance of the international legal solution). Benedict has serious reservations of what any theological affirmation would entail regarding the status of Jewish groups. However, there is an important ambiguity in Benedict's position that I think aligns itself with the arguments I have advanced. Benedict writes:

> The question of what to make of the Zionist project was also controversial for the Catholic Church. From the beginning, however, the dominant position was that a theologically-understood acquisition of land (in the sense of a *new political messianism*) was unacceptable. After the establishment of Israel as a country in 1948, a theological doctrine emerged that eventually enabled the political recognition of the State of Israel by the Vatican. At its core is the conviction that a strictly theologically-understood state—a Jewish faith-state [*Glaubenstaat*] that would view itself as the theological and political *fulfillment* of the promises—is unthinkable within history

15 See International Theological Commission, *In Search of a Universal Ethic: A New Look at the Natural Law* (Catholic Truth Society, 2012), chap. 5.

according to Christian faith and contrary to the Christian understanding of the promises.[16]

There are good grounds for Benedict's rejection given the precise specification of what he is rejecting. These rejections add to the argument I have been advancing by bringing in a new dimension: how Jews understand the state. I have intentionally disregarded this issue to be able to focus on a Catholic discernment of history, rather than a Catholic evaluation of Jewish views of the land. The latter would require a further stage of engagement and reflection. No doubt, Catholics can learn much from Jewish reflections, but that is not our propose in this essay. Catholics cannot go into this engagement without establishing their own orientation to the question first—which might then be sharpened, questioned, and even reframed by Jewish views of the land. Benedict rejects two or possibly three specific Jewish conceptions: "a theologically-understood acquisition of land (in the sense of a *new political messianism*)"; "a Jewish faith-state [*Glaubenstaat*] that would view itself as the theological and political *fulfillment* of the promises."

It is not clear from these options whether a Jewish faith state that did not view itself in these ways would be acceptable to Benedict. What is clear is this: any Jewish claim related to the land that is incompatible with Catholic doctrine is inadmissible. Such would be the case if Jewish claims related to the land excluded the Christian messianic truth claim, that Jesus of Nazareth is the Jewish messiah. It is understandable that the Jewish claims do not accept the claims made about Jesus. Benedict then adds, before moving to a different topic: "the Vatican . . . has recognized the State of Israel as a modern constitutional state, and sees it as a legitimate home of the Jewish people, the rationale of which cannot be derived directly from Holy Scripture. Yet, in another sense, *it expresses God's faithfulness to the people of Israel*."[17]

The final sentence raises two questions. First, what other Jewish (secular or religious) conceptions of the land are present in the debate, and would such conceptions be acceptable, especially if Jewish views saw the land in terms of John Paul II's outlook: as showing God's providential care for his people and not primarily in messianic/eschatologically realized terms? Rabbi David Rosen, who contributes to this collection, makes the point well:

16 Pope Benedict XVI, "Grace and Vocation without Remorse: Comments on the Treatise 'De Iudaeis,'" trans. Nicholas J. Healy, *Communio: International Catholic Review* 45 (2018): 178; and original text: Emeritus Pope Benedict XVI, "Gnade und Berfung Ohne Reue. Ammerkungen zum Traktat 'De Judaeis,'" *Communio: IKaZ* 47 (2018): 387–406.

17 Benedict XVI, "Grace and Vocation without Remorse," 178; emphasis added.

> Benedict's distinction between seeing Divine Providence in the return of the Jewish People to its ancestral homeland (with the reestablishment of independent Jewish national sovereignty) testifying to Divine fidelity and love toward the Jewish people, versus an event of Messianic significance parallels a debate within Religious Zionism itself whether or not the establishment of the State of Israel should be viewed in Messianic religious terms or not.[18]

Rosen's point helps us to see that the conceptions proposed by Benedict are limited—if we are to engage with the significant variety of Jewish views on this matter. Benedict cannot be blamed for this as his attention to this issue is limited in the context of his overall essay. However, he is setting forth important principles: no Jewish view can be accepted in its own terms if it is incompatible with Catholic doctrine. This is right and proper. However, I have been arguing for a position that theologically affirms the land promise without compromising any Catholic doctrine but rather arising from Catholic doctrines on Israel. The position is not reliant on any Jewish view, although it may overlap with some Jewish views and be in antagonism with others. I am aware that the Catholic doctrine on the land is not yet settled within the Church and thus the real challenge is to advance this position without undermining the finality and fulfillment of Jesus Christ so that it may commend itself to the wider Catholic community. I believe this fulfillment view is compatible with the rejection of supersessionism, but this requires further argument and I will return to this point below.

The second question is related to the ambiguity of Benedict's position and is posed to his position. On the one hand he seems to wish to keep the international legal affirmation of Israel intact, like White in this collection; but on the other hand, he moves toward a theological affirmation of God's providential care for the Jewish people related to their settling in the land of Israel since 1948. The last sentence on the matter notes that the Holy See sees Israel "as a legitimate home of the Jewish people, the rationale of which cannot be derived directly from Holy Scripture. Yet, in another sense, *it expresses God's faithfulness to the people of Israel*." This moves away from the legal recognition to a theological one.

There is a way in which this ambiguous sentence could be read which seems more plausible. Could it be that Benedict's point is that since the modern State of Israel is not the subject of direct address in revelation,

18 Lisa Palmieri-Billig, "Correspondence between Pope Emeritus Benedict XVI and Arie Folger, the Chief Rabbi of Vienna," 2018; available at jcrelations.net/articles/article/the-pope-and-the-rabbi.html.

the "legitimate home of the Jewish people" in this context is not "directly derived" from Scripture, but indirectly derived. Analogously, one might say that Scripture does not directly address the question of the legitimate use of embryos for medical experimentation. To address this question using Scripture, we would have to make indirect derivations depending on analogous cases or arguments from principles related to one matter (the valuing of human life) being applied appropriately to another (the assumption that the embryo should be treated as human life at the stage of conception).

Catholic thinking on these matters is thus derived indirectly from scriptural principles and insights and through analogical reasoning and evolving tradition. However, for Benedict if Scripture says nothing about the "legitimate home" in relation to the modern State of Israel, Scripture clearly provides grounds for possibly indirectly affirming that such a home "expresses God's faithfulness to the people of Israel." It is difficult to determine whether the people and the land, rather than the nation-state distinctions I have employed, underlie Benedict's subtle position or whether some other determinations are operating, such as viewing this particular land in a general providential manner rather than related to the Jewish people specifically.[19]

In Benedict's published letter to Rabbi Arie Folger after Benedict's initial article, in response to Folger's questions, Benedict restates the matter slightly differently, which allows for slight clarification on the two points we have been discussing.[20] Benedict writes:

> Today, a proper interpretation of the land promises is vital for all sides in the context of the birth of the State of Israel. Without repeating everything I have said in my essay, I would like to reiterate the thesis, which is important not only for Christians, that the State of Israel as such cannot be theologically classified as the fulfillment of the land promise, but is in itself a secular state, which certainly has religious bases. For the fathers of the State of Israel—Ben Gurion, Golda Meir, etc.—it was quite clear that the state they created had to be a secular state—simply because it was the only way to survive. I believe that the development of the idea of a secular state is substantially indebted to Jewish thought, according to which sec-

19 Perhaps White's essay in this collection best reflects Benedict's approach thus resolving the issues? White writes: "The covenant of faith, hope, and love for God that animates Judaic believe in God, and in the Torah and the prophets, implies only an indirect relation to the modern state of Israel, whatever its territorial boundaries."

20 Both texts can be found at the following websites. For Folger, see ccjr.us/dialogika-resources/themes-in-today-s-dialogue/emeritus-pope/folger-2018sept4; for Benedict's response, see https://www.ccjr.us/dialogika-resources/themes-in-today-s-dialogue/emeritus-pope/benedict-2018aug28.

> ularism does not mean being anti-religious. The Holy See was only able to establish diplomatic relations with the State of Israel on such terms. And the dispute with the Arabs and the search for peaceful coexistence with them are also bound to this view. It is not difficult, I believe, to see that in the creation of the State of Israel the fidelity of God to Israel is revealed in a mysterious way.

A number of points should be made about this restatement of Benedict's view. First, the "secular state" of Israel that Benedict supports is seen as being indebted to Jewish thought in not being anti-religious and is also the grounds for possible peace with non-Jews, the Arab people. The assumption is that a secular state can be tolerant of religious pluralism and embrace Jews, Christians, Muslims, and others—which is the bedrock for eventual peace in the Middle East. There is no reason why a Jewish state could not permit religious pluralism. This position has been argued for by David Novak with some rigor.[21] And it is not self-evident that a secular state might not discriminate against non-Jews, as was the claim made against a law passed a month before Benedict's text. The Basic Law of 1998 defines Israel as the "Nation State of the Jewish People" and defines Israel first and foremost as a Jewish state. Among its eleven provisions, it describes Israel as "the national home of the Jewish people" and says the right to exercise national self-determination there is thus "unique to the Jewish people." At the level of political science, there are so many options and models that theology cannot make a pre-judgment of every sort of model but can only provide general principles to assess the various models that arise.

Second, the general principle theologically affirmed by Benedict, from my perspective, provides the grounds for minimalist Catholic Zionism. The grounds of this theological affirmation by Benedict are now given a "mysterious" grounding. Previously, it could not be directly derived from scripture, now it is "mysterious," but it is not clear whether "mysterious" might be equated with "indirect derivation" such as I have argued. I admit that I have not addressed the objection fully as I am unable to locate the source of Benedict's concerns precisely. He is too excellent a theologian to dismiss, so it is valuable at least to discriminate between his many legitimate objections with which I agree, to recognize an aspect of the problem not treated at all in my paper (religious Jewish Zionist views of the land), and to show how even Benedict's concerns still leave a door open toward the solution I am proposing.

21 David Novak, *Zionism and Judaism: A New Theory* (Cambridge University Press, 2015), 153–97.

Another Catholic objection would be that the term *supersessionism* is not clearly defined and cannot be applied to assume that every promise in every form stands intact. This is an objection raised again by Benedict in the article cited above. I believe he is right. The debate about the meaning of the term is very complex; there are different forms of supersessionism (punitive, economic, and structural)[22] and there are those who argue that fulfillment theology is incompatible with post-supersessionism.[23] So as not to lose focus on the specific question of the land and the generic meaning of supersessionism, I should make clear some of my own assumptions to indicate how I would navigate this question.

First, I agree that supersessionism has no clear meaning and in that sense, neither does post-supersessionism. Second, the supersessionism I object to would be the nullifying of the promises made to Israel, that is, claiming that the land gift is now abrogated. Third, from a Christian point of view, those promises cannot be understood as a contemporary Jew understands them but must be understood Christologically by a Catholic. This Christological orientation will be incompatible with present-day Jewish beliefs—Christians believe that the messiah has come in Jesus Christ. Each group will read the significance of the events differently: the settling of the Jewish people in the land promised by God to his people. And within each group, Jewish and Christian, there is considerable internal diversity. In the view developed in this paper, more attention is required to Christologically understand the significance of the land promise. I have pointed to its possible eschatological dimensions which are Christological. More scriptural work is required to elaborate this dimension.[24]

Let me turn to one Jewish objection, although that is hardly an end to Catholic and other Jewish objections. How can Catholics develop a theology of Jews without taking Jewish self-understanding as the starting point?[25] Such a critic would argue that my position exemplifies this problem. I have outlined an understanding of the promises of the land to the Jewish people without any reference to Jewish viewpoints. Catholic internal discourse generates the image of the Other so that the real Other is not present in Catholic

22 R. Kendall Soulen, *The God of Israel and Christian Theology* (Fortress Press, 1996).

23 Ed Kessler says there is a "danger" of fulfillment slipping back to supersessionism in Edward Kessler, "Reflections from a European Jewish Theologian" (2015), available at ccjr.us/dialogika-resources/documents-and-statements/analyses/crrj-2015dec10/kessler-2015dec10.

24 See Gerald R. McDermott, ed., *The New Christian Zionism: Fresh Perspectives on Israel and the Land* (IVP Academic, 2016).

25 This is one of the subtle themes of Karma Ben-Johanan, *Reconciliation and Its Discontents: Christians and Jews after Vatican II* (Harvard University Press, 2021).

doctrinal formation. Thus, the discourse is always in danger of occluding rather than engaging with the Other which is the aim of the discourse. Sometimes this critique is fed by the words of the 1974 Catholic document that requires that Catholics learn how Jews describe themselves, in their own terms.[26] While this is an important objection in showing that my approach requires another step—engagement with Jewish views of the land—I believe that my approach is methodologically sound for doctrinal development. While questions may arise to Catholics from outside the Catholic world (when Jews ask, "What is the meaning of the land promise to the Jewish people to you Catholics?"; or when some Protestants ask, "What is the basis for proclaiming the Assumption of Mary into heaven?"), such doctrinal questions can only be answered from the traditional sources: Scripture, tradition, and the magisterium. Jewish exegesis and tradition, however important, are not authorities for doctrinal theology, while at the same time this is not to deny God's presence and inspiration in Jewish exegesis and tradition.

The Orthodox Jewish Rabbi Joseph B. Soloveitchik recognized this internal primacy for doctrinal thinking as do other Orthodox thinkers.[27] The experience of Christians is important but not itself a source of authority until or unless the magisterium deems these experiences decisive. An example of the latter would be how popular piety can eventually generate a dogmatic decision about who is a saint (popular piety, attestation of miracles by the saint) or whether a Marian apparition has taken place or not (usually through popular devotion at a site of an apparition). Hence, there are internal Catholic authoritative sources that must first be examined (steps one and two in the first part of this paper) and then applied to contemporary history (the third step, Israel in 1948). Insofar as the question relates to the explication of the meaning of revelation, the Jewish viewpoint on the land is not logically relevant at this point. It only becomes relevant in the process of engaging with different Jewish views to better understand the other in their own terms

26 See the preamble to "Gifts": "We may simply restate here that the spiritual bonds and historical links binding the Church to Judaism condemn (as opposed to the very spirit of Christianity) all forms of antisemitism and discrimination, which in any case the dignity of the human person alone would suffice to condemn. Further still, these links and relationships render obligatory a better mutual understanding and renewed mutual esteem. On the practical level in particular, Christians must therefore strive to acquire a better knowledge of the basic components of the religious tradition of Judaism; *they must strive to learn by what essential traits Jews define themselves in the light of their own religious experience*" (emphasis added).

27 Joseph B. Soloveitchik, "Confrontation," in *Bridges: Documents of the Christian-Jewish Dialogue, vol. 1: Road to Reconciliation (1945–85)*, ed. Franklin Sherman, Studies in Judaism and Christianity (Paulist Press, 2011); and see also Michael Wyschogrod, *Abraham's Promise: Judaism and Jewish-Christian Relations*, ed. R. Kendall Soulen (SCM Press, 2006); David Novak, *Talking with Christians: Musings of a Jewish Theologian* (Eerdmans, 2005).

and to engage in debate—as is happening in this book. Jewish viewpoints are spurs and challenges to the internal logic of the Catholic tradition in its present developments. This is witnessed by the constant Jewish request to clarify where Catholics stand on the land promise.[28] However, Jewish voices cannot be authorities in the articulation of the Catholic view, which does not mean that the doctrines developed are not thereby tested and require traction with what happens on the ground. By tested, I mean that if no religious Jew were a Zionist, it might cause a Catholic to ask whether they are misreading the Old Testament. Of course, back in 1897 there were very few to no Jewish religious Zionists; secular Zionists spearheaded the Zionist movement.

There are many further questions that must be addressed, but I hope to have made a case for a minimalist Catholic Zionism that is sensitive to different Catholic, Jewish, and Palestinian voices and that stands on the solid doctrinal grounds of Scripture and the magisterium.

28 For example, see Rabbi David Rosen at vatican.va/roman_curia/pontifical_councils/chrstuni/relations-jews-docs/rc_pc_chrstuni_doc_20151210_ebraismo-nostra-aetate_en.html; and also "Reflections from Israel" (2015), available at ccjr.us/dialogika-resources/documents-and-statements/analyses/crrj-2015dec10/rosen-2015dec10. See also Rabbi Henry Siegman, "A Decade of Catholic-Jewish Relations—A Reassessment," *Journal of Ecumenical Studies* 15 (1978): 251.

5

THE ELECTION OF THE LAND OF ISRAEL AND THEOLOGICAL JEWISH ZIONISM

Rabbi Jehoschua Ahrens

The land of Israel represents an integral part of Judaism. The Jewish faith is fundamentally based on three pillars: *Avodat Yisrael* ('service,' meaning worship or anything religious in the broader sense), *Am Yisrael* ('people,' meaning a connection between all Jews, not necessarily in the ethnic sense, but rather as 'peoplehood'), and *Eretz Yisrael* ('land,' meaning the connection with a particular land and with the Temple as the center of holiness). These components run like a thread through the history of Israel, from its biblical beginnings to the present day. This shows that Israel is more than just a religion. Israel is a religion, nation, land, culture, language, and many other things, but in summary, Jewish identity is a religious *and* a national identity.

In this paper I start with a short analysis of where we are in Jewish-Catholic relations concerning the land. Afterward, I would like to give a short introduction to the significance of the land of Israel for the Jewish people from both the Bible and rabbinic literature. Thereafter, I will present some known and less-well-known modern Jewish religious Zionist approaches—theological perspectives on not only the land, but also the State of Israel—and also discuss Israel in contemporary Jewish thought, including the question of the status of non-Jews in Israel and Palestinian self-determination.

THE LAND OF ISRAEL AND JEWISH-CATHOLIC RELATIONS —WHERE ARE WE?

The question of the land of Israel and the State of Israel is an important focal point in Jewish-Christian, especially Jewish-Catholic, relations. It is often the unspoken-of elephant in the room. Most official Catholic writings have not yet really touched this hot potato. In the 2015 "Gifts" document, we find this brief statement: "In Jewish-Christian dialogue the situation of Christian communities in the State of Israel is of great relevance, since there—as nowhere else in the world—a Christian minority faces a Jewish majority. Peace in the Holy Land—lacking and constantly prayed for—plays a major role in dialogue between Jews and Christians."[1] It is no secret that the Vatican adopts a neutral position, not least because of considerations concerning Christians in Arab lands. Therefore, the State of Israel is usually treated in a political context rather than a religious one.

For example, in the 1985 *Notes on the Correct Way to Present the Jews and Judaism in Preaching and Catechesis in the Roman Catholic Church*, it is written: "The existence of the State of Israel and its political options should be envisaged not in a perspective which is in itself religious, but in their reference to the common principles of international law."[2] Rabbi Arie Folger, former Chief Rabbi of Vienna and a member of the Standing Committee of the Council of European Rabbis and chairman of its Nostra Aetate Response Committee, quite rightly asked how exile and misery of the Jewish people should have religious significance, but that their happiness—especially the return to the Holy Land and its reconstruction—is described as a purely secular matter.[3]

Even when elaborated at length by leading Catholics, such as by Pope Benedict XVI, the State of Israel is considered secular in nature,[4] as outlined in his article "Grace and Vocation without Remorse: Comments on the Treatise *De Iudaeis*,"[5] which led to a major controversy, not least for his

1 "Gifts," 46.

2 *Notes on the Correct Way to Present the Jews and Judaism in Preaching and Catechesis in the Roman Catholic Church* (1985), VI, 1; available at christianunity.va.

3 Jehoschua Ahrens, "Christen bleiben Christen: Zur Debatte um einen Aufsatz Benedikts XVI. über den christlich-jüdischen Dialog," *Herder Korrespondenz* 73, no. 5 (2019): 51.

4 Philip A. Cunningham and Adam Gregerman, "'Genuine Brotherhood' without Remorse: A Commentary on Joseph Ratzinger's "Comments on '*De Iudaeis*," *SCJR* 14, no. 1 (2019): 18.

5 Pope Benedict XVI, "Gnade und Berfung Ohne Reue. Ammerkungen zum Traktat 'De Judaeis,'" *Communio: IKaZ* 47 (2018): 387–406. An English translation is available: Pope Benedict XVI, "Grace and Vocation without Remorse: Comments on the Treatise 'De Iudaeis,'" trans. Nicholas

conclusions on the land and State of Israel. Benedict's apodictic proposition is that "a theological interpretation of the State of Israel that relates the founding of the state to the biblical promise of land is impossible according to Christian understanding." While the State of Israel's right to exist was not questioned in the article, it appears, however, that this state is just by accident in its present geographic location.[6] Benedict minimizes the land promise, or at least its relevance in Christianity.[7] Similarly, David Neuhaus argues: "The transformation of understandings of land and election in the New Testament as compared to the Old is notable, as the land and peoplehood are universalized . . . The Land of Israel is no longer exclusively the place for covenant fidelity, as wherever the Gospel is preached, disciples enter the covenant. Christ came to bring down the borders that separate, this being central to his mission (cf. Eph 2:14–18)."[8]

From a Jewish perspective it is highly problematic that our dialogue partners remain "neutral" when it comes to the land or State of Israel or even question the theological connection between the people and the land of Israel. The land and State of Israel are more than just a political facet or a minor theoretical point in theology; they are at the core of the discussion about Jews and the relations of Jews and non-Jews.

Jewish Orthodoxy found it very difficult in the past that the Vatican did not maintain diplomatic relations with Israel, because ultimately the State of Israel always stands symbolically for dealings with Judaism in general. Thus, the establishment of diplomatic relations between the Holy See and the State of Israel in 1993 was seen as much more than a political or diplomatic matter, as Rabbi David Rosen pointed out several times.[9]

As we have moved forward so much in Catholic-Jewish relations in recent decades, maybe it is due time for the Catholic church to recollect some positions from the past and take them to the future. As early as the third international Christian–Jewish Conference in Fribourg, Switzerland, in 1948, a group of Catholic theologians centered around the future Cardinal Charles Journet defined a remarkable position on the State of Israel: "Further, in view

J. Healy, *Communio: International Catholic Review* 45 (2018): 163–84, with the original text available at ccjr.us/images/Ratzinger_Grace__Vocation_without_Remorse_-_English.pdf.

6 Jehoschua Ahrens, "Christen bleiben Christen: Zur Debatte um einen Aufsatz Benedikts XVI. über den christlich-jüdischen Dialog," *Herder Korrespondenz* 73, no. 5 (2019): 49.

7 Cunningham and Gregerman, "'Genuine Brotherhood' without Remorse," 20.

8 David M. Neuhaus, "Where to from Here? Continuing Challenges in Jewish-Catholic Conversation," *Religions* 12, no. 929 (2021): 6.

9 See David Rosen, "Reflections on the Recent Orthodox Jewish Statements on Jewish-Catholic Relations," in *From Confrontation to Covenantal Partnership: Reflections on To Do the Will of Our Father in Heaven*, ed. Jehoschua Ahrens et al. (Urim, 2020), 89–90.

of this national restoration of Israel, even if it seems to go against widespread, perhaps all-too-human opinions about the destiny of Israel, it is our task to seek and prove its importance ln God's plans."[10] Pope Benedict XVI, Joseph Cardinal Ratzinger, mentions this concept also in his *Communio* article and Cardinal Koch refers to it in his correspondence with the Orthodox Rabbinical Assembly in Germany, in which he writes that the land of Israel remains a central topic, but so far unresolved. He continues: "I am grateful to note that in your letter you too consider the reference to 'God's faithfulness to the people of Israel' as an idea 'which could be further developed'—and in my opinion should be, since the relationship between the biblical promise of land and the concrete reality of the State of Israel is a topic that needs to be intensively discussed in Jewish-Catholic dialogue."[11]

THE LAND OF ISRAEL IN THE BIBLE AND CLASSIC RABBINIC LITERATURE

The land of Israel is a crucial part of the first covenant with Abraham: "And I will maintain My covenant between Me and you and your offspring to come, as an everlasting covenant throughout the ages, to be God to you and to your offspring to come. I assign the land you sojourn in to you and your offspring to come, all the land of Canaan, as an everlasting holding; and I will be their God."[12] The land is not only an indispensable part of the covenant, but also Abraham's goal. This promise is also reaffirmed later to the other forefathers, that is, Isaac and Jacob. God owns the land.[13] He can decide what He does with it and to whom He gives it. The medieval commentator Rashi (Germany/France, 1040–1105) explains this very vividly in his commentary on Genesis 1:1:

> Rabbi Isaac said: The Torah which is the Law book of Israel should have commenced with the verse [Ex 12:2] "This month shall be unto you the first of the months" which is the first commandment given to Israel. What is the reason, then, that it commences with the account of the Creation? Because of the thought expressed in the text [Ps 111:6] "He declared to His people the strength of His works (i.e. He gave an account of the work of Creation), in order that He might give them the heritage of the nations."

10 Charles Journet, "Le Congrès de l'association internationale des chrétiens et des juifs à Fribourg," *L'Amitié judéo-chrétienne* 2 (1948): 13.

11 Jehoschua Ahrens, "Christen bleiben Christen: Zur Debatte um einen Aufsatz Benedikts XVI. über den christlich-jüdischen Dialog." *Herder Korrespondenz* 73, no. 5 (2019): 51.

12 Gn 17:7–8. Notably, all Tanach quotations are taken from the JPS translation.

13 See Lv 25:23.

> For should the peoples of the world say to Israel, "You are robbers, because you took by force the lands of the seven nations of Canaan," Israel may reply to them, "All the earth belongs to the Holy One, blessed be He; He created it and gave it to whom He pleased. When He willed He gave it to them, and when He willed He took it from them and gave it to us" [Yalkut Shimoni on Torah 187].[14]

It is not the Jewish people who own the land of Israel and make it holy—it is God's decision. The people and land of Israel belong to God and therefore He will rule over both, as the prophet Joel put it: "For, behold, in those days, and in that time, when I shall bring back the captivity of Judah and Jerusalem, I will gather all nations, and will bring them down into the valley of Jehoshaphat; and I will enter into judgment with them there for My people and for My heritage Israel, whom they have scattered among the nations, and divided My land."[15]

The land of Israel is the place of Jewish sovereignty and security, a place of freedom.[16] The exodus from Egypt is directly related to statehood in the land of Israel—as the goal and culmination of liberation.[17] It is also a Holy Land and within Israel there are different levels of holiness, the walled cities are holier than normal cities, Jerusalem is holier than the other walled cities, within Jerusalem the Temple Mount is holier, on the Temple Mount the Temple is holier, and within the Temple certain areas within the Holy of Holies is—as the name indicates—the holiest place.[18] This special status of the land of Israel is also reflected in the commandments.[19]

There are, according to the *Sefer HaChinuch* (a compendium of commandments and prohibitions in Judaism), more than forty-five *mitzvot hatluyot ba'aretz*, commandments that are directly related to the land of Israel. The commandments and prohibitions associated with the land of Israel encompass almost the entire order of *Sera'im* (with the exception of Tractate *B'rachot*), meaning almost a sixth of the Talmud is devoted exclusively to these commandments. This illustrates that the land of Israel comes with great responsibility and obligation: it is the land in which Jews are to fulfill their mission as the chosen people, that is, to be a light unto the nations, an

14 Rashi on Gn 1:1, available at sefaria.org/Rashi_on_Genesis.1.1.1.

15 Joel 4:1–2.

16 See Ex 14:13–14.

17 See Ex 3:8.

18 M Kelim 1:6–9.

19 See Dt 6:1, 12:1.

example of how to live a life pleasing to God.[20] Only then can the Jewish people have the right to dwell in the land of Israel and enjoy its benefits, as affirmed in the Torah: "Keep, therefore, all the Instruction that I enjoin upon you today, so that you may have the strength to enter and take possession of the land that you are about to cross into and possess, and that you may long endure upon the soil that the Lord swore to your fathers to assign to them and to their heirs, a land flowing with milk and honey."[21]

However, not keeping God's commandments has fatal consequences.[22] The prophets repeatedly warned of what would happen if the people of Israel turned away from God, practiced idolatry, and behaved unethically, which is already clearly stated in the Torah: "Do not defile yourselves in any of those ways, for it is by such that the nations that I am casting out before you defiled themselves . . . So let not the land spew you out for defiling it, as it spewed out the nation that came before you."[23] This is very explicit language. Later the prophet Jeremiah expressed it likewise, in his vision which unfortunately came true:

> Assuredly, thus said the Lord of Hosts: Because you would not listen to My words, I am going to send for all the peoples of the north—declares the Lord—and for My servant, King Nebuchadnezzar of Babylon, and bring them against this land and its inhabitants, and against all those nations round about. I will exterminate them and make them a desolation, an object of hissing—ruins for all time. And I will banish from them the sound of mirth and gladness, the voice of bridegroom and bride, and the sound of the mill and the light of the lamp. This whole land shall be a desolate ruin. And those nations shall serve the king of Babylon seventy years. When the seventy years are over, I will punish the king of Babylon and that nation and the land of the Chaldeans for their sins—declares the LORD—and I will make it a desolation for all time.[24]

So, the Jewish people indeed had to go into exile, but was this the end of Judaism? With the destruction of the First Temple in 586 BCE and the exile in Babylonia, many Jews actually believed that the covenant with God was no longer valid, and that this was the final end of Jewish statehood. At that

20 See Rabbi Yehudah HaLevi, Sefer HaKuzari, 2:16; and Rabbi Samson Raphael Hirsch on Gn 48:3–4.

21 Dt 11:8–9.

22 See Nm 35:33–34.

23 Lv 18:24, 28.

24 Jer 25:8–12.

moment of devastation and mischief, however, the prophets Ezekiel and Jeremiah (who previously vehemently prophesied the destruction) proclaimed that this was not the end and that the Jewish people will return to the land of Israel after seventy years and rebuild the Temple and the state. This sounded of course completely absurd in those desolate times, but history proved the prophets right. Ezekiel's famous vision of the "dry bones" expresses the feelings of the people at that time.[25] "And He said to me, 'O mortal, these bones are the whole House of Israel.' They say, 'Our bones are dried up, our hope is gone; we are doomed.'"[26]

This is a metaphor for the Jewish people: they are without hope, feeling de facto dead, like dry bones, but God promises to fill the bones with life and bring the people back to Israel: "Prophesy, therefore, and say to them: Thus said the Lord God: I am going to open your graves and lift you out of the graves, O My people, and bring you to the land of Israel."[27] In fact, three generations later this vision came true, the Babylonians were defeated and King Cyrus the Great allowed the Jews to return to their homeland and to rebuild the Temple. Ezra celebrates this miracle:

> In the first year of King Cyrus of Persia, when the word of the Lord spoken by Jeremiah was fulfilled, the Lord roused the spirit of King Cyrus of Persia to issue a proclamation throughout his realm by word of mouth and in writing as follows. Thus said King Cyrus of Persia: The Lord God of Heaven has given me all the kingdoms of the earth and has charged me with building Him a house in Jerusalem, which is in Judah.[28]

The redemption was, however, not complete, the prophecy remained a potential—a potential not fully applied.[29] The Second Temple was not like the First Temple, as it lacked the most important features. The Talmud explains that there are five differences between the two temples: "The ark with the cover plate and the cherubim, the [altar] fire, the Divine Presence, the Holy Spirit [Prophecy], and the Oracle Shield."[30] The main reason the Talmud gives for this unfulfilled, temporary redemption is the fact that many Jews

25 See Hayyim Angel, *Haggai, Zechariah, and Malachi: Prophecy in an Age of Uncertainty* (Maggid, 2016), xvi.

26 Ezek 37:11.

27 Ezek 37:12.

28 Ezr 1:1–2.

29 See Malbim on Hag 1:1.

30 bT Yoma 21b.

did not return to Israel.[31] The time of prophecy ended and God concealed His face, *hester panim*, an important concept in Judaism.[32] In mystical Judaism, in kabbalah, a similar concept is *Sod haTzimtzum*, literally "the secret of [God's] constriction."[33] Both concepts are later used in Jewish Holocaust theology and are also connected to the reestablishment of Jewish statehood in Israel. So, redemption may not have been complete and God's presence may have been concealed; nevertheless hope has always remained, throughout all centuries of exile. The Torah explicitly states:

> When all these things befall you—the blessing and the curse that I have set before you—and you take them to heart amidst the various nations to which your Lord God has banished you, and you return to your Lord God, and you and your children heed God's command with all your heart and soul, just as I enjoin upon you this day, then your Lord God will restore your fortunes and take you back in love. [God] will bring you together again from all the peoples where your Lord God has scattered you. Even if your outcasts are at the ends of the world, from there your Lord God will gather you, from there [God] will fetch you. And your Lord God will bring you to the land that your fathers possessed, and you shall possess it; and [God] will make you more prosperous and more numerous than your ancestors.[34]

This hope and desire to return to the Holy Land that God has given to us is deeply rooted in our tradition. In the *Amida* (main prayer) of Jewish liturgy, Jews pray every day: "Sound the great shofar for our freedom, raise high the banner to gather our exiles, and gather us together from the four quarters of the earth. Blessed are You, Lord, who gathers in the dispersed of His people Israel."[35] In the introductory prayers are many more examples, quotations from the prophets and the psalms, as well as liturgical poems that likewise pray for the return to Israel. This attitude is also reflected extensively in Talmud and midrash. There were some voices advocating no return to the land of Israel before the messianic era, but throughout the times for leading rabbinic authorities it has been a commandment to settle in the land, "even in a town full of non-Jews in Israel, [it is] better than [in a] Jewish city

31 bT Yoma 9b; bT Brachot 4a; Rashi, available at sefaria.org/Rashi_on_Genesis?tab=contents.

32 Dt 31:17.

33 See Aryeh Kaplan, *Inner Space: Introduction to Kabbalah, Meditation and Prophecy* (Moznaim Publishing, 1990), 120–28.

34 Dt 30:1–5.

35 The Koren Sachs Siddur (2009), 120.

outside," the sins of those living in Israel are forgiven and whoever walks "four *amot* [approximately six feet] in Land of Israel," has a "place in the world-to-come."[36]

THE LAND OF ISRAEL—THE LIVING ROOM OF GOD

Jews believe today that God is not physical in any way. This is an influence from Maimonides. There may be, however, some form of physicality of God, connected with the land of Israel. Rabbi Eliyahu Dessler wrote the following about the connection between the Jewish people and the land of Israel:

> It is amazing to consider how over the last two thousand years of exile from our Land, the love for the Land has remained in our hearts. How is this love possible? [The answer is that] the Land of Israel does not represent a center of our nationhood the way it does for other nations. If that were the case, the Holy Land would already have been forgotten, like other nations who forget their homeland after long periods of exile. Rather, the love for the Land is rooted in holiness. The holiness of this land—in which God is [readily] found—is the same holiness that is inside of us. It is an inheritance located in our souls, which we received from Avraham, after he overcame the test of *Lech lecha* [in which he had to leave his home, his birthplace, and his country to come the Land of Israel].[37]

Hence, there is indeed a dwelling place of God. Rabbi Chaim of Volozhin elaborates on this further and speaks about the Jewish people in the land of Israel as the vessels of the divine presence.[38] The incarnation of God is not anywhere, but connected with a locality, with the Temple in Jerusalem in Israel.[39] This is what makes it holy—that God dwells there in a way He does not do anywhere else.[40]

36 bT Ketubot 110b–111a.

37 Rabbi Eliyahu Dessler, Michtav M'Eliyahu 1:11.

38 Rabbi Chaim of Volozhin, Nefesh HaChaim 1:4.

39 Ex 40:35, 1 Kgs 8:13.

40 Michael Wyschogrod, "Inkarnation aus jüdischer Sicht," *Evangelische Theologie* 55, no. 1 (1995): 21–22.

HISTORICAL RELIGIOUS ZIONISTS

Despite the importance of the land of Israel in Jewish tradition and a continued Jewish presence there, mass immigration starts only in the nineteenth century under the aegis of Zionism. One branch, religious Zionism, was usually based on messianic motives. One of the most important religious Zionist thinkers was Rabbi Abraham Isaac Hakohen Kook, the first Chief Rabbi of the *Yishuv* (modern Jewish settlement in Israel). He was convinced that the Jewish people could only fully unfold and develop their mission as an independent nation in Israel. In his essay "Israel and Its Renaissance" in *Orot* (his primary teachings about Israel, originally published in 1921), he wrote:

> [This was the basis of] of the desire to establish one nation on earth as "a kingdom of priests and holy nation" (Exodus 19:6)—to be a demonstration of the supernal divine light that penetrates the lives of people. Only when [this nation will be] strong and free, having returned to its intact and protected state—after all its many manifestations in the past, after all its difficult tribulations, after all its catharses and refinements—[this nation] will return with . . . all the wealth of its soul and the talents of its life, with all its purity—of flesh, race and belief, with all the content of the divine revelation, which is its inheritance and which is nurtured and broadened by the gift of its land—only then through the inner friendship that Israel will show to the nations of the world despite all the hatred and persecutions it received from them . . . Only then will it be apparent to all that the gift for holiness is not a cheap trinket to be seized by any impure hands, but rather a treasure purchased with awesome toil, with constant self-sacrifice, and through the merit of the holy heritage of parents to children who bear their yoke with love and guard the way of God with all might. Then the fog, the mask, will be lifted off the faces of all the peoples . . .[41]

Rabbi Kook initially had positive attitudes toward Christianity, but because of World War I, he believed that Western (Christian) civilization had failed. He believed that Jews could not grow spiritually in such societies but must establish their own Jewish society.[42] Despite his critique of Christianity, his understanding of Zionism was not an ideology of separation and exclusivity. On the contrary, it is a vision of universalism:

> The heart must be filled with love for all. The love of all creation comes first, then comes the love for all humankind, and then follows the love for

41 Abraham Isaac Hakohen Kook, *Orot* (Maggid, 2015), 154–55.

42 Yehudah Mirsky, *Rav Kook: Mystic in a Time of Revolution* (Yale University Press, 2014), 129–32.

> Israel, in which all other loves are included. It is the destiny of Israel to serve toward the perfection of all things. All these loves are to be expressed in practical action, by pursuing the welfare of those we are bidden to love, and to seek their advancement . . . The love for people must be alive in heart and soul, a love for all people and a love for all nations, expressing itself in a desire for their spiritual and material advancement. Hatred may direct itself only toward the evil and the filth in the world . . . The degree of love in the soul of the righteous embraces all creatures, it excludes nothing, and no people or tongue . . . The highest level of love for people is the love due to the individual person; it must embrace every single individual, regardless of differences in views on religion, or differences of race or climate . . . The entire Torah, the moral teachings, the commandments, the good deeds and their studies have as their objective to remove the roadblocks so that this universal love should be able to spread, to extend to all realms of life.[43]

His Zionism is not an exclusive theology, but seeks to build bridges to the non-Jewish world, where a Jewish state in Israel is understood as the necessary prerequisite for Israel's positive mission to the world and to do good for all humankind.[44]

RELIGIOUS ZIONISM DURING AND AFTER THE SHOAH

Already during the Shoah, but much more afterward Zionism developed from a minority to a majority opinion within Judaism. The Shoah accelerated this development, but, as David Novak points out correctly, it was not the key factor.[45] There were and are anti-Zionist voices for whom Zionism is even the root of the Shoah, just as Rabbi Yoel Teitelbaum claimed the "[Zionist] heresy" was the reason for punishment by God.[46] This was and is, however, a small minority within the Jewish community, and today the majority of Jews within all denominations, from Reform, to Conservative, to Orthodox have a positive image of Israel or understand it even as *reshit tzmichat ge'ulateinu* ("the beginning of the sprouting of our redemption").[47] Within the religious Zionist camp, the voices are quite diverse. Some are

43 Abraham Isaac Hakohen Kook, *Midot HaRaya*, Chapter *ahava* (love). An English translation is available at blogs.timesofisrael.com/rav-kook-on-what-we-need-to-do-to-fix-the-word-step-4-grow-love-erase-hate/. For the Hebrew original, see he.wikisource.org/wiki/מידות_הראי"ה_אהבה

44 See Abraham Isaac Hakohen Kook, *Orot me-Ofel*, chap. 9.

45 David Novak, *Zionism and Judaism: A New Theory* (Cambridge University Press, 2015), 225.

46 Ibid., 230–31.

47 See Gilbert S. Rosenthal, *What Can a Modern Jew Believe?* (Wipf and Stock, 2007), 144.

anti-Gentile and extreme in their positions, but not all religious Zionists are automatically politically right-wing or religious fanatics. This chapter focuses on the many and important moderate voices and sources that offer a constructive base for Jewish-Christian relations.[48]

Rabbi Chaim Zwi Taubes, Chief Rabbi of Zurich from 1936 to 1966 and pioneer of Jewish-Christian dialogue in Switzerland and Europe, wrote in 1943 an essay entitled "Living Judaism," in which he envisions a new Jewish religious commonwealth, with a new Sanhedrin, based on a renewed covenant out of Zion. Under the impression of the Shoah he understood Israel to be the only option for Jews and, if not making *aliya* immediately, at least a strong connection between a newly stablished state and the diaspora communities were vital for Taubes. The character of the new Jewish state must be both religious and national:

> In reality, Judaism is not only a people and not only religion, but a covenant, a commonwealth, the first commonwealth in world history. A commonwealth is the association under the power of an idea, to which it commits under an oath . . . "I will be your God and you will be My people," this is the double idea of the Jewish covenant. It is therefore right from the beginning at once religious and national.[49]

Taubes gives examples from the Bible to prove that Israel has always been successful when religion and nation merged harmoniously into a higher unity. Therefore, the new Jewish state must be the new Jewish center, culturally, socially, politically, and religiously, where the holy covenant should be regularly renewed though a common federal act. For Taubes, the answer to the most severe situation of the Shoah must be renewal.[50] This is exactly why he chose the title "Living Judaism" for his book. At the same time, Rabbi Taubes envisioned a brotherly partnership of Judaism, Christianity, and Islam, which had an eschatological dimension.[51]

Similarly, Rabbi Eliezer Berkovits understood nationhood as a necessity for Judaism and wrote in 1943, in the same year as Taubes: "The creation of an autonomous Jewish body corporate is the sine qua non for the regeneration of Jewish religion and culture. Without it, further development of Judaism

48 See Marc D. Angel, Shlomo Riskin, et al., "Religious Zionism Revisited: A Symposium," *Tradition* 28, no. 4 (1994): 6–7.

49 Chaim Zwi Taubes, *Lebendiges Judentum* (Midgal, 1946), 17.

50 See ibid., 32–44.

51 Chaim Zwi Taubes, "Das Gemeinsame in Judentum, Christentum und Islam" [The common in Judaism, Christianity and Islam], Religious Zionist Archives Jerusalem, Nachlass Taubes (2–29–12, 1940), 5–6.

is impossible; without it Judaism can hardly be saved in the present circumstances."[52] The Shoah proved the vulnerability and weakness of the Jewish people, but also of Judaism. For Berkovits the establishment of statehood was not only about protection or political independence, but crucial for the development of Judaism. Judaism can only thrive and further develop the theology of the written and oral Torah in a sovereign Jewish entity that creates nationhood. He emphasizes the communal, collective aspect of religion, rather than the individual. Only then can the Jewish people fulfill its central mission of being an example to the world.[53]

Berkovits based this Zionist vision on his Holocaust theology. The concept of *hester panim* is central to his theology. For him God's self-hiding is necessary, since "responsibility requires freedom, but God's convincing presence would undermine the freedom of human decision. God hides in human responsibility and human freedom."[54] It is, however, "not a reaction to human behavior . . . God's self-hiding is an attribute of divine nature. Such is God. He is a God, who hides himself . . . God's hiding himself is an attribute of the God of Israel, who is the Savior. In some mysterious way, the God who hides himself is the God who saves."[55] God must respect the freedom of choice and freedom of decision of man, for "freedom and responsibility are of the very essence of man. Without them, man is not human. If there is to be man, he must be allowed to make his choices in freedom. If he has such freedom, he will use it. Using it, he will often use it wrongly; he will decide for the wrong alternative. As he does so, there will be suffering for the innocent."[56] For Berkovits, God is not completely absent, He is present in history. God must be

> absent and present concurrently. He hides his presence. He is present without being indubitably manifest; he is absent without being hopelessly inaccessible. Thus, many find him even in his "absence"; many miss him even in his presence. Because of the necessity of his absence, there is the "Hiding of the Face" and suffering of the innocent; because of the necessity of his presence, evil will not ultimately triumph; because of it, there is hope for man.[57]

He continues:

52 Eliezer Berkovits, *Essential Essays on Judaism*, ed. David Hazony (Shalem, 2002), 164.

53 David Hazony, "Eliezer Berkovits, Theologian of Zionism," *Azure* 17 (2004): 90–91.

54 Eliezer Berkovits, *Faith after the Holocaust* (KTAV Publishing, 1973), 64.

55 Ibid., 101.

56 Ibid., 105.

57 Ibid., 107.

> [God] reveals his presence in the survival of his people Israel. Therein lies his awesomeness. God renders himself powerless, as it were, through forbearance and long-suffering, yet he guides. How else could his powerless people have survived! He protects, without manifest power . . . The Talmudic conclusion was correctly reached: God was silent. Yet, the dilemma was resolved, not in theory, but, strangely enough, in history itself.[58]

The State of Israel is such a manifestation of God in history and offers the opportunity to reconnect to what was lost nearly two thousand years ago. Potentially, Jewish statehood can create what Berkovits calls a "Holy Nation," something the communities in the diaspora can never achieve, no matter how strong or autonomous they are or if they are connected in associations or federations. Similarly to Taubes, Berkovits understands the Jewish ideal as a combination of the religious and the national, the holy and the nation. Only the unfolding of spirit and action in its own state can enable the Jewish people to represent the divine on earth in the fullest way possible. This presupposes, however, that the Israelis live according to the commandments.[59]

Rabbi Joseph Ber Soloveitchik, who was influenced by Rabbi Kook,[60] went along the line of Rabbi Berkovits. In his famous speech *Kol Dodi Dofek*, which he delivered 1956 at Yeshiva University in New York on the occasion of Israel's Independence Day, he identifies six knocks, six signs that proved how miraculous the establishment of State of Israel really was.[61] The Zionist idea of Rabbi Soloveitchik differed from other religious Zionist philosophies, which identified an intrinsic messianic manifestation within the State of Israel. For Soloveitchik, the State of Israel was first and foremost a historical chance, which Jews should take.[62] He understood it nevertheless as a manifestation of God within history, similarly to Berkovits. For both Soloveitchik and Berkovits, the concept of *hester panim* is central to their land theology.

58 Ibid., 109.

59 Hazony, "Eliezer Berkovits," 99–100.

60 Jeffrey Saks, "Rabbi Soloveitchik Meets Rav Kook," *Tradition* 39, no. 3 (2006): 91–92.

61 Joseph B. Soloveitchik, *Kol Dodi Dofek: Listen—My Beloved Knocks*, trans. David Z. Gordon, ed. Jeffrey R. Woolf (Yeshiva University, 2006), chap. 4.

62 Zsolt Balla, "Das Land Israel und der Staat Israel im interreligiösen Dialog," in *Rabbiner im Gespräch mit dem Vatikan: Jüdisch-katholische Beziehungen nach Nostra Aetate und Korrespondenzen mit Benedikt XVI.*, ed. Jehoschua Ahrens and Arie Folger (LIT-Verlag, 2021), 113.

ISRAEL IN CONTEMPORARY JEWISH THOUGHT

The political developments and the founding of the State of Israel had a deep impact on many Jewish thinkers. For Rabbi Arye Kaplan the ingathering of the Jewish people to the land of Israel has theological significance beyond the political facts:

> One of the most important traditions regarding the Messianic Era concerns the ingathering of the Diaspora and the resettlement of the Land of Israel. There are numerous traditions that the Jewish people will begin to return to the Land of Israel as a prelude to the Messiah. The ingathering will begin with a measure of political independence (Rabbi Chama, Sanhedrin 98a), and according to some, with the permission of the other nations (Ramban, Shir HaShirim 8:13). As the holiest spot in the Land of Israel, Jerusalem is the most important city that must be rebuilt there (Responsa Chassam Sofer, Yoreh De'ah 234). There is a tradition that the ingathering of the exiles and the rebuilding of Jerusalem will go hand in hand as the two most important preludes to the coming of the Messiah. According to this tradition, first a small percentage of the exiles will return to the Holy Land, and then Jerusalem will come under Jewish control and be rebuilt. Only then will the majority of Jews in the world return to their homeland. It is thus written, "God is rebuilding Jerusalem; [then] He will gather in the dispersed on Israel" (Tehillim 147:2) (see Berachot 49a, and Rashi there).[63]

This collective aspect is very important, since ethics and values are not understood individually, but—as Rabbi Shlomo Riskin, the Chief Rabbi of Efrat, points out (similar to rabbis Kook and Berkovits):

> The Jewish nation qua nation, *Knesset Yisrael*, is endowed with a unique mission to spread ethical monotheism throughout the world, and this is what is meant by our national (and not individual) *segula* or *inyan Elohi* . . . in a very real sense, our national dedication to the Torah and land of Israel is perceived by the Bible as the necessary gateway for our mission to the world . . . Our prophets perceived that it was only against the backdrop of a nation-state, with is possibility of creating a national culture and the concomitant challenges of a just economic system, proper use of power, and societal justice and compassion devoid of discrimination, that we can begin to influence a world of nation-states. Hence it may correctly be said that our nationalism is a means toward our universalism—and the messianic goal for which we yearn depends upon a sovereign Israel

63 Aryeh Kaplan, *Handbook of Jewish Thought*, vol. 2 (Moznaim Publishing, 1992), 24:18.

> which succeeds in leading the world to a period in which "nation shall not lift up sword against nation and humanity shall not learn war anymore" (Isaiah 2:4).[64]

Messianic times, as outlined by the prophets and the *Rishonim*, for example Maimonides, can only come about, however, through human action and *tshuva*, which Rabbi Riskin understands literarily as return—return to Israel and Torah (ethics/values). This means that the chosenness of Israel and the realization of the Jewish messianic ideal depend on the dedication to Torah—in a correct way, as Rabbi Riskin explains it:

> [Based on Nachmanides's] interpretation of the commandment "Thou shalt be holy": it is not enough to study and practice Torah; unless one studies and practices Torah from the proper perspective it is possible to be a scoundrel "(who thinks he is) within the domains of the Torah." I would therefore submit that our Torah authorities and religious educational institutions must unequivocally declare any justification of Jewish racism in any form whatsoever, or the harming of innocent Gentiles, as being totally unacceptable to normative Judaism.[65]

Similarly, Rabbi Marc Angel, at that time the president of the modern Orthodox Rabbinic Council of America, argues that

> Religious Zionism qua Religious Zionism has *not* been guilty of cultivating a negative attitude toward non-Jews. If individuals who call themselves Religious Zionists do cultivate such attitudes, this is to be lamented and criticized. Even before the rise of the State of Israel, Rabbi Uziel had emphasized that all human beings, Jewish and non-Jewish, are created in the image of God and are entitled to respect and dignity. Rabbi Hayyim David Halevy has written an important response (Ase Lekha Rav 8:687, 689) in which he demonstrates that Judaism rejects racism and discrimination. He has also described the positive responsibilities of Jews toward non-Jews (7:70, 71, and 9:30). Other Religious Zionists have spoken in similar terms.[66]

Rabbi René-Samuel Sirat, former Chief Rabbi of France, goes further. Commenting on various parts of the medieval Sephardic-Jewish classic *Kuzari* by Rabbi Yehuda HaLevi, and other biblical and post-biblical sources,

64 Angel et al., "Religious Zionism Revisited: A Symposium," *Tradition* 28, no. 4 (1994): 31.

65 Ibid., 32–33.

66 Ibid., 6–7.

he understands the Jewish return to Jerusalem as the peak of Jewish history. However, on the other hand, Jews have a major obligation to promote peace and harmony. For Sirat, it is "in this sense that a Jewish Jerusalem cannot be negotiated. But that is not to say that it is impossible to conceive of a Palestinian sovereignty over the Christian and Muslim Holy Sites. This might be the only way that Jerusalem might one day live up to its etymological meaning: City of Peace."[67] His vision is that

> Christians can go unhindered to the churches in Jerusalem and Bethlehem. Muslims can come from Ramallah or Hebron on Fridays to pray in the Mosques of the Haram al-Sharif. That one can go and pray without security checks, unfortunately necessary in the present situation. . . . There all the sons of Abraham will be recognized as such. I dream of a Jerusalem, City of Fraternity. There all men and women will experience the links of brotherhood as they are all children of Adam. I dream of Jerusalem, City of Peace. There peace is appreciated as the most precious of resources and reflects what is lived as a day to day reality. I dream of Jerusalem, City of Liberty. There each one feels free to live according to their conscience, as long as they do not infringe on the liberty of their neighbor. There all citizens are respected and respect one another. I dream of Jerusalem, City of Equality. There the stranger living among you suffers no prejudice. All have the same rights. The stranger is loved like your own self, for you too were strangers in the land of Egypt.[68]

For the realization of such visions, it is essential to create new understandings of the biblical land promise. Rabbi David Hartman, for example, sees Zionism as "on one level, a revolt against Jewish tradition and, on another level, as a renewal of Biblical covenantal theology. That dialectic is fundamental for the understanding of Israel."[69]

67 René-Samuel Sirat, "I Dream of Jerusalem," transcript of speech delivered at the Second Colloquium of Jesuits in Jewish-Christian Dialogue, June 27 to July 2, 2000, available at individual.utoronto.ca/mfkolarcik/texts/jesuit_jewish_dialogue_02.html.

68 Ibid.

69 David Hartman, "Israel: The Rebirth of a People," transcript of speech delivered at the Second Colloquium of Jesuits in Jewish-Christian Dialogue.

THE STATUS OF NON-JEWS AND PALESTINIAN SELF-DETERMINATION IN THE STATE OF ISRAEL

The State of Israel is liberal-democratic, and not a religious entity, even when defining itself as a Jewish state. Therefore, minority rights and religious freedom are first and foremost decided in political-secular processes and is less a religious issue. Nevertheless, Judaism is formative for Israel, and it is important to consider how religious leaders deal with this issue.

Soon after the establishment of the State of Israel, Chief Rabbi Herzog referred to the precedent concept of *Ger Toshav* about the status of minorities in Israel. He wrote in "The Rights of Minorities in Jewish Law" about Muslims and Christians:

> 2. What is the status of Arabs of the Muslim religion? Are they to be considered as resident aliens [*ger toshav*]? That Muslims are in no way categorized as idolators is quite clear; this is the definitive ruling of Maimonides. The question is only whether, even if they are no longer idolators, they are not yet resident aliens [*ger toshav*]. For even though they observe the seven commandments, and much more, observe the commandments to do charity and that of the prayer to the one God, and so, they never accepted even the seven commandments in the presence of an Israelite court [. . .]
>
> 4. [With respect to] purchasing real estate in the Land of Israel: Sale of real estate to gentiles in the Land of Israel is explicitly prohibited. This does not mean that the government [*malkhut*] of Israel is legally empowered to expropriate their holdings . . .
>
> 5. With regard to tolerance toward their worship: This certainly presents no difficulty . . . We are only commanded to uproot idolatry from our land and to disallow gentiles from practicing idolatry in it. But as the Ishmaelites are not idolators, there is no question here at all.
>
> [. . .] Just as the sages said that heathens outside the land are not real idolators—rather, "they [merely] maintain their ancestor's practices" (Hullin 13b)—so too contemporary Christians, even Catholics, are not idolators in the original sense of the term; rather, their heart is to heaven, even though they cannot resolve the contradiction between monotheism and the Trinity in their own minds.
>
> 7. With regard to their worship: As to the Protestants, their faith is in the worst case [only a matter] of adding to the deity, and their worship does not involve statues but only the cross, which is clearly not an object of

> worship but a symbol. Yet even regarding the Catholics, we know that they do not worship statues as deities but rather by way of adoring the persons therein. Now, although we are certainly forbidden to enter their places of worship . . . the question here is whether we are commanded to forcibly bar this worship in a Jewish state. With regard to this, I say that we would not be sinning against our holy Torah were we to tolerate its existence.[70]

While Chief Rabbi Herzog basically did not permit sales of land and property to non-Jews in Israel (although he accepted that the state authorities could do so), other halachic authorities, such as the Rambam, do allow it, since the prohibition applies to idol worshippers, but not to a *ger toshav*. Even those who do not share this opinion have grounds to permit it nevertheless. One reasoning is that the de facto acknowledging of non-Jewish landownership in Israel through the modern halachic ruling of *shmita*. Another reasoning is value-based. On ethical grounds we cannot forbid non-Jews from living in the land of Israel (and having lived there for a long time) to keep their property or acquire new land. Moreover, major rabbinic authorities, such Rabbi Chaim Ozer Grodinsky, Rabbi Zvi Pesach Frank and, later, Rabbi Ovadia Yosef (the Sephardic Chief Rabbi of Israel) and Rabbi Joseph B. Soloveitchik argued that halacha does permit in principle a deal of land for peace.[71] These approaches can offer a religious base for land ownership of Palestinians and answer some of the key issues over land in Israel.

Certainly, a peaceful solution for Palestinian self-determination is long overdue and can be achieved only with new concepts. Lately, the idea of an Israeli-Palestinian (Con-)Federation gains momentum, in religious circles,[72] and in secular circles,[73] on both the Israeli and the Palestinian side. Perhaps by way of such new ideas it is possible to come to a solution that pragmatically combines vision and reality. The Abraham Accords, although harshly criticized by the Palestinian side, could be a game changer when including the Palestinians and other regional players in the Near East. The Abraham Accords have religious connotations and, as Rabbi Menachem Froman put it: "If religion is part of the problem, then it must necessarily be part of the

70 Isaac Halevi Herzog, "The Rights of Minorities in Jewish Law," quoted in *The Jewish Political Tradition*, ed. Menachem Lorberbaum et al. (Yale University Press, 2006), 2:525–29.

71 Anthony Manning, "Land for Peace (Part 1)," available at outorah.org/p/85697/.

72 See Yoel A. Oz, *Abrahamic Confederation: A Solution to the Israeli-Palestinian Conflict* (self-published, 2018).

73 Yossi Beilin and Saliba Sarsar, "Israeli-Palestinian Confederation Is a Way Forward for Peace," *Jerusalem Post* (February 17, 2022), available at jpost.com/opinion/article-696830.

solution."[74] Interreligious dialogue has flourished in Israel over the last years and is constantly intensifying.[75] Religion can play a crucial part in finding a just and fair solution for both Israelis and Palestinians—and pacifying the entire region. Rabbi Taubes had already in 1943 laid out the vision that Israel can "play a mediating and connecting role between the Orient and other parts of the world" and bring "great benefit also to the Arab countries," since Jews have "a peaceful attitude toward the Arabs" and can "prove the Arab population that we don't want to oust them from the land."[76]

CONCLUSION

To summarize, the land of Israel is not only an eminent part of Jewish identity, but an intrinsic part of the covenantal relationship between God and His people Israel. God chose to give it as an infinite inheritance to the Jewish people so that they can fulfill their mission in this world as God's partners in the ongoing creation. Therefore, it is much more than only a place of sovereignty and security, but is also a place of holiness, of God's presence. The land of Israel has always remained in the hearts and the souls of the Jewish people and deeply embedded in Jewish tradition, even in exile. It was and is therefore an important part of Jewish self-conception. It is home.

Further, not only the land of Israel, but also the State of Israel has a theological and covenantal dimension. God manifests Himself in history through the renewed Jewish presence in His land, not only as a Jewish majority in Israel, but as a majority of the Jews in the world. This is not just a coincidence or an accident. True, it is not the fulfillment of the prophetic visions of redemption either, but it is a first step. It is a historical chance, given by God to us, a chance of "renewal of Biblical covenantal theology," as Rabbi David Hartman put it. New approaches are needed for the new challenges we face, which includes the question of the status of non-Jews in Israel, particularly the Palestinians and their rights on the land.

There are voices that open up a perspective for a pragmatic solution on the land of Israel, but it is also important that non-Jews, for example the churches, not only tolerate a Jewish presence in Israel or speak out against violence, but actively acknowledge and engage with Israel and the Israelis

74 Yakov Nagen, "The Abrahamic Union: A confederate solution to the Israeli-Palestinian conflict," *The Times of Israel* (May 29, 2017), available at blogs.timesofisrael.com/the-abrahamic-union-a-confederate-solution-to-the-israeli-palestinian-conflict/.

75 See Jehoschua Ahrens, "Jüdisch-christlicher Dialog in Israel," *ZfBeg* 1 (2019), available at zfbeg.org/ojs/index.php/cjbk/article/view/504/472.

76 Zwi Chaim Taubes, *Lebendiges Judentum* (Midgal, 1946), 111–14.

and develop a Christian theology and vision regarding the land of Israel that respects or at least considers the Jewish viewpoint. This could create a common base. New visions are needed to bring us forward and eventually achieve final redemption, as in Iggerot ha-Re'ayah, Letters of Rabbi Abraham Isaac ha-Kohen Kook: "The old shall be renewed and the new shall be sanctified; together, they will become torches that illuminate Zion."

6

THEOLOGICAL ZIONISM

Rabbi David Novak

CHOICES: DIVINE AND HUMAN

Jewish theology is most deeply concerned with election: the choices God makes and their significance for human thought and action.[1] These choices seem to be (1) God's choice to create the world as God's total possession; (2) God's choice to create humans as the unique "image of God" (*tselem elohim*), that is, for a singular mutual relationship with Godself; (3) God's choice of Israel / the Jewish people (*am yisrael*) as the optimal community for the God-human relationship (the *berit* or "covenant") to develop in; and (4) God's choice of the land of Israel (*eretz yisrael*) as the optimal earthly locus of the God-Israel relationship. Finally, there is a fifth choice: a human choice, that is, the political choice of the Jewish people to primarily live in the land of Israel, to choose the kind of polity (*medinah* in Hebrew) that they judge to be the best means for keeping the divine commandment to settle the land of Israel as the earthly center of the covenant between God and the people Israel. Only that political choice, it seems, does the Jewish tradition leave to the Jewish people to decide by themselves for themselves voluntarily. In fact, Jewish history shows several different options have been tried by the Jewish people.

Accordingly, theocracy is a theological concept that properly characterizes God's governance of the universe, God's governance of the human world, God's governance of the Jewish people, and God's governance of the Jewish people in the land of Israel. Only the people's choice of what kind of

1 The following draws upon the theological thesis in my book, *Zionism and Judaism: A New Theory* (Cambridge University Press, 2015), 99–152.

government they want to administer their communal existence is not and should not be considered a theocratic enterprise, even though it is devised for the sake of the theocratic enterprise.

The Torah teaches that the four aforementioned choices are all made by God. Indeed, one could not speculate about the options not chosen had the actual choices and their results (*desiderata*) not been explicitly revealed in the Torah. Humans could know nothing of what God does in the world had not God revealed in the Torah what God does in and for the world, plus what God expects our human responses to these divine activities to be.

Let us look at the first two choices, that is, God's choice to create the universe and God's choice to create humans in His image. Thinking about these two choices first enables us to appreciate the ontological significance of the last two choices, that is, God's choice of the Jews and God's choice of the land of Israel for the Jews. In other words, the election of the Jews and the election of the land for us are consistent with the way we can think about God's relationship with the universe and with humankind. With this ontological grounding, these latter two choices seem to be less capricious than would be the case were we to think about them in a more mundane way. Let us now look at these first two choices more closely.

GOD CHOOSES TO CREATE THE UNIVERSE AS GOD'S POSSESSION

First, let us distinguish between "the universe" and "the world." The universe is everything God has created. The world is the earthly part of the universe that humans can experience, know, and inhabit, which is not even all of the earth (*ha'arets*). It is what the rabbis called "the habitable world" (*yishuvo shel olam*) or what we would call "civilization."

Accordingly, the context of God's next three choices regarding humankind, the people Israel, and the land of Israel is *the world*, not the universe. The meaning of the universe for the world is that God has freely chosen to create the universe in such a way that a habitable world can arise *therein*. It is where humankind, the people Israel, and the land of Israel could be chosen by God. "The Lord creator of the heavens, He is the God who forms the earth, who makes it and establishes it; He created it to be a habitation [*la-shevet*], not chaos [*tohu*]" (Is 45:18). God's choice to found the world as the place of human habitation, though, presupposes that God has first chosen to create a universe where the three choices just noted are all of cosmic or universal significance. They are not, therefore, cosmic flukes. Responsible election lies at the core of reality. Nevertheless, God's chosen interest in the world is not confined here, any more than God's chosen interest in the entire universe is confined there.

God's purpose in creating the universe is, as Maimonides taught, the purpose God created *for* the universe. The purpose of the universe or "Nature" is not immanent within the created universe itself. So choices are considered to be rational when they are made for a purpose; choices are capricious or arbitrary when they are made for no purpose. It would be an insult to God to presume that God's choices are made for no purpose, that God is capricious, arbitrary, and thus irresponsible. For us, the purposes or ends for which we choose to act one way rather than another are *already there* before our choice or rejection of them, eliciting our response to them. But God's creative choosing or electing creatures is also God's creation of the purposes that ultimately structure or inform these creatures; hence they are what God creates *for* the universe *while* God simultaneously creates their substance. These purposes, though, are not what God finds *already within* the universe. To presume that would be to assign the universe itself (or its intelligible "nature") priority over God Himself. God's choices, then, are infinitely more radical than our own.

Of course, because free choice requires more than one option before it can be chosen or else it would not be free, God could have just as easily chosen not to create the universe, that is, to remain in and by Godself. So, why did God create the universe? Even though we can only surmise why, we first need to assume that God's action has a purpose, nonetheless. What could the purpose of this just or righteous Creator God be?

Perhaps God desired that there be something other than God, which could be the object of God's continuing concern. To fulfill this desire could be God's purpose in creating the universe, a universe different from God, and a universe that is not part of God. To be the object of God's continuing concern, though, means that the universe is meant to always stand *before* God, that is, to face God [*lifnei*] rather than turn "away from [*mi-lifnei*] God" (Gn 4:16). That is, the universe cannot transcend God as God transcends the universe. The universe has no life of its own independent of God, but God has a life independent of the universe and His concern for it. That would not be so, however, if God had chosen to create a truly self-sufficient, absolute, autonomous universe, a universe turned loose, as it were, to run on "automatic pilot." Were that so, to assert that the universe *was* created by God to be independent of God would make God Himself superfluous by the time such an assertion could be made by any creature. If the Creator is indifferent to His creatures once the creatures have been created, do the creatures not have good reason to be similarly indifferent to their Creator thereafter?

The God-universe relation is asymmetrical: the universe is not related to God like God is related to the universe. God is not correlated with this universe or with any other possible universe. No matter what relation God has to the universe or any of its parts, there is always a divine surplus.

God's choice to will *that* the universe come-to-be (its existence), plus God's willing *what* the universe is-to-be (its essence or nature), like all choices, take place in time with its possibilities. Thus the universe itself was once only a possibility for God. The universe is a temporal reality in which choices, both divine and human, can take place, because there are always possibilities *as yet* unrealized. An essentially temporal universe has an open future. An essentially temporal universe is not one that is wholly determined by strict causal laws from top to bottom, so to speak. In such a universe, human choices are as undetermined as are divine choices. Nevertheless, there is an essential difference. Divine choices involve an infinite range of possibilities, whereas human choices are confined to a quite finite range.

Now even after God makes a choice, God is not correlated with what God chooses, that is, God has a life of God's own not only *before* creation, but also *outside* and *alongside* creation (and maybe even *after* the created universe has run a finite temporal course). Yet what that pre-universal/extra-universal life of God is, that cannot even be known by anyone other than God.

GOD CHOOSES TO CREATE THE HUMAN PERSON

Humans are distinctly different from all other creatures, and so Scripture clearly describes our creation differently. Throughout the creation narrative in the first chapter of Genesis we are told that God "made" this or that by speaking it into existence, and that immediately afterward God *approved* what He made. For example, "God saw the light that it is good [*ki tov*]" (Gn 1:4).

"Good" here seems to mean: God was pleased with what He made, as it turned out the way God wanted it to turn out. (We should not be wary of attributing an emotion like pleasure to God, because God's creation of an "other" in which God is concerned means that God has chosen not only to create or *effect* that other, but also to be *affected* by that other.) However, when it comes to the creation of "man" or humans (*adam*), it says: "Let us make [*na'aseh*] man in our image [*be-tsalmenu*] like us [*ki-demutenu*] . . . male and female He created them" (Gn 1:26). Moreover, it does not say that God was pleased or happy with this human creation: God did not conclude that his human creatures are "good" (*tov*). That absence of approval seems to be because God is not the sole maker of humans; instead, it seems as though God made us humans as His partners in our own making. That is, interacting together with God we humans make our lives. God does not yet approve or disapprove of this human life, that is, the life of every single human person, because we and God are not finished working with each other.

God's special concern seems to be God's purpose in creating humans in His image to be like Him, that is, God's concern intends an object *with whom* to be in a relationship. God's purpose in creating humans in his image seems to be that God desired companions to whom God could speak and who could respond accordingly. Thus God calls Abraham "my beloved friend [*ohavi*]" (Is 41:8). And, about Moses, the Torah says: "And the Lord spoke to Moses face to face, like a man speaks to his companion [*re'ehu*]" (Ex 33:11). Unlike us, though, God can live without companions.

God could have chosen some sort of *symbiosis* with God's human image, that is, to reduce Godself to a correlation with humankind alone. But that would make God as answerable to humans as humans are answerable to God. Thus God declared to Job: "Where were you when I founded the earth? Tell it if you have any insightful understanding!" (Job 38:4). "Do you know the laws of heaven [*huqqot shamayim*]; could you apply their governance [*mishtaro*] on earth?" (Job 38:33). God's concern with the human world is not exhausted here. God is still concerned with what lies beyond the human world, just as God's concern with the universe does not prevent God from having his own life totally independent of his being the Creator of the universe. Just as God's transcendence of the universe is affirmed when God is not reduced to God's creative relation to the universe, so God's transcendence of the world is affirmed when God is not reduced to only being the "Master of the [human] world" (*ribbono shel olam*). Even God's relation to the universe is more complex than simply making the earthly part of the universe fit for life and human habitation.

The question now is: Why is God's relationship with every human person, for which every human person has a capacity, not sufficient? Is the election of humankind not enough for God? Why does God want to choose Israel, and choose the land of Israel for His people to settle there?

GOD CHOOSES ISRAEL

From the creation narrative in Genesis, we learn that from the beginning God first relates Godself to humans in community, that is, as *humankind*. So, before we can properly understand why God is related to *this* people Israel, we need to understand why God would desire to relate to *any* people, that is, to any specific human community in the world. This is *the* political question that requires a theological answer.

As Aristotle astutely noted, humans are political animals because they speak with one another; and humans speaking with one another thereby constitute their common political world. But what is the content of this political communication?

The content of intelligent conversation or dialogue is "teleological" or purposeful. Indeed, these purposes become known when we know with whom we are speaking as the addressees of that speech. As we have seen, speech emerges in the world from two speech situations. First, God speaks to the human person, commanding us (him and her) to act a certain way in the world that is pleasing to God, who is the master of our world (*ribbono shel olam*). Second, the man speaks to the woman, inviting her to build up the world we have been placed in by God. In both situations, the parties to the conversation have freely chosen to participate in it.

The first speech-constituted relationship is what obtains between humans and God (*bein adam le-maqom*). The second relationship is what obtains between humans themselves (*bein adam le-havero*). The two relationships are themselves interrelated. We humans are ultimately interested in God because God has created each of us and all of us for a free normative relationship with Godself. And we humans are ultimately interested in each other because we are all participants in the common world God has created for the divine-human relationship to be conducted coherently therein. So the essential purpose of the interhuman relationship is to enable the human community to be related to God insofar as we are to be ruled by God. And the optimal divine-human relationship can be conducted only in a human community who have freely accepted this to be their transcendent purpose, their raison d'être. We humans are both the divinely oriented image of God and political beings oriented to each other. However, when our "religious" nature is reduced to our "political" nature, we become the servants of political idolatry or the divinization of the state. And, when our religious nature is separated from our political nature, it is like when Plato urged us "to fly from the world and become like God." Then, the world either ignores us or, more usually, it banishes us. Thus each aspect of our nature checks the excesses of the other.

This is what human community per se is supposed to be: one community under God and living for the sake of God. Already before the Flood, however, the interrelation of the divine-human and the interhuman realms began to unravel. Humans established societies apart from their relationship with God. Regarding Cain, who had offended God by murdering his brother Abel, it is said: "Then Cain went away from the Lord [*mi-lifnei adonai*] . . . Cain knew his wife and she conceived and gave birth to Enoch; and he then built a city, and called the city by the name of his son Enoch" (Gn 4:16–17). Yet, in the scriptural narrative, about another man also named "Enoch" (*hanokh* or "dedicated one"), it is said: "Enoch walked with God and he was no more, for God took him away [from this world]" (Gn 5:24). In a number of rabbinic speculations about this enigmatic character, Enoch is portrayed as a man whose devotion to God could not be correlated with involvement in contemporary politics. Therefore, he had to leave his polity and become a virtual recluse. Apparently, religious commitment and political commitment were incompatible; hence Enoch had to choose between the two. He chose devotion to God over political involvement. Thus the first Enoch, son of Cain, is dedicated to the polity his father established "away from the Lord," while the second Enoch, son of Jared (Gn 5:18), is dedicated to God away from his polity. Surely, loyalty to God and loyalty to the state were on a collision course; one would inevitably try to displace the other.

Political estrangement from God comes to a head when humankind does come together, but not under God's kingship. Instead, they come together in order to storm heaven and displace God altogether, replacing God's kingship with their own international authority. Thus the verse, "The whole earth had one language [*safah ahat*] with similar words" (Gn 11:1) has been interpreted to mean that all humankind conspired together for one purpose: to wage war against God, replacing God with the Tower of Babel, the product of their own industrial ingenuity. "Let us build for ourselves a tower [*migdal*] whose head goes up into heaven; so let us make a reputation [*shem*] for ourselves" (Gn 11:4).

God's response to this universal human audacity is to undo such perverse human unity by scattering now divided humankind "all over the earth" (Gn 11:9). Moreover, God undoes their stated desire for political unity, which could be constituted only by linguistic unity, by causing that elusive unity to unravel into linguistic/cultural diversity. There is no unity among such radical, antagonistic divergence. Therefore the desideratum of humankind truly united for the sake of a transcendent goal, that is, to be united under God's universal sovereignty, becomes in scriptural teaching the eschatological desideratum only God can and will realize. "For then I [God] shall turn to the peoples with clear speech [*safah berurah*], to call all of them in the name of the Lord, to serve Him with one consensus [*shkhem ehad*]" (Zeph 3:9). In other words, the true and final unity of humankind will come only when God chooses to reestablish the universal authority He exercised at creation. "On that day the Lord will be one, and His name one" (Zech 14:9), which is interpreted to mean that the God who is now worshiped by Israel alone will be worshiped by everybody later; and the God who now rules Israel directly through His Torah revealed to Israel will directly rule everybody later.

Because of universal political estrangement from God, the only human relationship with God possible under these circumstances becomes God's relationship with lone individuals, who have either separated themselves or who have been separated from political life, as we have just seen above. Thus in rabbinic speculation about the life of Abraham before his election by God, Abraham (or "Abram" as he was called before his election by God) is portrayed as a lone God-seeker in a society essentially hostile to God. And, in such a society hostile to God, it is inevitable that there will be violence and oppression among the human inhabitants who, lacking a truly equal commonality, have no real basis for seeking justice and peace among themselves. Abraham is both a religious and a political rebel.

Nevertheless, instead of being commanded to become a sort of hermit in an uninhabited wilderness (which would be a utopia, there being no such place on earth), Abraham is commanded to go to a particular land, one already inhabited and therefore inhabitable, there to found an altogether new sort of human community. Hence this new community is a theological-political entity, one where the religious and political sides of human nature are interrelated, and where neither is neglected for the sake of the other. This community is founded through a covenant between God and this special people, who become "the unique nation [*goi ehad*] on earth" (1 Chr 17:21), that is, they are uniquely related to "the singular [*ehad*] God" (Dt 6:5). The election of Abraham, then, makes the God-human relationship in this world a specific public relationship instead of a private one with particular individuals outside human society. All that notwithstanding, that relationship is not yet the actual kingdom of God on earth (*malkhut shamayim*) with universal humankind.

The present state of God's relationship with humans in the political world is better than the relationship with lone individuals outside the political world. Moreover, this *communal* relationship is not one we humans ourselves could have established with God any more than individual humans could have established the God-human relationship by themselves. How could we do so, as nothing in the world tells us that God is concerned with us at all, that God wants a relationship with us at all, that God desires us? That information can only come from God. (That also explains why humans cannot really love God unless we are convinced that God loves us first.)

God's choice of a special people, who become a people because of God's election of them for a covenantal relationship, seems to be the best choice God could have made under the circumstances. The other options would have been to leave the divine-human relationship at the level of a divine-individual relationship, or to redeem all of humankind by making the covenant become truly universal. The first option is similar to what is called today the "privatization of religion," which makes living a religious life ultimately untenable politically, as religion like language is an essentially public matter. The theological-political realm does not function as a public-private relation. The second option, that is, the redemption of the whole world sounds best;

nevertheless it seems that God did not think that humankind is yet ready for the end of history that this ultimate universality entails.

This only tells us, though, *that* God's desire to elect *a* people is in God's best interest; it does not tell us, however, *why* God actually did choose *this* people Israel. Now the answer to this question could be either retrospective or prospective. (The election of the covenanted people, like any divine choice as we have seen, should not be taken to be capricious, which would impugn God as irrational and unjust.) The Torah rules out a retrospective answer: "Not because of your great numbers did God desire [*hashaq*] you to choose you, for you are the least of the nations. It is because of the Lord's love [*me'ahavat adonai*] for you, and His keeping the promise [*ha-shevu ʿah*] He made to your ancestors . . ." (Dt 7:7–8). Hence, whatever the people Israel are able to accomplish is not due to their own meritorious efforts in the past, but rather because God "upholds His covenant [*brito*] that He promised your ancestors" (Dt 8:8). And that promise is not a promise of payment for services rendered to God by Israel. Instead, it is a promise of divine grace or charity. "You should not say in your heart . . . because of my righteousness [*be-tsidqati*] the Lord has brought me to inherit this land" (Dt 9:4). It does seem better to assume that the answer to the question "Why Israel?" is prospective rather than retrospective. Israel's election is not because of what the Jews have been in the past. It is because of what they will be in the future, a future only God can truly anticipate.

One cannot assert an explicit reason why God chose *this* people Israel, as that would require one to locate some unique natural or historic factor in the life of the people that they possess and that they know they possess. If the people knew that it is because of that factor they were in fact chosen, then their election would become their worldly possession rather than their task to fulfill in the world. But their task in the world is to show God, themselves, and the world that God did not make a mistake by choosing this people in the first place. That task always lies before them; it is never a *fait accompli*. So, when we Jews blatantly reject the task of actually proclaiming the sanctity of God's name or reputation (*qiddush ha-shem*) to the world or to ourselves, the reputation of God in the world is tarnished (*hillul ha-shem*).

The election of Israel is not due to any inherent properties, either biological (with their racist implications) or cultural (with their chauvinistic implications), by which Jews can claim to be inherently superior to the rest of humankind. The Jewish people differ from the rest of humankind only because of God's claim upon us to live with God in what is a monogamous relationship, that is, on our side of the covenant. Thus the same prophet who says to Israel in God's name, "Only you have I intimately known of all the families of the earth" (Amos 2:3), also reminds the people that just as "I have brought Israel up out of the land of Egypt," God has also rescued "the Philistines from Caphtor and Aram from Kir" (Amos 9:7). Outside that covenantal relationship with God, the Jewish people are no different from any other people; hence we should not represent ourselves to be the only humans God is concerned with. Israel's unique relationship with God, which is essentially God's relationship with us, is a reality *between* Israel and God alone, not between the Jewish people and the world. Even despite the Holocaust, Jews have no special claim on the world; we only have the claim any people has to be treated justly by the world, both as individuals and as a people. But the Jews do have a claim on God to redeem us, even though we have no right to set the date or even know it. "I know My Redeemer lives, though he be the last to arise on earth . . . then from my own flesh I shall see God" (Job 19:25).

To cogently affirm that God chose the people Israel is to thereby deny that the Jews chose God. And, that affirmation thereby denies that the Jews chose themselves to be different from every other people as end in itself. That affirmation also denies that the Jews choose to be a conquering people (*Herrenvolk* in German), that is, a people dedicated to obliterating every other people's difference from them by absorbing these other peoples into our own political and cultural domain. That is a counterfeit universalism, for it makes one particularity universal by default. It becomes universal by obliterating in one way or another every other particularity. That is now what we call a "zero-sum game." Conversely, "Then I [God] shall turn to the peoples [including Israel] with clear speech, calling all of them [*khulam*] in the name of the Lord, to serve Him with one shoulder" (Zeph 3:9).

The people Israel only have the choice to either confirm or deny their election by God. When they do confirm that covenantal election, they are given much authority or voluntariness to interpret and develop the Torah, which is the constitution of that covenantal relationship, as they see fit. But, when they attempt to repudiate their election by God, God does not accept their illegitimate autonomy to do so with impunity. When this happens (and it happens regularly), God reiterates His covenantal claim over and over again, often through that minority of Jews, the "remnant of Israel" (*she'erit yisra'el*), who have always remained faithful to the covenant all along. God does not allow us to un-elect ourselves and thereby nullify the covenant with Him, no matter how far we have strayed away from it. The rabbis emphasize that God's choice to elect the people Israel is irrevocable because, even though God did not have to choose the people Israel, once God did choose this people, that choice may not be undone. God is responsible for the choice He has made insofar as that choice was not capricious. That choice was made by means of an oath (*shevuah*). Were God to break His oath, He would thereby cease to have any moral authority over this people, as a liar is no longer to be trusted, and all moral authority is based on trust.

GOD CHOOSES THE LAND OF ISRAEL

Being confined to the world, the people Israel need a place to call home in this world, a place in which to center the God-Israel covenant. It seems that Abraham was regarded by the people of Canaan to be a nomad, a designation even he accepted by calling himself a "transient resident" (*ger ve-toshav*, Gn 23:4). But is that his permanent status and that of his people in the world or not? Now there have been both Jews and non-Jews who have thought that being "the Wandering Jew," forever homeless in any and all lands, is an essential strength of the Jewish people, one Jews should take special pride in. In this view, the Jews' strength is that they are not tied down to any land, thus making the real homelessness of all humans in this world an asset rather than a liability. But, if this were the true status of the Jewish people, they would have the same dichotomy we saw when considering what the God human relationship would be like were it to be an essentially private relationship between God and some isolated individual humans. For if that were the case, the essentially political nature of humans would be left out of the God-human relationship, as the relation of a polity to a particular *territory* is a political necessity.

To be sure, even in exile, Jews can still retain their communal life, but they are still living *under* the political domain of some other people. The Jews would still be living as aliens in any society whose warrant comes from a non-Jewish historical revelation (like that of Christianity or Islam), or they would be living as anonymous individual citizens of a society whose warrant comes from a social contract among equals that does not directly stem from their different prior communal commitments. And in this type of liberal society, a Jewish community (*qahal*) can only be a private association of individuals. This is why the optimal existence of the Jewish people is in a special land of their own. Thus the Torah teaches that just as God chose the people Israel to be his special covenanted people, so did God choose the land of Israel to be the special locus of that covenant in the world, that is, the place (*maqom*) where the covenant is to be lived primarily. It would seem that God's other options vis-à-vis the land for His covenanted people Israel would be to either let the people choose whatever land they wanted for themselves, or to let the people conquer one land to be the headquarters of the universal project to conquer the world for the Jews' covenant with God, or to let the people think of themselves as aboriginal natives of the land, that is, that the land is their natural location in the world.

The first option or possibility would be similar to the view that God created the universe as a *fait accompli* and then turned it loose to function autonomously on its own. In this case, allowing the people to choose their own land by conquest would be like saying that God chose to create the people Israel back then, but that they are now on their own to do as they see fit for themselves. Contrary to this opinion, however, the Torah states: "You should know that it is not because of your righteousness [*be-tsidqatekha*] that the Lord your God gives you [*noten lekha*] this good land to acquire it [*le-rishtah*]" (Dt 9:6). This means that the people Israel have no right or claim to take any land because of what they have made of themselves. Thus the verse concludes: "for you are a stiff-necked people." The land, then, is a gift to the people from God, not as recompense for their righteousness, but rather as a task for the people to fulfill: "to acquire it." In other words, Jewish settlement of the land of Israel is a divine commandment (*mitsvah*), a task the Jews are to fulfill for the sake of their communal covenant with God. So, it is not the land that is given to them as passive recipients, but rather the commandment to settle the land that is given to them by God. The commandment is what God has chosen for them to do; the land of Israel is where God has chosen for them to do it.

Like all the divine commandments, this is not a task humans have chosen for themselves autonomously. Were the choice of the land of Israel theirs to make autonomously, this autonomy could then lead them to pick any land they thought best for themselves here and now, or they could decide there is no land here and now that suits them.

The historic connection of the Jewish people to the land of Israel is most cogently expressed in our claim on the nations of the world to let us fulfill the duty God has placed upon us to acquire and settle the land God has chosen for us. And in today's world, we can do that only by becoming a nation-state among the other nation-states of the world. This duty (*hovah*) is one that we Jews cannot abrogate, any more than we could repeal a commandment of the Torah, even when we could not fulfill a commandment because of circumstances beyond our control. Indeed, throughout much of Jewish history, when most Jews could not live in the land of Israel because of insurmountable physical, political, and economic obstacles, we still did not despair or lose hope (*ye'ush*) of resuming an independent communal life there. Perhaps it could be said that the historic right of the Jewish people to the land of Israel is our right to return there to fully become the people God wants us to be, there especially, and which we have tried to be throughout our history, even when we have been prevented from living there due to insurmountable political and economic factors.

Of course, this theological claim is primarily a claim to be made by Jews among ourselves. Jews need our own internal Jewish reasons for being Zionists before we can argue externally for our Zionism to the nations of the world, with reasons that seem genuine and not apologetic. These secular reasons can be made anywhere to anybody, but they must still come from somebody somewhere in the world. The authenticity of these external claims is suspect, though, if they come from anonymities who are nowhere or everywhere in their own minds. Nevertheless, contrary to the view of extreme secularists (who only argue *ad extra*) and extreme religious nationalists (who only argue *ad intra*), the two claims are not polar opposites. Instead, they can be coordinated rationally. So, Jews can claim that we are fulfilling the task assigned to us by God of acquiring and settling the land of Israel, and we are doing that by means of standards accepted internationally for the exercise of political sovereignty (*shilton* in classical Hebrew) by a particular people in a particular country.

Furthermore, because Jews and Christians share the Hebrew Bible as divine revelation, the Jewish theological claim on the land of Israel is one that is theologically valid for Christians as well. Christians who are faithful to their own tradition, therefore, believe or should believe that God's covenant with the Jewish people and with the land of Israel as their inheritance is everlasting and forever valid. It has only been supplemented, not superseded or replaced, by Christianity.

The claim that God chose the land of Israel for the people Israel is also contrary to the claim that Jews have a natural right (as distinct from an historic right) to the land of Israel. Yet the fact is that the Jews (or Israelites) are not the aboriginal people in the land. Like Abraham, they come from somewhere else to the land at God's explicit command. "The Lord said to Abram: 'Go, get yourself out of your land, and from your birthplace [*u-mi-moladetekha*], and from your patrimony, to the land I will show you" (Gn 12:1). So when Abraham deals with the aboriginal people of Canaan, he acknowledges: "I am only a transient resident [*ger ve-toshav*] among you" (Gn 23:4). From this it follows that just as the special covenantal status of the people Israel is not a natural fact, neither is the connection of the people to the land a natural fact. Every fact in the world, whether natural or historic, is taken by the Jewish people to be either the result of a divine choice or the result of a human choice. That is because neither historic facts nor natural facts themselves explain why they exist rather than not exist. Nothing is "just there." Everything has been "put there" by someone or other. That is why the land does not belong to the Jews—or to anybody else—for nothing in creation belongs to any creature. Everything and everybody belong to God alone. As such, God assigns the land of Israel to the people Israel like an innkeeper assigns the room he or she wants a guest to inhabit during his or her brief sojourn there. Therefore, our place in the world, our "somewhere," is to be in the land of Israel. The Jews are not meant to be anywhere (like nomads) or nowhere (like "rootless cosmopolitans").

That the Jewish connection to the land of Israel is not a natural fact makes one think of why God chose *a* land for the Jewish people, but not why God chose *this* land for us. Ordinarily, it would seem that the only reason for the choice of a special land would have to be because of its natural or geographic properties, that is, that it has more useful resources for the people than any other land has. However, what would these natural resources be, and how could we show that they are unique to this land? Therefore, just as we cannot know what inherent genetic characteristics the Jewish people have that would make them naturally superior to the other peoples of the world, so we cannot know what inherent geographic properties make the land of Israel superior to the other lands of the world.

To presume that the Jews are naturally superior and that the land is naturally superior suggests a type of racism that the Jewish tradition largely rejects. For, if the Jews are naturally or biologically unique, then how could the tradition encourage them to accept converts from non-Jewish stock? If the land of Israel is naturally or geographically unique, then how could the tradition permit Jews to live anywhere else? Thus we can assume that God's specific reasons for both the election of this people Israel and this land of Israel do exist in the mind of God (who is not to be believed to be a capricious God), but they are unknown and unknowable to humans, at least while we are still in this world. "My plans [*mahshavotai*] are not your plans" (Is 55:8). Hence the connection of the people Israel to the land of Israel is best thought of as being a fact of divine election. The Jewish connection to the land of Israel is not the result of the choice of the Jews. Our choice is only to either confirm or deny that connection, that is, to be or not to be a Zionist in the deepest sense. This human choice is subsequent to God's choice to elect whomever God elects. Perhaps the specific reasons for God's election of the people and of the land will be revealed in the "end-time" (*ahareet ha-yamim*), when other secrets will also be revealed to those whom God elects to be alive then.

By limiting the full national existence of the people Israel to the land of Israel, Jews are best able to live their specific covenantal relationship with God. In the land of Israel, that relationship is truly centered. Jews can thus overcome the sundering of their communal existence from their national existence, which would be the case were they to be an essentially "stateless" community in the world. And Jews thus overcome the imperialist temptation to regard the redemption of the whole world to be their own project, of which they could brag "my strength and the might of my hand have accomplished for me this success" (Dt 8:17).

Just as God's concern is not confined to the people Israel alone, God's relationship with them is special; yet it is not a symbiosis. So too, the relationship of the people Israel with the land of Israel is special, not exclusive. That means that the Jewish people are centered in the land of Israel; they are not confined there, however. Though inferior to Jewish life in the land of Israel, Jewish life outside Israel, in the Diaspora (*golah*) has Jewish legitimacy. Moreover, we can acknowledge in good faith that the land of Israel is not confined to Jews. As such, Jews can recognize the right of non-Jews to live in the land of Israel: either as individual citizens in a Jewish state there, or even having a state of their own within the boundaries of the entire land of Israel. That is because, even though the land of Israel has been given to the Jews to govern, inhabit, and primarily develop, nonetheless we may not regard that land to be our own possession to do with as we please, that is, to act here in our *own* perceived self-interest. "You too are resident-aliens [*gerim ve-toshavim*] with Me" (Lv 25:23). An old rabbinic text has God saying to the people Israel in the land: "Don't make yourselves the chief factor [*iqqar*] . . . whatever is yours is Mine." All this presupposes that "the earth is the Lord's and all that fills it; the world [*tevel*] and all who inhabit it" (Ps 24:1). Even God's elect people should not assume they are like God in this respect. We can only use what God has permitted us to use in this world, and in the way God has commanded us to use it.

The Jews are not God's vicarious landlords. Like the first humans in the Garden of Eden, they are only placed in the land "to work it and to guard it" (Gn 2:15). So, is there no legitimate covenantal life whatsoever except within the boundaries of the land of Israel? If so, that not only disenfranchises the Jews in the Diaspora, but it also seems to reduce the Creator God who chooses Israel (among His other choices) into some sort of tribal deity confined to a particular territory like the people themselves are confined there.

To be sure, the optimal life of the Jewish people can only be lived in the land of Israel, and now, even more so, in the Jewish state therein. Yet that only makes the difference between Israeli Jewry and Diaspora Jewry a difference of degree, not a difference of kind. Thus the land of Israel exists for the sake of the people Israel; the people Israel do not exist for the sake of the land of Israel. The "sanctity" (*qedushah*) of the land of Israel means it is the site of certain commandments that can be kept only there.

In the same way the State of Israel is for the sake of the people Israel in the land of Israel, the people Israel in the land of Israel is not for the sake of the State of Israel. And, most importantly, the people, then the land, then the state all exist for the sake of God. Indeed, the Jewish people's relation to all these entities are to be responses to the God who has chosen this people, chosen this land for us, and whose commandment to settle the land and inhabit it gives the Jewish state its true warrant.

7

BRIEF REFLECTIONS

THEOLOGY AND THE PROMISED LAND

Tehila Wenger

My reflections focus on the role of conditionality in any theological consideration of the land promise. I will argue that the conditional nature of the divine land promise at any given historical moment, acknowledged to different extents by Prof. D'Costa and Rabbi Ahrens, would make Catholic recognition of the theological significance of recent historic events in Israel at worst an opening for external evaluation of the Jewish nation's moral and spiritual level based on geopolitical developments, and at best an assertion so heavily qualified as to become devoid of significance. Instead of demanding the Church's recognition of Israel on theological grounds, Jewish thinkers and dialogue interlocutors should be challenging and qualifying the dogmatic theological significance that contemporary dominant voices in religious Zionism have increasingly bestowed upon the Jewish people's recent return to the land.

In their papers, Ahrens and Novak both argue for some form of Catholic recognition of the theological significance of Jewish return to Israel. Ahrens writes that a Catholic theological position regarding the relationship between Jewish people and land is overdue: "It is highly problematic that our dialogue partners remain 'neutral' when it comes to the Land or State of Israel or even question the theological connection between the People and the Land of Israel."[1] Novak asserts that "Christians who are faithful to their own tradition . . . should believe that God's covenant with the Jewish people and with the

1 Ahrens, 41.

land of Israel as their inheritance is everlasting and forever valid."[2] D'Costa is more restrained in proposing a "form of minimalist Catholic Zionism."[3] He argues for Catholic acknowledgment of the theological significance of events following 1948, while cautioning against prematurely (and arrogantly) concluding that modern Israel must signify the end of days or uncritically endorsing the State, government, and policies of Israel as divinely sanctioned, by interpreting the land promise as fulfilled by modern political developments.

As all three scholars point out, God's covenant and promise of the land of Israel to the Jewish people is considered irrevocable in both Jewish and Catholic theology. In the Jewish tradition, this is rooted in Genesis: "I will maintain My covenant between Me and you, and your offspring to come, as an everlasting covenant throughout the ages, to be God to you and to your offspring to come. I assign the land you sojourn in to you and your offspring to come, all the land of Canaan, as an everlasting holding."[4] In a Christian context, one can also quote Paul's confirmation of the irrevocable nature of God's "gifts" in Romans 11:29. However, D'Costa and Ahrens both point out that the implementation of the eternal promise at specific historical moments is conditional upon the Jewish people's fulfillment of their side of the covenant. D'Costa quotes Leviticus 18:28, the textual warning that Jewish sojourn in the land can be revoked if the people violate the law, and adds that this conditionality makes it impossible to affirm current Jewish return to the land as the beginning of the end of days.[5] Ahrens also cites this verse, but contextualizes the conditional nature of residence in the land within the first and second Temple periods.[6] He does not directly discuss the possibility that the current return of Israel to the land may end in similar exile, depending on the nation's present moral and religious behavior.

Novak pays the least attention to the conditional nature of residence, attributing repeated and protracted Jewish exile from the land to "insurmountable political and economic factors,"[7] instead of to a Jewish national failure to keep their terms of the covenant. The closest Novak comes to acknowledging the conditional nature of the land promise is in refuting the idea that Jews have a natural right to the land: "God assigns the land of Israel

2 Novak, 73.

3 D'Costa, 28.

4 Gn 17:7–8; emphasis added.

5 D'Costa, 23.

6 Ahrens, 44.

7 Novak, 73.

to the people Israel like an innkeeper assigns the room he or she wants a guest to inhabit during his or her brief sojourn there."[8] While this sidesteps the ethical and spiritual prerequisites delineated in the Bible for continuous residence in the land, the analogy does underline some level of contingency in the nation-land relationship.

The possibility of Jewish exile, and replacement in the land by other nations, is raised in multiple places in the Torah. The warning from Leviticus mentioned above is further developed in rabbinic sources. The Talmud refers to three sins as primary causes of exile: idolatry, sexual immorality, and violation of the Sabbatical and Jubilee year restrictions.[9] Interestingly, these transgressions cover every actor in the God-people-land relationship: idolatry is an offense against God, sexual immorality impacts internal Israelite relations, and the Sabbatical/Jubilee commandments are the strongest expression of our relationship with the land itself. In addition to Leviticus, Moses enjoins the people to be faithful to God multiple times in Deuteronomy, lest "God scatter you among the nations."[10] Several chapters on, he warns them again about the consequences of idolatry: "God's anger will flare up against you, shutting up the skies so that there will be no rain and the ground will not yield its produce; and you will soon perish from the good land that God is assigning to you."[11] This verse is repeated three times a day by observant Jews in the *Shema*, one of the most important prayers in Jewish tradition. While the land promise is immutable, the conditionality of this promise at any given historical moment on Jewish national behavior is enshrined in biblical, Talmudic, and even liturgical tradition.

The conditional nature of the land promise adds a layer of complexity, and potential friction, to Catholic theological recognition of the Jewish people's return to Israel today. Reading the success or failure of Jewish flourishing in the land as theologically significant leaves an opening for Catholic evaluation of the Jewish people's current spiritual level based on current geopolitical developments. Do the Jewish dialogue partners arguing for Catholic recognition of the land promise really want the Church to measure the Jewish people's relationship with God and adherence to our own religious mores by the degree of sovereignty we exert over the land of Israel?

Any serious Catholic consideration of the theological significance of Jewish return to Israel will necessarily acquire a Christian messianic framing.

8 Novak, 74.

9 Tractate Sabbath 33, William Davidson edition, Sefaria.

10 Dt 4:27.

11 Dt 11:17.

As D'Costa writes, "We must ask whether the restoration of the land to the people of Israel in 1948 should be considered an eschatological sign of Jesus's return."[12] The implications of this discussion are potentially much more harmful for Catholic-Jewish dialogue than ignoring the theological aspect of the issue entirely. A case study is provided by Christian Evangelical Zionists in the United States; these strange bedfellows of Israeli settlers in the West Bank actively support the most radical right-wing policies of maximum territorial expansion for Jews in the West Bank and rebuilding the third Temple, the ultimate violation of the fragile status quo over the Temple Mount/Haram Al-Sharif Compound.[13] Contemporary Israeli zealots and Evangelical Zionists both aspire to ethnic supremacy and violent escalation in the Holy Land. For the first, the fears and divisions stoked by nationalist and interreligious violence are a means of consolidating political and territorial control, drawing nearer to a messianic vision of a third Temple period in which the Jewish people (specifically, the Zionist nationalist camp) assert full national, territorial, and religious dominance within the ancient borders of Israel. For their Evangelical allies, this project is in itself a means to their own messianic endgame.

I am not suggesting that Catholic theological thought, in embracing the significance of Jewish return to the land, would take the same route as Evangelical American Zionism. However, it cannot be denied that there are significant political consequences for the attribution of theological significance to the return of the Jewish people to Israel, and certainly to the establishment of a Jewish state. This by itself will not necessarily convince Catholic scholars to shelve the discussion. As D'Costa notes, the political ramifications by themselves cannot outweigh the pursuit of religious truth: "if there are valid theological arguments deriving from revelation applied to history, should revelation and its teaching and application be subject to political prudence?"[14] It should, however, give pause to Jewish dialogue partners advocating for upgrading Jewish-Catholic relations through theological confirmation of the land promise in today's context. This improvement will necessarily be expressed on a political level, and the question of who stands to benefit within Jewish religious and political movements is of paramount importance, given the demonstrated impact of other Christian movements on Israeli politics and society today.

12 D'Costa, 25.

13 See Victoria Clark, *Allies for Armageddon: The Rise of Christian Zionism* (Yale University Press, 2007).

14 D'Costa, 31.

The political expression of theological recognition, whether Jewish or Catholic, is fundamentally shaped by what (if any) emphasis is placed on conditionality. We can approach Jewish connection to the land of Israel through a theologically supported right to the land. As Novak points out, it is an inherited rather than inherent right, but this does not significantly alter the political consequences of such an approach. Alternatively, we could approach it through a covenantal connection, which in the biblical context means a contractual relationship with God, such that the Jewish people's sojourn in the land is directly tied to their fidelity to God and adherence to the law, particularly in the books of the prophets, to moral and social law.

Robert Cover discusses the differences of using right and obligation as sources of law and ideology in a detailed contrast of Western and Jewish jurisprudence. Although he does not explore the consequences of these different approaches as applied to the land promise, he affirms that the Jewish tradition is firmly rooted in obligation rather than rights, and further notes the weakness of rights language "in providing for the material guarantees of life and dignity flowing from the community to the individual . . . Taken alone it only speaks to a need. A distributional premise is missing which can only be supplied through a principle of 'obligation.'"[15] For example, the Palestinian people may have a right to a state, but without a relevant party (Israeli, international, or reflexively Palestinian) obligated to work toward the realization of this right, the principle is immaterial.

Discussion of right to a state in a Jewish theological context relies on borrowed terminology. The moral and spiritual standard required to maintain a theologically justified Jewish presence in the land arguably provide a more authoritative Jewish basis for approaching this topic. Right to land and state is rooted in international law, and for a variety of reasons beyond the scope of this paper, international law has little to no standing in the mainstream Orthodox Jewish community today. It is difficult to ground a compelling theological Jewish argument in the principles of a liberal world order because of these different starting points of obligation and right. As Ahrens notes in his paper, Judaism is not solely a religion;[16] it is also a culture and a nation, and as a nation in particular the discussion of rights is relevant today. However, that is not a theological discussion.

A right by its nature cannot be revoked or conditioned. A covenantal framework, on the other hand, ties our sojourn in the land directly to our fidelity to God and adherence to the law, particularly (in the prophets) moral

15 Robert Cover, "Obligation: A Jewish Jurisprudence of the Social Order," *Journal of Law and Religion* 5 (1987): 71.

16 Ahrens, 39.

and social law. Cover notes that "in a jurisprudence of mitzvoth the loaded, evocative edge is at the assignment of responsibility."[17] In the case of the land promise, a framing based on obligation and conditionality means that the receiver is accountable for actions that will maintain or threaten their status on the land. Righteous national behavior ensures continued dwelling and flourishing in the land. Corrupt, unethical, ungodly behavior can lead to exile.

Establishment of the State of Israel can be read as a manifestation of God in history, but to then extend this interpretation into a view of the State of Israel as a necessary and irreversible step toward permanent Jewish presence in the land is closer to an inauthentic discourse of religious entitlement than to a framing of obligation and covenant. The rights approach lends itself to the kind of religious extremism that is expressed in violence and oppression of the other, and denies the contractual nature of the land-God-people relationship outlined in the Bible. It turns the land into an inalienable right of the people, instead of the basis of a covenant with obligating terms and consequences in the event of violations.

Understanding the land as a conditional promise helps reconcile the dilemma between the recognition of the miraculous nature of recent historical events insofar as the creation of the State of Israel has been instrumental in allowing Jewish return to and dwelling in the land today, and the equally unavoidable acknowledgment of the problematic role that the State has played in denying similar Palestinian flourishing in the land. If God's promise of the land is not the establishment of an immutable right, but rather a covenantal promise, its realization is dependent on the fulfillment of a moral standard of national righteousness. From a Jewish Israeli perspective, such an approach underlines the pressing motivation for achieving peace with our neighbors as soon as is humanly possible.

17 Cover, "Obligation," 72.

SECTION 2

THE BIBLE/TANAKH ON THE LAND PROMISED TO THE JEWISH PEOPLE

8

THE JEWISH PEOPLE AND THEIR SACRED SCRIPTURES IN THE CHRISTIAN BIBLE AND THE PROMISED LAND:

A HERMENEUTICAL RETROSPECT AND PROSPECT

William M. Wright IV

In 2001, the Pontifical Biblical Commission issued the document *The Jewish People and Their Sacred Scriptures in the Christian Bible* (hereafter *JPSSCB*).[1] This text makes a welcome contribution to the Catholic Church's ongoing reevaluation of its relationship with Jews and Judaism, following the horrors of the Shoah and the teachings of the Second Vatican Council in *Nostra Aetate*.[2] *JPSSCB* has three principal chapters of unequal length. The first chapter (§§2–18) focuses on the ways in which the New Testament recognizes the authority of the Old Testament scriptures, as well as convergences and divergences between ancient Christianity and Judaism on matters such

1 The Pontifical Biblical Commission, *The Jewish People and Their Sacred Scriptures in the Christian Bible* (Libreria Editrice Vaticana, 2002). As Charles Miller has shown, the official English tradition of *JPSSCB* is in many ways deficient, requiring consultation of the French original; see Charles H. Miller, "Translation Errors in the Pontifical Biblical Commission's *The Jewish People and Their Sacred Scriptures in the Christian Bible*," *Biblical Theology Bulletin* 35 (2005): 34–39. Accordingly, all English citations of *JPSSCB* will be taken from the aforementioned English edition but with consultation of the French original (and amended as needed). References to the French edition of this text are taken from vatican.va/roman_curia/congregations/cfaith/pcb_documents/rc_con_cfaith_doc_20020212_popolo-ebraico_fr.html. All references to this document will be given parenthetically in the body of the text or, when appropriate, in the footnotes.

2 See *JPSSCB*, §1, 22.

as the relationship of Scripture and tradition, exegetical method, and canon. The second chapter (§§19–65) examines a series of theological themes which are established in the Old Testament and variously developed in the New. The third chapter (§§66–83) examines the presentation of Jews in the New Testament writings. Since its publication, *JPSSCB* has been generally well-received, though some aspects of it have been critiqued.[3]

When it comes to the promised land,[4] *JPSSCB* surveys major expressions of this motif in both testaments and does so from a generally historical-critical perspective.[5] In so doing, *JPSSCB* aims to let the major Old Testament witnesses be heard on their own terms and in relation to their interpretation in the New Testament. Both of these are laudable and important goals. But *JPSSCB* has also been criticized on theological grounds for the way in which it relates the two biblical testaments and conceptualizes the interpretation of the Old Testament in the New.[6] These matters affect the interpretation of the promised land, and some conceptual adjustments can offer fresh possibilities for thinking about the promised land in the Christian Bible. In this essay, I wish to contribute to the Catholic thinking about the biblical presentation of the promised land by building upon *JPSSCB* and making some adjustments

3 For instance, Richard Clifford, SJ, "Changing Christian Interpretations of the Old Testament," *Theological Studies* 82 (2021): 509–30; Denis Farkasfalvy, "The Pontifical Biblical Commission's Document on Jews and Christians and Their Scriptures: Attempt at an Evaluation," *Communio: International Catholic Review* 29 (2002): 715–37; Reinhard Hütter, "'In.' Some Incipient Reflections on *The Jewish People and Their Sacred Scriptures in the Christian Bible*," *Pro Ecclesia* 13 (2004): 13–24; Roch Kereszty, "The Jewish-Christian Dialogue and the Pontifical Biblical Commission's Document on 'The Jewish People and Their Sacred Scriptures in the Christian Bible,'" *Communio: International Catholic Review* 29 (2002): 738–45; Jon D. Levenson, "Can Roman Catholicism Validate Jewish Biblical Interpretation?," *Studies in Christian Jewish Relations* 1 (2005–6): 170–85; Mathew Levering, "The Pontifical Biblical Commission and Aquinas' Exegesis," *Pro Ecclesia* 13 (2004): 25–28; Amy-Jill Levine, "Roland Murphy, the Pontifical Commission, Jews, and the Bible," *Biblical Theology Bulletin* 33 (2003): 104–13; Roland E. Murphy, "The Biblical Commission, the Jews, and Scriptures," *Biblical Theology Bulletin* 32 (2002): 145–49; Henry Wansbrough, OSB, "'Can Catholicism Validate Jewish Biblical Interpretation?': A Reply to Jon D. Levenson," *Studies in Christian-Jewish Relations* 2 (2007): 86–93.

4 As *JPSSCB* notes (§56), the Old Testament does not describe the land as "promised" but as the land that the Lord "swore to give" to Israel. Thus, Ex 6:8 (a text which *JPSSCB* does not reference) reads: "I will bring you into the land *that I swore to give to you* [נָשָׂאתִי אֶת־יָדִי לָתֵת אֹתָהּ] to Abraham, Isaac, and Jacob." Heb 11:9 does speak of Abraham as dwelling for a time in "the land of the promise [γῆν τῆς ἐπαγγελίας]"; my translation and emphasis added. Mindful of these lexical matters, I will use the expression "the promised land" or "the land" on account of the conventionality of the phrase. Unless otherwise noted, all biblical citations in English are taken from the NRSV.

5 On the *JPSSCB*'s treatment of the land promise, see Gavin D'Costa, *Catholic Doctrines on the Jewish People after Vatican II* (Oxford University Press, 2019), 64–104; Adam Gregerman, "Is the Biblical Land Promise Irrevocable?: Post-*Nostra Aetate* Catholic Theologies of the Jewish Covenant and the Land of Israel," *Modern Theology* 34 (2018): 137–58.

6 Esp. Farkasfalvy, "Biblical Commission's Document," 717–31.

to its hermeneutical substructure. I will first offer a retrospect of *JPSSCB*, focusing on its hermeneutical commitments and treatment of the promised land. After introducing some conceptual adjustments, I will set forth a prospective account for how Catholics can honor and affirm the abiding character of God's promise of the land to the people Israel while also holding that this promise is transposed and fulfilled in the eschatological situation established by the life, death, and resurrection of Jesus.

JPSSCB AND THE PROMISED LAND: A HERMENEUTICAL RETROSPECT

Hermeneutics

The interpretive program of *JPSSCB* incorporates Catholic faith commitments and grants methodological primacy to the historical-critical method. In this respect, *JPSSCB* follows in large measure the program set forth in the 1993 Pontifical Biblical Commission document *The Interpretation of the Bible in the Church*.[7] In this way, *JPSSCB* works within a paradigm of text, meaning, and interpretation which is much shaped by historical-critical commitments. While it never explicitly defines the category, *JPSSCB* effectively understands the literal sense to be what a text would have meant to its first readers in its historical context of origin. The document speaks of biblical texts' "literal and historical sense" (§13), their "original meaning" (§§13, 19–20), a meaning that is "original, obvious" (§54), and the need to understand texts "in their historical and literary contexts" (§87). Beyond these descriptors, it is not clear whether *JPSSCB* understands the literal sense (to employ the parsing of Olivier-Thomas Venard) more in terms of a "psychological-historical asymptote" (i.e., the text's ostensive reference or its author's psychological intention) or a "textual asymptote" (i.e., the literary sense of the words).[8] Clarity on these matters is important. Not only has the literal or plain sense of Scripture been defined variously throughout the history of Christian exegesis, but the way in which one defines the literal sense informs how one understands the more-than-literal senses of Scripture and relates them to the literal.[9]

7 See William M. Wright IV, "*Dei Verbum*," in *The Reception of Vatican II*, ed. Matthew L. Lamb and Matthew Levering (Oxford University Press, 2017), esp. 94–99.

8 Olivier-Thomas Venard, OP, "Les deux asymptotes de sense littéral des Écritures," in *Le sens littéral des Écritures*, ed. Olivier-Thomas Venard, OP (Éditions du Cerf, 2009), 11.

9 See Brevard S. Childs, "The *Sensus Literalis* of Scripture: An Ancient and Modern Problem," in *Beiträge zur Alttestamentlichen Theologie: Festschrift für Walther Zimmerli zum 70. Geburtstag*, ed. Herbert Donner, Robert Hanhard, and Rudolf Smend (Vandenhoeck and Ruprecht, 1977), 80–93.

For instance, within classic Christian hermeneutics, the literal sense has a foundational character vis-à-vis other meanings of Scripture. Representative of the exegetical tradition before him, Thomas Aquinas in one location defines the literal sense as "that first signification whereby words signify things" and the spiritual sense as "That signification whereby things signified by words have themselves also a signification."[10] For Aquinas and much of the preceding tradition, the literal sense pertains primarily to the words of Scripture as signifiers, whereas the spiritual senses are proper to the things (or *res*) signified by the words.

JPSSCB wants to retain the foundational character of the literal sense for more-than-literal interpretations but does so on terms set by the historical-critical method. To do so, *JPSSCB* employs a version of the *sensus plenior* (or fuller sense).[11] As defined in the 1993 *Interpretation of the Bible in the Church*, the *sensus plenior* is "a deeper meaning of the text, intended by God but not clearly expressed by the human author."[12] This divinely intended, yet concealed, meaning of the language is uncovered by later developments.[13] Whereas the spiritual senses of Scripture traditionally pertain to the things signified by the words, the *sensus plenior*, as Raymond Brown writes, "exists *in the words of a text*."[14]

JPSSCB does not appeal overtly to the *sensus plenior*, but much of its argumentation squares with this basic theory. Commenting on the New Testament interpretations of Israel's prophetic writings, the text reads, "All the texts, including those which were later read as messianic prophecies, already had an immediate import and meaning for their contemporaries before attaining a fuller meaning [*une signification plus pleine*] for future

10 Thomas Aquinas, *Summa Theologiae* I, q. 1, a. 10, co. All citations of Aquinas's *Summa Theologiae* are taken from *Summa Theologica*, trans. Fathers of the English Dominican Province, 3 vols. (Benziger, 1947–48). All Latin citations of Aquinas's texts are taken from the corresponding online edition at corpusthomisticum.org.

11 *JPSSCB* does not employ the specific phrase *sensus plenior* but it does speak of "fuller meaning" (*une signification plus pleine*) (§21). Moreover, Henry Wansbrough ("Reply to Jon D. Levenson," 89–90), a member of the Biblical Commission which produced this text, discusses it with regard to the *sensus plenior*.

12 The Pontifical Biblical Commission, *The Interpretation of the Bible in the Church* (St. Paul Books and Media, 1993), II.B.3 (87).

13 Ibid., 87–88.

14 Raymond E. Brown, *The "Sensus Plenior" of Sacred Scripture* (St. Mary Seminary, 1955; reprinted by Wipf and Stock, 2008), 92. He goes on to make this same point: "This clearly distinguishes it from the generally accepted notion of the typical sense which is primarily a sense of 'things' written about in the text: the *sensus plenior* needs so such intermediary . . . The fuller sense thus presupposes the literal sense of the passage and is a development of that literal sense" (ibid.).

hearers" (§21). Elsewhere, *JPSSCB* identifies the Christological interpretation of the Old Testament as a development of something in those texts: "Christian readers were convinced that their Old Testament hermeneutic, although significantly different from that of Judaism, corresponds nevertheless to *a potentiality of meaning that is really present in the texts*" (§64).[15] On this account, there is something in the language or original sense of the biblical writings—or even in the history of their composition—which gets actualized or developed when the New Testament interprets the Old.

This manner of relating literal and more-than-literal interpretations dovetails with another way in which *JPSSCB* articulates the relation of the testaments: a blending of "continuity, discontinuity, and progression" (§64). Through the *sensus plenior*, *JPSSCB* affirms genuine continuity between Old Testament texts' original meaning or language and their Christological interpretation in the New Testament. At the same time, this continuity is not perfectly straightforward. There are also real differences between the testaments as regards texts, themes, and institutions (§64). But this blend of continuity and discontinuity is such that the discontinuity does not override the continuity. Put positively, *JPSSCB* speaks of this discontinuity-within-continuity as "progression" (§65). The text states, "Jesus, far from being in opposition to the Israelite Scriptures, revoking them as provisional, brings them instead to fulfillment in his person, in his mission, and especially in his Paschal mystery" (§65). Given *JPSSCB*'s commitment to preserving the lines of continuity between the testaments, progression or fulfillment is understood as a development of certain texts or trends in the Old Testament which culminates in Jesus.

The Promised Land

JPSSCB discusses the promised land in its lengthy second chapter which examines themes connecting the two testaments of the Christian Bible (§§23–65). One such theme is entitled "Promises" (§53), and it is here that *JPSSCB* treats the land (along with the posterity of Abraham, the salvation of Israel, God's kingly rule, and Davidic kingship and the messiah).

The paragraph which opens the section on biblical promises situates them within the relationship between the testaments and the interpretation of the Old Testament in the New. The treatment begins: "Many of the promises made by God in the Old Testament are re-read in the light of

15 Emphasis added. Similar to the notion of "dynamic aspect" in the 1993 *Interpretation of the Bible in the Church* (II.B.1 [83–84]), the 2001 PBC text speaks of an "internal dynamism of the Old Testament which finds its goal in Jesus" (§21; see §86).

Jesus Christ in the New Testament" (§54). It acknowledges that the New Testament's interpretations of these promises differ in real ways from how they are variously understood in the Old Testament. These elements of continuity, discontinuity, and progression lead to the second critical issue: "the legitimacy of an interpretation of the promises over and above their original, obvious meaning" (§54). Here, *JPSSCB* reveals its anxiety about establishing a hermeneutical warrant for the New Testament's interpretation of Old Testament promises, and more specifically, a warrant which is amenable to historical-critical commitments to the "original, obvious meaning."

The discussion of the promised land occurs at §§56–57. Beginning with God's promise of the land to Abraham's posterity who would come to receive it, *JPSSCB* moves through the plotline of the Old Testament canon: the exodus from Egypt and the entrance of the next generation of Israelites into Canaan under Joshua; the division of monarchy after the reign of Solomon and calls from the prophets during the divided monarchy to repent or be exiled from the land; and then the return to the land as an element within scenarios of eschatological restoration. Within this epitome, there is an aside which discusses the distinctive presentation of the land in the Priestly tradition. Here, *JPSSCB* adduces scriptural texts that temper Israel's claim vis-à-vis the land. Since the land is where God dwells with his people Israel, there is a consequent need for Israel to live in a state of moral purity. The text reads, "The gift is therefore conditioned [*Le don est . . . conditionné*] by moral purity and by service to the Lord alone" (§56). *JPSSCB* also references Leviticus 25:23—"the land is mine; with me you are but aliens and tenants"—which likewise qualifies Israel's relation to the land. Here, God is the landlord, and the people Israel are his tenants. The treatment of the land in the Old Testament concludes with a substantive discussion of the ban (חֵרֶם) and its place in the Deuteronomic accounts of the conquest of Canaan.

When it comes to the New Testament, *JPSSCB* correctly observes, "the New Testament does not develop much further the theme of the promised land" (§57). It appeals to only four New Testament passages as concerns the land. The first text is the return of the Holy Family to Israel after their flight into Egypt in Matthew 2. Here, the infant Jesus's return to the land of Israel from Egypt recapitulates the movement of the people Israel from slavery in Egypt to the promised land. The second text is the beginning of Stephen's speech in Acts 7, wherein Stephen references God's promise of the land to Abraham and his posterity. Third, there is the interpretation of the Land in Hebrews 11:9–16, which *JPSSCB* interprets to mean that "the 'land' of Israel is only for pointing symbolically toward a different land, a 'heavenly homeland'" (§56).[16] Lastly, it cites the third Matthean beatitude—"Blessed are the meek, for they will inherit the earth" (Mt 5:5)—and in this beatitude, *JPSSCB* discerns a similar kind of reinterpretation that is going on in Hebrews 11. The text states that this beatitude "effects the same kind of passage from a historical and geographical meaning to a more open one . . . in a horizon of eschatology, both present and future" (§56).[17]

JPSSCB concludes its discussion of the land with three qualifying remarks. First, the text states, "The authors of the New Testament are only pushing forward a process of symbolic deepening already engaged in the Old Testament and intertestamental Judaism" (§56). When introducing its section on the promises, *JPSSCB* raises the issue of the "legitimacy" (§54) of New Testament interpretations of the promises. *JPSSCB* seemingly finds warrant for regarding these Christological interpretations as legitimate because they continue some interpretive trends in Second Temple Judaism.

Second, the text qualifies this statement about the symbolic interpretation of the land by stating, "This, however, must not make us forget that a concrete land was promised by God to Israel and actually received as an inheritance."[18] *JPSSCB* rightfully reminds Catholic readers that the symbolic or eschatological interpretation of the land in the New Testament should not eclipse the fact, given in the Old Testament, that God gave a specific land to a specific people who in turn received it as an inheritance from him. But *JPSSCB* adds a third statement that in turn qualifies the second one. Shifting its language from "promise" and "heritage" to "gift," *JPSSCB* recalls its earlier exposition of the Priestly tradition and speaks of the land as conditioned: "this gift of land was conditioned by fidelity to the covenant (Lv 26; Dt 28)."[19]

Assessment

JPSSCB is a valuable contribution, and there is much about it to be applauded. Acknowledging that the Jews and Christians read these same scriptures differently, the document affirms the interpretive legitimacy of "the Jewish reading of the Bible [as] a possible one, in continuity with the Jewish Sacred Scriptures from the Second Temple period, a reading analogous to the Christian reading which developed in parallel fashion" (§22). It is concerned with preserving the integrity of the plain sense voice of Old

16 My translation.

17 My translation.

18 My translation.

19 My translation.

Testament texts, and it rightfully encourages Christians to study and learn from Jewish interpreters of Scripture past and present (§22). Furthermore, one can agree with Reinhard Hütter that this text constitutes genuine fruit in inter-faith relations borne by the incorporation of historical-critical exegesis in Catholic biblical interpretation.[20]

To further Catholic theological thinking about the promised land in Scripture, more attention should be given to several matters. First, further consideration should be given to the substance of the relationship between what is said about the land in the Old Testament and what is said about it in the New. *JPSSCB* correctly points out that the symbolic and eschatological interpretation of the land in the New Testament should not displace recognition that God promised a specific land to the people Israel in the Old Testament. But the text does not explore how the specifically material land, promised by God to the people Israel in the Old Testament, relates to its eschatological or symbolic character in the New. Instead, *JPSSCB* seems more concerned with interpretive method, that is, how can a more-than-literal New Testament interpretation of an Old Testament text be regarded as legitimate in light of the document's own hermeneutical requirements. Put differently, there is the need to move beyond the *verba* of the texts to consider the *res* of which they speak.

Second, despite its laudable goal to integrate modern biblical criticism with traditional Christian hermeneutics, the *sensus plenior* does not seem conceptually able to bear the exegetical and theological weight it is asked to carry. From the heyday of its discussion in the middle third of the twentieth century, the theory of a *sensus plenior* has been criticized as a conceptually inadequate way for articulating the relationship between literal and more-than-literal readings of Scripture.[21] Kevin Duffy offers the following summary observations: "This distinctive theory does not work because, in the last analysis, it is incoherent. Methodologically, it involves conflating distinct stages in interpretation into a single process where the *sensus plenior* of a

20 See Hütter, "Some Incipient Reflections," 21; Wright, "*Dei Verbum*," 98–99.

21 See, e.g., Lewis Ayres and Stephen E. Fowl, "(Mis)reading the Face of God: *The Interpretation of the Bible in the Church*," *Theological Studies* 60 (1999): 513–28; Raymond E. Brown, "The Problems of the *Sensus Plenior*," *Ephemerides Theologicae Louvanienses* 43 (1967): 460–69; Jean Daniélou, review of Joseph Coppens, *Les harmonies des deux Testaments* (Louvain, 1949), *Dieu vivant: Perspectives religieuses et philosophiques* 16 (1950): 149–53; Kevin Duffy, "The *Sensus Plenior* of Scripture: A Debate and Its Aftermath," *Louvain Studies* 38 (2014): 228–45. That being said, the *sensus plenior* has been receiving attention in Evangelical Protestant circles, especially in light of speech-act theory. See Kit Barker, "Speech Act Theory, Dual Authorship and Canonical Hermeneutics: Making Sense of *Sensus Plenior*," *Journal of Theological Interpretation* 3 (2009): 227–39.

text is, and is not, located in the original meaning [of] a text."[22] Moreover, as pointed out by Daniélou and Farkasfalvy, the *sensus plenior* effectively collapses the distinction between the literal sense of the Old Testament texts and their Christological senses by making the latter somehow ingredient to the language of the former.[23] Redolent of Alasdair MacIntyre's critique of the Enlightenment's attempt to justify inherited morality on alternative conceptual grounds, the *sensus plenior* attempts to fit classic Christian hermeneutics into a historical-critical paradigm, a paradigm which cannot adequately justify those hermeneutics on its own terms.[24]

The place of the biblical land promise in the Christian account of the divine economy and the relation between the material land to its eschatological or symbolic disclosure in the New Testament are, properly speaking, theological questions. They are biblical questions but ones which historical and literary analysis alone cannot answer. There is thus the need to move the historical and literary discussion of scriptural witnesses into the properly theological sphere. As taught by Benedict XVI in *Verbum Domini* and elsewhere, this task involves an integration of exegetical analysis and theological thinking as well as a consideration of matters at a more theoretical level.[25] Reframing some conceptual aspects of this discussion can, I think, provide a way for Catholics to honor and affirm the abiding character of God's promise of the land to Israel while also confessing that God's promises are transposed and fulfilled in the eschatological register situation established by Jesus. To do so, I will draw on some of what Francis Martin and I discuss in *Encountering the Living God in Scripture: Theological and Philosophical Principles for Interpretation*.[26]

22 Duffy, "*Sensus Plenior*," 244.

23 Daniélou, review of Coppens, 150–51; Farkasfalvy, "Biblical Commission's Document," 728.

24 Alasdair MacIntyre, *After Virtue: A Study in Moral Theory*, 2nd ed. (University of Notre Dame Press, 1984), 36–61.

25 Benedict XVI, *The Word of the Lord: Verbum Domini* (Pauline Books and Media, 2010), esp. §§29–49; Joseph Cardinal Ratzinger, "Biblical Interpretation in Conflict: On the Foundations and Itinerary of Exegesis Today," trans. Adrian Walker, in *Opening Up the Scriptures: Joseph Ratzinger and the Foundations of Biblical Interpretation*, ed. José Granados, Carlos Granados, and Luis Sánchez-Navarro (Eerdmans, 2008), 1–29.

26 William M. Wright IV and Francis Martin, *Encountering the Living God in Scripture: Theological and Philosophical Principles for Interpretation* (Baker Academic, 2019).

A HERMENEUTICAL PROSPECT

The Land as a Mystery-Bearing Reality

Instead of framing things in terms of the *sensus plenior*, I propose a resourcing and conceptual updating of the classic Christian hermeneutical schema and suggest that the more-than-literal meanings of Scripture be understood not as a property of the language of texts but of the reality, or *res*, which the text mediates.[27] God employs created realities, such as the land, in his dealings with the world. When God acts and reveals himself through these realities, they acquire new and more intensive dimensions of significance.[28] *Dei Verbum* 2 affirms this point when it teaches that the realities of the divine economy contain "mystery" which the words of Scripture elucidate.[29] On this account, God reveals himself and his will and exercises his power through the various realities of the divine economy, and as such, these realities bear the divine mystery. The various authors and editors of the biblical books bring to light some of the mystery, or theological significance, of the *res* and display it through their compositions.

The promised land is such a mystery-bearing biblical reality, for the Lord God incorporates it into his activity in the world. In addition to those aspects cited in *JPSSCB*, we can cite the following as speaking to the inner mystery—or theological dimensions—of the land in the divine economy.[30] Genesis forges a close connection between the identity of the Abraham's family and the land. Not only is the land promise repeated to each of the three patriarchs (Gn 12:7; 15:18–21; 22:17–18; 26:4; 28:13), but in Genesis 17:9, the Lord announces that he will give the land to Abraham and his descendants "as a perpetual holding." In Deuteronomy 12:9 and Psalm 95:11, the land is the place of "rest" which the Lord will give to his people. Through the land and its produce, God provides sustenance for his people (Dt 8:9–10). Indeed, when the Israelites celebrated their first Passover in Canaan and then ate of the land's produce, the supply of manna stopped (Jos 5:12). The land is holy, for it is here that the Lord draws near his people and dwells among them in a special way (e.g., Nm 35:34; Dt 12:5; 1 Kgs 8:27–29). The land is also the arena for the Lord's blessings and punishments. Not only is exile and scattering

27 On the reframing of the biblical *res* in terms of a phenomenological "categorial object," see Wright and Martin, *Encountering*, 186–87 and 197–201.

28 On the matters discussed in this paragraph, see Wright and Martin, *Encountering*, 202–10.

29 Second Vatican Council, *Dei Verbum* 2; available at vatican.va.

30 See Waldemar Janzen, "Land," in *The Anchor Bible Dictionary*, ed. David Noel Freedman et al., 6 vols. (Doubleday, 1992), 4:143–54.

stipulated as a covenantal punishment for sin (Dt 28:63–64), but restoration to the land from exile is an eschatological hope and promise (Dt 30:5).

Transposed Into a New Context

These theological dimensions of the land, which the Old Testament texts bring out, appear within the horizon established by the revelation of God and his covenant with Israel. Within the Christian account of the divine economy, this biblical horizon undergoes a modification with the incarnation.[31] As Robert Sokolowski has shown, the incarnation establishes a new theological context within which the realities of the divine economy come to light.[32] The incarnation—and the Paschal mystery—thus establish a new horizon within which the textually-mediated realities of the divine economy appear to Christians.[33]

As mentioned, the biblical writers draw out some of the theological dimensions of the realities of the divine economy in their textual renderings. When the presentational context is modified with the incarnation, other dimensions of the inner mystery borne by the realities of the divine economy come to light. Namely, the biblical *res* appear as having dimensions whereby they participate in the life and work of Jesus by way of anticipation. Whereas the *sensus plenior* theory attempts to connect Christological and non-Christological senses in a text's language or original meaning, the theory advanced here locates the Christological aspects as dimensions of the *res* mediated by the text. Sokolowski writes, "It is not the case that there was one meaning in the mind of the human author and another meaning intended by God, but that the one *thing* intended by the human author had dimensions that had not yet come into view, dimensions that could not appear until more had happened."[34]

By locating the Christological dimensions in the textually-mediated *res* and as being becoming visible only in horizon established by the incarnation and Paschal mystery, one can affirm that the disclosure of these new dimensions do not displace or annul those aspects of the textually-mediated realities which have already come to light in the Old Testament writings. As Christians believe that Jesus reveals the aspects of the God of Israel that are not visible in the horizon of the Old Testament—but which do not displace

31 See Robert Sokolowski, *Eucharistic Presence: A Study in the Theology of Disclosure* (The Catholic University of America Press, 1994), 34–54; Wright and Martin, *Encountering*, 207–10.

32 Sokolowski, *Eucharistic Presence*, 54.

33 Wright and Martin, *Encountering*, 214–15.

34 Sokolowski, *Eucharistic Presence*, 149.

that already given revelation—so might Christians think of Christ as revealing dimensions of the textually-mediated realities of the divine economy which are not visible in the horizon of the Old Testament but which likewise do not displace those already disclosed dimensions.

This manner of conceiving the relationship between the senses of Scripture encourages Christians to recognize the validity and abiding value of the Old Testament presentation of biblical realities. On their own terms, the Old Testament scriptures illuminate some ways in which God is actively present in the realities of the divine economy. While the interpretive traditions of Judaism and Christianity may receive the plain sense and negotiate its various challenges differently, Jews and Christians can nevertheless study the biblical texts together profitably in this respect. Historical and literary analysis can be a sphere of mutual learning and collaboration as we both strive to understand the scriptures, their historical, cultural, and intra-textual associations, as well as seeking a better understanding of their claim.[35]

When the Christological senses are understood to be dimensions of the textually-mediated *res*, Christians can affirm that the literal sense of Old Testament texts—understood as the verbal presentation of things—may have no direct Christological bearing. At the same time, the identification of the Christological senses as dimensions of the mystery-bearing realities allow Christians to also see these realities as participating in the mystery of Christ as "anticipated participations."[36] With regard to the promised land, Christians can thus affirm God's promise of the land to Israel as "a perpetual holding" (Gn 17:9), while also believing this promise to be transposed to a new theological and eschatological register and there fulfilled.

Explaining the Relationship

JPSSCB observes that the New Testament sometimes treats the promised land in a symbolic and/or eschatological way and that these dimensions do not displace the material reality of the land promised by God to Israel. But *JPSSCB* does not explore how the land as an eschatological reality in the New Testament relates to the material reality of the land in the Old Testament. Where *JPSSCB* seeks to legitimate the New Testament interpretation in light of its historical-critical commitments, this proposal to understand the more-than-literal senses as dimensions of the realities articulated and mediated by

35 Thus Jon D. Levenson, *The Hebrew Bible, the Old Testament, and Historical Criticism: Jews and Christians in Biblical Studies* (Westminster John Knox Press, 1993), 83–84; Kereszty, "Jewish-Christian Dialogue," 740.

36 On "anticipated participations," see Wright and Martin, *Encountering*, 210–15.

the texts, rather than texts themselves, opens up a new direction for exploring this matter theologically.

Consider the third Matthean beatitude: "Blessed are the meek, for they will inherit the earth" (Mt 5:5). This beatitude echoes Psalm 37:11 with its declaration, "The meek shall inherit the land," and through this Psalm, it recalls the land promise to Abraham in Genesis 15:7 and other scriptural loci. While the exact sense of "the earth [τὴν γῆν]" in Matthew 5:5 is debated, it is likely that "the earth" has an eschatological meaning, pointing to the world as having been eschatologically transformed in the "renewal of all things [παλιγγενεσίᾳ]" (Mt 19:28).[37]

As the *JPSSCB* text rightly claims, such an interpretation fits with ways in which the land promise was interpreted in some Second Temple circles. For instance, 1 Enoch 5:6 envisions the eschatological judgment and announces, "to the elect there shall be light, joy, and peace, and they shall inherit the earth."[38] As Nickelsburg and VanderKam note, several elements in 1 Enoch 5 allude to the eschatological scenario in Isaiah 65, and in that light, the mention of "the earth" as an eschatological blessing to the elect should be taken as referring to the "new heavens and a new earth" in Isaiah 65:17.[39] The "land" here is not simply the historic land of Israel, but the whole earth eschatologically renewed. Other Second Temple witnesses likewise interpret the land promise as extending to the entire world, and Paul picks up this interpretive tradition in Romans 4:13.[40]

The eschatological interpretation of the land promise also appears in 4 Ezra and 2 Baruch. In 4 Ezra 6, Ezra laments regarding why the Lord has subjected his people Israel to the nations and asks when he will reverse this state of affairs. He continues, "If the world has indeed been created for us, why do we not possess our world as an inheritance?" (4 Ezra 6:59).[41] The implication is that Israel will come to possess "the world" when God works

37 So too Hans Dieter Betz, *The Sermon on the Mount*, Hermeneia (Fortress Press, 1995), 124–29; W. D. Davies, *The Gospel and the Land: Early Christianity and Jewish Territorial Doctrine* (University of California Press, 1974), 359–65; W. D. Davies and Dale C. Allison, Jr., *The Gospel According to Saint Matthew*, 3 vols., The International Critical Commentary (T&T Clark, 1988–97), 1:449–45; Ulrich Luz, *Matthew 1–7: A Commentary*, trans. Wilhelm C. Linss (Minneapolis, 1989 [1985]), 236.

38 Cited from James H. Charlesworth, ed., *The Old Testament Pseudepigrapha*, 2 vols., Anchor Bible Reference Library (Doubleday, 1985), 1:15.

39 George W. E. Nickelsburg and James C. VanderKam, *1 Enoch 1: A Commentary on the Book of 1 Enoch, Chapters 1–36; 81–108*, Hermeneia (Fortress Press, 2001), 161–62.

40 See James D. G. Dunn, *Romans 1–8*, Word Biblical Commentary (Word Incorporated, 1988), 213. He likewise cites Jubilees 17:3, 22:14, 32:19; Philo, *Som* 1.175; and *Mos.* 1.155 as exemplifying this interpretive trend.

41 Charlesworth, *Old Testament Pseudepigrapha*, 1:536.

his eschatological action. The text of 2 Baruch similarly interprets the land promise eschatologically as referring to the world to come. Speaking of the transformation and destiny of the righteous in the resurrection, 2 Baruch 51:3 reads: "the shape of their face will be changed into the light of their beauty so that they may acquire and receive the undying world which is promised to them" (2 Bar 51:3; see 14:13).[42]

Further indications in Matthew's Gospel suggest that the third beatitude speaks to the world as eschatologically transformed. The third beatitude exhibits the same tension between the present and future tenses ("Blessed *are* . . . they *will be* . . .") which characterizes other beatitudes and envisions an eschatological reversal of fortunes. So understood, to "inherit the earth" is an eschatological blessing promised to "the meek" (Mt 5:5). The declaration that "the meek" are "blessed" also places this beatitude in thematic parallel with the first beatitude: "Blessed are the poor in spirit, for theirs is the kingdom of heaven" (Mt 5:3). In his study of the pairing of heaven and earth language throughout Matthew, Jonathan Pennington argues that in this Gospel these two realms are presently contrasted but this contrast "will be resolved at [the] eschaton when heaven and earth are reunited through Jesus."[43] The eschatological conjoining of heaven and earth is what Matthew 19:28 refers to as παλιγγενεσία, "the renewal of all things."[44] Pennington thus sums up Matthew's teaching on the matter: "the Christian hope is *not* for an ethereal heaven-situated existence, but the consummation of the heavenly realities coming into effect *on the earth*; not for a destruction of the earth and a kingdom that exists only in heaven, but for a παλιγγενεσία, a new genesis."[45]

JPSSCB is correct to observe that the eschatological interpretation of the land in the New Testament fits with interpretive trends in the Second Temple period. But instead of focusing on the hermeneutical legitimacy of such readings, we might explore theologically the relationship between a created reality in its present mode of existence and what its mode of existence may involve once it has been eschatologically transformed in "the new heavens and the new earth" (Is 66:22; see 65:17). From a Christian perspective, the best point of departure for thinking about this relationship is the bodily resurrection of Jesus.[46]

42 Ibid., 1:638.

43 Jonathan T. Pennington, *Heaven and Earth in the Gospel of Matthew* (Brill, 2007; reprinted by Baker Academic, 2009), 343; emphasis removed.

44 See also Davies, *Gospel and the Land*, 363–65; Davies and Allison, *Matthew*, 3:5–58.

45 Pennington, *Heaven and Earth*, 326–27.

46 Matthew Levering and Gregory Vall have likewise pointed to Jesus's resurrected body as a way for Christians to think theologically about this topic. See Matthew Levering, *Engaging the Doctrine of Israel: A Christian Israelology in Dialogue with Ongoing Judaism* (Cascade Books,

A belief established in Second Temple Judaism and later incorporated into rabbinic tradition, the resurrection of the dead is an event which figures into scenarios of God's eschatological action.[47] Christian belief in the resurrection of Jesus means that the eschatological age, or new creation, has taken irrevocable root in the world. The glorified, resurrected humanity of Jesus is the anchor point for the general resurrection of the dead and the renewal of creation which Christians look to occur at Jesus's Parousia.

The resurrection of Jesus involves the transformation of a created reality (i.e., Jesus's humanity) into an eschatological mode of life. In the resurrection, Jesus's entire humanity is divinized, totally transformed by divine glory, and raised up to an eschatological mode of embodied existence. As described by Paul in 1 Corinthians 15 and as presented in resurrection appearance narratives, the resurrected state is a mode of eschatological existence which is both continuous and discontinuous with bodily life as we presently know it. Particularly important for this topic is the *bodily* character of Jesus's resurrection. When the New Testament writings depict Jesus's risen humanity, they identify it as the same body which died on the cross. But his body has been transformed into a different mode of existence, one no longer bound by created limits. Thus in resurrection appearances, the risen Jesus both suddenly appears and disappears (Lk 24:31, 36) but also shows his body as bearing the wounds of the cross (Lk 24:39–40; Jn 20:20). Similarly, the vision of heavenly liturgy in Revelation 5 presents the risen and ascended Jesus as the Lamb who was slain, a Lamb which is alive and also bears the wounds of his slaughter.

Important for present purposes is that the humanity of Jesus, before and after the resurrection, is the same humanity, although it exists in different modalities. Jesus's humanity is not annihilated, displaced, or left behind when it is transformed into its eschatological, glorified state. Rather, the resurrected humanity of Jesus is the same humanity with which he was born (and continues to possess) even if it now exists in a different mode than when he walked the earth.

The bodily resurrection of Jesus provides a point of reference from which Christians can think about the land promise. A core New Testament claim is that God fulfills his promises in Jesus, who reconfigures many of the eschatological expectations and realizes them in unanticipated ways. For

2021), 32; Gregory Vall, "'Man is the Land': The Sacramentality of the Land of Israel," in *John Paul II and the Jewish People: A Jewish-Christian Dialogue*, ed. David G. Dalin and Matthew Levering (Rowman and Littlefield, 2008), esp. 151–53.

47 See Jon D. Levenson, *Resurrection and the Restoration of Israel: The Ultimate Victory of the God of Life* (Yale University Press, 2006); N. T. Wright, *The Resurrection of the Son of God* (Fortress Press, 2003).

Christians, the bodily resurrection of Jesus shows that eschatological transformation does not obliterate the material reality and goodness of what is transformed. The eschatological reconfiguration and fulfillment of the land promise in Jesus no more displaces the material realism of the land or the abiding nature of God's promise of the land to Abraham's descendants as a "perpetual heritage" (Gn 17:9) than the transformation of Jesus's humanity in the resurrection does away with its corporeal reality. The land promise is extended and eschatologically fulfilled, but its material realism and abiding importance is not thereby erased.

CONCLUSION

Refitting the classic Christian account of the senses of Scripture enables the non-competition between a plain-sense interpretation of Old Testament texts and a Christological interpretation. This situation results from relocating the Christological meanings from the language of the Old Testament texts to the ontological-spiritual constitution of the realities which those texts articulate and present. Since those dimensions of the mystery borne by the realities given in the Old Testament are not displaced by those Christological dimensions which appear in light of the incarnation and Paschal mystery, Christian readers can affirm abiding nature of God's promise of the land to Abraham's family as a "perpetual heritage" (Gn 17:9).

At the same time, the new theological context established by the incarnation (and the Paschal mystery) not only causes new aspects of these textually-mediated realities to appear but it also transposes them into an eschatological situation wherein their full realization occurs. With Jesus's bodily resurrection as an analogue for Catholic thinkers, we can recognize that such eschatological transformation or fulfillment of created things does not erase their reality, demean their goodness, or deny their place within the divine economy. Just as the resurrection does not annul the reality of Jesus's humanity but takes it up and transfigures it into a new mode of existence, so too might Catholics look similarly at the land promise: it retains its abiding realism and integrity when it is beginning to be fulfilled in the eschatological renewal of creation that starts with Jesus's glorified humanity.

Accordingly, Catholics can acknowledge the return of the Jewish people to live in their ancestral homeland as an instance of God's loving-kindness and faithfulness to his covenant people. Catholics can do so in a manner akin to honoring the abiding value and religious significance of the plain-sense dimensions of the Old Testament and the realities which it presents. Such honoring does not necessitate that Catholics view the return of the Jewish people to the land in decidedly eschatological terms. Catholics would understand the eschatological fulfilling (and transposing) of the land promise in terms of the resurrection of Jesus as the starting point of the new creation. For the New Testament writings configure around Jesus a trajectory regarding the land promise already established in Second Temple Jewish texts. Catholics might affirm thus that the land promise is one that is made by God to the Jewish people, though the significance of that having come to pass will be different for Jews than for Catholics.

9

HOW TO THINK ABOUT ZIONISM

Gary A. Anderson

Few movements are as difficult to understand as modern Zionism.[1] In conversations with well educated people, I often meet with great surprise when I inform them that Zionism began in the nineteenth century among secular Jews. They are even more surprised to learn that when the movement started nearly all religious Jews opposed any effort to establish a Jewish homeland. To be sure, the prayer book used on the Sabbath and festival days was chock-full of petitions for the day when God would gather His people from the four corners of the world and draw them to the land He holds so dear. But those prayers were all cast in highly theocentric terms. The end of the Diaspora was to be accomplished by the hands of the Holy One, not by mere mortals; and certainly not by mortals who had little or no interest in the life of the Torah as it was traditionally understood. Although many religious Jews became avid Zionists over the course of the last century, these tensions did not disappear. To this day, one still sees secular Israelis infuriated when one of the ultra-orthodox religious parties in their country is able to negotiate a large government subsidy for its religious schools and housing complexes while its members refuse to serve in the military.

Yet for all the controversy over the identity of the State of Israel, most Jews are in agreement that the state itself is worthy of constant support and

1 I would like to thank the editor of *First Things* for giving me permission to republish this essay. It first appeared in the April issue of 2005; and later in abridged form in *The Christian Century*, January 13, 2009 issue. I am a bit embarrassed by the title which the editors of *First Things* gave to this article—I fear it claims too much. This essay was intended to be more of a proposal than a final answer. But in the interests of clarity, I have chosen to republish it under the same title. Biblical texts in this article are taken from the NRSV.

prayer. Better to be an unhappy Jew in Israel than to be at the mercy of the country's Arab neighbors. The situation in the Christian West, however, is not so tolerant of what is sometimes dismissively called the "Zionist entity." Indeed, over the past several decades various mainline church bodies have called for an international effort to isolate Israel, and they routinely compare the Jewish state to apartheid South Africa. Given the political and theological significance of Zionism, we should expect and encourage an honest airing of different opinions. But one is struck by how few arguments about Zionism seem informed by any real theological knowledge. One is not surprised that secular journalists have been so flat-footed in this area, but the response of the mainline churches has been almost as bad. Few Western Christians seem willing or able to examine the theological challenge that Zionism presents both to religious Jews and to Christians.

Any discussion of the modern Zionist movement must begin with the biblical claim that the land of Canaan was given by God to the people Israel. And any discussion of that claim leads back to the call of Abraham in Genesis 12 and its immediate literary context. The first eleven chapters of Genesis depict a growing rebellion in the human community. Each story presents the reader with a new form of sin, and many such stories culminate in an act of dispersion. Adam and Eve are exiled to a place just east of Eden; Cain, in turn, must absent himself from the vicinity of Adam and Eve (a similar fate will greet the survivors of the Flood); and the proud generation that set to work on the Tower of Babel is dispersed across the face of the earth. All of humanity shares in the condition that would come to be Israel's special lot after the invasion of the Babylonians: exile. But there is one important difference: Israel remembers that she is in exile and prays for her exile to end, while the gentiles remain blissfully ignorant of their condition and its origins. (Christians have been allowed to share in this memory; Latin hymnody, in particular, is full of references to the human race as the "exiled children of Eve.")

All seems to be lost until God addresses Abram, son of Terah: "Go from your country and your kindred and your father's house to the land that I will show you. I will make of you a great nation, and I will bless you, and make your name great, so that you will be a blessing. I will bless those who bless you, and the one who curses you I will curse; and in you all the families of the earth shall be blessed" (Gn 12:1–3). In this striking message Abraham is called to leave all that he holds dear and set off for an unknown land. Through this paradigmatic migration God intends to rectify the created order that has spun so badly out of control.

It may be worth pausing for a moment on this audacious promise. In terms of the larger tableau of the Old Testament it is a promise that is both irrevocable and unfulfilled. It is irrevocable because it is a promise made by God. To this particular people (and to no other) God has tied His identity; to their fate His very nature is bound. As the apostle Paul puts it, the advantage of the Jews lies in the fact that "they were entrusted with the promises of God." Could their apostasy erase these promises? "By no means," Paul answers, "Let God be true though every man be false!" (Rom 3:2, 4).

It is not so easy to see that this promise is also unfulfilled. Some would insist that it has been fulfilled. They would point out that much of the Book of Joshua is devoted to showing precisely how the land promised to Abraham came under the control of the Israelite tribes. But to this it must be answered that the Book of Joshua is not part of what the Jewish canon (and Jesus himself in the Gospels) identifies as "the Torah." At the end of this collection of five books, Moses and the Israelite tribes are still waiting to enter the promised land.

> Then Moses went up from the plains of Moab to Mount Nebo, to the top of Pisgah, which is opposite Jericho, and the LORD showed him the whole land: Gilead as far as Dan, all Naphtali, the land of Ephraim and Manasseh, all the land of Judah as far as the Western Sea, the Negeb, and the Plain—that is, the valley of Jericho, the city of palm trees—as far as Zoar. The Lord said to him, "This is the land of which I swore to Abraham, to Isaac, and to Jacob, saying, 'I will give it to your descendants'; I have let you see it with your eyes, but you shall not cross over there." (Dt 34:1–4)

And so with the entire promised land in his sights, Moses breathes his last and the account of Israel's beginnings—Israel's Torah—comes to a close.

As many have noted, the very last words of the last book of the Jewish Bible end on a similar note. "Thus says King Cyrus of Persia: The LORD, the God of heaven, has given me all the kingdoms of the earth, and he has charged me to build him a house at Jerusalem, which is in Judah. Whoever is among you of all his people, may the LORD his God be with him! Let him go up" (2 Chr 36:23). The similarity between the passage in Deuteronomy and this passage in 2 Chronicles cannot be accidental. The status of the Israelite people at the close of the biblical period is drawn into alignment with her founding charter. Israel is a people waiting just outside the land for the moment when God will bring it home.

Seen in this way, the return to Zion represents the completion of the promise made to Abraham. For this reason, it does not belong in any solely anthropological category; it constitutes a true *opus Dei*, or "work of God." It is an eschatological event in the sense that it requires the push of the divine hand to set it in motion. And there is more. When the moment arrives and God finally vindicates the claims He has made on behalf of His chosen people, the righteousness He displays will resound to the ends of the earth. Through the choice of Abraham, all nations will find blessing. The prophet Isaiah is most clear on this point:

> In days to come the mountain of the LORD's house
> shall be established as the highest of the mountains,
> and shall be raised above the hills;
> all the nations shall stream to it.
> Many peoples shall come and say,
> "Come, let us go up to the mountain of the LORD,
> to the house of the God of Jacob;
> that he may teach us his ways
> and that we may walk in his paths."
> For out of Zion shall go forth instruction,
> and the word of the LORD from Jerusalem.
> He shall judge between the nations,
> and shall arbitrate for many peoples;
> they shall beat their swords into plowshares,
> and their spears into pruning hooks;
> nation shall not lift up sword against nation,
> neither shall they learn war anymore. (Is 2:2–4)

How, then, are we to understand the modern State of Israel in light of the irrevocable promise made to Abraham that still awaits fulfillment? The Bible would seem to allow only one answer: the return to Zion is the beginning of the messianic era. And indeed many fundamentalist Christians have asserted precisely this. Because the modern State of Israel is an objective sign of the messianic end times, Christians should unite with their Jewish brothers and sisters and defend the modern State of Israel against its many adversaries. As if in reaction to this unyielding attitude, many thoughtful Christians err in the opposite direction. They approach the question of the Jewish state as a purely political affair, ignoring any sort of theological framework—or, even worse, they approach the State of Israel from the classical position of *adversus Judaeos* and so try to make Israel a pariah among the community of nations. The relationship of the Jewish people to the land of Palestine is thus viewed, even by many Christians, from an entirely secular perspective.

Here, then, is the central question I would like to consider: If we truly believe that God's promises to the Jewish people have not come to an end, and that those promises are linked inextricably to the land, what are we to make of the current return to Israel? We seem to be left in a quandary. It would appear that in order for Christians to sympathize with Zionism, they must believe that we now live in the shadow of the end times. But this is not the only way to read the biblical evidence. To get another perspective on the matter it would perhaps be useful to see how Judaism has struggled with the very same issue.

To the surprise of many Christians, a fair number of religious Jews are equally puzzled over how to assess the current resettlement of the land of Israel. And not a few Jews remain devout non-Zionists both in and outside of Israel. The grounds for their position are twofold. The first is the Bible's admonition to those who naïvely presume that it is their simple human right to live on this hallowed ground. According to Leviticus 18:24–30, the moral standards of the land are so high that it will vomit forth anyone who conducts himself improperly while living on it. This was the reason that the Canaanites were evicted from the land, and it is presumably a standing threat to anyone else who wants to settle there. Holiness has its privileges but it also comes loaded with important responsibilities. One thinks here of Shai Agnon's novel *Only Yesterday*.[2] The protagonist of the story is a young, spirited Zionist named Isaac. On his boat ride to Israel, he meets an older religious Jew who asks the young man where he is headed. When the older man learns that Isaac plans to move to Israel and participate in the resettling of the land, he breaks out in anger and reproaches Isaac for profaning the sacred bequest of Israel. Does he think the land of Israel is a land just like any other, a land to which you can simply migrate in hopes of attaining a better life?

The other reason for Jewish skepticism about the claims of Zionism comes from the biblical story of the spies sent to reconnoiter the land in preparation for the arrival of the Israelites. After the spies have returned and warned the people about the terrible dangers that will attend their march forward to take possession of the promised land, all Israel rises up in rebellion. "Would that we had died in the land of Egypt!," they complain before Moses and Aaron, "or would that we had died in this wilderness! Why is the LORD bringing us into this land to fall by the sword? Our wives and our little ones will become booty; would it not be better for us to go back to Egypt?" So they said to one another, "Let us choose a captain, and go back to Egypt" (Nm 14:2–4). After this rebellion God decrees that the entire generation is to die in the wilderness over the next forty years and only after a new generation has arisen will the promise of entering the land be fulfilled. But after Moses has conveyed this divine decree, a number of Israelites reconsider the matter and decide on their own to enter Canaan. Moses admonishes them sternly but

2 Shay Agnon, *Only Yesterday*, trans. B. Harshav (Princeton University Press, 2000).

to no avail. They defiantly march into the hill country of southern Canaan and are vigorously repelled: "Then the Amalekites and the Canaanites who lived in that hill country came down and defeated them, pursuing them as far as Hormah" (Nm 14:45).

As the historian of Jewish thought Aviezer Ravitsky has shown in his book *Herut al ha-Luhot*, biblical texts such as Leviticus 18 and Numbers 14 led many Jewish thinkers to express grave misgivings about returning prematurely to the land of Israel.[3] In the thirteenth century Meir of Rothenberg declared:

> Let him be abstinent in the Land and beware of any transgression, for if he sins there, he will be punished most severely. For God supervises the Land and watches over its inhabitants. He who rebels against the king from within the king's palace is not the same as he who rebels outside it. This is the meaning of "a land that devours its inhabitants" (Numbers 13:32). As for those who go there and think they can get away with levity and reckless contentiousness, I would invoke the verses, "But you entered you defiled my land" (Jeremiah 2:7) and "Who asked of you to trample my courts?" (Isaiah 1:12).

Still, such pointed reservations need to be set in proper historical context. Despite all his worries about the danger of return, Meir of Rothenberg made his own plans to settle in the land of Israel. Only his premature death prevented him from doing so.

How should we understand this ambivalence about the land of Israel? Certainly Ravitsky is correct when he remarks that the longer Jews remained in exile, the more they were in awe of the Holy Land. How, they wondered, could God's own land be a fit habitation for mere mortals? Indeed, for some Jewish thinkers a return to the promised land is so tied to moral and spiritual purity that the very nature of the human person would have to be transformed in order for the return to be safe—and even then it would have to come as the result not of human decision but of an explicit act of God, lest Jews repeat the sin of the spies by "hastening the end."

It would be hard to overestimate the historical importance of Jeremiah's dictum to those who suffered the first exile of 587 BCE: "Seek the welfare of the city where I have sent you into exile, and pray to the LORD on its behalf, for in its welfare you will find your welfare" (29:7). Indeed the siddur, or Jewish prayer book, honors the advice of Jeremiah by including a prayer on

3 Aviezer Ravitzky, *Freedom Inscribed: Diverse Voices of the Jewish Religious Thought* [Hebrew] (Am Oved, 1999). See the second chapter, "The Land of Israel: Desire and Trepidation in Jewish Literature."

the Sabbath or festival day for the government of the country in which the local community of Jews resides. For all the spiritual attraction of the land of Israel, there were good scriptural reasons to wait patiently before "going up to Zion."

But the vagaries of human history have a way of jarring one loose from once-settled convictions. The God of the Bible is not some ethereal Gnostic spirit but a personal God covenanted to the people He chose. To slightly alter a biblical maxim, their ways are not inseparable from His ways. In the wake of the Holocaust, and of the stupendous victory of Israel's armed forces over its Arab neighbors in the Six-Day War of 1967, it seemed to many Jews that the traditional Jewish reservations about modern Zionism were in need of revision. God was again at work in this land on behalf of this people. The question now becomes how to conceptualize this work of God in light of biblical antecedents. Some secular Jews such as Michael Walzer have argued that the policy advocated by Jeremiah has been dramatically disconfirmed by the events of the twentieth century, and that, as a result, Jews should follow the example of the Israelite rebels of Saul's day who demanded a king in order to be like the rest of the nations (1 Sm 8).[4]

Though not without its own internal rationale, such an explanation does not convince the religious. An act of rebellion in the Bible's day cannot become the inspiration for an act of obedience in ours. The question for the religious Jew—and, I would argue, for the sympathetic Christian observer as well—is whether the return to Zion can be articulated in a manner that is biblically and theologically compelling.

There is, I think, no better guide to this question than the Israeli biblical scholar Uriel Simon, who distinguishes between two sorts of claims a people can make on a land.[5] One is a natural claim—a claim that the land in question belongs to a people because that is where they have dwelt for several generations, where they have raised their children, buried their ancestors, and created a distinctive local culture. The Jews, by contrast, claim a very different sort of connection to their land. Canaan is theirs not by dint of any set of conventional circumstances; it came to them as a gift from God. Israel's claim to the land is of a supernatural order.

As Simon notes, each sort of claim has its own advantages and disadvantages. A natural connection to one's land results from a history of continuous occupation, so that legal title to the land comes to be felt as a kind of natural

4 Michael Walzer, *Exilpolitik in der Hebräischen Bibel* (Mohr Siebeck, 2001). Though the title is in German, the book has printed the English original on facing pages.

5 Uriel Simon, *Seek Peace and Pursue It* [Hebrew] (Yediot Aharonot, 2002), see chap. 12, "Biblical Destinies—Conditional Promises." Translations from this book are my own.

right. In such a case, one may not even consider what would become of one's people if it lost its land, so complete is the identity between the people and its place. "The population feels an obligation to defend its land and its independence," Simon writes, "but in general it does not worry about being uprooted in toto. The danger of exile [is not perceived] as a real threat, nor does it impinge on their consciousness." But once such a connection is broken, it is broken forever: when, for example, the Hittites were driven from their land, their identity as a people came to an end.

Israel's supernatural claim to Canaan is not continuous in the same way, since its relationship to the land is marked by rupture. What God has given He can also take away, and on at least two occasions—the destruction of Jerusalem in 587 BCE and 70 CE—Israel has been driven into exile. And yet, unlike the Hittites, the people of Israel have perdured. Wherever they are driven they remain unassimilated.

The fact that Israel has lasted two millennia without a homeland or any sort of native rule is miraculous. If we could go back in time and quiz those who lived in the ancient Near East about which people had the firmer claim to its land and which culture would most likely stand the test of time, they would more likely have chosen the Hittites than the Israelites. A natural connection to the land, supported by a large standing army, is far more impressive by worldly standards than the promissory note of a national god.

The first to note the peculiar fact of the perdurance of Jewish identity was Haman, the notorious antisemite in the book of Esther. In his advice to King Ahasuerus he declares:

> There is a certain people scattered and separated among the peoples in all the provinces of your kingdom; their laws are different from those of every other people, and they do not keep the king's laws, so that it is not appropriate for the king to tolerate them. If it pleases the king, let a decree be issued for their destruction, and I will pay ten thousand talents of silver into the hands of those who have charge of the king's business, so that they may put it into the king's treasuries" (Est 3:8–9).

To be a people set apart has its attendant dangers. Augustine was also cognizant of this fact, though he regarded it in a more favorable light. That the Jews still survive in spite of their role in having God's messiah crucified is proof that God acts in accord with the teaching of the Gospels and continues to love His enemies. Though Augustine's position is considerably better than that of Haman, one still winces at the description of the Jews as "God's enemies." Yet what is important for our purposes is Augustine's historical observation that the Jewish identity has survived in spite of the Diaspora and in contrast to conventional historical patterns. This fact, Augustine argued, demanded a theological explanation.[6]

The Catholic novelist and occasional philosopher Walker Percy comments on this fact in a far more sympathetic way. He argues that the Jewish people, as a people, point toward the reality of the God who has tied His identity to them:

> Where are the Hittites?
>
> Why does no one find it remarkable that in most world cities today there are Jews but not one single Hittite even though the Hittites had a great flourishing civilization while the Jews nearby were a weak and obscure people?
>
> When one meets a Jew in New York or New Orleans or Paris or Melbourne, it is remarkable that no one considers the event remarkable. What are they doing here? But it is even more remarkable to wonder, if there are Jews here, why are there not Hittites here?
>
> Where are the Hittites? Show me one Hittite in New York City.[7]

It is worth noting how Percy's assessment of the matter overlaps with that of Simon. The Hittites, of course, had a natural connection to their land, a connection that would have been understood by them and their neighbors as enduring. Yet history has defied their expectations; enter rapacious invaders and whatever was left of a venerable Indo-European culture went into rapid decline. The Jews cannot possess their land without interruption until the end of days, but their identity as a people is a promise guaranteed by God. They have lost their land twice—and could lose it for a third time—but their identity remains, and will remain, intact by virtue of God's gracious hand.

Israel's claim to its land is to be distinguished from that of other peoples in another important way. The choice of Abraham and the people he would engender was not an end in itself. Rather, through that choice God sought to bring a blessing to a troubled world. Through Abraham the nature of God's relationship to humanity was to be made known. Thus, when God was about to destroy Sodom and Gomorrah for their flagrant wickedness, He decided to bring Abraham into His confidence, and the reason for this is important: "For I have chosen him, that he may charge his children and his household after him to keep the way of the LORD by doing righteousness and justice;

6 The exposition of Augustine's thinking about the Jews is Paula Fredricksen, *Augustine and the Jews* (Doubleday, 2008). On the issue of the survival of Jewish identity in the diaspora, see her discussion on 271. On God's love for his "enemies" see the discussion of Augustine's treatment of Ps 59 in her final chapter, 290–352.

7 Walker Percy, *The Message in the Bottle* (Farrar, Straus and Giroux, 2000), 6.

so that the LORD may bring about for Abraham what he has promised him" (Gn 18:19).

But God's dealing justly with the nations of the world is not something that Abraham learns about only by way of dialogue. His own life and the lives of many of his descendants will be witness to this principle in a far more concrete way. For God has bequeathed this land to Abraham's people on the surprising condition that they patiently wait hundreds of years before they actually take possession of it. "Know this for certain, that your offspring shall be aliens in a land that is not theirs, and shall be slaves there, and they shall be oppressed for four hundred years." Why this surprising codicil to the promise? Because the wickedness of the Amorites, who were the current inhabitants of the land, had not yet reached its tipping point. God will not give this land away until its former occupants have relinquished their rights. So Israel's right to the land, though the result of a divine grant, is not without its restrictions. And the Torah warns that should Israel violate the rules incumbent upon those who would dwell in that land, it will be thrown out, just as the Amorites were. To be sure, God's promise to Israel is eternal, but this does not mean that Israel's presence in the land will be continuous and without interruption. Only in the messianic age, the Tanakh promises, will Israel's settlement in the land be secure and final.

Of course, God's promise to Israel is not to be understood as just a settling of accounts with the Amorites. Through His choice of Abraham, God makes known to the world the superabundance of His love and graciousness toward all creation. And the graciousness of God finds a fit recipient in the person of Abraham, who responds with unparalleled obedience. Abraham offers back to God that very part of his own being that he holds most dear: his beloved son Isaac. But even more important for the present discussion is another example of Abraham's generosity. In Genesis 13, just after Abraham has escaped from Egypt and brought great wealth back to the land of Canaan, he finds that his possessions and those of his nephew Lot are too numerous for the land to support. One option that lies well within Abraham's rights is to send Lot back to his home in Mesopotamia. But rather than do this, Abraham allows Lot to choose whatever portion of land he wishes. Lot immediately responds by choosing for himself the very best portion—a piece of land Scripture compares to Eden. (Of course, this land turns out to be in the territory of Sodom and Gomorrah, but only the reader is aware of this detail. At the time of Abraham's offer, the valley Lot chose was lush and attractive beyond measure, and neither Abraham nor Lot had any inkling of what fate lay before it.) The original beneficiary of the divine promise, Abraham, concedes the very land that seemed most conducive to the fulfillment of that promise.

It is precisely at this point in the narrative, when Abraham shows himself willing to give up this choice territory, that God intervenes and rewards Abraham with explicit title to all the land that had been promised: "Raise your eyes now, and look from the place where you are, northward and southward and eastward and westward; for all the land that you see I will give to you and to your offspring forever . . . Rise up, walk through the length and the breadth of the land, for I will give it to you" (Gn 13:14–17). Whereas Lot had raised his own eyes (Gn 13:10) in order to select the choicest land, it is God who raises up Abraham's eyes (Gn 13:14) to bestow upon him a far better portion. Whereas Lot is asked to look to the north and south to determine the land that would be his (Gn 13:9), Abraham is instructed to cast his glance toward all four points of the compass (Gn 13:14). The generosity of Abraham does not put the divine promise at risk; on the contrary, it becomes part of the fulfillment of that promise.

Where does this leave us with the Jewish claim to the land of Palestine? We need not agree with the Christian Zionists who insist that because this is the onset of the messianic era, anything Israel does in Palestine is part of its larger divine mandate. Even if we are witnesses to the beginning of the final messianic age—and this possibility can never be wholly dismissed—we should certainly expect that whatever God does with the Jews during this time will conform to the character of His relationship to this people as it is revealed in the Bible. A unilateral land-grab that takes no moral cognizance of the plight of Israel's neighbors is not consistent with Israel's foundational story.

Still, we must also insist that the promises of Scripture are indeed inviolable and that Israel's attachment to this land is underwritten by God's providential decree. The miraculous appearance of the Israeli state just after the darkest moment in Jewish history is hard to interpret outside of a theological framework. Certainly this is one reason (though not the only reason) why Islam has such difficulties with the modern State of Israel. The Jews are a protected people in the Koran but also a people who must know their place. Many Muslims believe that the Jews have gone far beyond their limited set of rights by possessing an independent state with authority over Muslim holy sites. Many Arab nations continue to draw maps of the Middle East in which the State of Israel does not even appear. But even worse is the silence of those mainline church bodies that ignore such blatant non-recognition while loudly attacking Israel for its shortcomings.

Nevertheless, the acknowledgment of Israel's right to some form of sovereignty in Palestine leaves many pressing moral questions open. How is Israel to view the present moral quandary in which it finds itself? What is the relationship of Israeli Jews to the people with whom they dwell? The close of

Uriel Simon's essay on the role of the Bible in modern Zionism is worth citing in full, since it presents us with a perspective that the Church could assent to:

> I believe that we are living in an era in which the divine promises are being enacted, a time in which God is extending assistance to his people, a time in which a portion of our biblical destiny is taking bodily form. This faith ought to instill in us patience, personal and spiritual trust, a readiness to assume great personal sacrifice, and above all this faith should support us in marshalling our energies for a fitting embodiment of this destiny. Along with this, it is incumbent upon us to take every precaution against "false messianism," from an advancement of the course of human history by dint of sheer human will and the refusal to distinguish between an era in which the ways of this (fallen) world still remain in force and the messianic age wherein the wolf shall lie down with the lamb. The failure to make precisely this distinction will occur when we convince ourselves that what we have has been promised from above and that our return to the land is indeed final. Precisely this sort of false confidence is liable to lead to our spoiling once more, [God] forbid, the great opportunity that has been given us. On the other hand, our hold on this land will grow stronger the more we remember that it has been given conditionally, that is, on the nature of our deeds. These deeds must include a zealous pursuit of peace.[8]

For Simon, Israel's providential right to the land is secure. It is the subject of a divine promise. The nature of Israel's present return was unanticipated by many Jewish thinkers and posed a serious challenge to many thoughtful religious Jews. But then, so were the many horrors visited upon this chosen people in the twentieth century.

The problem, as Simon understands it, derives from the presumption that any Jewish return to the land must, by definition, be understood as the final fulfillment of Israel's prophetic hopes. The novelty of Simon's answer to this challenge is his assertion that the present return does have a theological grounding yet at the same time does not necessarily constitute the fulfillment of God's eschatological plans. In this sense, Simon's position differs only slightly from what Benedict XVI has recently written. Like Simon, he denies that the present return to the land constitutes a fulfillment of prophetic expectations. Though his own formulation tends in a more secular direction, it is not without a theological core. The Vatican, he notes, has recognized the State of Israel "as a modern constitutional state" fully consistent "with the standards of international law." But at the same time he is also willing to

8 Simon, *Seek Peace*, 247–48.

confess that the formation of this modern state "expresses God's faithfulness to the people of Israel."[9]

The return of the Jews to Israel has also posed a challenge to Christians. For ever since the days of Augustine, Israel's landlessness was commonly thought to be a punishment for the death of Christ. Events of the previous century showed us where this type of thinking can lead. Happily, many thoughtful Christians have moved beyond this position. Certainly the visit of Pope John Paul II to the Holy Land in the spring of 2000—walking the streets of the Jewish state and praying at the Western Wall—was a powerful expression of this. The question now is whether we can move from an attitude of toleration and acceptance to bold theological affirmation. Is the return to Zion part of God's providential design and eternal promise to His people Israel? I believe that it is. Is Israel's most recent return to this land final and permanent? No one can know for sure. That will depend, as Uriel Simon wisely argues, on the providential plan of our benevolent Creator and on the actions of Israel.

As an addendum to this article, I must confess that many readers, including all the scholars that *The Christian Century* charged with responding to my essay, failed to grasp the crucial point of Uriel Simon which provided the center of my own position near the close of this article. Recognizing the inviolable promise that God made to Israel regarding the land does not necessitate in any way some sort of recalcitrant, right-wing position regarding peace with the Palestinians.[10] I believe that I gave sufficient emphasis to this dimension of Simon's argument and I ask the reader to ponder carefully what he says about the important model established by Abraham in Genesis 13 and his repeated emphasis that Israel's claim on the land is radically conditional: it relies on the character of her deeds while she possesses the land.

9 Benedict XVI, "Grace and Vocation without Remorse: Comments on the Treatise *De Iudaeis*," *Communio* 45 (2018): 179. One wonders whether Benedict could have expressed himself a bit more strongly had he been familiar with Simon's own position. Nevertheless, though the challenge for Benedict is—to a degree—similar to that of Simon (Israel's current return to the land cannot be viewed as a culmination of Israel's eschatological hopes), there is also an important area of disagreement: Christian hopes for the way in which God will bring history to its close necessarily differ and as a result a Jewish approach to what is ultimately at stake in a return to the land cannot agree with Christian expectations. For this reason, Benedict must underscore that a "strictly theologically-understood state—a Jewish faith-state [*Glaubenstaat*] . . . is contrary to the Christian understanding of the promises" (178).

10 Uriel Simon, himself, is a man of the left and many of my Israeli acquaintances who stand to the right of me oppose his position and have criticized my employment of his work.

But most disappointing to me is the failure of so many Christian readers to avoid the theological dimensions of the problem altogether and head directly for the various geopolitical options that are currently on the table. Israel's relationship to the land is unlike the relationship of any other people to their land. And the difference is grounded in the covenantal promises God bequeathed to the Jewish people. I believe it behooves all persons committed to the theological importance of the Bible to ponder carefully the nature of this profound theological mystery But most disappointing to me is the failure of so many Christian readers to avoid the *theological* dimensions of the problem altogether and head directly for the various geopolitical options that are currently on the table.[11]

11 See the responses in: *The Christian Century*: January 13, 2009 issue and March 10, 2009 issue.

10

THE PLACE OF THE LAND OF ISRAEL IN THE HEBREW BIBLE, RABBINIC TRADITION, AND ITS ONGOING SIGNIFICANCE FOR THE JEWISH PEOPLE

Rabbi David Rosen

The divine covenant with Abraham and his descendants,[1] ratified with the children of Israel at Sinai where they are called to be "a kingdom of priests and a holy nation,"[2] is inextricably bound up with the promise of the land which plays both an integral role in the covenant as well as an instrumental one. The children of Israel fulfill their commitment first and foremost through the observance of the divinely revealed commandments.[3] By living this way of life, the people testify to the revelation and its divine source,[4] and this way of life is ideally meant to be lived in the land of the forefathers' sojournings.[5] While the purpose of such is not explicitly stated, we may easily conclude that if the children of Israel are to serve as a paradigm of a holy nation, then the normative needs of a nation require that it has a national home in which to strive to fulfill this destiny. Exile from the land is presented as the consequence of the children of Israel's disregard of the commandments and the instrument by which they are punished for their failure.[6]

1 Gn 15:18, 17:8; Ex 6:4; Dt 1:8.

2 Ex 19:6.

3 Dt 26:17–18; Jos 24:22.

4 Dt 4:6–8.

5 Dt 4:5, 11:21; Lv 26.

6 Lv 27:32–33; Dt 29:23–27.

Nevertheless, because the divine covenant is eternal, the people will be given another chance; and thanks to divine fidelity and compassion, they will be returned to the land to try again to fulfill the covenantal way of life.[7] Thus, Israel testifies to the divine presence in the world, through its very fate and survival reflecting the transcendent nature of the people's covenanted existence ("for the name of the Lord is designated upon you").[8] Accordingly, Isaiah describes the Jewish people as the "witnesses" of the Lord.[9] Moreover, the land is not just the land of divine destiny, but it is the land that contains "the place where He chose His Name to dwell"[10] embodied in the Temple.

Indeed, the sages describe Jerusalem as the place where heaven and earth meet, generating "a vortex" of holiness,[11] and in the first chapter of tractate Kelim, the Mishnah describes the ever-widening circles of sanctity generating out from the Holy of Holies to the world at large.[12] The sages highlight this idea describing the Land and Jerusalem as the *umbilicus mundi*, the spiritual navel of the world:

> As the navel is set in the middle of a human being, so the Land of Israel is located in the centre of the world, Jerusalem is in the centre of the Land of Israel, the Temple in the centre of Jerusalem, the Sanctuary (*heikhal*) in the centre of the Temple, the ark in the centre of the Sanctuary and in front of the Sanctuary is the Foundation Stone from which the world began.[13]

Eliezer Schweid describes the significance of the concept as follows:

> The uniqueness of the Land of Israel is thus "geo-theological"... This is the land which faces the entrance of the spiritual world, that sphere of existence that lies beyond the physical world known to us through our senses. This is the key to the land's unique status with regard to prophecy and prayer, and also with regard to the commandments.[14]

7 Lv 27:44–45, 30:3–5; Dt 30:3–6.

8 Dt 28:10.

9 See Is 40–55.

10 Dt 12:5.

11 Babylonian Talmud (hereafter TB) *Ta'anit* 5a; see also TB *Hagigah* 12b.

12 Mishnah (Oral Torah): *Kelim* 1:6–9.

13 *Tanhumah Ylamdenu* Leviticus 78; See TB *Sanhedrin* 37a. See also Philo, *Legatio ad Gaium 294*, and Josephus, *Wars of the Jews* 3:51–52.

14 Eliezer Schweid, *The Land of Israel: National Home or Land of Destiny*, trans. Deborah Greniman (Fairleigh Dickinson University Press, 1985), 56.

However, the Hebrew Bible is not explicit as to whether this sanctity is intrinsic or extrinsic and there are different views in this regard in rabbinic thought. Even the above mentioned Mishnah in tractate Kelim is open to interpretation in both ways. Nevertheless, the sanctity of the land (*kedushat ha-aretz*) developed rich associations in rabbinical thought, where it assumed a highly symbolic and mythological status infused with promise, though always connected to the geographical location.[15]

In addition, the centrality of the land became inextricably intertwined with the people's very identity and this was reflected in the degree to which exile from the land, especially in the wake of the destruction of the Temple, was seen as the ultimate national catastrophe. The Book of Lamentations presents the destroyed city and land as the very embodiment of the humiliated and desolate people itself: "Judah . . . dwells now among the nations but finds no resting place."[16] "Zion stretches out her hands but there is none to comfort her . . . the Lord has ruled against Jacob."[17] Yet there is hope that when "the punishment of the daughter of Zion's iniquity will be accomplished, He will keep (her) in exile no longer."[18]

Accordingly, Jeremiah refers to the Jewish people as "Jerusalem," when communicating the promise of redemption: "Go and proclaim in the ears of Jerusalem saying, thus says the Lord 'I remember the devotion of your youth, your love as a bride. How you followed me in the wilderness in a land not sown.'"[19] And Isaiah continuously identifies the place and the people with one another, such as where he declares that God will once again "say to Zion, you are my people."[20] Indeed, the anticipated return of the people is described as the "return *of* Zion" and not as "the return *to* Zion."[21]

I am not sure if such total identification of a people and a place has ever existed elsewhere. To be sure, Athenians saw their identity as bound up with Athens, but I do not think that they would ascribe to the city a personality that is exiled, let alone redeemed. Thus, Judaism developed rituals to continuously recall the trauma of the destruction of the Temple and our exile from the land, both in order to learn from our own tragic mistakes, but above all

15 See Michael L. Satlow, *Creating Judaism: History, Tradition, Practice* (Columbia University Press, 2006), 160.

16 Lam 1:3.

17 Lam 1:17.

18 Lam 4:22.

19 Jer 2:2.

20 Is 51:16.

21 Ps 127:1.

to sustain the hope for the return and reconstruction of Jerusalem and the land of Israel as a whole.

The calendar contains a number of fast days in this regard, the main one being the full night and day fast of Tisha B'Av, the ninth day of the month of Av, as the anniversary of the destruction of the two Temples. The rabbis declared that one should really mourn the destruction and exile every day and in every place, but that it is not possible to mourn so much:

> The sages have therefore ordained thus. A man may whitewash his house, but he should leave a small area unfinished in remembrance of Jerusalem. A man may prepare a full-course meal, but he should leave out an item of the menu in remembrance of Jerusalem. A woman may put on all her jewelry except one or two in remembrance of Jerusalem.[22]

Most of all, it was through Jewish liturgy that the memory and centrality of the Holy Land and city were maintained continuously in Jewish consciousness.

In addition to the fast days, daily mention of the destruction and prayers for the people's return to the land became an obligatory part of all statutory services, as well as in grace after every meal. In the daily morning service, leading into the declaration of the Jewish credo "Shema Yisrael" ("Hear O Israel"),[23] we recite the words "and bring us back in peace from the four corners of the earth and lead us upright (in dignity) back to our land, for you are God who performs salvation."[24] Indeed, the biblical messianic concept of salvation refers first and foremost to the return of the exiles to the land and the establishment of independent Jewish life within it once again, in keeping with divine promise.[25]

The fourteenth blessing in the central weekday *Amidah* prayer, is devoted entirely to the idea of the return to and the restitution of Jerusalem, and the seventeenth blessing concludes with the words "and may our eyes witness Your return to Zion in compassion, Blessed are You, Lord, who restores His Presence to Zion."[26] The idea that God Himself is in exile from Jerusalem and the land of Israel with His people, was developed by the rabbis in homiletical exposition of biblical texts, for example:

22 *Tosefta Sotah* 15:12–14; TB *Bava Batra* 60b.

23 Dt 6:4–9.

24 *The Authorized Daily Prayer Book of the United Hebrew Congregations of the Commonwealth*, 4th ed. (Collins, 2007), 67.

25 Lv 26:45.

26 *Daily Prayer Book*, 91.

> Rabbi Shimon ben Yohai says, come and see how beloved Israel (the Jewish People) is before the Holy one Blessed be He; for wherever they are exiled, the Divine Presence is with them . . . and when they will be redeemed, the Divine Presence will be (redeemed) with them,[27] as it is said "and the Lord will return (with) your captivity." It is not written, He will return *you* from your captivity; but that *He* will return, which teaches that the Holy One Blessed Be He will return with them from amidst the exile."[28]

The *Mussaf* (additional) *'Amidah* prayer on the Sabbath and the new moon, but most of all on the pilgrim festivals, reinforces this yearning and expectation. "Bring back our scattered ones from among the nations and gather our dispersed people from the ends of the earth. Lead us to Zion, Your city, in jubilation and to Jerusalem, home of Your Temple, with everlasting joy."[29] Similarly with the grace after meals, the third benediction is largely devoted to the expectation of return to the land, with the restoration of the Davidic dynasty, and the rebuilding of the Temple. It concludes with the words "blessed are you Lord who in His compassion will rebuild Jerusalem, Amen."[30]

The practice of sending the earthly remains of Jews from the Diaspora to the land of Israel traces its origins to the patriarch Jacob.[31] This custom both reflected the bond between the land and the people, and also the particular view of the intrinsic sanctity of the location. In the words of Rabbi Anan,[32] "Anyone buried in the Land of Israel is considered as if he was buried beneath the altar; it is written 'An altar of earth (*adamah*) you shall make for me,'[33] and it is written 'His land (*admato)* will atone for His people.'"[34] (The rabbis here intentionally reinterpret the literal meaning of the verse.)

Not all sages encouraged such practice, as reflected in the story told in the Jerusalem Talmud about Rabbi Bar Kiri and Rabbi Elazar who saw coffins arriving in the land of Israel from the Diaspora. Rabbi Bar Kiri said to Rabbi Elazar, "What are they achieving? I apply to them the verse 'You make My inheritance desolate (during your lives), and you came and defiled My

27 TB *Megilah* 29a.

28 Dt 30:3. See also Is 52:8.

29 *Daily Prayer Book*, 677.

30 Ibid., 765.

31 Gn 49:29.

32 TB *Ktubot* 11a.

33 Ex 20:21.

34 Dt 32:43.

land (in your death).'"[35] (That is, they should have lived in the land rather than send their dead bones to it.) However, Rabbi Elazar replied "When they arrive in the Land of Israel, a clod of earth is placed in the coffin, as it is written, 'His land will atone for His people.'"[36]

While this memory and the hope for the return to the land sustained the Jewish Diaspora, a continuous Jewish presence remained in the land awaiting messianic deliverance, and in virtually every generation there were Jews who returned to live in the land out of religious motivation, despite the overwhelming poverty and adversity.

The name of the modern Jewish political movement to establish independent national life in the ancestral homeland, Zionism, reflects the profundity of the relationship between the people and the land, so deeply rooted in the religious tradition. As David Ben Gurion famously declared when testifying before the British Royal (Peel) Commission "the Bible is our (national) mandate."[37] However, the movement was overwhelmingly led by secular Jews (often rebelling against what they saw as the constraints and impotence of religion) and was substantially born out of secular forces, above all eighteenth-century rationalism and nineteenth-century nationalism. This in part explains the opposition in Orthodox Jewish circles to Zionism. On the other side of the denominational spectrum, it was also opposed by the nascent liberal Judaism that saw this movement as an unwelcome tribal regression. Nevertheless, Orthodox religious leaders are identified as both precursors and source of inspiration for political Zionism,[38] and the religious Zionist movements grew significantly. Moreover, religious language and terminology nurtured and oriented the movement as a whole. Attitudes within liberal Judaism also changed radically in the course of the twentieth century, especially in the wake of the Shoah, and with the establishment of the State of Israel.

In 1920, the Jewish members of the first High Commissioner's Advisory Council objected to the official use of the Hebrew transliteration of the word "Palestine," on the grounds that the traditional name was *Eretz Yisrael* (the land of Israel).[39] As the Arab members of the Council would not agree to

35 Jer 2:7.

36 Jerusalem Talmud *Kilayim* 9:3 and *Ketubot* 12:3.

37 Nur Masalha, *The Zionist Bible, Biblical Precedent, Colonialism, and the Erasure of Memory* (Acumen Publishing, 2013), 50.

38 See rabbis Zvi Hirsh Kallischer, Joseph Mohilever, and Judah Alkalai, in *The Zionist Idea*, ed. Arthur Herzberg (Jewish Publication Society of America, 1959).

39 This designation is mentioned in the Bible in 1 Sm 13:19, 1 Chr 22:2, and 2 Chr 2:17 in reference to Solomon's census of all of the "strangers in the Land of Israel." Ezekiel, though generally

the use of the term "land of Israel," the High Commissioner Herbert Samuel decided that the Hebrew transliteration of the name Palestine should be used, but followed always by the two Hebrew initials of "Eretz Yisrael."

> He was aware that there was no other name in the Hebrew language for this land except "Eretz-Israel." At the same time he thought that if "Eretz-Israel" only were used, it might not be regarded by the outside world as a correct rendering of the word "Palestine," and in the case of passports or certificates of nationality, it might perhaps give rise to difficulties, so it was decided to print "Palestine" in Hebrew letters and to add after it the letters "Aleph" "Yod," which constitute a recognized abbreviation of the Hebrew name. His Excellency still thought that this was a good compromise.[40]

On May 14, 1948, the day that the British mandate over Palestine expired, the Jewish People's Council gathered at the Tel Aviv Museum to approve a proclamation declaring "the establishment of a Jewish state in Eretz-Israel, to be known as the State of Israel." The Israeli Labor Party which governed for three decades after independence accepted the partition of mandatory Palestine into independent Jewish and Arab states as a pragmatic solution to the political and demographic issues of the territory, with the description "land of Israel" applying to the territory of the State of Israel within the "green line" of the 1948 ceasefire lines. However, the then opposition "revisionists," to be known as the Herut party and evolving into today's Likud party, regarded the rightful land of Israel as *Eretz Yisrael Ha-Shlema* (literally, the whole land of Israel), which came to be referred to as Greater Israel.

The 1955 Israeli government yearbook stated: "It is called the 'State of Israel' because it is part of the land of Israel and not merely a Jewish State. The creation of the new State by no means derogates from the scope of historical Eretz Israel."[41] Following the Six-Day War in 1967, the Israeli military government in the Occupied Territories issued an order on December 17 of that year, stating that "the term 'Judea and Samaria region' shall be identical in meaning for all purposes . . . to the term 'the West Bank Region.'"[42] This change in terminology, which has been followed in Israeli official statements since that time, reflected a historic attachment to these areas and rejection

preferring the phrase "soil of Israel," uses the name "Land of Israel" twice (40:2 and 47:18). However, the term became normative in rabbinic usage.

40 "Minutes of the Meeting on November 9, 1920," quoted in Memorandum No. 133, "Use of the Name Eretz-Israel," in the *Report by the Palestine Royal Commission*, 1937.

41 "Israel, the State and the Nation," in *Israel Government Yearbook* 5716 (1955): 320.

42 Shlomo Gazit, *Trapped Fools: Thirty Years of Israeli Policy in the Territories* (Routledge, 2003), 162.

of a name that was seen as implying Jordanian sovereignty over them.[43] However, the use of this terminology, especially after the 1977 elections which saw the Labor party replaced by a Likud-led coalition, became increasingly associated with those who not only sought to conform the borders of the state with those described in the Bible,[44] but also to resist the idea of territorial compromise. Nevertheless, even though Menachem Begin preached undying loyalty to Judea and Samaria and promoted Jewish settlement there, he did not annex the West Bank and Gaza to Israel after he took office, reflecting a recognition that absorbing the Palestinians could turn Israel it into a binational state instead of a Jewish one.[45]

The Jewish return to the biblical heartland of the land of Israel, and the "unification" of Jerusalem as a result of the Six-Day War had galvanized world Jewry's identification with Israel as central to contemporary Jewish identity and proved to be a watershed in the evolution of religious Zionist attitudes. While there had been different strands within religious Zionism ranging from the pragmatic to the neo-messianic, the latter came to increasingly dominate. With the events of June 1967 that seemed to confirm the unstoppable unfolding of a preordained historical process, the expansion of Israel's borders became a central priority in the agenda of Israeli religious Zionism. This idea also proved attractive to some non-religious nationalists who could not justify their territorial claims purely on political or military grounds.

The religious Zionist parties which had sought to be a bridge between the Jewish religious tradition and modern Israeli secular society had been part of Labor-led coalitions and had generally adopted compromising positions on territorial issues. However now as part of the Likud-led coalition, maximalist territorial positions became increasingly prominent.[46]

Gush Emunim, the national religious settler movement established in 1974, explicitly based its policies on the biblical narrative. Its leaders argued that the West Bank should be annexed permanently to Israel for both ideological and religious reasons. Over the decades *Gush Emunim*'s ideology became increasingly normative among religious Zionists, and today in effect it serves as the manifesto of the party that presumes to officially represent

43 Emma Playfair, *International Law and the Administration of Occupied Territories: Two Decades of Israeli Occupation of the West Bank and Gaza Strip* (Oxford University Press, 1992), 41.

44 See Raffaella A. Del Sarto, "Israel's Contested Identity and the Mediterranean," *Mediterranean Politics* 8, no. 1 (2003): 27–58.

45 "The World: Pursuing Peace; Netanyahu and His Party Turn Away from Greater Israel," *New York Times*, November 22, 1998.

46 Aviezer Ravitzky, "The Revealed End: Messianic Religious Zionism," in *Messianism, Zionism, and Jewish Religious Radicalism*, translated by Michael Swirsky and Jonathan Chipman (University of Chicago Press, 1996).

religious Zionism. It should be noted however that not all Israelis who describe themselves as religious Zionists vote for that party, and that there is also a religious Zionist constituency which advocates territorial comprise as an existential political and moral necessity. Nevertheless the "neo-Messianic" strain within religious Zionism became overwhelmingly dominant. This is to be seen inter alia in the religious fervor with which both Israel's Independence Day and especially Jerusalem Day (celebrating Israel's victory in the Six-Day War and the "unification" of Jerusalem) are celebrated within these circles.

The establishment of the State of Israel in the wake of the Shoah had led to fissures within ultra-Orthodox rejectionism. The latter was not only related to the overwhelmingly secular character of Zionism; but it was also predicated on a theological argument based on the Talmudic reference to the Three Oaths which included a prohibition to initiate a mass return to the land of Israel to restore Jewish sovereignty.[47] After the establishment of the state, while the majority of ultra-Orthodox leadership still opposed political collaboration with the government, they nevertheless trafficked with it in order to preserve and promote their own sectorial interests. Even though some remained implacably hostile to the Zionist enterprise, it should be noted that this did not mean opposition to individuals and communities settling in the land; on the contrary, many of them do believe that it is

47 The Three Oaths is the popular name for a homily in the Talmud (TB *Ketubot* 111a) which relates that God adjured three oaths upon the world. Two of the oaths pertain to the Jewish people, and one of the oaths pertains to the other nations of the world. The Jews for their part were sworn not to forcefully reclaim the land of Israel and not to rebel against the other nations, while the other nations in turn were sworn not to subjugate the Jews excessively. Responses to this argument include the following: (1) The Three Oaths are an aggadic homily and have no halachic legal standing. Accordingly, Maimonides's Code (Mishneh Torah), Joseph Karo's Code of Jewish Law (Shulhan Aruch) and other halachic sources do not even refer to the Three Oaths let alone rule accordingly. (2) It is not clearly established in the text or commentaries what precisely would constitute permission from the nations. As such, the Balfour Declaration, the San Remo Conference, League of Nations Mandate for Palestine, and UN GA Resolution 181 are to be understood as representing permission and approval from the nations of the world. Accordingly, the Jewish people cannot be considered to have rebelled against the nations. (3) The Three Oaths simply meant that God had decreed an exile for the Jewish people. The fact that the Jewish people have successfully returned to the land of Israel, and that the State of Israel has survived, is evidence that the oath is void and the decree has ended. Religious Zionists often point to Israel's seemingly miraculous survival in the numerous Arab-Israeli wars as proof of divine support for the State of Israel. (4) The Jewish people did not return *en masse* to the land of Israel, but rather through individual immigration as well as a series of five group immigrations. There was never a point in history where a majority of world Jewry collectively migrated to the land of Israel. Thus, many authorities understand the oath of "not ascending as a wall" as only including an immigration of the entire (or at least a majority of the) nation. (5) Some of these authorities also require that this mass immigration be one of force in order for the oath to be considered violated. This is a position held by many rabbinic authorities both mediaeval and modern.

incumbent on individuals to live in the land of Israel if they can. This is in accordance with Nachmanides's affirmation that Jews "are commanded (by the Torah) to inherit the land in every generation, even during exile."[48] As collaboration with the State increased, the number of ultra-Orthodox hard-liners diminished and only a small minority remained determined to avoid trafficking with the secular state. This group is often known by the name of its most vociferous constituent, *Neturei Karta* (Guardians of the City). As mentioned, most of ultra-Orthodoxy adopted a more pragmatic approach, even if generally avoiding being part of a governing coalition.

With the Likud's electoral success in 1977, Begin brought in the ultra-Orthodox parties into his government, leading to increasing ultra-Orthodox access to and dependency upon the state's resources. This inevitably led to (and even required) a religious ideological justification and an increasing identification with right-wing political ideology, which was reinforced by the emergence of Shas—the "Sephardic" ultra-Orthodox party—the majority of whose voters came from the right wing of the Israeli political spectrum.

As a result, the religious attachment to the land has increasingly become part and parcel of the discourse even within ultra-Orthodox circles, despite the theological reservations regarding the secular state. All of this has impacted on political debates in Israel across the political spectrum, even for those secular parties for whom religious sentiment carries little weight. This was particularly evident in the public discourse and discussion in the Knesset over the Jewish Nation State law.[49] Perhaps a testimony to this process in the overall national context, was the establishment by the Knesset in June 2016, of Aliyah Day (i.e., Immigration Day; the Hebrew word "Aliyah" means literally "going up" to the land, and is used in Israel specifically in relation to Jewish immigration) as an annual Israeli national holiday, explicitly celebrating the anniversary of the Israelites crossing the Jordan River into the land of Israel while carrying the Ark of the covenant.[50]

The importance of the State of Israel for the identity of the vast majority of world Jewry is overwhelmingly perceived as rooted in this biblical attachment. Accordingly, Jewish perceptions of other peoples and religions are significantly influenced by their approaches toward Israel and the degree to which this historic attachment is respected or not.

48 Nachmanides, addendum to Maimonides's book of commandments (positive commandment #4).

49 See Eugene Kantorovich, "A Comparative Constitutional Perspective on Israel's Nation-State Law," *Israel Studies* 25, no. 3 (Fall 2020): 137–52.

50 Jos 4:19.

Even though the theology behind widespread Evangelical Christian support for Israel is highly problematic for Jewry in terms of its prevalent eschatological intent, this support for Israel has impacted positively on Israeli views of Christianity. The establishment of full diplomatic relations between the Holy See and the State of Israel was widely seen throughout Jewry in a similar light. Indeed, until then many Jews (and perhaps many Christians?) had wondered how genuine the Church's changed approach toward Jews and Judaism was without such full bilateral relations. At the press conference in Rome announcing the Fundamental Agreement between the Vatican and Israel, Yossi Beilin, Israel's Deputy Minister of Foreign Affairs and co-chair of the Bilateral Commission, recalled the Holy See's past opposition to the creation of a Jewish state and declared the Agreement to be "a triumph for Zionism."[51] Even though the Fundamental Agreement placed itself within "the historic process of reconciliation between Catholics and Jews," the Vatican sought to minimize any theological significance to the Agreement and even opposed Israel's rumored intent to appoint a rabbi as Israel's first ambassador to the Holy See,[52] apparently precisely out of concern for Catholic communities in Muslim countries.[53]

The official position of the Vatican on the significance of the State of Israel was referred to in the document issued by the Holy See's Commission for Religious Relations with Jewry issued on June 24, 1985, and titled *Notes on the Correct Way to Present the Jews and Judaism in Preaching and Catechesis in the Roman Catholic Church*. Inter alia it declared that "Christians are invited to understand this religious attachment (of the Jews to the Land) which finds its roots in Biblical tradition." However, the document not only refrained from but even cautioned against Christians "making their own any particular religious interpretation of this relationship." At the same time, it affirmed that the permanence of Israel is to be perceived as an "historic fact and a sign to be interpreted within God's design."[54]

In 1993 I had a private audience with Pope John Paul II when attending the Prayer for Peace in the Balkans, held in Assisi. It was by no means my first meeting with him, but it was my longest conversation with him. In receiving my colleague Lisa Palmieri Billig and me, he reformulated the message of *Nostra Aetate* with phrases he had used previously in relation to the Jewish

51 Personal testimony of the author who joined Beilin in the press conference.

52 Chemi Shalev, *Maariv*, December 1993.

53 Conversation between Professor Zvi Werblowsky and Cardinal Joseph Ratzinger reported to the author.

54 *Notes on the Correct way to Present the Jews and Judaism in Preaching and Catechesis in the Roman Catholic Church* (1985), VI.1; available at christianunity.va.

people. "You know," he said to us, "I have said that you are the people of the original Covenant, never abrogated and never to be abrogated." Around the same time, I had the pleasure of an extended private conversation with the then-Cardinal Joseph Ratzinger, who was visiting Jerusalem. During our discussion he said to me "God's Covenant with the Jews is fundamental for the Church and everything that is holy for you, must be holy for us." I said to him "you know, whether it is intrinsic or extrinsic, Judaism sees the land as holy and thus the reestablishment of Jewish life within it, as being of great *religious* significance." He replied: "Of course, I know, and indeed we have not yet plumbed the full meaning of *Nostra Aetate* for us."

Some twenty-five years later and after his retirement as pope, there was some controversy concerning an article by Benedict published in the German edition of *Communio* entitled "Grace and Vocation without Remorse: Comments on the Treatise *De Judaeis*," in which he reflected on theological aspects of the new Catholic-Jewish relationship that was ushered in by the promulgation of the conciliar declaration *Nostra Aetate* more than fifty years earlier.[55] The article was a response to the 2015 "Gifts" document, which had summarized the developments and achievement in terms of Catholic-Jewish relations over that period.[56] One of the main concerns in various quarters both Jewish and Catholic about Benedict's article was his clear and categorical rejection of any soteriological significance of the State of Israel. However, an incorrect conclusion was drawn by many that he had thus rejected any religious significance to the establishment of the state. In fact, in the article Benedict specifically refers to the state as an expression of "God's faithfulness to the people of Israel" (179), in keeping with the position mentioned above in the 1985 "Notes."

Benedict's distinction actually echoes that of certain Jewish religious Zionist thinkers in the internal debate regarding whether the establishment of the Jewish state was to be seen in messianic terms or not. As opposed to the latter position very much personified by Rabbi Abraham Isaac HaCohen Kuk, the first Ashkenazi chief rabbi of the Jewish community in the land of Israel prior to establishment of the state, the distinction that Benedict makes echoes that of Rabbi Yitzhak Yaacov Reines, founder of the religious Zionist Mizrahi movement.[57]

55 Joseph Ratzinger / Benedict XVI, "*Grace and Vocation without Remorse: Comments on the treatise De Judaeis*," *Communio/IZAK* (Spring 2018): 387–406.

56 See the "Gifts" document.

57 Eliezer Don-Yehia, "Jewish Orthodoxy, Zionism, and the State of Israel," *The Jewish Quarterly* 31 (1984): 10–30. See also Eliezer Don-Yehia, "Ideology and Policy in Religious Zionism:

However, to the best of my knowledge, this recognition of the Jewish polity in the land of Israel as an expression of divine fidelity to the covenant has barely been theologically explored in any official document of the Catholic Church. Moreover, if the idea of the replacement of the Jews is rejected, does the Church not have a responsibility to itself and its faithful to explain where this expression of divine fidelity finds its place in its own theology? In this sense, Joseph Ratzinger's personal acknowledgment to me of the task still not yet fulfilled, is pertinent. Of course, any position of the Holy See that relates to the Jewish state cannot and must not disregard the interests and wellbeing of its own faithful and indeed of all religious and ethnic communities living in the land. Just as Israel's own moral integrity depends on the way it treats its minorities and the way it seeks to resolve the conflict with the Palestinian people struggling for their own self-determination and independence, so a Catholic position must take into account the interests and aspirations of the Palestinian people as a whole, in addition to its own communities and holy sites.

Nevertheless, while most Israelis and indeed most Jews are not very concerned with the theologies of other religions, a positive statement from the Church on the religious significance of the State of Israel for Christian theology in light of the biblical attachment of the Jewish people to the Land, in keeping with the transformation ushered in by *Nostra Aetate*, would undoubtedly impact very positively on Jewish views of the Church and its relationship to the Jewish people and Judaism.

Rabbi Yitzhak Yaacov Reines' Conception of Zionism and the Policies of the Mizrahi under his Leadership," *Zionism* 8 (1981): 103–46.

11

BRIEF REFLECTIONS
BIBLE/TANAKH ON THE LAND PROMISED TO THE PEOPLE

Fr. Joseph Sievers

William M. Wright IV emphasizes biblical hermeneutics and concentrates on a critical analysis and appraisal of the 2001 (2002) document of the Pontifical Biblical Commission, *The Jewish People and Their Sacred Scriptures in the Christian Bible* (hereafter *JPSSCB*). Gary Anderson discusses some of the biblical bases of Zionism and offers an approach to the question of the land that emphasizes the element of generosity. Rabbi David Rosen brings an impressive sampling of biblical, liturgical, and other traditional texts concerning the promise of and attachment to the land and then moves on to a historical survey of recent attitudes and developments.

David Rosen vividly demonstrates how for Jews everywhere and at all times, the connection with the land of Israel, Jerusalem, and Zion has been an essential ingredient of their identity, expressed in the Hebrew Bible, in rabbinic literature, in liturgy, and in other traditional writings, in art, in travel habits, and in much else. This attachment is in various ways linked to the promise of the land expressed in the Bible beginning with the Abrahamic covenant formulations.

Rosen cites ancient tradition that considers Jerusalem the navel or center of the country or of the entire world. Evidently this is symbolic language, especially where the discourse in *Tanhuma Yelamdenu* turns to the Temple and even to the Ark of the covenant, apparently depicted as present realities. Much of this is known or should be known to many Christians, but rarely have these views occasioned an adequate response. Maybe the time for this is about to come.

Rosen, however, does not stop at the classical traditions about the promised land. He expertly guides the reader through the history of the past century, especially since the founding of the State of Israel in 1948. He clarifies how religious and secular elements have mingled in recent approaches. He knows what he is talking about also from personal experience, since he has been an active and decisive player in some of these processes, especially in the negotiations between Israel and the Holy See on the establishment of full diplomatic relations.

Although he mentions Palestinians explicitly only once, in the context of Menahem Begin's decision not to annex the West Bank and Gaza, he is clearly sensitive to the issue of the need to take them into serious consideration in any discussion of the promised land today. One important point he courageously raises is the fact that a religious ideology became dominant that focused disproportionately on territorial and messianic components of Jewish tradition.[1]

The implications of such a view are considerable. It may be appropriate to ask if despite all asymmetries we may say that for generations Catholics and other Christians have been focusing disproportionately on non-territorial and non-messianic components of Jewish tradition? Perhaps a relearning is necessary on both sides, without denying or diminishing the importance of the asymmetries.

David Rosen ends his paper with a plea: "A positive statement on the religious significance of the State of Israel in light of the biblical attachment of the Jewish people to the Land would undoubtedly impact very positively on Jewish views of the Church and its relationship to the Jewish People and Judaism." Whether, and if so how, this plea will find an echo remains to be seen.

That plea, however, leads us to the chapter by William M. Wright IV. Its purpose is to provide some underpinnings and some tools for such a possible statement. He states: "I wish to contribute to the Catholic thinking about the biblical presentation of the promised land by building upon *JPSSCB* and making some adjustments to its hermeneutical substructure."[2] One of the main problems he finds with that document is its mostly implicit reliance on the so-called *sensus plenior*, thought to bring out "a deeper meaning of the text, intended by God but not clearly expressed by the human author."[3] How far the document goes in relying on this concept is not clear to me,

1 Rosen, 124.

2 Wright, 86–87. On *JPSSCB*, see Wright, 85n1.

3 The Pontifical Biblical Commission, *The Interpretation of the Bible in the Church* (St. Paul Books and Media, 1993), II.B.3 (87), cited in Wright, 88n12.

since it has only one allusion to it, as Wright correctly notes. Caveats about its use were included even in the presentation in the earlier document *The Interpretation of the Bible in the Church*, cited by Wright.

As to the strengths and weaknesses of the 2001 PBC document (*JPSSCB*), both acknowledged by Wright, we may ask: What is the baseline against which we ought to measure these strengths and weaknesses? Can we judge progress or lack thereof, rather than perfection?

In discussing the question of the promised land, he concentrates on hermeneutical and theological questions. In some ways he follows W. D. Davies and others who proposed that the New Testament "personalizes 'holy space' in Christ . . . For the holiness of place, Christianity has fundamentally, though not consistently, substituted the holiness of the Person: It has Christified holy space."[4] Wright goes a step further by comparing the spiritualization of the land to the spiritualization of the risen Christ's body. Whereas such spiritualization has its place in theology, one needs to be careful not to forget the concrete reality on the ground. An article on New Testament perspectives on the land speaks of some Christians who "consider the actual land in which Palestinians and Israelis live as unimportant, surpassed by a vision that looks toward a heavenly future."[5] At least in the present contribution, Wright's approach seems to fit into that category. He provides no hint at the complex present situation in which a land promise, which is still valid, must be legitimized in the face of rights acquired by a different population.

In line with the Pontifical Biblical Commission's 1993 document, *The Interpretation of the Bible in the Church*, considerations on a more practical level would be needed. It states: "Dialogue with Scripture in its entirety, which means dialogue with the understanding of the faith prevailing in earlier times, must be matched by a dialogue with the generation of today. Such dialogue will mean establishing a relationship of continuity. It will also involve acknowledging differences" (III.A.3).

Therefore, the jump from the Old Testament texts to an eschatological situation established by the life, death, and resurrection of Jesus seems to leave out the present circumstances, in which the "already" has to be balanced against the "not yet" of a difficult situation on the ground in the land and State(s) of Israel/Palestine.

4 W. D. Davies, *The Gospel and the Land: Early Christianity and Jewish Territorial Doctrine* (JSOT Press, 1994), 367–68; originally published by the University of California Press, 1974.

5 Michael F. Trainor and J. Cornelis de Vos, "New Testament Perspectives on the Land," in *Enabling Dialogue about the Land*, ed. Philip A. Cunningham, Ruth Langer, and Jesper Svartvik (Paulist Press, 2020), 21.

Thus, undoubtedly Catholic teaching cannot address the issue of the promised land today without addressing the question that it is a land in which diverse populations have a vital stake. The question arises: What kind of a statement would be able to provide a balanced approach without causing more polemics than understanding, in other words more harm than good?

We may thus ask: Why is it that *JPSSCB* (at least in the English version) uses the term "land" some forty-eight times and devotes an entire section (II.B.9b §§56–57) to it, yet has little to say about the postbiblical status of the question? Does it carefully avoid addressing the question? Is it because of current concerns? How legitimate are these concerns? If we want to improve on *JPSSCB*, how may these concerns be addressed?

Nostra Aetate was a much criticized and fought-over document. Yet it opened new paths toward revised attitudes toward Jews and Judaism and other religions. It had seemed an impossible task, but in the end about ninety-five percent of the bishops present at the Second Vatican Council voted in its favor and the influence of this very imperfect document continues unabated, although its message has not been able to reach everyone adequately.

The more specific issue of the land is important, as ought to be recognized by Catholics at least based on the 1974 *Guidelines*[6] and the 1985 *Notes*.[7] A question is how far one may be able to go beyond the latter statement and still achieve results that are open toward a consensus, even in non-Western parts of the Catholic Church? Concerning practical approaches to the land, I think one can profitably include consideration of varying attitudes to the size and structure of the land within the Hebrew Bible itself, as suggested, for example, by Tamara C. Eskenazi and J. Cornelis de Vos.[8]

6 "On the practical level in particular, Christians must therefore strive to acquire a better knowledge of the basic components of the religious tradition of Judaism; they must strive to learn by what essential traits the Jews define themselves in the light of their own religious experience." *Guidelines and Suggestions for Implementing the Conciliar Declaration Nostra Aetate (no. 4)*, preamble; available at christianunity.va.

7 Christians are invited to understand this religious attachment which finds its roots in biblical tradition, without however making their own any particular religious interpretation of this relationship (see the *Declaration* of the U.S. Conference of Catholic Bishops, November 20, 1975). The existence of the State of Israel and its political options should be envisaged not in a perspective which is in itself religious, but in their reference to the common principles of international law. The permanence of Israel (while so many ancient peoples have disappeared without trace) is a historic fact and a sign to be interpreted within God's design; see *Notes on the Correct Way to Present the Jews and Judaism in Preaching and Catechesis in the Roman Catholic Church*, VI.1; available at christianunity.va.

8 Tamara C. Eskenazi and J. Cornelis de Vos, "The Land in the Hebrew Bible," in *Enabling Dialogue about the Land* (ed. Cunningham et al.), 3–20, esp. 17.

The thoughtful essay by Gary Anderson addresses some of these questions admirably. Although Anderson modestly argues that the title "How to Think About Zionism," chosen by the original editors for publication in the April 2005 issue of *First Things*, claims too much, it certainly points the reader in an appropriate direction. The essay has withstood the passage of time admirably well for the issues it covers. Unfortunately the questions it poses have in part become even more acute and the answers more polarized through recent developments on the ground. In many ways, Anderson's essay complements Rosen's in providing further elements on the biblical roots, the secular origins, and the history of Zionism. Anderson takes seriously the connection between Zionism and the promise of the land to Abraham and his descendants. Therefore, he sees the Jewish return to the land and the birth of the State of Israel in a theological framework. In this context, however, he also emphasizes the requirements to be fulfilled for the land promise to come true, namely acting with justice and concern for one's neighbor. He forcefully states: "A unilateral land-grab that takes no moral cognizance of the plight of Israel's neighbors is not consistent with Israel's foundational story." On the other hand, he also emphasizes that the silence or one-sided pro-Palestinian pronouncements of mainline churches, even in the face of the non-recognition of the existence of the State of Israel, is not helpful.

As a biblical paradigm for better relations Anderson offers the example of Abraham's generosity to Lot, in Genesis 13. Although God had promised the land to Abraham and his descendants, he offers the first choice to Lot, his nephew, rather than to his descendant. Such generosity in sharing portions of what has been a promised land can certainly be taken as an antidote to the claim that all the land and all its parts have to be put exclusively under Israel's control. While this may be an important and good starting point, the situation on the ground is much more complicated. Even if both sides agree to share the land—a proposition that is not currently accepted by many of the stakeholders—the sharing cannot be based on the generosity of one side. There must be a recognition of mutual rights—and obligations—even if they are seen as asymmetrical: on the one side, a divine promise that is still valid, on the other side the presence on the land for many, or at least several, generations.

SECTION 3

THE PEOPLES IN THE LAND

PALESTINIANS AND JEWS AND THE MEANING OF THE PROMISE

12

THE PROMISE OF THE LAND AND PALESTINIAN CHRISTIANITY

Rev. Yazid Said

THE BROADER CONTEXT

The escalating constitutional crisis in the State of Israel in early 2023 over the nature and purpose of the legal branch of government and the increasing attacks of Jewish extremists on Church property provide a helpful opportunity to consider Jewish and Christian perceptions and understanding of the biblical promise of the land—with all its meanings and challenges. The crisis has shown that the rhetoric and dichotomies between Palestinian and Jewish narratives about "the land" are being further complicated by the polarity and divisions within Israeli society after the return of Benjamin Netanyahu as prime minister. This might be a good time to take stock, given the ongoing tragedy of the land and the daily cases of death and suffering, especially in the Palestinian territories.

In this chapter, I propose to examine the implication of the debate on the promise of the land for Palestinian self-understanding and the wider significance for the Israeli-Palestinian equation. This contribution is neither satisfied by the increased visibility of a particular type of religious Zionism, Christian or Jewish, that exudes a scripturally-based political xenophobia of Palestine and its history, nor by a fairly uncritical and apologetic rejection of certain segments of the Hebrew Bible led by some Palestinian activists and writers. A serious engagement with the meaning and purpose of covenant and the land should in theory bring good news to both Palestinians and Jews. However, the intimations of this argument for the wider atmosphere in which a Palestinian and Jewish engagement is conducted is harder to pin down, for the approach on all sides lacks accuracy of expression in the face of the wider regional complexity.

Indeed, determining a generic Palestinian or Jewish view on the promise of the land is hardly possible: sectarian and educational variables are a clear proof of that difficulty. Palestinian Christian or Muslim elites tend to conform to Western approaches to "religion" and prefer not to allow "religion" to play a role in the politics of nation-states. The secular Arab Christian political leader and former member of the Israeli Knesset, Azmi Bishara, now in exile, argued in one of his journalistic articles in the Egyptian *al-Ahram* that while the New Testament contains "a universal message of love," American Puritan support for Israel is based on the ancient "moral code of the Old Testament."[1] Palestinian Christian thinkers who genuinely struggle with finding legitimate answers to the challenges of Palestinians under occupation present a slightly more nuanced engagement with the Bible. Nonetheless, many of the Palestinian liberation theology advocates who call for a one-state solution to the Israel/Palestine conflict are ultimately shaping their views on the basis of a Western understanding of the nation-state and a secular understanding of human rights, reasoning away any reference to the "scandal of particularity" that defines both Jewish and Christian history.[2] The engagement with the biblical text requires a deeper struggle with the purpose and challenge of covenant and a more nuanced method of textual exegesis.

Some Christian and Jewish Zionists, on the other hand, exaggerate the official religiosity of the modern State of Israel, appealing to audiences who think in polemical religious terms against liberal secular democracies, thereby creating what one could call an idolatrous cult of the highly self-conscious and ethnic nature of the modern State of Israel.[3] After all, one should not forget that the mutual perceptions or misconceptions between Israeli Jews, Palestinian Christians, and Muslims are tied up with the confusions about wider international support for Israeli government decisions, especially regarding American policies in the Middle East. Indeed, reading the

1 Quoted in Tim Winter, "America as a Jihad State: Middle Eastern Perceptions of Modern American Theopolitics," *The Muslim World* 101 (2011): 398.

2 Naim Ateek, *A Palestinian Christian Cry for Reconciliation* (Orbis Books, 2008), 158.

3 Eugene Korn, a religious Zionist contributor to this volume, in his chapter affirms that "any form of Zionism that sees residence on the Land as constituting messianic redemption *per se* or constituting the *actual* fulfillment of the covenant comes perilously close to idolatry."

press in the wider Middle East, one might conclude that America had an evangelical Christian crusade against the Muslim Middle East.[4]

Arab Christians in the region were among those trying to make sense of how American military expansionism is rooted in an American religious quest and not simply in traditional colonial power struggles.[5] This American religious quest is defined by American Christian Zionism, which constantly pushed for support of any decisions made by an Israeli government. The roots of Christian Zionism, as has often been pointed out, are not in America.[6] But the influence of Christian Zionism on American foreign policy decisions has been the most obvious when considering the strong resentful attitude of local Muslims and Christians in Palestine toward Israeli claims to the land as well as American dominance in the region. For Middle Eastern Christians, Christian Zionism has always been an embarrassment, especially in relationship to Muslims in Palestine.

American governments, however, do vary and one could say that the influence of the Christian Right could be overestimated. In the aftermath of George W. Bush's presidency, there seems to be a shift away from the excessive influence of Christian Zionism on Washington's foreign policy. The victory of President Obama coincided with the death of Samuel Huntington, the author of *Clash of Civilizations*, and brought a different measure of engagement with the Middle East. When Donald Trump was a candidate for the presidency there was no clear sign at the beginning of an effective "religious Right"—this not really being his background. However, with Trump and Pence at the helm, we saw the moving of the American embassy to Jerusalem, which is one of the aims of American Christian Zionists, such as John Hagee; the move is tied up with the rebuilding of the Temple in Jerusalem as part of an apocalyptic scenario.[7]

4 Tim Winter, "The Inception of *A Common Word*," in *The Future of Interfaith Dialogue: Muslim-Christian Encounters through A Common Word*, ed. Yazid Said and Lejla Demiri (Cambridge University Press, 2018), 16–20.

5 Ibid., 19.

6 Donald M. Lewis, *The Origins of Christian Zionism: Lord Shaftesbury and Evangelical Support for a Jewish Homeland* (Cambridge University Press, 2014). Lewis situates the origins of Christian Zionism with Lord Shaftesbury and the English evangelical support for a Jewish homeland. Palestinians had to face the beginning of the effects of Christian Zionism from these early days. The collapse of the Ottoman Empire made Zionism play a role in Arab political imagination and in the formulation of inter-communal unity. There was a shift from the millet-structured society of the Ottoman era to the early mandate manifestations of non-religious nationalism. This had already started in the late Ottoman period and Imperial reforms but was enhanced also by fears of Zionist encroachment in Palestine.

7 John Hagee, *Jerusalem Countdown* (Frontline, 2006), 54; Hagee, *Beginning of the End* (Thomas Nelson, 1996), 183.

Such public engagements with government policies are ultimately based on curious modern religious readings of the Bible. John Hagee and others like him have a clear affinity with the premillennialism of John Nelson Darby (1800–1882) and its dispensationalist reading of the Bible; according to this view, the Bible is to be taken literally but should be divided into various dispensations that explained away apparent contradictions in the text.[8] This was an ideology that helped fuel their anti-communism in the past as much as it provided the basis for the evident support of the modern State of Israel today.[9]

At the same time, this ideology stems from a dualistic mindset, which, while having an affinity with premillennial dispensationalism, is a dualism found in the rhetoric of some Israeli leaders from the far right affirming similar trends and characteristics.[10] However, although in America leaders such as Marion (Pat) Robertson failed spectacularly after running for the U.S. presidency, showing their limited power overall, their ideology seems to shore up greater support for the Israeli political scene.[11] Indeed, as some American commentators of the past have noted, Prime Minster Netanyahu saw the significance of this alliance for the Jewish State and of modern Zionism.[12]

These religious, historical, and political developments unsurprisingly played into the fears and anxieties of Palestinian and regional communities creating various interreligious tensions and conflicts.[13] These tensions arose partly because of the inability to differentiate between different contexts for dialogue. The Greek Catholic bishop of Galilee, Elias Chacour, noted once that "Western Christians who live in our country and in our milieu apparently believe that they have been entrusted to monopolize contacts with the Jews and often claim that the 'Arab Christians do not know how to deal

8 George Marsden, *Fundamentalism and American Culture* (Oxford University Press, 1980), 4–5 and 27; and Charles C. Ryrie, *Dispensationalism* (Moody Publishers, 1995), chap. 4.

9 Marsden, *Fundamentalism and American Culture*, 90 and 208–10.

10 Peter Beinart, *The Crisis of Zionism* (Times Books, 2012), chap. 7.

11 Stephen D. Johnson, Joseph B. Tamney, and Ronald Burton, "Pat Robertson: Who Supported His Candidacy for President?," *Journal for the Scientific Study of Religion* 28, no. 4 (1989): 387–99.

12 Available at latimes.com/archives/la-xpm-1998-mar-18-mn-30074-story.html.

13 As some Palestinian Christian commentators have noted in their various local publications; see the contributions of Geries Khoury and Yuhanna Katanasho to Mundher Isaac's *Madkhal ila al-lahut al-filastini* [An Introduction to Palestinian Theology] (Diyar Press, 2017), 222, 225–30, 243–45. See also T. W. Hervert, *Faith-Based War from 9/11 to Catastrophic Success in Iraq* (Equinox Publishing, 2009).

with the Jews' . . . One thing is true; we never persecuted the Jews."[14] Now the history of the Jews in the Middle East is far more complicated than Fr. Chacour suggests. But he does have a point. While in Europe, Christians and Jews have been engaged in dialogue in the light of Europe's history, given the uniqueness of the context of the Church in the Holy Land, "the covenant" and "the land" will require specific attention to that specific context.

After all, for most Christians, Christian Zionism in its American fundamentalist shape is, as Rowan Williams once described it, "deeply eccentric."[15] On the one hand, behind the fundamentalism at play, there is of course a theological vision, parts of which are not new to mainline Christians: the stress on human sin, the need for redemption, the emphasis on individual faith with a 'low view' of the church and the sacraments, the 'high view' of scripture as all-sufficient and uniquely constitutive of doctrine, and even the use of isolated decontextualized verses; all of these have an impeccable pedigree. But, on the other hand, despite these obvious continuous pedigrees and despite its own claims to be Christianity as it always was, this form of Christian Zionism remains essentially modern. As George Marsden noted, the fundamentalist conception of truth is derived from a scientific age. It is formed on the analogy of natural science as seen in the Newtonian mold. Therefore, fundamentalists tend to have a "scientific view" of the Bible; a series of "hard facts" apprehensible by the "common sense" of the sincere believer.[16]

It is of interest that this movement flourished in North America more than in any other traditional context.[17] Its foundational method of reading the Bible is not dissimilar to the foundation of modern America with its disregard for history, local tradition, and law. Early immigrants came to consider America as the new free land, where they can do what they wish with total disregard to the local traditions, and with no sense of belonging to the indigenous culture of America.[18] This formative narrative, one might suggest, is fertile soil for eccentric fundamentalisms.

While Christian Zionism has produced a thoroughly modern phenomenon in the Christian world, just as Wahhabism in Islam appeared to be a modern reform, Jewish religious Zionism is also a modern movement, which has forever changed the traditional understanding and reflection of

14 Elias Chachour, "An Arab Christian Speaks Out," *Face to Face—an Interreligious Bulletin* 2 (Winter 1977): 9–10.

15 Rowan Williams, "Holy Land and Holy People," in *Challenging Christian Zionism: Theology, Politics and the Israel-Palestine Conflict*, ed. Ateek Naim et al. (Melisende, 2005), 293.

16 Marsden, *Fundamentalism and American Culture*, 7–8.

17 Ibid., 221–28.

18 As the story narrated in Dee Brown's *Bury My Heart at Wounded Knee* all too clearly reveals.

what it means to be a Jew in the last hundred years or so. Most Jews today are Zionists in a way that they might not have been prior to the nineteenth century. The publication of relevant cabinet papers and government office files in the run up to the Balfour Declaration carries with it the trace of such a distinction between Zionist and anti-Zionist views among Jews in a way that would not have been possible prior to the development of Zionism in nineteenth-century Europe.[19]

The historical and religious development under consideration here relates to the image of Judaism transformed from being a millennial enterprise of faith and promise, which, though it had a centuries-old longing for the land, did not express itself in the form of the land-grab rabbis who did not seem to care for tradition and law any more than Christians in North America. Today, certain forms of Jewish and Christian Zionism invoke the past. But they do so with reference to scriptures stripped of their normative exegetical tradition. So, they recall the Maccabees as achieved Zionism but not the prophets Amos or Isaiah.[20] Indeed, all of today's Zionist apologists, whatever their lesser differences, see the State of Israel as a redemption in history of which the land is the core and crux.[21]

It is in this impossible condition that Palestinians have had to form their self-identity. The establishment of the State of Israel in 1948 brought a challenging new factor into the equation in which Palestinian Muslims and Christians found themselves caught in a sharply tragic form of experience that complicates the relationship between the secular and the sacred. There was the identity of Palestinians as refugees in the face of Zionism, some of them displaced twice over; the pain of displacement and exile, the tragedy of whole generations reared in camps. This has engendered an identity of bitterness and violent resentment. It seems that from this suffering there is no escape.

One might say that there is nothing different in the Zionist enterprise in Palestine regarding the power struggle and equation *per se*. That is normal politics: a zero-sum game. We can see similar politics elsewhere in the world. Islam too had its imperialist territorial ambitions. What is exceptional in religious Zionism is the endowing of the political state equation with the faith (in the religious sense) of inherent messianic sanctity that is transcendentally conferred in a way that classical Islam never did. Faith, nation, and land

19 Doreen Ingrams, ed., *Palestine Papers 1917–1922: Seeds of Conflict* (John Murray, 1972), 16–17.

20 Kenneth Cragg, *Palestine: The Prize and Price of Zion* (Cassell, 1997), 74, 168, 191.

21 Ibid., chap. 2.

have undoubtedly been inseparable here.[22] It is, therefore, full of paradox. It has brought Jewish communities from across the world who have reached a climax in their inability to agree on the nature and coherence of their state today. It depends on external support for the sinews of its own self-sufficiency. As such, the modern political State of Israel with a majority of secular Jews makes use of a religious narrative to justify an effectively secular political power that is often against the call of the prophetic tradition in the Hebrew Bible. This in turn has complicated the spiritualized picture familiar to most Palestinian Christians and indeed caused problems for some religious Jews[23] and was seen as a violation of the divine justice in Islamic theology.[24]

To make things more difficult, the competing claims to the land were compounded by being conducted in the aftermath of the horrors of the genocide of European Jewry. Many Western Christians sought to express solidarity with those whom they have increasingly come to speak of as their elder brothers in faith.[25] This kind of support was more convincingly justified than what we have seen coming from American Christian Zionists. Can Palestinians learn something from this kind of European support facing the guilt of the Holocaust, even if they did not persecute the Jews, as Fr. Chacour noted?

When one hears of the rising attacks on Christian churches by Jewish settlers in recent months,[26] one begins to see how fear has become the basis of people's lives on all sides. More disturbingly, it is not clear to what extent political leaders are able to see this as a moral problem. As the current Israeli government pushes to change the independence of the legal system, one wonders whether the government is capable of approaching these challenges as matters regarding vision and choice that makes sense of what it is to be in the land; this is especially true when the law aims to guarantee the truth that human beings deserve. Is the Israeli government rhetoric capable of turning

22 Eliezer Schweid, *The Land of Israel: National Home or Land of Destiny* (Fairleigh Dickinson University Press, 1985), 171–72.

23 Danny Ben-Moshe and Zohar Segev, eds., *Israel, Diaspora and Jewish Identity* (Sussex Academic, 2007).

24 Suha Taji-Farouki, "A Contemporary Construction of the Jews in the Qur'an: A review of Muhammad Sayyid Tantawi's *Banu Isra'il fi al-Qur'an wa al-Sunna* and Afif Abd al-Fattah *Tabbara's al-yahud fi al-Qur'an*," in *Muslim-Jewish Encounters: Intellectual Traditions and Modern Politics*, ed. Ronald L. Nettler and Suha Taji-Farouki (Harwood Academic Publishers, 1998), 15–38.

25 John Paul II, "To the Jewish Community of Rome," April 13, 1986, available at jewinthepew.org/2015/04/13/13-april-1986-pope-john-paul-ii-tells-rome-synagogue-you-are-our-elder-brothers-otdimjh/.

26 Nir Hasoon, "Anti-Christian Hate Crimes in Jerusalem Soaring This Year," *Haaretz*, March 26, 2003, available at haaretz.com/israel-news/2023-03-26/ty-article/.premium/anti-christian-hate-crimes-in-jerusalem-soaring-this-year/00000187-1b89-d4ca-afff-1b89bd020000.

a critical eye on itself, asking how far the condition of chronic insecurity it experiences has roots in its own decisions? The dream that Herzl envisioned has never been untroubled.[27] The anxiety about security contributes to the perpetuation of the jeopardy that warrants it.

In this situation, dialogue, as an agent of reconciliation, could be in danger of becoming a factor in a pseudo-dialogue. If there is to be reconciliation, it will necessitate a radical acknowledgment of tragedy without assuming simplistic innocence on one side or the other. Surely true religious faith must teach us that holiness is an attribute of our behavior, rather than our location, or simply our land as an abstraction. One cannot deny that the modern State of Israel has exemplified a successful economic, physical, and cultural Zionism. However, it can be made good spiritually by mutual forgiveness, sought and given, by each knowing the other's fault and one's own evil. As Rowan Williams once said: "If you wish to know the pertinence of religious faith to the political realm, here is one answer, in the summons to a recognition of the need and possibility of shared repentance."[28] For the purposes of this chapter, the mutually challenging conversation should be informed by the complexity of the history of Palestine as well as the tradition of longing for the land in light of scriptural exegesis. I focus on two different Jewish contributions in this volume, that of Eugene Korn and David Meyer, to explore my concerns.

THE LAND IN CONTEXT: JEWISH AND PALESTINIAN CHRISTIAN REFLECTIONS

When at various points after the first Zionist Congress in 1897 suggestions were made about the creation of a Jewish homeland, various possibilities were considered from Africa to America and Asia. At the end, only one serious option could be considered, which was Palestine.[29] As Eugene Korn noted in his chapter, "the Jewish claim to its homeland is grounded in the covenant between God and the Jewish people as indicated in Hebrew Scripture."[30] Indeed, all of the contributors to this volume are in general agreement that the promise of the land is part of the covenant with God, which stands irrevocable. Even the language of a new covenant that appears

27 Beinart, *The Crisis of Zionism*, 11–13.

28 Rowan Williams, *Open to Judgment* (Darton, Longman and Todd, 1996), 128–29.

29 Barnet Litvinoff, *Road to Jerusalem: Zionism's Imprint on History* (Weidenfeld and Nicolson, 1965), 100–113.

30 Korn, 159 above.

in Jesus's eucharistic words has a precedent in Jeremiah 31:31, which requires examining Jesus's words in the context of the Jewish scriptures as well.

The biblical narrative and the history of the land over the last two millennia, however, suggest that one cannot assume that this covenant is simply about sustaining the people's identity in abstraction, in an empty land, or that one can just so easily equate it with the modern reality of the State of Israel. To begin with, the piece of land that the Romans called Palestine has been the home of Christianity since its inception from the early Hebrew Christian communities until today. According to the late Dominican scholar Jerome Murphy O'Conner, when Christians escaped the city after the Roman destruction of Jerusalem in 70 CE, they did not have to go far away to stay safe; they stayed within the environs of Jerusalem. He suggests that there was "an absence of some three years," which "is unlikely to have perturbed their memories of places which they would have been able to identify quite easily."[31] This explains why Pope St. Paul VI noted in 1974 how the various Christian communities today are communities whose members "live there where Jesus lived . . . and are the successors of the ancient and wholly primitive Church, which has given birth to all the other Churches."[32]

For the indigenous Palestinian Christians, that history cries out for a broadly informed engagement from various elements locally and internationally. It is obvious that the Arab story in Palestine is neither simple nor linear. The question that arises here for modern Zionism, including those perspectives represented in this volume, is: To what extent did the Zionist movement know the history and complexity of Palestinian Christianity? When Christian Zionists advocated that "Israel still remains a peculiar people and are to be restored to their own land,"[33] the question becomes significant. While Old Testament prophecy is never abstract for the Jewish people, the fate and history of the Palestinian people has been one of the forgotten tragedies of the twentieth century. Barnett Litvinoff noted long ago that early European Zionists,

> in true nineteenth century spirit . . . made every conceivable allowance in their calculations for a reborn Zion except to consider the local population. They had no formulated Arab policy. True, they did not plan deliberate domination, but their reconstruction of a Jewish homeland made exclusion

31 Jerome Murphy O'Connor, *Keys to Jerusalem: Collected Essays* (Oxford University Press, 2012), 172.

32 Pope St. Paul VI, Apostolic Exhortation *Nobis in Animo* (March 25, 1974).

33 Lewis, *The Origins of Christian Zionism*, 123.

of the Arab implicit. Events quickly overtook the Zionists and the Arabs, just as there is now only faint prospect of moving forward to one.[34]

Palestinian Christians have, in response, had to accommodate to new realities in the land. Noah Haiduc-Dale's study of Palestinian Christian engagement with the political changes during the British Mandate gives a sociological reading on how Palestinian Christians learnt to negotiate their place in society and the meaning of their religious affiliation. They shaped their relationship to Palestinian nationalism in debates among themselves, the wider Palestinian community, and with the British and Zionist authorities at the time.[35] This relationship had to take a more active participation from Palestinian Christian leaders in national political life considering the political developments in Palestine. It was inconceivable to accept that the modern State of Israel can be so easily equated with the biblical Israel given the history as well as the difference in time, context, and imagination.

The Melkite Archbishop of Galilee, Joseph Raya (1916–2005), was thought to be one of the first church officials to speak for the Christian victims of the *Nakba* ("the catastrophe," as the events of 1948 are remembered among Palestinians).[36] Others included later political figures such as George Habash, Emile Habibi, and Hanan Ashrawi. The list of names is not exhaustive. It was in the 1970s and 1980s, however, that we witnessed a more visible Palestinian Christian engagement with public political concerns that tried to present a Christian voice, which is less marred by certain forms of nationalism or religious fundamentalism (Hamas and the Jewish settler movement).[37]

Notable among Palestinian Christian activists and writers was Canon Naim Ateek (b. 1937), the Anglican priest who led the movement that became known as Palestinian liberation theology, creating and maintaining a local theological voice and activism for the confused and hurt Palestinian communities in the region. As with other liberation theology movements, Palestinian liberation theology proposed a Christian presence that is politically engaged and culturally decentralized. As such, central to his writings is

34 Litvinoff, *Road to Jerusalem*, 56.

35 Noah Haiduc-Dale, *Arab Christians in British Mandate Palestine* (Edinburgh University Press, 2015).

36 Ateek, *A Palestinian Theology of Liberation: The Bible, Justice and the Palestine-Israel Conflict* (Orbis Books, 2017), 124. He refers to him as well in his first book, *Justice and Only Justice*, 57.

37 Elizabeth S. Mareijn, "The Revival of Palestinian Christianity: Developments in Palestinian Theology," *Exchange* 49 (2020): 257–77. See also D. Christiansen, "Palestinian Christians: Recent Developments," in *The Vatican-Israel Accords: Political, Legal and Theological Concerns*, ed. Marshal J. Breger (University of Notre Dame Press, 2004), 309.

a counter-critique of Christian Zionism, especially as it evolved in the United States.[38] With the cataclysmic impact upon the church's history in Palestine prior to and after 1948, his activism, in turn, had an important impact upon the Western church's perception of Palestinian Christianity.

However, as Ateek espoused liberationist ideas, he broke out of the normative categories of reading the Bible. For him, Palestinian Christians cannot affirm Old Testament promises, most notably the promise of the land, as exclusive to the Jews. There is also a clear distinction in his writings between the God of Jesus, as universal, loving, and compassionate, and the God of the Old Testament who appears in certain parts of the Bible to be exclusively loyal to the people of Israel.[39] The promises of the Old Testament for Ateek have been superseded in Jesus Christ with the church as the New Israel, giving no significance to the land as a territorial fixity.[40] He also makes a clear distinction within the Old Testament between the covenant with the Davidic royal family (2 Sm 7:8–13, Ps 89) and the covenant with Jonah. Jonah's covenant appears to be more promissory, a covenant that engages wider humanity.[41]

There are unavoidable difficulties with the approach adopted by Canon Ateek—and not just for religious Zionists. The readiness to edit scripture on his part so as to remove what this or that generation will find difficult has a risky precedent, with *The Deutsche Christen* being the most obvious example.[42] Western reviewers of Ateek's books tend to point to an uncomfortable supersessionism that could have devastating anti-Jewish claims.[43] As such, even those who are sympathetic to the cause of the Palestinian people point out a failure to understand the theological basis of covenant in Israel.[44]

38 Christiansen, "Palestinian Christians," 81–91. Christian Zionism here means "the belief that the Jewish people were destined by God to have a national homeland in Palestine and that Christians were obliged to use means to enable this to take place." See Donald M. Lewis, *The Origins of Christian Zionism: Lord Shaftesbury and Evangelical Support for a Jewish Homeland* (Cambridge University Press, 2013), 5.

39 Ateek, *A Palestinian Cry for Reconciliation*, 58.

40 Naim Ateek, Cedar Duaybis, and Maurine Tobin, eds., *Challenging Christian Zionism: Theology, Politics and the Israel-Palestine Conflict* (Melisende, 2005).

41 Ateek, *A Palestinian Cry for Reconciliation*, chaps. 5, 7, 10.

42 Susannah Heschel, "Nazifying Christian Theology: Walter Grundmann and the Institute for the Study and Eradication of Jewish Influence on German Church Life," *Church History* 63, no. 4 (1994): 587–605.

43 Amy-Jill Levine, *The Misunderstood Jew: The Church and the Scandal of the Jewish Jesus* (HarperOne, 2006), 183.

44 Todd Walatka, book review of Naim Stifan Ateek, *A Palestinian Theology of Liberation: The Bible, Justice, and the Palestinian Conflict*, in *Studies in Christian-Jewish Relations* 14, no. 1 (2019): 1–3. See also Peter Waddell's book review in *Religion and Theology* 25, no. 4 (2018): 620–22.

They also point to an oversimplified contrast between law and Gospel.[45] Ateek's emphasis on the universalism of Christ makes him lose touch with the importance of the particularity of Christians in Palestine across history, let alone accepting the Church's understanding of the canon of Scripture.

This makes it difficult to engage with the nuances of the historical relationship between the Jewish people and the Church in context. If the Church supersedes the Jewish people in that simple sense, then what is the basis of dialogue with the Jewish people? Ateek seems to reflect what Rowan Williams called "an ersatz universality, a large-scale tribalism with Christ as source and guarantor of the authoritative and comprehensive system of meaning purveyed by the Church."[46] One needs to pay greater attention to where the theology of the early Church comes from: a story of conflict between how we (Jews or Christians) envisage God and how God actually appears. The cross in the context of first-century Palestinian Jewishness is a central challenge to any understanding of the incarnation or claim to finality.[47]

While one can find similar supersessionism among some other Arab Christians,[48] other Palestinian thinkers are a bit more nuanced in their approach. For instance, Bishop Jamal Khader, former academic dean of Bethlehem University, does not quite cancel out the biblical narrative. He suggests that God's faithfulness to Israel can be understood as a faithfulness to the particular and to the Church without editing the text itself.[49] In other words, the fidelity of God to God's promises in the Bible shows what sort of God the God of Israel is—a God that can be trusted. Faithfulness to Israel in all its failures and triumphs is shown to be of a piece with what sustains the Palestinians as well. Khader's approach here seems to be more aligned with the recent publication of Colin Chapman, *Christian Zionism and the Restoration of Israel: How Should We Interpret the Scriptures*. Chapman challenges Christian Zionism from a position regarding the inspiration and authority of scripture that most evangelical Christians would accept.

45 Colin Chapman, an unpublished response to Ateek, *A Palestinian Cry for Reconciliation*.

46 Williams, *On Christian Theology*, 100.

47 Ibid., 229.

48 Paul Charles Merkley, *Christian Attitudes towards the State of Israel* (McGill-Queen's University Press, 2001), 187. See also Gavin D'Costa, *Catholic Doctrine on the Jewish People after Vatican II* (Oxford University Press, 2019), 125.

49 See his Arabic chapter, "nahwa qira'atin masihiyya falastiniyya li-'l'ahd al-qadim," in *madkhal ila al-lahut al-falastini*, ed. Munther Isaac (Diyar Press, 2017), 113–23. See also Salim Munayer, "Reconciliation as a Christian Response to the Israel-Palestine Conflict," in *Christians and the Middle East Conflict*, ed. Paul S. Rowe, John H. A. Dyck, and Jens Zimmerman (Routledge, 2020), 16 and 21.

Korn dismisses Khader as another Palestinian Christian supersessionist.[50] However, the difference between these various Palestinian Christian approaches is a positive sign that prompts us to keep the door open for dialogue between Palestinian Christian writers and Jewish thinkers.[51] Many evangelicals in America may dismiss Ateek's work precisely because of his cherry-picking approach to scripture. Although the stumbling blocks are there with Khader, there is a better opening for engaging his more serious reading of scripture.

Also, as was suggested above, considering the context remains important for this dialogue. The context of the Holy Land today is not dissimilar to New Testament times, in that the Jewish people now has the benefit of being the more powerful majority over against the local Christians. Even if one did not agree with simple supersessionism, for the Palestinian Christians to define Jewishness as superseded could be read as a reaction to the role of what Palestinians often see as the exclusive Jewish ideologue and overlord in modern political Israel who appears as an opponent, especially when Christianity itself seems to be under attack by some Jews. And the further implication is that the marginal or powerless Christian community in the Holy Land, unlike the European one, might feel that it has a bit more freedom to challenge the majority community. This was also seen as a reason behind the evident various anti-Jewish verses in parts of the New Testament.[52]

Today, Palestinian Christians would equally find it difficult to understand why it is that a notable Jewish religious leader such as Eugene Korn cannot speak loudly in his contribution to this volume about the historic wound of the Palestinian people. Indeed, there is a good deal of blame regarding what the Palestinians have failed to do in the last few decades in Korn's chapter. If *tikkun olam* is central to the covenantal promise, as he points out, it becomes incumbent to ask whether the Jewish community in Israel is fulfilling a covenantal obligation to embody the promise of peace. It is always easy to find the blame in the other. What does the concrete power of an Israeli government in relation to the poorest and most disadvantaged of its Palestinian neighbors say about the aim of the covenant?

50 Korn, 150.

51 There are of course other notable Palestinian Christian writers today such as Mitri Raheb in Bethlehem. Both he and Jamal Khader are members of the group that produced the *Kairos Palestine* documents. For the purposes of this piece, I am focusing on two examples of Palestinians who present different readings as a way of engaging and responding to Eugene Korn and David Meyer.

52 Rowan Williams, *On Christian Theology* (Blackwell, 2000), 98–99 and 229, and Williams, *Christ on Trial* (HarperCollins, 2000), 73–74.

JEWISH CHRISTIAN CONSENSUS? DAVID MEYER AND ROWAN WILLIAMS

There remains an important aspect to Korn's argument which leaves the door open for conversation. In contrast to what is sometimes assumed, he shows that we do not simply have a standoff between two rival legal positions when it comes to the relationship of Israel with the Palestinians, one of Jewish law and one of human rights. He shows how ultimately Jewish law, when it deals with the difficult positions of sharing the land, does not depend on votes or preferences, but on the conviction that it represents the will of God. And precisely because it is so, it is unfinished business insofar as codified and precise provisions are concerned. It can change in accordance with broader Jewish values. Therefore, to recognize *halakhah* is a bit like the classical understandings of Sharia in Islam. It is to recognize a method of jurisprudence governed by revealed texts rather than a single system or an abstraction called "human rights."

David Meyer's contribution here takes this unfinished nature of *halakhah* to a new level, which reflects the diversity of Jewish thinking on the issue and makes a positive engagement with Palestinian history more possible. By relying on the *halakhic* methodology of Rabbi Meir Simkha HaCohen of Dvinsk, Meyer finds it possible to define the Land as an *hefker*-object, which is a gift to Israel to be shared with others. By doing so, he is implicitly asking: "What do we expect the promise of the land to be *for*?" When the religious history of the Jewish people speaks of the irrevocable nature of the covenant, what kind of relation are we taking for granted between the promise and the system of human language and meaning in the text and its context? As such, he uses a definition of Gershom Sholem about the Hebrew language so as to be "volcanically" erupting with prospects of sharing the gift of the land.[53] His task turns out at the end not to construct a metatheory of religious Zionism in the way that Korn seems to start with, but to explore how the identity of the land as gift and as an *hefker*-object can in practice open and sustain different schemes of language and meaning based on the text and drawing toward the reality of peaceful coexistence with non-Jews.

The gift of land in this way becomes a crucial historical question rather than a final claim; it becomes like a sacrament. In that gift, all our engagement with the world around us is judged and defined with God as the gift giver and the gentile neighbor as our interlocutor. Though both Korn and Meyer are careful to warn against the land becoming idolatrous, Meyer, unlike Korn, seems to steer away from either an exclusive claim to the land or from allowing no more than unquestioning coexistence. Resorting to Meir Simkha

53 Meyer, 245.

HaCohen, he enquires about the nature of the foundational text, not as a possession, but as an agenda, and tries to see what is being said about the meaning of gift and the place of the Other.

In this way, Meyer allows for the possibility of conversation with a Christological and sacramental insight as articulated by some Anglican theologians. The Anglican bishop and nineteenth-century New Testament scholar, Brooke Foss Westcott, once gave an image of the empty tomb of Christ as the mercy-seat of the ark: the empty tomb as the holy of holies of the Temple.[54] Like Meyer's gift of the land, the body of Christ appears as the gift, which we cannot possess, cannot own. He is the gift that is always ahead, to be given away as it were. In that, we see "something about the character of divine presence or action."[55] Rowan Williams, in his writing on the finality of Christ, shares some of the concerns raised by David Meyer above which ultimately form the foundation of another important lecture he sent to the Sabeel international conference in Jerusalem in 2004 entitled "Holy Land and Holy People."

The lecture aimed to discuss the idea of liberation theology within the Hebrew scriptures and the contemporary Jewish context in the modern State of Israel. It begins by pointing out that a discussion of Christian Zionism should not just be an exercise in critique, but also "an opportunity to clarify something of what Christians can say about Israel, as one dimension of a 'liberation theology' that will carry good news to all in the Holy Land and more widely."[56] The lecture goes on to distinguish the concept of Israel in terms of "two distinct but overlapping realities": the first is Israel under God, and the second is the contemporary State of Israel, which he defines as "the sole place in the world where Jewish people have a guaranteed place." Williams states explicitly, however, that "the modern state of Israel is not biblical Israel"; those who use "Israel under God" to justify contemporary Israeli policies need to think again, as these arguments are incomplete within the Jewish tradition itself. For this reason, the covenant for Williams is not simply about a land grant in the abstract but must be seen within the broader calling and responsibility of the people as "a paradigm nation."[57]

For Williams, one needs to pay closer attention to the meaning and purpose of covenant and the place of the new dispensation in Christ.[58] The

54 Brooke Foss Westcott, *The Gospel According to St. John* (John Murray, 1882), 291.

55 Williams, *On Christian Theology*, 186.

56 Ateek et al., *Challenging Christian Zionism*, 293.

57 Ibid., 294.

58 The text of the lecture is found in ibid., 293–303. The chapter on the finality of Christ in Williams, *On Christian Theology*, spells out some of the foundational points that shaped

lecture attempted to tread that narrow path that Meyer alludes to. The Sabeel conference organizers, led by Canon Naim Ateek, did not engage positively with the content of the lecture at the time any more than Meyer's writing would in a contemporary Jewish Zionist context.[59] Nonetheless, it remains important to engage both Palestinians and Jewish thinkers with what Rowan Williams has to say here, simply because history has to be confronted with all its complexity. Just as contemporary Jews need to face the complexity of Palestine's history and story, Palestinians need to face the complexity of the biblical narrative and its significance for the Jewish people today. Being critical of Israeli government policies does not in and of itself legitimize cancelling out the narrative of Israel in the Bible.

Unlike what Ateek stipulates, Williams's methodology of engaging the Old Testament is in reading it in its entirety. By engaging Deuteronomy and Leviticus with Amos, Ezekiel, and Isaiah, Williams was able to point to the self-critical dynamic that is in the Hebrew scriptures themselves.[60] The foundation for any constructive dialogue for Williams with Jewish interlocutors at the theological level cannot diminish any part of Hebrew scriptures. This methodology remains significant not just to give Hebrew scriptures their due, but Christian scriptures as well. When exploring the meaning and purpose of the new covenant or the mission of Christ, Williams cannot separate Jesus or Paul from their Jewishness; to do so, even by implication, is to cut at the heart of all the themes of foreshadowing and restoration in Paul (especially Rom 9–11),[61] and the grounding of Jesus's mission and his understanding of his passion in Jewish concepts.[62]

Instead of editing the scriptures, as Ateek does, Williams asks a similar question that was proposed by Meyer: how a full-blooded engagement with the whole of the Jewish scriptural corpus, including the promise of the land, can be turned to the service of a comprehensively liberating agenda for theology and action. The critical Palestinian interlocutors did not quite understand how this might be "good news for all."[63] As Williams is reflecting here on the nature and purpose of the Church in relation to the Jewish people, he points to what could be achieved from Jewish and Christian dialogue:

Williams's thinking on Israel.

59 There are two contributions responding to the lecture in Ateek's *Challenging Christian Zionism* which express Palestinian Christian frustrations with the content of the lecture.

60 Ateek et al., *Challenging Christian Zionism*, 294–96.

61 Ibid., 300.

62 Williams, *On Christian Theology*, 96–99.

63 Ateek et al., *Challenging Christian Zionism*, 304–18.

discerning a common understanding of covenant as sacramental and therefore as a sign of God's peace.

It is precisely because of this rigorous attention to the text and to the complex historical varieties of Jewishness in first-century Palestine that Williams in another context can point to the crucified Jesus as the one who "puts God's question to the various styles of political defense of Jewishness in the first century of the Christian era." This question appears to be the challenge to "the reversed image of messianism, displayed in the story of Jesus," which "can be part of a contemporary critique of the *ersatz* messianism of the modern state of Israel."[64] Hence his distinction in the Sabeel lecture between "Israel under God" and the modern State of Israel. Whilst this might be ironic for a Christian to say in the light of the history, the challenge is also for the Church's claim for institutionalized finality: "The history of Jesus enacts a judgment on tribalized and self-protecting religion, on the confusion between faith and ideology."[65] Christ's finality and universality is not at the end what Ateek anticipated:

> A finished account of Christ as containing all meanings would make Christology non-eschatological. What we have to do is to discover how our commitment to the question Jesus poses may make itself audible and intelligible beyond the bounds of the Christian institution.[66]

The same might be said of Meyer's methodology: a finished account of a land possession would close off the possibility of discovering how the commitment and the longing for the land might make it intelligible as good news beyond the bounds of the Jewish people.

CONCLUSION

It is an understatement to say that we have a double situation which appears to be difficult to reconcile in the first instance between Palestinian history and Jewish metahistorical claims. Politics in the Holy Land has failed in establishing stable trustworthy relationships. As I noted earlier, for the State of Israel, achieved Zionism has meant a redemption in history of which the land is the core. It has been a reaffirmation of identity through territorial possession, a Hebrew language and national independence. As such, it has incurred and aroused inevitable conflict with a resolute refusal to allow its

64 Williams, *On Christian Theology*, 101–2.

65 Ibid., 104.

66 Ibid., 94.

future to be vulnerable to others. Therefore, it has been inherently power-based and in that sense essentially secular.

On the other hand, the religious thrust from some of the arguments above suggest that the existence of the covenant people is like a sacrament communicating the nature of God as the one we can trust. How is it possible to redeem this tragedy of *ersatz*-messianism? The implication of the Meyer/Williams contributions to the Israeli-Palestinian question is important. If their arguments are considered seriously, they form good news; for we are not dealing it appears with a collision of institutions or systems, neither is it a simple supersession of one of the other. Meyer opens up the possibility, through Scripture, for a dialectical engagement that shapes Israel and the Palestinian people when they both meet what they do not own, and each learns that they live from these encounters. The vision proposed by Williams suggests that only resources beyond human power can save or restore or reveal holiness to the land and the people, not the modern reality of the nation-state. He does so through the narrative of the political history of the Jewish people to which Jesus stands as a question. The Christian it seems is always held to the question that Jesus poses before his judges, which is the tragic dimension where the redemptive nature of love is the only inclusive answer. The universal can only be revealed through the scandal of particularity.

I do not believe that the promise of the land as it appears in the Bible needs necessarily to mean that political power is also hallowed by divine authorization. It certainly cannot be learned readily through the historical events of the Holy Land as it has suffered up until today. The way has been long and hard for all involved. It does not look very hopeful going forward either. The events as they have evolved in Palestine since 1917 carried with them many vicissitudes with a brood of emotive reactions: anger, clamor, and despair. Indeed, the history itself became a propaganda tool aided by American Christian Zionism.

Today, with the evident collapse of a two-state solution, one wonders whether the Holy Land is heading toward what Rowan Williams called elsewhere a "society of societies."[67] That will require another reflection. Whatever shape it takes, it needs to be governed by law and order and it needs prophets who can stand up for the forgotten and marginalized in the land. Practically, the State of Israel needs to face the full challenge of the origins of the conflict and be exposed to some level of self-criticism; without any of this, long-range calculations about its future become less important. The recent internal divisions within Israel testify to this and warn of a fatalistic attitude.

67 Rowan Williams, *Faith in the Public Square* (Bloomsbury, 2015), 50.

While one cannot separate the political theology of Zionism from the history of European Jewry, we need to pay more attention to the local context. If Palestinian Christianity has roots in the Hebrew history of the land, what sort of convergences and political coherence do we need to aspire to today, and how should our understanding of the covenant help us in defining that political entity today? It would not hurt to heed the words of the Psalmist: "except the Lord build the house they labor in vain that build it" (Ps 126:1).

13

THE COVENANTAL LAND

JEWISH THEOLOGY, GENTILES, AND PALESTINIANS

Rabbi Eugene Korn

As a prologue I take the liberty of introducing myself in the hope that a knowledge of my personal values will help to illuminate the arguments that follow. I am an unrepentant Zionist, meaning that I believe it is historically warranted, morally permissible, and theologically important for the Jewish people to reconstitute itself in a sovereign political entity in at least part of its ancient homeland between the Mediterranean Sea and the Jordan River. It is this personal conviction that impelled me to leave America, and as did Abraham of old to migrate to The Land[1] and the State of Israel, whose *de jure* status is established by Jewish historical claims and by international law when in July 1922 the League of Nations approved the British Mandate for Palestine and ratified the Balfour Declaration. This was further confirmed by UN Resolution 181 in November 1947.[2]

Moreover, I am a *religious* Zionist, and this religious dimension imposes additional claims and responsibilities on my Zionist philosophy. Religious Zionism entails a theologizing of Zionism, namely that the Jewish claim to its homeland is grounded in the covenant between God and the Jewish people as indicated in Hebrew scriptures, of which The Land is a central and inextricable element. Throughout the Bible The Land appears as the necessary means for Jews to realize their covenantal purpose. This singular mission

1 Gn 12:1. As a proper noun, the biblically covenanted land is capitalized.

2 The full text of the League of Nations resolution can be found at israelforever.org/state/Mandate_for_Palestine_Jewish_State/

and its attributes are sometimes referred to as "election" or "chosenness." In the words of the Bible (which Jews call Torah), "You shall be My treasured possession among all people."[3]

God's covenant also carries with it legal and moral responsibilities for the Jewish people, ones that are inseparable from the gift of Jewish entitlement and residence on The Land—particularly with respect to the treatment of others. Contrary to the exclusivist Zionist conceptions espoused by some nationalist-religious Israelis today, it is precisely this theological dimension that imposes critical moral demands and that can yield fruit in creating legal and ethical space for others in The Land.

I will unpack these ideas in what follows, first outlining my theological understanding of the biblical covenant, then presenting considerations of Jewish law (*halakhah*) in striving to realize the covenantal promise today. Since Jewish law is essential to—but not exhaustive of—Jewish religious life, halakhic considerations are critical to the subject at hand. Finally, I will grapple with the problematics of applying these theological and halakhic conceptions to the empirical reality and its dour realpolitik that Israelis and Palestinians experience today.

THE BIBLE'S COVENANTAL DRAMA, CHOSENNESS, AND THE LAND

Jews understand themselves theologically as a covenantal people. The covenant appears at the dawn of the Jewish people and Jewish spiritual destiny, when God called on Abraham to migrate to The Land and, promised that Abraham will become "a father of a great nation," that "through him all the families of the earth will be blessed," and that God "will give the Land to Abraham's descendants" (Gn 12:1–7). Soon thereafter (Gn 18:18–19), God again asserts Abraham's election and Abraham's covenantal responsibilities: he must "teach his children and his children's children after him to follow the way of the Lord by doing what is right and just" (*tsedakah u'mishpat*). These responsibilities together with the mandate to be a blessing to the families of the earth (Gn 12:3) constitute the Jewish theological mission over sacred history.

Throughout Genesis, Abraham, Isaac, and Jacob repeatedly "call the name of the Lord," which rabbinic tradition understood to be the covenantal obligation for Abraham and his descendants to bear witness to God's presence and the divine morality of righteousness, justice, and compassion. In this way the Jewish people would fulfill the mandate of Genesis 12 to function

3 Ex 19:5. Hebrew: *Am segulah mikol ha-amim*.

as the agents of blessing to humanity.[4] Thus the covenantal Jewish people was created for the world, not the world for the Jewish people.[5] So important is this universal mission of blessing that God reiterates it five times throughout Genesis,[6] and rephrases it in Exodus as the mandate to "be a nation of priests."[7] If all the people of Israel are priests it can only be the gentile nations of the world that the Jewish people is called upon to bless. God also places this mandate in the mouth of Isaiah, who demands in God's name that the Jewish people be "My witnesses" and "a light to the nations."[8]

Hence the central paradox pervading the Hebrew Bible: a particular people on a particular land is called upon to realize a universal covenantal mission given by the universal God, the Creator of all humanity. Throughout the Bible, this particular land is inseparable from covenantal sacred history. The Land is the second most popular substantive in the Hebrew scriptures, referenced either explicitly or implicitly more than a thousand times. The Land theme is so ubiquitous that "it may have greater claim to be the central motif in the Old Testament than any other."[9] And The Land is tied essentially to the biblical covenant: out of the 250 times the covenant is mentioned in the Hebrew Bible, in 176 instances (70 percent) it is connected to The Land . Moreover, in 73 percent of the instances where the covenant appears in the Pentateuch, The Land is present either explicitly or implicitly.[10]

Zion, then, is no mere Jewish political interest. Rather, it is constitutive of Jewish biblical theology and Jewish spiritual identity. And The Land of which the Bible speaks is real land—gritty physical earth with geographical borders where people live, plant, harvest, and over which they fight wars—not some de-hypostasized metaphysical entity. Only a supersessionist or

4 For a fuller explication of the ways that Jewish theological tradition saw how this blessing would be spread, see Eugene Korn, "Israel as Blessing: Theological Horizons," in *Judaism's Challenge—Election, Divine Love and Human Enmity*, ed. Alon Goshen-Gottstein (Academic Studies Press, 2020), 50–70.

5 See commentary of Rabbi Naftali Zvi Yehuda Berlin, *Ha-emeq Davar* [Hebrew], introduction to the Book of Exodus.

6 Gn 12:2–3, 18:18, 22:18, 26:4, 28:13–14.

7 Ex 19:6. See also the Bible commentaries of Rabbis Abraham ben Maimonides, Obadiah Seforno, and Samson Raphael Hirsch on this verse.

8 Is 42:6, 43:10, 60:2–3.

9 Waldemar Janzen, "Land," in *Anchor Bible Dictionary*, ed. David Noel Freedman (Doubleday, 1992), 4:146.

10 Gerald R. McDermott, *Israel Matters* (Brazos, 2017), 139–40 and 146n7. McDermott has also tracked critical references to the Land and the enduring validity of the land promise in the New Testament. See "Israel in the New Testament?," available at thebullelephant.com/israel-in-the-new-testament.

universalist reformulation of the particularist biblical promise can eliminate the centrality of The Land .[11]

The Bible is clear that God's covenant with the Jewish people is irrevocable, and because the gift of The Land is an essential component of the covenant, title to The Land is thus similarly irrevocable.[12] *Residence* on The Land is conditional on covenantal fidelity,[13] but the covenantal *title* to the land remains unconditional and eternal.[14] Even amidst the punishment of exile, the Bible promises that Jewish penitents will return to The Covenantal Land to which they still hold title.[15] Leviticus 26:42 is particularly explicit in reinforcing this pervasive biblical understanding: after the Jewish people's repentance in exile, God "will remember My covenant with Jacob; I also will remember My covenant with Isaac; and also My covenant with Abraham, and I will remember the Land," thus stressing that (1) the covenant is irrevocable even while Israel sins, and (2) the land promise is an inextricable element of the covenantal implementation. Moreover, the original Hebrew text indicates that the Jewish return to God and the Jewish people's return to The Land are linguistically and spiritually linked.[16]

Another central covenantal demand is for the Jews to become a holy people, that is, to be distinct from the peoples around them and committed to developing unique covenantal values. This is part of the dialectical

11 When classical Christian theology universalized the covenant, it rendered the specific land promise superfluous. For contemporary examples of supersessionist and universalist transformations of the land promise, see Munther Isaac, *From Land to Lands, from Eden to the Renewed Earth: A Christ-Centered Biblical Theology of the Promised Land* (Langham Monographs, 2015), and Jamal Khader, "Christian-Jewish Relations from a Christian Palestinian Perspective," in *Contemporary Catholic Approaches to the People, Land, and State of Israel*, ed. Gavin D'Costa and Faydra L. Shapiro (The Catholic University of America Press, 2022), 234–50.

12 Gn 13:14–18. The Catholic Church has officially acknowledged the irrevocability of God's covenant with the Jewish people in both *Nostra Aetate* (1965) and "Gifts" (2015). Given that the land promise is an essential component of the covenant, the need for the Church to consider the theological significance of the present Jewish return and residence on The Land seems logically compelling.

13 Lv 18:24–28, 26:27–33; Dt 4:25–28.

14 The Catholic Church, too, acknowledges the unconditionality of the land promise and the rightful return of the Jewish people to residence on The Land. See The Pontifical Biblical Commission's *The Jewish People and their Sacred Scriptures in the Christian Bible* (2001), 37 and 42; available at vatican.va.

15 Gn 15:13–18; Lv 26:39–42, 44–45; Dt 30:1–5. Return to Jerusalem is also a given in all the messianic visions of Isaiah, Jeremiah, Zakariah, and Micah. In rabbinic literature, title and future return to the land is always assumed. See Sifre, *Parashat Eikev* 41.

16 The Hebrew word for "return" is *shuvah*. It is the key word in Dt 30, where this verb is employed repeatedly connoting both the Jewish return to God/repentance (*teshuvah*) and the resulting Jewish return to the land (*shuvah*).

tension of Exodus 19:6 containing the divine double imperative "to be a kingdom of priests" (requiring connection to other people) and "to be a holy people," which entails a distancing from surrounding cultures. The latter is why Deuteronomy 20 insists that when the Jewish people enter The Land , they should not tolerate coexistence with the idolatrous Canaanite tribes. Corporate holiness, then, implies that the people of the covenant neither acculturate to ungodly foreign values, nor ideally should be subordinate as a people to the political domination of others. The covenantal project demands both spiritual independence and national self-determination.

Critically, residence and sovereignty on The Land are not for the objective of political power *per se*, but function only as necessary preconditions for realizing the theological and ethical vision of being a holy people living under the kingship of God and divine values.[17] Here we arrive at another existential and spiritual paradox: human politics is necessary for achieving the prophetic theological vision of "non-politics" under God's rule. Independence, sovereignty, and residence in The Land are instrumental values, necessary because they afford the *possibility* of the chosen people fully developing and living out God's covenantal values. The Land is not an end in itself, but merely the means to potentially fulfilling The Land promise. Any form of Zionism that sees residence on the land as constituting messianic redemption *per se* or constituting the actual fulfillment of the covenant comes perilously close to idolatry. Redemption is realized only with security, justice, compassion, and the sanctification of human life under God. Called to be living witnesses to God and national exemplars of the biblical holiness, *tsedakah,* and *mishpat*, any residence on the Land that is devoid of this biblical *paranesis* would be a betrayal of the covenant and the Jewish spiritual mission.

I add that the biblical link between residence and independence in The Land on the one hand, and effective covenantal witness on the other, has been confirmed by empirical history. In the Jewish people's nearly-two-thousand-year exile—particularly in Christendom—Jews were most often condemned to live as a weak and disrespected minority. During this exile Jews were rarely allowed to possess the physical means or cultural independence to develop freely as a people.[18] This truth continues today. As someone who

17 This is best expressed by Maimonides: "The Sages and the Prophets did not long for the days of the Messiah because they wanted to rule the world or because they wanted to have dominion over gentiles or because they wanted the nations to exalt them . . . Rather, they desired this so that they would have time for Torah and its wisdom." *Mishneh Torah*, Laws of Kings 12:4.

18 This was also often the case for Jews under Islam. Arguably the second most famous and influential book of medieval Jewish philosophy was *The Kuzari*, written by Yehudah Halevi in the twelfth century. The work's complete title, *The Kuzari: A Book in Defense of the Despised Religion*, testifies to the defensive, weak, and humiliated state of the Jewish people even during

came from America and whose DNA is indelibly imprinted with American values, I easily feel the difference between the emerging majoritarian Israeli culture characterized by freedom, creativity, and spiritual independence, and American Jewish life as a minority, for all its affluence, enticements, and blandishments. Also significant is that throughout the exile, the idea of giving up the dream of return to The Land never took root.[19]

There is one more critical element in the biblical picture of Jewish sovereignty on the Land. While the Bible categorically proscribes coexistence with the primitive Canaanite tribes, the Torah also provided for the presence of non-idolatrous gentiles in the covenantal Jewish polity on The Land. This is the "stranger" or resident alien (Hebrew: *ger toshav*),[20] who the Torah is careful to warn the Jewish majority repeatedly not to oppress or harm, and who the Talmudic rabbis demanded that Jews sustain, protect, and provide a secure residence on The Land.[21] Nor is this gentile presence on The Land a mere concession to demographic reality. The Bible's insistence on treating the stranger ethically, even to the extent of loving him and her,[22] indicates that the rights of strangers on The Land is part of the covenantal ideal.

JEWISH RELIGIOUS LAW: OBSTACLES AND OPPORTUNITIES

Because Jewish law is fundamental to both Jewish theology and religious behavior, two questions are critical for theological Zionism today regarding life on The Land with non-Jews: first, can Israeli Arabs and other gentiles in Israel be accorded equal political rights in the Jewish state according to Jewish law and religious philosophy? Second, are there circumstances under which Jewish law permits the existence of gentile sovereignty on parts of the covenantal Jewish homeland, or would such national coexistence constitute a violation of the biblical and rabbinic imperatives to settle The Land? In other words, is territorial compromise and sharing the land with a sovereign

---

the so-called Spanish Golden Age in the eleventh and early twelfth centuries. Under such conditions, Jews were hardly in a position to be effective witnesses to the world.

19 See Ruth Langer, "Israel in Jewish Theologies," in Cunningham et al., *Enabling Dialogue about the Land* (Paulist Press, 2020), 43–62.

20 In rabbinic law, the *ger toshav* is the gentile in the Jewish polity who accepts the basic civilizing prohibitions against killing, stealing, sexual wildness, cruelty, idolatry, and blasphemy, as well as the positive obligation to live under a system of just laws, i.e., not to live in a primitive Hobbesian jungle.

21 BT, Gerim 3:3.

22 Lv 19:33–34.

Palestinian entity a theological and legal option for the Bible's covenantal promise and God's chosen people?

While the biblical picture provided for the presence and rights of individual gentiles in the sovereign Jewish polity on The Land, resident aliens were not granted full equality according to the biblical and Talmudic models. The biblical polity is a monarchy, whose king must be a native-born Jew, not a convert, foreigner, or resident alien (Dt 17:15). Moreover, normative Jewish law extended this restriction to all positions of authority.[23] Resident aliens are protected by the Jewish majority, but they remain subordinate to Jewish sovereignty. Nor were they allowed to own territory or plots in The Land permanently. We can view their status as similar to the *dhimmi* status of non-Muslims in tolerant Muslim societies, but without the onerous head tax that *dhimmis* were required to pay to Muslim authorities.

The biblical and classic rabbinic conception of Jewish sovereignty on The Land is hierarchical—a polity where Jews hold authority and determine culture and values, while non-idolatrous gentiles are granted non-permanent rights and privileges on the basis of Jewish sufferance. A modern pluralistic democracy characterized by full equality was unknown to the Bible or to the rabbis who framed classical Jewish law. This is why some Jewish religious extremists who insist on hewing close to the original biblical or Talmudic models sometimes seek to deny full rights to gentiles in the State of Israel today,[24] even though that position violates the Bible's imperatives to love and protect the stranger in The Land and contravenes Israel's Declaration of Independence and its democratic laws guaranteeing legal equality irrespective of religious identification.[25] As such, faithful Jews as well as Zionists committed to Israel's founding vision have a religious and national responsibility to fight this Jewish exclusiveness and intolerance. And certainly a binational entity shared by Jews and gentiles was not conceivable in the Bible or in traditional Judaism.

I take as self-evident that the ancient political model described above will not work morally or politically for us, nor will it help to ease the political morass and ideological conflict that entangles Israelis and Palestinians

23 Maimonides, *Mishneh Torah*, Laws of Kings 1:4, based on Dt 17:15.

24 One particularly blatant example of this is the 2010 proclamation signed by fifty nationalist rabbis forbidding Jews from selling land in the State of Israel to non-Jews, since non-Jews have no rights to own land according to the original biblical and Talmudic legal conceptions. For a rabbinic refutation of the claims in this letter, see Shlomo Riskin, "Selling Land in Israel to Gentiles," *Meorot* 9 (2011), available at library.yctorah.org/files/2016/07/Riskin-Selling-land-in-Israel.pdf.

25 The Declaration of Independence ensures "complete equality of social and political rights to all its inhabitants irrespective of religion, race or sex," and that guarantees "freedom of religion, conscience, language, education and culture."

today. Fortunately, however, this is not the only possible model within Jewish law or religious philosophy. While the concept of a pluralistic democracy is absent from the ancient political conceptions, Jewish law and religious policy can accommodate such a liberal arrangement under a different conceptual structure—one that goes to the heart of our issue, and one that, perhaps providentially, has played a significant role for Jews in the history of Jewish-Christian relations.

Democracy is governance "of the people, by the people, and for the people," in the words of American president Abraham Lincoln. In theory it is a voluntary political partnership among equal parties. Thus in considering the possibility of a pluralistic democracy for the State of Israel in classic Jewish categories, the question might be reformulated as, "is a formal *de jure* political partnership possible within Jewish law?"

Partnership (*shutafut*) is a well-known concept in rabbinic writing, albeit in the context of commercial relationships. Because rabbinic law attempted to regulate and sanctify all areas of Jewish life, it had to enter the domain of commercial transactions and relations between parties. This is also a biblical requirement, since the Bible prohibits charging and paying interest on loans between a Jewish creditor and a Jewish debtor.

The legal concept of partnership also entered the domain of Jewish theology, when the Talmud forbade Jews from entering into commercial partnerships with idolators as a precautionary measure against violating the biblical prohibition against Jews causing idolators to mention the name of their false gods (Ex 23:13).[26] This prohibition did not apply to Jewish-Muslim commercial relations, since Islam has a purely monotheistic understanding of God, similar to that of Judaism. Yet owing to the doctrines of the Trinity and the incarnation, rabbinic authorities in the Middle Ages considered whether Jews were allowed to enter into commercial partnerships with Christians. We need not go into the extensive rabbinic dialectics and debates around this question.[27] For our purposes it is sufficient to note that the majority of rabbinic authorities living in Christendom from the sixteenth century onward concluded that Jews are permitted to partner with Christians because Christianity is not like the idolatrous religions to which the Bible and Talmud refer.[28] Christianity indeed worships the single Creator of heaven and earth.

26 BT, Sanhedrin 63b.

27 See Jacob Katz, *Exclusiveness and Tolerance* (Oxford University Press, 1961), chap. 3.

28 For rabbinical attitudes and halakhic categorization of Christianity, see Eugene Korn, "Rethinking Christianity," in *Jewish Theology and World Religions*, ed. Alon Goshen-Gottstein and Eugene Korn (Littman Library of Jewish Civilization, 2012), 190–215.

The upshot is that there is no legal or theological barrier for Jews to enter into commercial partnerships with Muslims or Christians. If so, may we not consider a conceptual shift by creatively applying this license to the arrangement of a political partnership on The Land in which there is Jewish sovereignty and in which all citizens have equal rights irrespective of their religion or ethnic background? This approximates the principles articulated in Israel's Declaration of Independence that constitute the foundation for Israel's democratic structure, and which religious Zionists accept on pragmatic grounds even though it does not conform to the biblical or talmudic political conception. Some contemporary rabbinic thinkers have begun to move in this direction,[29] but a systematic halakhic conception of Israel as a democratic partnership needs to be developed. As such, I see no problem with the long-standing Zionist requirement of Jewish sovereignty on The Land coexisting with egalitarian democratic principles as long as Israel retains its Jewish majority—an empirical reality that will continue to obtain for a very long time.[30]

In addition, the prophet Ezekiel provides grounds for gentiles to hold territory in The Land permanently: "You shall allot it as a *heritage for yourselves and for the strangers who reside among you, who have begotten children among you. You shall treat them as Israelite citizens;* they shall receive allotments along with you among the tribes of Israel. You shall give the stranger an allotment within the tribe where he resides—declares the Lord God" (Ezek 47:22–23).[31] Ezekiel's vision seems to pertain only to the messianic

29 Notably, all texts cited in this footnote are in Hebrew. See Yehuda Brandes, *Judaism and Citizens Rights* (Israel Democracy Institute, 2019), 281–403; Shaul Yisraeli, "The Gentile as Knesset Member and Municipal Member," *The Oral Torah* 16 (1974): 72–79, and *The Right Pillar* (Moreshet, 1966); Yehuda Zoldan, "The Appointment of Gentiles to Public Positions," *Tehumim* 21 (2003): 348–57; Aviad Hacohen, "The Essence of Authority in Hebrew Law," in *Collection on Religious Zionism*, ed. Simcha Raz (World Center of Mizrachi and Poel Mizrachi, 2002), 488–500. Chief Rabbi Isaac Herzog detailed the halakhic arguments for the rights of Christians and Muslims in Israel in "The Rights of Minorities according to Jewish Law," *Tehumim* 2 (1951). While Herzog argued for the rights of Israeli minorities primarily on pragmatic grounds rather than ideal halakhic principle, his approach of legal realism to secure these rights is firmly entrenched in halakhic tradition and yields conclusions that are often meant to be permanent, not temporary.

30 According to Israel's Central Bureau of Statistics, the population of Israel at the end of 2021 was estimated at 9,449,000 residents; 73.9 percent of the total population is Jewish, while 26.1 percent is non-Jewish. Births in 2021 conformed to the same percentage distribution, implying that the overall percentage of Jews to non-Jews in Israel will remain relatively constant for the foreseeable future. The Jewish percentage will likely increase slightly due to Jewish immigration to Israel. These data are available at cbs.gov.il/en/mediarelease/Pages/2021/Population-of-Israel-on-the-Eve-of-2022.aspx.

31 Note that the allotment of land to the non-Jewish residents becomes *a heritage*, not merely a temporary grant. See commentary of Abravanel *ad loc*, who implies that this future allotment of the land to the gentile is a permanent allotment.

future, yet its legitimacy is not contested in Jewish writings. It thus remains as a possible covenantal desideratum for today. There is no legal or theological problem, then, acknowledging the individual rights of Palestinians and other gentiles in a sovereign Jewish state.

The second question is more difficult. Can a territorial compromise of The Land be consistent with the covenantal promise, Jewish law, and theology? This is complex, in both theory and practice, and the issue continues to be hotly debated in Israel today. One need only note the passionate arguments, toxic rhetoric, public distress, and sporadic violence that took place during the implementation of the Oslo accords in the 1990s as well as during Israel's 2005 withdrawal from Gaza to see how much this question goes to the heart of Zionist identity and politics. The ideal of the full and exclusive Jewish possession of The Land is so deep that it led one prominent religious Zionist leader to claim that "dividing The Land is like cutting up God's body"—a remarkably Christological metaphor that in the context of Jewish theology borders on the heresy mentioned earlier. And so volatile was this idea in 1995 that it led a religious Zionist to assassinate Israel's Prime Minister Yitshak Rabin.

The Bible views The Covenantal Land as one integral unit, delineating its borders and even allocating its specific regions to the twelve individual tribes descended from the sons of Jacob.[32] Although the scriptural borders of The Land are sometimes inconsistent, the talmudic rabbinic authorities resolved that problem and defined the borders in a clear manner. This was necessary for Jewish law, since observing some biblical commandments such as the restrictions on planting and harvesting The Land's crops during the Sabbatical and Jubilee years required knowing the precise boundaries of The Land.

Nevertheless, there appears to be no biblical or halakhic imperative for the chosen people to settle or control *the entire Covenantal Land*, while admittedly such full control is the ideal. Moreover, there are two significant religious precedents for dividing The Land or at least intentionally not extending Jewish control over all The Land. The first is the biblical narrative found in Genesis 12:7, in which God pledges to Abram that the Lord "will assign this land to your [i.e., Abram's] offspring," that is, Abram and his descendants have full title to all The Land. Yet not long after, the covenantal patriarch forgoes exclusive ownership of The Land by ceding parts of it to his nephew Lot: "Let there not be strife between you and me, between my herdsmen and yours. Is not the whole of the land before you? Let us separate . . . Thus they parted from each other; Abram remained in the Land of Canaan while Lot settled in the cities of the plain, pitching his tent near Sodom" (Gn 13:8–13).

32 Nm 32 and Jos 14–19.

Significantly, it was for the purpose of achieving peace that Abram (and by implication his descendants) voluntarily gave up control of parts of The Covenantal Land.[33] Also noteworthy is that neither the Bible nor Jewish legal tradition evinces any critique of Abram for this practical decision. Second, the Mishna and Talmud record that when the Jewish people returned to The Covenantal Land from their exile in Babylon around 516 BCE, they did not settle in all of the territory originally settled by Joshua and the Israelites. No doubt they did this for pragmatic reasons. Significantly, Jewish tradition adopted the borders of the second immigration for normative religious law regarding the Sabbatical and Jubilee years.[34] It appears that the borders of The Land to which the unique holy status applied depended upon the later historical experience of the Jewish people, that is, where they chose to settle, rather than the fixed territory defined in the Bible. If so, could not the borders of The Land on which Jews claim rights to covenantal title and sovereignty be similarly adjusted in light of pragmatic realities prior to the ideal messianic era, and be limited to where Jews actually live on The Land today?[35]

The fact that religious precedents exist for dividing and sharing of The Land is important for Jewish theology and tradition. Also significant is the justification for this sharing. In the case of Abraham, dividing The Covenantal Land was prompted by the yearning for peace; in the case of the returnees from Babylon, it was pragmatic considerations. And if these justifications were sanctioned in days of yore, may they not also be considered a legitimate possibility in our day?

SUPERSESSIONISM AND REALPOLITIK

I have tried to outline the possibilities for a Jewish covenantal theology that respects the Bible, Jewish law, and the centrality of The Land for Jewish identity, while at the same time leaving dignified space on The Land for non-idolatrous gentiles and their faith—both as individual citizens within sovereign Israel as well as in a coexisting national entity on part of The Land. Crucially, both Jewish conceptions are possible only when the gentiles on

33 I could find no other biblical evidence for sharing The Land. Moreover, one can argue textually and legally that Abraham's ceding part of the land to Lot preceded the later formal ratification of the covenant found in Gn 15. After ratification, division may not have warrant.

34 Mishna Shiv'it 6:1; BT, Yebamot 16a. See also Maimonides, *Mishneh Torah*, Laws of Sabbatical and Jubilee Years 4:26, and Laws of Terumot 1:2–6.

35 While the borders of the land were fixed for all time by the Jews returning from the Babylonian exile, the requirement to inhabit all The Land within those borders may be applicable only to the ideal messianic era rather than today.

The Land acknowledge the sovereign rights of Jews to live in peace and security in their covenantal homeland.

As the Christian scholar Barbara U. Meyer recently noted, "supersessionism has been neither true nor good theology."[36] I add that it has also led to moral disasters and political dead ends. I refer not to the eschatological supersessionism of Pope Benedict XVI, who maintained that the "theological unification is hardly possible within our historical time, and perhaps not even desirable,"[37] or any soft supersessionism that allows for concurrent validity of the Mosaic covenant and the Jewish people alongside the purported superior new covenant of Christianity. Interestingly, both of these supersessionist forms appear also in traditional Jewish belief and liturgy.[38] Indeed, it seems that for serious believers some type of supersessionism is unavoidable, as David Novak has correctly pointed out.[39]

The toxic, dead-end form of supersessionism is "hard imminent supersessionism," that is, supersessionism that rejects the ongoing validity of any other faith in the present and denies extending full dignity and rights to any persons or any people *extra ecclesiam*, *extra synagogam*, or *extra mosque*. If I understand Christian theology correctly, this was the normative form of Christian supersessionism throughout history until it was rejected by the

36 "Engrafted and Rooted Ways of Belonging—Alternatives to Abrogation in Post-Shoah and Palestinian Theologies," in Cunningham et al., *Enabling Dialogue about the Land,* 283.

37 Joseph Ratzinger, *Many Religions, One Covenant: Israel, the Church and the World* (Ignatius, 1999), 109. Ratzinger left the precise meaning of "theological unification" undefined. Although ambiguous, the complete disappearance of the Jewish people and its particularist covenant as distinct entities by a full assimilation into the Church is an unlikely possibility. John Paul II seems to have foreclosed that possibility in his explicit 1980 statement that later became official doctrine when it was incorporated into *Notes on the Correct Way to Present the Jews and Judaism in Preaching and Teaching in the Roman Catholic Church* (1985): "Jews are the people of God of the Old Covenant, which has never been revoked by God . . . The permanence of Israel is a historic fact to be interpreted within God's design. It remains a chosen people" (available at christianunity.va). Ratzinger was John Paul II's primary theological advisor and thus presumably agreed with this claim. In 2015, the "Gifts" document made Israel's permanence and the Jewish covenant's irrevocability official Church teaching.

38 The prayer of eighteen blessings that is central to Jewish daily statutory prayer includes this eschatological hope: "Let all that lives thank You, *Selah*, and praise Your name in truth, God our Savior and Help, *Selah*!" Similarly, the *Alenu* prayer recited thrice daily by religious Jews includes Zech 14:9: "In that day God will be one and his Name one," i.e., all people will come to recognize the unity of God as understood by Judaism. More recently, Rabbi Joseph Soloveitchik articulated this Orthodox eschatological supersessionism: "Only a candid, frank and unequivocal policy reflecting our unconditional commitment to God . . . believing with great passion in the ultimate truthfulness of our views, praying fervently for and expecting confidently the fulfillment of our eschatological vision when our faith will rise from particularity to universality will impress our peers of the other faith community." "Confrontation" in *Tradition* 6, no. 2 (1964): 25.

39 David Novak, "Supersessionism Hard and Soft," *First Things* (February 2019).

Church at the Second Vatican Council in the 1960s.[40] This hard imminent supersessionism has intolerant religious and secular political counterparts today in the exclusivist ideologies and hyper-nationalist politics espoused by some Zionist extremists alluded to earlier.[41] Such exclusivist thinking is also prominently found in Muslim and Christian ideologies that deny the history of the Jewish people on The Land, the Jewish people's right to a homeland under international law, and the legitimacy of Jewish sovereignty on any part of the Land. Importantly, all of these exclusivist ideologies—Jewish, Muslim, and Christian—influence the realpolitik of Israelis and Palestinians.

My experience of Jewish-Christian theological dialogue in the United States and Europe has been that mainstream Christian officials and scholars almost universally reject the old hard imminent supersessionism. This Copernican turn in Christian thinking is one of the great blessings for faithful Jews and Christians today, opening up stunning possibilities of peaceful coexistence, mutual appreciation, and practical cooperation.

Living in Israel, I am acutely aware of the ongoing tragic physical and ideological conflict dominating the lives of Israelis and Palestinians. There seems to be little hope for peace, both now and in the foreseeable future. Sadly, the inclusive pluralistic theological orientations mentioned above are but distant theories, far removed from the intractable political and psychological realities on The Land. In light of these existential, military, and political realities pressing down on Israelis and Palestinians, inclusivist theologies carry little influence in their day-to-day lives.

Palestinians, of course, have their own historical narratives and theologies of The Land, which I read with great interest since I have an existential investment in the matter. It is important to note that my interfaith experience in Israel and the Palestinian territories does not match my experience in America and Europe. And here I offer a confession: throughout my

40 See Stephen McMichael, "The Covenant in Patristic and Medieval Christian Theology," in *Two Faiths, One Covenant?*, ed. Eugene Korn and John Pawlikowski (Rowman and Littlefield, 2005), 49–51. While the post-*Nostra Aetate* Church continues to deny full theological legitimacy and salvific status to other religions, it no longer denies religious and civic freedoms to worshippers of those religions. See Gavin D'Costa, "Christian Orthodoxy and Religious Pluralism: A Response to Terrence W. Tilley," *Modern Theology* 23, no. 3 (July 2007): 437–42.

41 Jewish religious and political extremism is a growing phenomenon today that demands urgent attention. It is important to keep in mind, however, that radical Zionists and their organizations always constituted but a small percentage among Zionist thinkers, and their exclusivist ideologies have never determined normative policy among Zionists, either prior to 1948 statehood or after the founding of the State of Israel itself. The rejection of exclusivism is amply articulated in Israel's Declaration of Independence whose pluralistic guarantees were cited earlier. The presence in the Israeli Knesset (parliament) of Muslim and Christian Arabs evinces this commitment to political pluralism. In 2021 and 2022, the Islamist party, Raam, even helped constitute the Israeli coalition that governed the State of Israel.

interactions with Palestinian Christian religious officials and my reading of their theologies, I am still in search of a non-supersessionist Palestinian Christian theologian of any influence. The Palestinian Christian theologies that I encounter are invariably pre-Second Vatican Council forms. That is, they are hard supersessionisms that deny the validity of Judaism today, reject any connection between the covenanted Jews of the Bible and today's Jews, and deny any *de jure* Jewish rights to The Land. They have erased contemporary Jews from the Bible, the covenant, and The Land. This is true for Palestinian liberation theology[42] as well as non-liberation theologies.

Rev. Can. Jamal Khader, auxiliary bishop for the Latin patriarchate of Jerusalem, provides one representative example: "We [i.e., Christians] were in Egypt; we came to the promised Land."[43] For him, Christians are the indigenous people of The Land; in his rereading of the Bible it is Christians who have Abraham, Isaac, and Jacob as forefathers. Christians, not Jews, are the heirs to the covenantal promises fulfilled and transformed through Jesus; after Jesus, Christians are the people of God. His theology obliterates from Scripture and sacred history all post-Second Temple Judaism and today's Jewish people. Again, this appears to be mainstream Palestinian theology, not the exception.

This orientation affects the relevance of inclusivist Jewish theology. Israelis and Jews have little incentive to promote their own inclusivist conceptions or pluralist arrangements on The Land in the face of Palestinian theological and political hard supersessionisms that emphatically reject the ongoing validity of Judaism and Jewish rights to their historical homeland.

I do not know what is in the hearts and minds of Palestinian laypersons or non-politicians. But I and other Israelis pay close attention to the words and aspirations of Palestinian leaders. Unfortunately, secular supersessionisms and exclusivist claims on The Land continue to dominate Palestinian discourse and, unlike the minority toxic radical Zionist rhetoric, drive normative Palestinian policies.[44] Despite Yasir Arafat's letters to Israeli Prime Minister Yitzhak Rabin in 1993 and to President Clinton in 1996 promising to delete clauses in the PLO Charter that deny the right of Israel to exist, these texts were never expunged.[45] Moreover, this rejection was burned into

42 See, e.g., the well-known expression of Palestinian liberation theology, *Justice and Only Justice* by Naim Ateek (Orbis Books, 1989), esp. 164.

43 Jamal Khader, "Theology of the Land—A Christian Perspective," in Cunningham et al., *Enabling Dialogue about the Land*, 63–85.

44 See footnote 41.

45 For the evidence indicating no such revisions of the PLO charter, see israelnationalnews.com/Articles/Article.aspx/11719.

Israeli flesh and memory in 2000, when after Arafat rejected the Clinton proposals for territorial compromise, Palestinian terrorism led to the murder of more than a thousand Israelis, the overwhelming majority of whom were innocent civilians.

More recently, the President of the Palestinian Authority, Mahmoud Abbas, publicly denied any Jewish historical or religious claim to The Land, Jewish indigeneity to The Land, as well as Israel's right to exist. In January 2018 he proclaimed: "Colonialism created Israel to perform a certain function. Israel is a colonial project that has nothing to do with Judaism, but rather used by the Jews as a tool under the slogan of the Promised Land."[46] Finally, the covenant of Hamas, the Palestinian branch of the Muslim Brotherhood that rules the Palestinians of Gaza, declares that "Israel is to be obliterated," that "Hamas strives to raise the banner of Islam over every inch of Palestine," that "Peace initiatives and peaceful solutions . . . are in contradiction to the principles of the Islamic Resistance Movement," that "there is no solution for the Palestinian problem except by Jihad," and that "Jihad is the duty of every Muslim individual."[47]

In light of these uncompromising theological and political rejections of Israel's right to exist, and the violence visited upon Israelis after failed peace negotiations and Israel's territorial withdrawals from Lebanon and Gaza, Israelis have little appetite for pluralistic theologies, dividing The Land, or Palestinian sovereignty in the near future. From the Israeli perspective, the consistent broad-based Palestinian rejection of Israel's right to exist as evidenced in word and violent deed is cause of the persistent, tragic, physical, and ideological struggle over The Land. A sense of deep cynicism about the theological and political conflict has set in among both Israelis and Palestinians. At best, the problems can be "managed" on an ad hoc basis, not solved.

RETURNING TO THEOLOGY AND HOPE

In addition to illuminating reality, deepening human experience, and maintaining faithfulness to Scripture, good theology should also provide hope for the future. It should pave the way for history to move toward its sacred fulfillment and eschatological horizon. In a word, good theology must be

46 Speech on January 14, 2022, in response to America's recognition of Jerusalem as Israel's capital; available at timesofisrael.com/ rewriting-history-abbas-calls-israel-a-colonial-project-unrelated-to-judaism/.

47 Hamas Charter, Preface, articles 6, 13, 15; available at avalon.law.yale.edu/20th_century/hamas.asp.

constructive, not merely descriptive. And the best constructive theologies influence societies and individuals. They make actual contributions to improving the empirical world as we experience it (what Jews call *Tikkun Olam*—repairing the world) not merely in a distant metaphysical or mystical way.

I have tried to lay out the possibilities for a constructive Jewish covenantal theology of The Land, one that provides for the rights and dignity of Palestinians and other gentiles on The Land concurrent with Jewish sovereignty. What would it take for that type of theology to become influential among Jewish theologians and religious Zionists today? What could transform the current tragic situation on The Land into conditions that provide serious hope that the vision of a constructive theology could be realized?

As mentioned, scriptures and Jewish law both presuppose that the gentiles coexisting with the Jewish people on The Land acknowledge Jewish covenantal claims to The Land and commit themselves to live peacefully amidst Jewish sovereignty. And as I read the Israeli political map today, to move toward peace Israelis also demand the same, namely that their neighbors accept that the Jewish people have the right to sovereignty, freedom and security on The Land.[48]

History indicates that when Israel's neighbors agree to such acceptance, peace indeed follows. When Egypt and Jordan recognized Israel's right to exist and signed treaties with Israel, the territorial disputes ended—even over those territories considered part of the biblical Covenantal Land. Peaceful relations emerged. More recently the Abraham Accords in which the United Arab Emirates and Bahrain recognized the State of Israel, also led to peace and cooperation. This political breakthrough had implications for The Land. Prior to the Abraham Accords, 48 percent of Israelis were in favor of annexing much of the Palestinian territories. However, when Israelis had to choose between the peace accords and annexation, only 20 percent favored annexation.[49]

These dynamics indicate that the disinterest of the overwhelming majority of secular and even religious Israelis to immediate peace initiatives and Palestinian sovereignty on The Land is based primarily on security and geopolitical considerations, not hardened theological principles. When Israeli security assessments and Arab intentions change, Israeli attitudes and the possibility of political progress also change. And in spite of the existing

48 These are reasonable requirements even for some Islamists. The Israeli Islamist party, Raam, was a part of the 2022 Israeli government under these assumptions.

49 Barak Ravid, *Trump's Peace: The Abraham Accords and the Shake-Up in the Middle East* [Hebrew] (Yedioth Press, 2021).

stagnation in resolving the dispute over the Land, the two-state solution with territorial compromise still remains the most favored option among both Israelis (42 percent) and Palestinians (43 percent) over all other scenarios.[50] When there is reliable evidence of commitments to peace, compromise, and coexistence, pluralistic theologies of The Land become credible; hope is renewed.

Tragically, this has never obtained in Israeli-Palestinian relations. The maximum peace offers that Israel has repeatedly made,[51] namely, division of The Land with Jewish sovereignty and security, together with termination of Palestinian claims on Israel, have never met the minimum Palestinian requirement, namely, the return of the Palestinian refugees to Israel proper and the continuation of territorial claims on Israel after peace agreements.

According to the talmudic rabbis, "The entire Torah was given for the sake of peace."[52] In its original context, this statement referred to innovative rabbinic legislation to promote internal harmony among Jews. Yet it cannot be denied that peaceful relations between the Jewish people and gentiles is a spiritual and covenantal objective for the Bible, the prophets of Israel, Jewish theologians, and rabbinic authorities throughout the ages. The talmudic statement indicates that real peace, a peace that lasts because one side no longer harbors aspirations to conquer the other, stands near the top of the Jewish spiritual and moral hierarchy, one for which most other values may be sacrificed.

Exclusivist supersessionist theologies and ideologies are the death knell for the possibilities of peace and of understanding. Fortunately, we have seen that alternatives exist in Jewish theology and law for inclusive pluralistic conceptions of The Land if there is recognition of Jewish sovereignty and security. When there are sincere commitments for coexistence and peace, we can follow the model of the biblical Abraham, and announce, "Let there not be strife between me and you . . . Is not the whole of the Land before you?"

50 "Palestinian-Israeli Pulse: A Joint Poll conducted by the Palestinian Center for Policy and Survey Research (PSR) and the Evens Program in Mediation and Conflict Management at Tel Aviv University," August 2020; available at pcpsr.org/en/node/823.

51 Before statehood, the Jewish community living on The Land ("the *yishuv*") accepted the 1947 UN Partition Plan. Israel accepted or offered plans for territorial division of The Land in 1977 (the Camp David Accords), 2000 (the Clinton proposals), 2008 (the offer by Israeli Prime Minister, Ehud Olmert), and 2020 (the Trump peace plan). See Josef Federman, "Abbas admits he rejected 2008 peace offer from Olmert," *The Times of Israel*, November 19, 2015, and Greg Sheridan, "Ehud Olmert still dreams of peace," *The Australian*, November 28, 2009, available at theaustralian.com.au/news/opinion/ehud-olmert-still-dreams-of-peace/story-e6frg76f-1225804745744.

52 BT, Gittin 59b, based on Prv 3:17.

Both Jews and Palestinians are traumatized peoples. Yet if each finds the courage to rise above his pain and reject hard supersessionist theologies denying the legitimate rights of the other, there is reason for hope. After the Holocaust, amid the smoldering ashes of Auschwitz, no one could have predicted the Jewish people's miraculous rebirth and flourishing today in their own sovereign state on The Land. And after centuries of Christian supersessionist anti-Judaism, eighty years ago no one would have predicted the Copernican revolution in the Church and the resulting amity between the Church and the Jewish people. For whatever reason, God threw the majority of the Jewish people and the Church together for two millennia, much of which was consumed by theological and physical warfare. Yet these enemies are now fraternal allies. This unimagined reconciliation should teach us that peace is possible between any two peoples, however long and bitter their dispute and alienation.

For the last hundred years, God has thrown Jews and Palestinians together. Perhaps a second Copernican revolution is also possible, one between Palestinians and Israelis sharing The Covenantal Land in peace. We will need God's grace to achieve this, but, as in the Catholic turning, grace from above will not suffice. We must assume responsibility and actively initiate this sacred fulfillment.

Faithful Jews, Christians, and Muslims share the obligation to keep hope alive. So let us learn to recognize the presence and dignity of others who are not like us and drop our hard supersessionist theologies in favor of lasting peace. Let us banish any thoughts of erasing others from God's kingdom above and from The Covenantal Land below. However distant this reality may appear at this moment, it is what God demands of us as a nation of priests bringing blessings to the world, and as a holy people committed to *tzedakah* and *mishpat*. And may our spiritual lodestar be the same as that of Isaiah: "'Peace, peace to those who are far and to those who are near,' saith the Lord" (Is 57:19).

14

BRIEF REFLECTIONS

TWO PEOPLE ON ONE LAND

Bishop Etienne Vetö, CCN

Two peoples live on one land and claim the right to that land. Of all the questions that surface when addressing the theological status of the ingathering of the Jewish people on the land and the establishment of the modern State of Israel, this may well be the thorniest. How can these be founded on the divine promises contained in the Hebrew Bible when the establishment of the modern State of Israel has provoked such intense suffering for the Palestinian people, while leaving the Jewish people frequently exposed to existential threat and in a situation in which they are often led to repress another people? The significant contribution of Eugene Korn and Yazid Said is that their papers offer a series of elements that, brought together, allow us to see quite thoroughly the theological and methodological framework for a just approach to these complex questions. I will start by showing what this framework is, including a correct reading of scriptures, the recourse to context and history, as well as to interpretative traditions, and the theological developments that complete the process. Secondly, I will point out what I see as the limits of each contribution and what is missing for a complete theological treatment of the relationship between Jews and Palestinians on the land.

THE FRAMEWORK: SCRIPTURE, CONTEXT, INTERPRETATIVE TRADITIONS, AND THEOLOGY

In my view, Said expounds the question of the right approach to the biblical promises in the most complete and balanced way, by underlining the complexity of the scriptures and their use. Said deftly and fruitfully navigates between two opposing extremes: the selective and "cherry-picked" readings of some Palestinian liberation theologians and the fundamentalistic approaches of some religious Zionists. Against the "cherry-picking" of the first, he insists on a "full-blooded engagement with the whole of the Jewish Scriptural corpus, including the promise of the Land," and rejects supersessionist readings of these promises. Said is in line with concerns expressed by Eugene Korn, who also underlines these irrevocable biblical promises and insists on the risk of 'supersessionism of the land' (my expression). However, Said points out that receiving the whole of scriptures means to consider the "self-critical dynamic" of the Hebrew Bible itself, where the voices of the prophets Amos, Isaiah, or Ezekiel offer a counterpoint to Deuteronomy and Leviticus, as they give priority to religious observance and the conversion of the heart to the possession of the land, and "stand up for the forgotten and marginalized in the land."

A second level of complexity, which challenges many biblically-based theologies of the land, is recognizing that the scriptures are not self-sufficient. Against fundamentalist readings, Said underlines the need to take into account "context," that is, local history, situations, and law. This is a specific contribution of Said's paper: because the land that the waves of *aliyot* came to in the early twentieth century, was not an empty one; because the people of the land had a long and rich tradition—whether Arab or Jewish, I would add—and that the Palestinian Christians can be considered the heirs of the local Church and its bimillennial presence (Said quotes Pope Paul VI), one cannot equate a biblical reality and a twentieth-century one. Scripture and context introduce a double level of complexity that challenges both Jews and Palestinians: "Just as contemporary Jews need to face the complexity of Palestine's history and story, Palestinians need to face the complexity of the biblical narrative and its significance for the Jewish people today."

Moreover, scriptures are not self-sufficient because they need to be interpreted according to "their normative exegetical tradition." Both authors show how each of their religious traditions offer a necessary and creative interpretative tool for the biblical land promise. Korn proposes a detailed and convincing reflection on the possibility, according to Jewish law, *halakha*, to grant equal rights to non-Jews and to allow them sovereignty on a part of the promised land, which is more than what the Bible presents as the rights of resident aliens (*gerim toshavim*). He grounds his answer on the precedent of allowing commercial partnerships (*shutafut*) with non-idolatrous gentiles, as developed by European rabbinic authorities in early modernity: by analogy, *de jure* political partnerships that give equal rights to all should also be possible.

Likewise, Korn recurs to the precedents of sharing of the land by Abraham with Lot (Gn 13:8–13) and of the way that the Mishnah and Talmud, to set normative religious law regarding Shabbat and Jubilee years, adopt the borders where the Jewish people settled on their return from the Babylonian exile, rather than the often larger territory provided by the borders according to some of the biblical promises. Korn thus grounds halakhically both the equality of rights of Palestinians and other non-Jews in the State of Israel and the possibility of establishing a Palestinian state. This halakhic argumentation is a novel contribution to the debate and a crucial one, because of the rising role of religious Zionism in Israel. More deeply, it also shows how halakha is not fixed but has a rich potential for development and adaptation. This makes it an excellent tool to interpret the biblical revelation in the correct way to confront contemporary questions.

Said develops, from a Christian perspective, what he sees as the New Testament's contribution to the correct interpretation of the Hebrew Bible's land promises. For Said, the hermeneutical key that the New Testament brings to the whole of Scripture is the cross, the passion of Christ. Indeed, the cross brings to light "a story of conflict between how we (Jews or Christians) envisage God and how God actually appears." The cross is not a "Christian" challenge for the "Jewish" perception of God, but a challenge for both of our understandings of God—indeed, for any understanding of God. It is, specifically, a challenge for the faith in the incarnation, which insists on the promises as accomplished and as realized in a concrete, historical, and physical reality of this world. Following Rowan Williams, Said draws the conclusions relevant to the land and State of Israel: this "reverse type of messianism" can be applied as a critique of any "contemporary *ersatz* messianism of the modern State of Israel,"[1] that is, assigning religious status to political messianism and to understanding any political reality as an accomplishment of the messianic promises. Perhaps it even means this accomplishment can only be an eschatological reality. Let us note that Korn also refuses to see the twentieth-century ingathering and establishment of the State of Israel as the messianic fulfillment, although he does not expound on the question in detail: "Any form of Zionism that sees residence on the Land as constituting messianic redemption *per se* or constituting the *actual* fulfillment of the covenant comes perilously close to idolatry."

Once the scriptural approach and its interpretative framework are set, it is possible to procced with a grounded theological reflection. Relying on the same biblical references that he evokes to present the land promises, Korn explains the twin mandate of the Jewish people: to teach their children the

1 Rowan Williams, *On Christian Theology* (Wiley-Blackwell, 1999), 101–2.

way of righteousness and justice of the Lord and to be a blessing and a light to the nations. Korn insists on this relationship to the gentiles: "the covenantal Jewish people was created for the world, not the world for the Jewish people." Now, Korn argues that the spiritual independence that is necessary to be a "holy nation," a "priestly people," requires land to be able to distance the Jewish people from other peoples, as well as political sovereignty to preserve this distance. However, the logic is the same as for the Jewish people who are "for the world" and not vice-versa: "the Land is not an end in itself, merely the means to potentially fulfilling the covenantal promise."

As a Christian theologian, Said expounds a sacramental conception of the gift of the land. Although it is not quite clear for Said of what the land is a "sacrament," that is, what it makes present and signifies, the limits that sacramentality sets in regard to possession of the land and historical accomplishment of the promises are easy to deduce. Like Christ's risen body of which the empty tomb is the sign, a sacrament cannot be possessed or owned. It is to "be given away, as it were." It always points to more, to its full accomplishment in the eschaton. As such, one can surmise that the land cannot be possessed; not only may it be shared, but, indeed, it is *made* to be shared. Moreover, confirming the reading of the land promises through the lenses of the cross, one can conclude that the promises cannot be realized as a strictly historical reality but rather only in the eschaton.

TOWARD A COMPLETE THEOLOGICAL ASSESSMENT: INCARNATION, LOCAL CONTEXT, HISTORY, AND RECONCILIATION

Both authors agree that there is a divine promise of the land made to the Jewish people and that the present ingathering and establishment of the State of Israel cannot be considered the messianic accomplishment of these promises. However, they differ on whether this present ingathering can be grounded on the land promises, that is, whether it can be validated not only geopolitically but also as conforming to a divine mandate, even if full conformity can only be eschatological.

Based on his understanding of the prophetical self-critical dimension built into the scriptures and of the cross as hermeneutical key to these, as well as of the sacramental dimension of the land, Said strongly dissociates the land promises and the political reality. He seems to conclude that the modern ingathering and establishment of the state cannot be grounded on the land promises. This is how I understand his assertion: "The present author does not believe the promise of the land as it appears in the bible needs necessarily to mean that political power is also 'hallowed' by divine authorization."

Indeed, insists Said, "it certainly cannot be learned readily through the historical events of the Holy Land as it has suffered them up until today." The historical process through which it came to be, in disregard and disrespect for the context of the longstanding presence of the Palestinian people on the land, shows that one cannot discern divine authorization and "hallowing."

However, the wording is subtle and open-ended. Would Said say that if the process had followed other paths, it might have been able to rightfully invoke the authority of the biblical promises? Is there, under certain conditions, a possible historical (non-definitive, non-messianic) accomplishment of these promises as divine promises takes place? Would it eventually be possible to find this path in the future? Or are the promises only eschatological? I believe that the latter perspective is reductive and does not fully take into consideration the framework of the incarnation. Indeed, the cross transforms what we believe to perceive and "hold" in the incarnation; but it does not cancel the incarnation, and only because Christ is incarnate can he suffer his passion and die. Likewise, the sacraments, although they are signs oriented to the "not yet" of the eschaton, are also tangible realities, real foretastes of the same eschaton's "already there." The incarnate and sacramental dimensions of Christian revelation allow for imperfect and never definitive but true realizations of God's promises in salvation history. Should it not allow, at least in principle, for a cautious invocation of the land promises to ground the presence of the Jewish people and their self-determination on this land? Said rightly quotes Rowan Williams in saying that "Israel under God" and "the modern State of Israel" are "distinct but overlapping" realities. The distinction is crucial, and this is one of Said's significant contributions, but one should not ignore or dismiss the possibility that they overlap.

Conversely, Eugene Korn does not hesitate to ground the ingathering of the Jewish people and the establishment of the modern State of Israel on the divine promises. However, his position is weakened because of a blind spot: the lack of attention to the historical and local context where this promise is accomplished. For instance, Korn expounds on the relationship between the Jewish people and Gentiles in general, but he does not take into consideration the specificity of the situation of the Palestinian people as such. Is the relationship to the people who are legitimately living on the same land the same as to all other nations? Indeed, how are the Jewish people specifically a blessing and a light to the Palestinian people? That the Jewish people receive a God-given mandate is a fundamental theological truth. But this mandate cannot not be oriented to those who are closest, to one's "neighbors." Indeed, they are the first who should benefit from it and whether they do is a fundamental criterion of the enactment of the mandate.

To take this a step further, one can wonder if the presence of the Palestinian people on the land is just an accident of history, or whether it can have a positive meaning. Korn says that "there appears to be no biblical or halakhic imperative for the chosen people to settle or control *the entire* covenantal Land, *while admittedly such full control is the ideal*" (emphasis added). Is "full control" truly so ideal? Can the presence of another people on the promised land not be a "sign of the times," in Catholic parlance, that is, a providential sign that sharing is the ideal for a "holy people," a people called to live differently from other people (see 1 Sm 8:20) and, in precisely this way, to be a light for the nations?[2]

Likewise, it is quite surprising that a paper that touches on the relationship between Jews and Palestinians on the land makes no mention of the suffering of the Palestinian people. Korn does address the history of their relationship but only to present the wrongs of the Palestinians who have repeatedly rejected the legitimacy of the State of Israel. It is obvious that the Palestinians bear a great responsibility for the present tragic situation. It is also clear that, through the occupation and settler movement as well as the constant humiliation imposed on so many, there is an undeniable responsibility on the part of the Israelis.[3] Korn rightly underlines that the land is not an end, but that it is relative to covenantal life. Does this not mean that fulfilling covenantal requirements of justice and equity are more important than possessing the land?

As regards this last question, one final critical comment seems necessary. Neither author refers to universal ethics (what Catholics call natural law) and the grounding that it gives to political and geopolitical law. I believe that, because of its nature, no reflection on any land or sociopolitical entity can go without it. Universal ethics are most probably an underlying principle in Said's attention to history and context and it would have helped him to bolster the full legitimacy of the centuries-long Palestinian presence on the land. Likewise, bearing in mind this full legitimacy, although of a different kind than the biblically-grounded one, would have allowed Korn to avoid considering sharing of the land as a simple concession and it would have strengthened his attention to the ethical criteria of justice and peace as conditions of residency on the land. Of course, this would entail grounding the

2 See E. Vetö, "Land and Redemption: Why Does God Promise a Land?," in *Contemporary Catholic Approaches to the People, Land, and State of Israel*, ed. Gavin D'Costa and Faydra L. Shapiro (The Catholic University of America Press, 2021), 21–41.

3 One also needs to recognize the ambiguities of the events that led hundreds of thousands of Palestinians to flee their land in 1948. See, e.g., Efraim Karsh, *Palestine Betrayed* (Yale University Press, 2010), and Robert I. Rotberg, ed., *Israeli and Palestinian Narratives of Conflict: History's Double Helix* (Indiana University Press, 2006).

possibility for religious law to take universal ethics into account. However, it is quite possible to consider natural or human ethics as an indirect expression of divine commandments and will. Both the religious and the universal ethics in this case can illuminate and offer guardrails to each other. The land promises are valid, but they need to be implemented according to the criteria set both by religious law (the land is a means, not an end) and universal ethics (injustice is simply unacceptable). When there seems to be a contradiction between religious law and ethics, this signals a serious problem that must be addressed.

In the end, Scripture, context, interpretative traditions, and universal ethics compose the full framework for a just theological approach to the relationship of Jews and Palestinians on the land. That is quite a handful. Where things go wrong, and they are bound to, it does not in the least imply that either peoples lose their legitimacy, but rather that confronting the tragic difficulty in living out the ethical commandments of the covenant in the present situation is a constitutive part of a theological reflection on the land and state. It also means, as Said underlines, that both peoples (and the international community as well) need to consider their wrongs: "the state of Israel needs to face the full challenge of the origins of the conflict and be exposed to some level of self-criticism." Also: "can Palestinians learn something from this kind of European support facing the guilt of the Holocaust?" Could this be an aspect of the *tishuv* (return to God/repentance) that Korn illuminatingly relates to the *shuvah* (return to the land)?

SECTION 4

THE THEOLOGY OF THE STATE UNDERLYING CATHOLIC AND JEWISH APPROACHES TO ISRAEL

15

THE STATE OF ISRAEL AND THE HOLY SEE:
A THEOLOGICAL AND ETHICAL PERSPECTIVE

Fr. Thomas Joseph White, OP

On December 13, 1993, the Holy See and the State of Israel signed a Fundamental Agreement that ratified previous diplomatic discussions and that led directly to the formal creation of official relations between the two parties. In this agreement, a number of core themes can be noted.[1] First, there is the recognition of the sovereignty of the State of Israel, in accord with international law and the norms of common accords of states in regard to human rights. A centrality underscored here pertains to the rights of religious freedom and of conscience, particularly as they pertain to those who practice Christianity within the territory of Israel and of the Holy Land.[2] Second, there is a common denunciation of antisemitism and anti-Judaic intolerance, allied with a recognition on behalf of the Catholic Church of the moral horror of twentieth-century crimes against the Jewish people, as well as historical forms of unethical prejudice perpetuated by Christians

1 See "Fundamental Agreement Between the Holy See and the State of Israel" (1993), available at vatican.va.

2 "Fundamental Agreement," article 1, §2. "The Holy See, recalling the Declaration on Religious Freedom of the Second Vatican Ecumenical Council, *Dignitatis humanae*, affirms the Catholic Church's commitment to uphold the human right to freedom of religion and conscience, as set forth in the Universal Declaration of Human Rights and in other international instruments to which it is a party. The Holy See wishes to affirm as well the Catholic Church's respect for other religions and their followers as solemnly stated by the Second Vatican Ecumenical Council in its Declaration on the Relation of the Church to Non-Christian Religions, *Nostra aetate*."

and non-Christians alike against the Jews.[3] Third, there is the acknowledgment that Christians and Jews share a common spiritual heritage and that Jerusalem and other sites in the Holy Land have a role in the common religious and spiritual patrimony of humanity.[4]

In later discourses of Pope John Paul II, there is a modest but real acknowledgment that these three ideas are connected with a fourth. On a Catholic theological rendering of the relationship of Christians and Jews, the Jews continue even after the time of Jesus Christ and the fulfillment of the revelation of God in the old covenant to play an essential and mysteriously prophetic and eschatological role in the ongoing economy of God's salvific plan, as affirmed by Paul's Letter to the Romans and taught at the Second Vatican Council.[5] There is a universal future orientation, then, to the ongoing relation of Jews and Christians, one that is proleptic or eschatological in horizon. In the words of the 1992 Catechism of the Catholic Church, Christians and Jews together await in differentiated ways a messianic fulfillment of the covenant of God with Israel, one that has implications for all peoples and for the creation itself.[6] Our history and destiny as human beings, in our common human finitude, in the presence of the goodness of the creation, but also in the face of injustice, suffering, and death, are to be interpreted in light of the realism of this prophetically and biblically warranted form of expectation.

In light of this modern agreement between the State of Israel and the Holy See, how might one evaluate, from within the purview of Catholic theology, the ongoing existence of the State of Israel as a theologically meaningful datum? Here I will note one way in which I think Catholic theologians ought to avoid rendering the argument, namely, based on the claim to an ongoing divine right of the Jewish people to the land of Israel, and I will mention why I think this line of argument paradoxically risks to threaten stable and enduring healthy relations between Christians and Jews. Second, I will argue

3 Ibid., article 2, §1. "The Holy See and the State of Israel are committed to appropriate cooperation in combatting all forms of antisemitism and all kinds of racism and of religious intolerance, and in promoting mutual understanding among nations, tolerance among communities and respect for human life and dignity. [§2] The Holy See takes this occasion to reiterate its condemnation of hatred, persecution, and all other manifestations of antisemitism directed against the Jewish people and individual Jews anywhere, at any time and by anyone. In particular, the Holy See deplores attacks on Jews and desecration of Jewish synagogues and cemeteries, acts which offend the memory of the victims of the Holocaust, especially when they occur in the same places which witnessed it."

4 See ibid., articles 3–9. See also Pope John Paul II, Apostolic Letter *Redemptionis Anno* (April 20, 1984), available at vatican.va.

5 See the *Address of His Holiness Pope John Paul II to a Symposium on the Roots of Anti-Judaism,* October 31, 1997, para. 2; available at vatican.va. See also the 2015 "Gifts" document.

6 See the 1992 *Catechism of the Catholic Church,* §§839–40; available at vatican.va.

for what I take to be three promising and fundamentally positive notions of Catholic thinking in this regard. First, the recognition of the rights of states to self-determination in accord with universal ethical norms and international law; second, the mutually implicating notion of respect and tolerance for the religious freedom of others; and third, the common spiritual patrimony and potentially convergent mission common to Jews and Christians within a singular divine economy. These three latter forms of argument provide, it seems to me, an important framework for thinking about a common relation between Catholics and Jews that affirms the ethical significance and the rights of the State of Israel, in accord with sound principles of the Catholic intellectual tradition and its dogmatic theological tradition.

A DIVINE RIGHT TO THE LAND?

There can be little question that the Old Testament provides evidence of a divine promise to the land of Israel, originally pledged to Abraham, reinstantiated in the course of the Torah and reiterated in the prophetic literature and history of the ancient people of Israel.[7] Modern secular biblical interpreters may envisage such ancient writings as a mere collection of human artificial literature designed, out of whatever outmoded religious sincerity, to justify under divinely authorized pretexts the pre- or post-facto militant and culturally imposed occupation of territories that were originally of disputed ownership or that were possessed unambiguously by non-Israelites.[8]

The Catholic Church, however, maintains with modern Jews who believe in divine revelation that the land in question was originally promised to the descendants of Abraham by divine decree and that the historical culture of ancient Israel, however complex its concrete internal history and sociological development, came into existence in some way most fundamentally due to the prophetic initiative of God and the supernaturally instigated covenant that he formed in and with the people of Israel, a covenant which is of divine origin, and which has implications for the land of Israel on which the divine law of the Torah was initially meant to be observed, at least in some of its key instances, not least for the purpose of sacrifice in the Temple.[9]

7 See, e.g., Gn 12:1, 12:7, 15:7, 15:18–21, 26:3, 28:13; Nm 34:1–12; Dt 1:8, 19:8–9.

8 See the argument of Friedrich Nietzsche, *On the Genealogy of Morality*, trans. C. Diethe (Cambridge University Press, 2006), which represents an early version of this argument, with respect to the Torah.

9 See the traditional theological argument in this regard of Matthew Levering, *Christ's Fulfillment of Torah and Temple: Salvation according to Thomas Aquinas* (University of Notre Dame Press, 2002).

It may be tempting for this reason, for Catholic Christians, merely to pursue a logic of a common assertion with religious Jews regarding the divine origin of the promise of the land, based upon a shared conviction regarding the divine origin of the Hebrew scriptures, and on this basis to seek a new Catholic theology regarding the land of Israel, in light of its modern historical reinstantiation in the mid-twentieth century, in light of the conciliar teaching of *Nostra Aetate* at the Second Vatican Council regarding the ongoing existence of God's covenant with the Jewish people (based on a reactualization of Rom 9–12), and as a response to the unspeakable inhumanity of the Shoah.[10]

Nevertheless I think this is an error, both theoretically and strategically, for four reasons. First, there is very little fundamental basis in classical Catholic theological tradition for this claim, to the point that I believe the idea to be virtually indemonstrable, from the perspective of New Testament theology, the primitive Christian theological tradition, and mature Catholic dogmatics. Why do I say this? The main reason is that the New Testament makes little or no pronouncement on the issue of Israel's right to the land after the coming of Christ. It is true that the Old Testament, as Catholics understand it, entails the promise of the land. And the New Testament does unambiguously affirm the ongoing theological signification of the Jewish people and their covenant with God, in some form, even if this fact of New Testament revelation has been at times eclipsed or under-examined in Christian history.

However, the Pauline doctrine of the fulfillment of the old law by the life, death, and resurrection of Christ, which is a normative part of Catholic theology, also entails the notion of the abrogation of certain aspects of the old law, such as the practice of temple sacrifices.[11] Of course there are many elements of Old Testament teaching that remain normative for Christians, not least the Decalogue as it is interpreted in the Christian tradition. But does the promise of the land fall on the side of what continues after the coming of Christ, such as the moral norms of the Ten Commandments, or is the promise of the land brought to an accomplishment in Christ, like the prohibitions of unclean foods or fabric requirements? If one follows the fulfillment logic, then Israel might still be a land for the Jews, but is also able to become a universal holy land for all peoples, those who recognize the God of Israel revealed in Christ. The New Testament does not take a decided stance on

10 See in this respect, the recent observations and arguments of Adam Gregerman, "Is the Biblical Land Promise Irrevocable?: Post-*Nostra Aetate* Catholic Theologies of the Jewish Covenant and the Land of Israel," *Modern Theology* 34, no. 2 (April 2018): 137–58.

11 Gal 2:14–21; Rom 2:14–15, 5:1–9, 7:4, 7:7–18:17, 10:4.

this, as far as I can tell. According to a variety of New Testament texts, the Temple sacrifices and various sacrificial and ritual practices of the Torah do seem to have only a temporal and provisional dispensation, now abrogated in Christ, but what consequence, if any, does this have regarding the land or the territory of Israel? Though I am not an expert in the historical treatment of the topic, it strikes me that there is little or no patristic and medieval speculation on the subject of the positive continuing significance of the land of Israel as a land of the Jews, after Christ. By contrast, the New Testament does stipulate that the Jewish people and the covenant of God with this particular people do have a continuing importance in the economy of salvation. In classical Christian theology this element of New Testament thinking is retained even alongside the idea that elements of the law are abrogated. Within this theological context, the actuality of the revealed command and divine right of the people to live on the land remains at best ambiguous or unclear.

Second, the Christian appeal to a divine right to the land runs the risk of building on unstable foundations that will shortly crumble. In short, if Catholic theologians provide a warrant for Catholic-Jewish relations and the respect of the political sovereignty of the State of Israel on a theology that is not sufficiently grounded in the New Testament and in long-lasting Catholic tradition, then their arguments will appear arbitrary and will have only a provisional effect. Indeed, such arguments could lead to the dialectical reaction by Christians unsympathetic to the nation of Israel, wherein one allies recognition of the State of Israel with unwarranted theological innovation of non-traditional Catholic theologians of unwarrantedly Zionist sympathies, and so also associate the rejection of the diplomatic recognition of Israel with a return to traditional theological sources and with theological orthodoxy. This would be an unhappy outcome but it is also, in my opinion, an entirely avoidable one.

Third, the notion of the land of Israel from a territorial perspective is inherently opaque. Historically and in the modern context it is related to serious concerns about territorial sovereignty and self-determination of non-Jewish people in the region of Israel. How is the ancient notion of a promised land meant to translate effectively into a modern concept of state sovereignty and diplomatic respect of territorial identity in the context of the modern nation-states after the treatise of Westphalia, and in Israel after the wars of 1948 and 1968, as well as in light of the modern conflicts regarding the Golan Heights, the West Bank, and the Gaza territories? Catholics should be careful about imposing anachronistically their historical reconstructions of Israel upon a modern historical and political situation that is in many ways novel and alien to the biblical text.

Fourth, not all Israelis identify with the claims of the Catholic Old Testament regarding the divine right to the land in the ancient context. Not all religious Jews affirm a living divine right to the land. Not all religious Jews who affirm a divine right to the land affirm it in any way like the various ways some Christians currently do or have done. Yet the Church rightly should engage with all Jews, religious or non-religious, however they respond to this point of controversy, and should do so constructively in regard to the state sovereignty and international legal rights and responsibilities of the State of Israel. To do so they are aided not by a concept of a divine right to the land but by a notion of state self-determination in accord with natural law, a point I will turn to at this juncture.

BASIS FOR A CATHOLIC RECOGNITION OF THE MODERN STATE OF ISRAEL

In the second part of this essay I would like to explore three notions that can serve as the basis for a constructive mutual cooperation between the Catholic Church and the modern State of Israel. The first notion pertains to the Catholic Church's natural law tradition, namely insofar as it practices the recognition of the rights of states to self-determination in accord with universal ethical norms and international law. The second notion pertains to a related idea, the respect and tolerance for the religious freedom of others, as it pertains not only to individuals but also to collective populations, and to religious and non-religious minority subgroups within states. Third and finally, there is the important Catholic notion of the common spiritual patrimony and potentially convergent mission common to Jews and Christians within a singular divine economy. Taken collectively these three notions provide an important framework for thinking about a common relation between Catholics and Jews that affirms the sovereignty rights of the State of Israel, in accord with sound principles of the Catholic intellectual tradition and its dogmatic theological tradition.

Natural Law and the Rights of States

In her natural law tradition as it pertains to social doctrine, the Catholic Church affirms a number of basic truths about human beings. First, human beings have a natural inclination to live in community and form families, clans, cities, civilizations, and nations, which can be organized in political ways as constitutional states, in view of the common good of all of the members.[12] Universal values of the pursuit of truth, justice, respect of freedom, and mutual solidarity should normally guide the existence of relations between states and the relations of persons within them. These aims should be expressed in national and international bodies of laws, which are meant to guarantee an order of justice in society.[13]

Within this context, member states of the international order are meant to enjoy state sovereignty even while collaborating with one another constructively. "Sovereignty represents the subjectivity of a nation, in the political, economic, social and even cultural sense."[14] Here the Church appeals not only to law but also to culture: "Culture constitutes the guarantee for the preservation of the identity of a people and expresses and promotes its spiritual sovereignty."[15] "National sovereignty is not, however, absolute. Nations can freely renounce the exercise of some of their rights in view of a common goal, in the awareness that they form a 'family of nations' where mutual trust, support and respect must prevail."[16]

We can make three relevant observations about this body of Catholic social teaching in regard to state sovereignty and international law. First, the notion can apply to a people simply because it has a common culture, shared history, legal tradition, and internal government system, as well as a territorial unity or continuous location in place and time, for however long or short. This criterion is not bound up with the particular mode in which a given people or nation came to be, its particular national history, or an ethical assessment of every facet of its national character. It is a criterion that is granted simply on the basis of a natural fact, that a given people in a shared collective history of self-governance have formulated and preserved a national character. These are the things human beings do, inevitably and naturally, through myriad diverse historical circumstances, and by this criterion of natural law, the modern State of Israel is clearly a sovereign nation.

12 The 2004 *Compendium on the Social Doctrine of the Catholic Church*, para. 433: "The centrality of the human person and the natural inclination of persons and peoples to establish relationships among themselves are the fundamental elements for building a true international community, the ordering of which must aim at guaranteeing the effective universal common good" (available at vatican.va).

13 Ibid., 434. "International law becomes the guarantor of the international order, that is of coexistence among political communities that seek individually to promote the common good of their citizens and strive collectively to guarantee that of all peoples, aware that the common good of a nation cannot be separated from the good of the entire human family."

14 Ibid., 435.

15 Ibid.

16 Ibid.

Second, this criteria also acknowledges the place of nation-states within a larger international order bound by common justice and called to a collaboration of universal brotherhood or fraternity, namely to a unified order of amicability and consensus in the pursuit of a shared universal common good and the equitable and peaceful distribution of resources, both spiritual and material. In this sense, if Israel is a sovereign nation, it also inevitably has a role to play in the larger world order in relation with other national partners, both regionally and globally, and its culture and spiritual and cultural patrimony as a country should be welcomed and engaged with within the larger context of the universal cultural patrimony of the nations. On this view, the State of Israel is both naturally accountable to international order and law, and can contribute to international order and law, as well as make contributions to the universal reflection of humanity regarding truth, justice, goodness, and beauty.

Third, while these natural law reflections can be acknowledged without overt and explicit appeal to biblical notions of the distinct identity of diverse peoples and nations, they are entirely compatible with a biblical Old and New Testament depiction of the human family, which acknowledges both distinct nations and their roles in the divine economy and the larger universal order of all nations, within the unity of the one human race. Within this context, the ancient nation of Israel is understood (in an admittedly quite complex way) through its texture of biblical law, ritual, covenantal self-understanding, prophecy, writings, tribal history, kinship, and state agency, to provide a distinct message of a given chosen people to the whole of the human race.

This idea of one people influencing all others through the unique covenant God has enacted with them is not contrary to the principles of natural law stated above, but is compatible with them, albeit in a very exceptional way.[17] If ancient Greece could contribute a heritage of philosophical inquiry to European culture and from that culture to the world, then one people, the Jews, can contribute the prophetic testimony of a divinely inaugurated covenant that has consequences for all of humanity. Christianity of course understands the ancient law of Israel as being capable in Christ of transforming all of the nations even while respecting and preserving unique elements of the national genius and originality of each people and culture. My point in making this third observation is simply to underscore that none of the points made above previously regarding a natural law acknowledgment of

17 Aquinas argues for the reasonableness of this claim in *Summa Theologiae* I-II, qq. 98–105; see *Summa Theologica*, trans. English Dominican Province (Benziger, 1947). I have argued along a similar line in theological commentary on revealed law in Thomas Joseph White, *Exodus* (Brazos, 2015).

the modern State of Israel stand in any kind of profound tension with a plenary acknowledgment of the teaching of either the Hebrew scriptures or the New Testament with regard to the prophetic origin of Israel, even as the natural law doctrine in question also does not depend per se upon one's reception or not of that biblical revelation. This is why the Catholic Church's natural law argument for the political sovereignty of the modern State of Israel is something that all peoples can recognize in principle, insofar as they are capable of recognizing the political sovereignty of any other state, including that of Israel's neighbor states and the autonomous political destiny of its adjacent peoples.

I express all this while remaining highly conscious of the question of the political destiny of the Palestinian people in the Palestinian territories and the Gaza Strip. The natural law principles I am appealing to here in favor of some form of state sovereignty of Israel might also apply in a different application to the question of Palestinian self-determination and legal self-government, as well as territorial autonomy, without prejudice to the legal recognition of Israel as a partner state. The Catholic Church in its diplomatic agency has advocated traditionally for the possibility of a two-state solution for the two peoples, with an insistence on the possibility of long-term peaceful coexistence in justice, equity, affability, and reasonable concord.[18]

The Rights of Religious Freedom and of Conscience

The second notion, as mentioned above, pertains to respect and tolerance for the religious freedom of others, not only for individuals but also for collective populations, and for religious and non-religious minority subgroups within states. It is significant that the original 1993 accord of mutual recognition on the part of the Holy See and the State of Israel appealed in a special way to the principle of the rights of religious freedom and of conscience. There are two significant features of this appeal that should be acknowledged.

The first has to do with the evident mutuality of the principle as it applies to this relationship. The State of Israel is constituted at least in part by a majority religious and cultural patrimony, that of Judaism and of Jews. The Jews are not a race, as has often been pointed out, but are a people born of a common religious movement and identity and defined effectively both historically and essentially by reference to that religious identity. Traditionally speaking, a Jew is one born of a Jewish mother, gradually inducted into the practices of Judaism by rituals of biblical origin. However, in a broader

18 Pertinent in this regard is the 2015 *Comprehensive Agreement between the State of Palestine and the Holy See*.

context, a Jew is a person born of Jewish lineage, capable of being identified sociologically and historically with the Judaic tradition. The Church's recognition of the modern State of Israel as a legitimate sovereign state cannot be understood integrally, then, without reference to a historical Judaic people. Their appeal to collective identity and political self-determination, as well as security and wellbeing, finds a natural complement, then, in the Church's appeal to the principle of the rights of religious freedom. Israel has a Jewish religious heritage and so the collective freedom of conscience of its members is a dimension of its civic life. This modern Catholic appeal to a principled religious freedom is also related to the Church's condemnation of antisemitism and the repudiation of various past Christian theologies of contempt of Jews, that led to or were associated with atrociously unjust historical practices of anti-Judaism and antisemitism on the part of Christian believers, both medieval and modern.

On the theme of mutuality, however, the appeal to this principle of religious freedom cuts both ways. The notion is meant, in the context of the 1993 Accord, to underscore not only the above-mentioned acceptance of Jewish self-determination, but also the religious rights of those non-Jewish communities and individuals living in Israel, not least the Christian populations and religious communities present in the Holy Land. This idea is further related to various Catholic institutions and works of the Church present in the Holy Land that serve the needs of pilgrims or religious, academic, or cultural visitors of various kinds. The Catholic Church does underscore the significance of Jerusalem as a universal pilgrimage site for the international community.

This point is important as signifying something more than the mutual recognition of dignity and freedom of religious conviction by Jews and Christians alike. It also sets out a format for engagement by appeal to a principle of natural law, one that is in fact of medieval origin but that has gained greater currency in the modern period.[19] The human being, and thus de facto all communities of human beings, are marked by a desire for religious truth, and therefore have not only obligations but also sacred rights to seek the truth about God in conscience, and that obligation and right cannot be supplanted or dismissed by extrinsic political impositions.[20] At the heart of the culture of political freedom is the freedom to seek the truth,

19 On the origins of the doctrine of the right of religious freedom, see Robert Wilken, *Liberty in the Things of God: The Christian Origins of Religious Freedom* (Yale University Press, 2019), and Dominic Legge, "Do Thomists Have Rights?," *Nova et Vetera* (English edition) 17, no. 1 (2019): 127–47, which specifically underscores Aquinas's affirmation of the rights of religious conscience of Jews in the medieval context.

20 See the argument in Thomas Joseph White, "The Right to Religious Freedom: Thomistic Principles of Nature and Grace," *Nova et Vetera* (English edition) 13, no. 4 (2015): 1149–85.

especially the truth about God, and so the respect for religious freedom is a kind of foundational freedom at the heart of modern political life that must be considered as something essential to the healthy exercise of civic polity both within individual states and between states.[21]

A second feature of this 1993 appeal to the right to religious freedom in the accords between the Holy See and the State of Israel is connected with the principle of Catholic social doctrine mentioned in the conclusion of the previous section of this essay. Namely, the sovereignty of nations is related to the cultural individuality of each nation that, in turn, should be able to communicate with and enrich the collective cultural patrimony of humanity. As I noted above, this natural law principle, which is defensible by an appeal to unaided human reasons as a norm for the just collective life of all peoples, receives a very special application, or is subject to a very special realization, in the case of the people of Israel in the ancient world. They not only contributed from their culture to the larger spiritual patrimony of the ancient Near East, and later to the Hellenistic and Roman civilizations. They also specifically contributed, within this historical dynamic, a supernatural or prophetic revelation of the truth regarding the one God in his relation with the human race.

I have argued above that in a modern context it makes little sense for Catholic Christians to appeal to a divine right to the land in Old Testament prophecy as a basis for thinking about the modern State of Israel and its state sovereignty in regard to international law. This being said, the appeal to the right to religious liberty, *when combined with* the Catholic social doctrine notion of the sovereignty of the state as a sovereignty of an individual culture, does produce the idea, stated in Catholic terms and on Catholic grounds by appeal to natural law, that the modern State of Israel should be allowed to exist in political freedom *at least in part* to perpetuate a living expression of modern Judaism, as a religious voice in the contemporary world.

Let us be clear about what this claim does not entail. It does not entail that the Catholic Church considers modern Judaism in its variegated forms to be simply identical with the Judaism of the ancient world or the Second

21 See in this respect the argument of Pope John Paul II, Encyclical Letter *Veritatis Splendor* (August 6, 1993), 79: "The primary and decisive element for moral judgment is the object of the human act, which establishes whether it is capable of being ordered to the good and to the ultimate end, which is God. This capability is grasped by reason in the very being of man, considered in his integral truth, and therefore in his natural inclinations, his motivations and his finalities, which always have a spiritual dimension as well. It is precisely these which are the contents of the natural law and hence that ordered complex of 'personal goods' which serve the 'good of the person': the good which is the person himself and his perfection. These are the goods safeguarded by the commandments, which, according to Saint Thomas, contain the whole natural law (Cf. *ST* I-II, q. 100, a. 1)" (available at vatican.va).

Temple period prior to the coming of Christ, nor that Judaism represents a voice that Christians consider equally valid or potentially more valid than that of the New Testament and the church's apostolic teaching. Nor does it entail that all that is taught by contemporary Jewish religionists is to be considered without error, even serious error at that; nor that Israel as a state exists somehow mystically only or primarily for religious self-expression, as if secular Jews were somehow undeserving of plenary rights or plenary judicial and political respect under the terms of international law. In fact, this claim only signifies that insofar as the modern State of Israel is a homeland for the expression and international communication of religious ideas pertaining to the Jewish tradition, it has the right to do so, in accord with the norms of respect given to religious traditions in accord with natural law. The modest nature of this statement is an advantage, I think, for Catholic relations with Jews. It does not require respect of Israel based on any strong theological grounds of concord or prearranged theological criteria, but rather based on the respect of religious conscience which is endemic to cultures and thus also in a particular way to various nation-states. This idea does not require one to renounce the Catholic practice of communication of the plenary truth of the Gospel, including to Jewish persons, in Israel or outside of Israel, but it does qualify the way that any such activity as this is conducted by recognizing the individual and collective rights of religious self-determination of peoples. After all, the proposal and communication of the Gospel to all peoples is also in accord with a plenary understanding and acknowledgment of the right of religious freedom and the universal human obligation to seek religious truth. The communication of the truth can take place in plenary respect of the religious consciences of human persons and out of charity for them, in respect for their capacity to reach the plenitude of the truth.[22]

22 Second Vatican Council, *Dignitatis Humanae* (December 7, 1965), 1: "All men are bound to seek the truth, especially in what concerns God and His Church, and to embrace the truth they come to know, and to hold fast to it. This Vatican Council likewise professes its belief that it is upon the human conscience that these obligations fall and exert their binding force. The truth cannot impose itself except by virtue of its own truth, as it makes its entrance into the mind at once quietly and with power. Religious freedom, in turn, which men demand as necessary to fulfill their duty to worship God, has to do with immunity from coercion in civil society. Therefore it leaves untouched traditional Catholic doctrine on the moral duty of men and societies toward the true religion and toward the one Church of Christ" (available at vatican.va).

Christians and Jews Within a Single Divine Economy: Collective Destiny and Potential for Common Aims

As I have noted above, there is a third principle that governs Catholic relations with the State of Israel. This notion is not one that pertains to natural law per se, but that is theological in nature, and proper to the Catholic Church's interpretation of the New Testament. It pertains to the theological notion of a common spiritual patrimony and potentially convergent mission shared by Jews and Christians within a singular divine economy. While this idea is specific to Catholicism, not Judaism, it is something that can be understood by Jews who explore or analyze Christian self-understanding, and such understanding of Christians on the part of Jews can be of assistance in thinking about mutual relations of the Holy See and the State of Israel, since it allows Jews to understand the deeper theological motivations of Catholics for the continued respect for the State of Israel, which color or qualify the natural law considerations mentioned above, without supplanting them or providing for their foundations and justifications per se.

Here we can note first, then, the major theological claim of the Second Vatican Council document *Nostra Aetate* which is well known to all: the Christian affirmation that God's covenant with the Jewish people, modern inheritors of the law and promises of ancient Israel, is unbroken and enduring.[23] Catholic Christianity holds to a nuanced or carefully qualified understanding of this claim. The Church generally maintains a kind of fulfillment theology of the law and the prophets, which sees the inner form of ancient Judaism as consisting in the spiritual life of faith, hope, and charity toward God and neighbor, embodied in the law and ceremonies of the Torah, and brought to fulfillment in the age of Christ, in his person.[24] Fulfillment does not indicate annulment or cancelation however, and so the classical Talmudic and more modern forms of expression of Israel's common faith in God are interpreted by some Catholic theologians as a testimony to the

23 Second Vatican Council, *Nostra Aetate* (October 28, 1965), 4: "The Church keeps ever in mind the words of the apostle about his kinsmen: 'theirs is the sonship and the glory and the covenants and the law and the worship and the promises; theirs are the fathers and from them is the Christ according to the flesh' (Rom 9:4–5), the Son of the Virgin Mary. . . . God holds the Jews most dear for the sake of their Fathers; He does not repent of the gifts He makes or of the calls He issues: such is the witness of the Apostle. In company with the Prophets and the same Apostle, the Church awaits that day, known to God alone, on which all peoples will address the Lord in a single voice and 'serve him shoulder to shoulder' (Zeph. 3:9)."

24 This is clearly the spirit of *Nostra Aetate* 4 as well as "Gifts" (2015). For a treatment of fulfillment themes in Catholic theology of the Jewish people, see Matthew Levering, *Engaging the Doctrine of Israel: A Christian Israelology in Dialogue with Ongoing Judaism* (Cascade Books, 2021).

enduring fidelity of God to the Jewish people and of the Jewish people to God.[25] Even less so does this fulfillment theology require or mandate contempt for the enduring legacy of Judaism, and indeed one can appeal to it precisely so as to underscore in Catholic terms the value and theological significance of the enduring reality of Judaism in the world. Furthermore, and importantly, the Catholic theology of the enduring mystery of the Jewish people and their role in salvation history underscores a shared eschatological destiny. Christians and Jews participate in differentiated ways in a common eschatological hope for the definitive coming of the messiah and the final redemption of the world.[26]

The shared destiny of the Church and the Jewish people, then, is obvious: they each appeal to a common source of revelation (in the Hebrew scriptures), and they have a shared messianic and eschatological hope, in part. What divides the two peoples is an irreducible difference of understanding of Jesus of Nazareth, who Catholic Christians acknowledge as both messiah and Lord. But what divides them is also, paradoxically, what unites them in part, under a distinct aspect. Jesus of Nazareth as a member of the Jewish people and an interpreter of Scripture clearly unites the gentiles of the world gathered into the Church to the Jewish people, with whom they associate themselves through Jesus, and because of Jesus and the early Christian movement (especially the New Testament writings), the gentiles of the Church receive the Torah, the prophets, and the writings of ancient Israel, acknowledging them as scripture, and bring these writings to all peoples of the world. For the duration of world history, then, so long as there is a Catholic Church and a Jewish people, there will be intra-historical relations of significance between the two. They share in a common witness to the one God, the prophetic revelation, the covenant, law and prophecy, messianic expectation, the importance of martyrdom, and eschatological hope in God.

How does this relate to the State of Israel? Not, so I have argued, by appeal to a divine right to the land but rather in virtue of the notion of *Nostra Aetate* regarding the enduring covenant and economic role of the Jewish people in the history of God's dealings with humanity. The unbroken

25 See the helpful considerations in Gavin D'Costa works: *Vatican II: Catholic Doctrines on Jews and Muslims* (Oxford University Press, 2014) and *Catholic Doctrines on the Jewish People after Vatican II* (Oxford University Press, 2019).

26 *Catechism of the Catholic Church*, §840: "And when one considers the future, God's People of the Old Covenant and the new People of God tend toward similar goals: expectation of the coming (or the return) of the Messiah. But one awaits the return of the Messiah who died and rose from the dead and is recognized as Lord and Son of God; the other awaits the coming of a Messiah, whose features remain hidden till the end of time; and the latter waiting is accompanied by the drama of not knowing or of misunderstanding Christ Jesus."

covenant doctrine of Romans 9–11 affirms the theological meaningfulness of the ongoing existence of the Jewish people and its eschatological horizon. The organization of the modern State of Israel is one way in which the Jewish people continue to understand themselves in relation to God down through time, in fidelity to the unbroken covenant and as an expression of that fidelity, but also in ongoing eschatological hope. Here is the salient theological point: The ongoing covenant of the people with God does not depend upon the modern State of Israel but the modern state may in some qualified ways embody or express the ongoing commitment to the pursuit of the covenant with God on the part of the Jewish people.

This notion of the modern State of Israel as animated by a desire of at least some significant portion of the Jewish people to remain faithful to the covenant with God is distinct from a divine right to the land. The covenant of faith, hope, and love for God that animates Judaic belief in God, and in the Torah and the prophets, implies only an indirect relation to the modern State of Israel, whatever its territorial boundaries. The spiritual life of the covenant is an essential element of theological significance in the Church's eyes, and does reach its teleological fulfillment eschatologically in Christ, whereas the land need not, or may not, even if there are natural law grounds for respect for the state sovereignty of the modern State of Israel in a given historical time and framework, that is, as a modern nation-state.

However, one can in a qualified sense speak here of the theological fittingness of the enactment of the covenant on the land of Israel. What is "fitting" in Catholic theology (*conveniens* in Latin) is not strictly necessary but it is also not merely arbitrary. It is not strictly necessary that the covenant of God and the Jewish people that continues down through the ages be lived in the State of Israel. But such a practice is not wholly arbitrary or meaningless either. There is a kind of reasonableness to the aim of modern Jews to live out their religious aspirations of absolute fidelity to God on the land historically associated with the prophetic life of ancient Israel. However, this point should not bear too much weight for Catholic theology, for two reasons. First, the appeal to a distinctly theological notion as a pretext for the justification of the aims of Jews to live in Israel today as a modern nation-state carries a risk of hollowing out the Catholic Church's basic commitment to the recognition of the State of Israel by founding this recognition on a theological grounding that is somewhat novel, not tested by time, and has no widespread acceptance. Second, the appeal to natural law and to international law is important as a structure by which to analyze critically and adjudicate rival claims to territorial sovereignty by peoples adjacent to Israel or living within its territories. Analysis of such natural law principles is essential to the search for just practices and to the aspiration for long-term collective peace and justice, shared between regional partners.

This does not mean that the notion of the theological fittingness of the privileged embodiment of the covenant within the modern State of Israel is merely empty or useless when thinking about the relation of the Catholic Church and Israel. On the contrary, this notion allows for one to think about shared spiritual and corporeal works of charity and mercy that the Holy See and the State of Israel—that Christians and Jews—can agree on and collaborate in, even while accepting disagreements and agreeing to discuss (or even perhaps not to discuss) their ongoing religious differences. Here we can name a few: the care of the poor, the respect of the rule of law and of principles of justice, the end of antisemitism, the respect of common human rights, the aspiration to world peace, and the just distribution and use of resources. These are shared biblical and prophetic moral aspirations, with eschatological implications: to incarnate the Torah in history in preparation for the coming of a new age, in which God's glory is manifest more perfectly, even most perfectly, within the context of world history and of creation. This is a messianic age we hope for in common, which Christians refer to in terms of the definitive coming of Christ.

Our mutual differences of understanding of this reality need not impede profound cooperation between Jews and Christians, including in tandem with works of the State of Israel in collective collaboration with Christian institutions and entities. Christians and Jews can work together intellectually as well, to reflect on common philosophical and theological, artistic and historical convictions that stem from the word of God. In pursuing all these measures, we are pursuing a greater order of international peace, constructive cooperation between the religious traditions of the world, appeal to norms of international law, but also a common witness, in differentiation, to the Torah and the prophets, and to messianic expectations, that all the nations collectively might come to recognize the God of Israel, and call on his name, the name above every other name, that every knee should bow and every tongue confess the Lord, the God of Israel (Is 45:22–24, Phil 2:6–11).

CONCLUSION

It can be noted that I have argued for a natural law approach on the part of Catholic Christians to the accords governing the relations of the Holy See with the modern State of Israel. This idea is coordinated closely in Catholic thinking with the idea of the respect of religious freedom and of conscience as it applies to the collective expression of religious cultures, manifest in this case in the form of modern Judaism in the State of Israel. By shying away from an appeal to a theology of divine right to the land, I have underscored instead the perennial natural law foundations for Christian respect for state sovereignty and self-determination by the people of Israel. However, I have also underscored the importance of the Catholic theological vision of the perduring covenant of God with the Jewish people, insofar as it relates indirectly but really to the ongoing life of the Jewish people today in the land of Israel. This life in a concrete place of shared legal sovereignty is not essential to the covenant as such but is a fitting expression of it and therefore one that Catholic Christians can respect for theologically motivated reasons, without thereby expressing a position in favor of a divine right to the land. Ethical and religious cooperation is possible between Christians and Jews, as is a partially common testimony to the sources of revelation and a partially common messianic expectation, and eschatological hope in God. These shared values and aspirations can affect relations between Christians and Jews not only generally but also specifically in relation to the State of Israel, insofar as the culture and activity of the modern State of Israel provide for a venue of exchanges and ethical collaborations between members of each of these religious traditions.

May the official relations between the Holy See and the State of Israel flourish, then, not only as an expression of abiding respect among peoples seeking a common justice and peace for the international order, but also as an expression of peoples seeking God, and finding God, in accord with a common witness to God's revelation to Israel, one that should be shared with all the nations.

16

ZIONISM THROUGH THE PRISM OF BIBLICAL 'GERISM'

A PROPOSAL

Yonatan Moss

I was struck by the fundamental differences between Marc Rastoin and David Meyer's presentations, so I begin with them as an entry into my own proposal.[1] For Marc Rastoin the heart of the problem is both theological and political. Theological in the sense that it is about ascertaining God's will; political, in the sense that it concerns the question of Zionism as a whole. Rastoin's question is how Catholic theology should "take into account the existence of the State of Israel?" That question, for him, boils down to whether we can say that "the actual Zionist state is a divine ordinance"? Rastoin's approach is careful and humble, as befits his weighty questions. He heeds to the prophetic lesson that the ways of God are different from our own, and he heeds to history's reminders that moments of deepest darkness can turn out to be beacons of salvation, as much as "what begins as salvation can finish in darkness." Thus, in the end, Rastoin's essay is a series of unanswered questions. He writes that "we cannot affirm as Catholics that God is *not acting* in the new Jewish political life on the land," and then he adds: "but we cannot affirm *with certainty* that modern political Zionism comes from God."

1 Editor's note: This essay was originally a response to Rastoin and Meyer but the editors requested that it be made into a main paper for the question of the relation of religion and the state. The reader may prefer to read Rastoin and Meyer's essays first (chapters 18 and 19), although this essay is clear in its own terms.

Rastoin's political theology is apophatic. Yet, despite his refusal to answer the questions he poses, he insists on one key principle that must guide Catholic discussions of the matter. Inspired by the Jewish values of Jesus and Paul, Rastoin beautifully calls this principle *ahavat Yisrael*, the love of Israel. This means, according to Rastoin, "willing the best for Israel" and it entails the belief "that God wants the people of Israel, his elect forever, to live till the end." Although he cannot say *where* and *how* God wants the Jewish people to live in prosperity and health, Rastoin is sure *that* this is something God wants. Thus much he is willing to discern the divine will.

Turning to David Meyer's paper we find ourselves on very different ground. God's will is not up for discussion. Meyer's challenge and proposal are linguistic and halachic; not theological, nor, really, political. While sharing Rastoin's caution and hesitation in speaking about such a sensitive topic as "the land, its holiness and the divine promise attached to it," Meyer's approach is far from apophatic. He seeks to rethink holiness, both our general religio-linguistic understanding of the category, and, more specifically, our halachic understanding of it. Unlike Rastoin, Meyer is not interested in the meaning or value of Zionism as a whole. It seems that for him, Jewish sovereignty is a practical and theological given. The question for Meyer is pragmatic: how to create "a religious language of peace" that would, as he says, "offer some prospect of hope and negotiation in the region." Meyer proposes to do so by a sophisticated, selective, and creative reading of Talmudic and later rabbinical sources that leads, ultimately, to the disassociation of holiness from possession. He articulates a halachic language of holiness that allows for voluntary relinquishment of land in exchange for peace. Rather than losing holiness from being decoupled from possession, the land gains it from that very act, both through the advancement of peace and through the restitution of justice to its inhabitants.

In my own thinking about these issues, I find that Rastoin and Meyer's papers complement each other. Put simply: in a way, Rastoin's question speaks to me more than Meyer's; but Meyer's answer, in a way, speaks to me more than Rastoin's. Let me explain. I am neither a Catholic nor a theologian. Discerning God's will in current affairs, whether it be from a Catholic perspective, or from a Jewish one, is not something I feel I can do. I think Rastoin did well to conclude that we cannot determine God's stance on Zionism. Yet, I think Rastoin was right on the "marc" (!) in still posing the bigger question of the theological meaning of Zionism, the religious meaning of renewed Jewish sovereignty. This to my mind is the primary challenge; not the questions of land for peace and the holiness of the land, which currently seem less relevant, as the two-state solution unfortunately seems very far off on the horizon. Yet as, on the one hand, Israel is becoming more integrated into its Arab surroundings, and Palestinians are (in a sense) becoming more integrated into Israeli society, on the other hand, relations between Jews and Arabs within Israel are also becoming increasingly fraught, including scenes of worrisome violence moving in both directions, we do well to ask at this time: What is the religious meaning of the existence of the Jewish polity? What is its meaning, not in terms of the land, but in terms of the people? In seeking to answer these questions, I sympathize with Meyer's creative, non-apophatic approach of looking for underexploited resources within our tradition.

Within the narrow confines of this short essay, I would like to make one such proposal, which I have not seen elsewhere, but which seems to me crucial to the understanding of the meaning of Zionism. Before proceeding I should stress that I speak not as a theologian (which I am not), nor as a comparative religionist (which I am supposed to be; yet what I propose here I do not do *ex illa cathedra*). I speak as a Jew, who turns to the Torah for insights about his existential questions.

I begin with a midrash, from Genesis Rabbah, on the famous words that Abraham says to God in his attempt to dissuade him from destroying the wicked town of Sodom: "Shall not the judge of all the earth do right?" (Gn 18:25). The midrash, taking characteristic exegetical liberty, reads this not as a rhetorical question, but as a statement:[2]

> Said R. Levi: 'The judge (*šōpēt*) of all the earth shall not do right (*mišpāt*).' If you wish to have a world (*'ôlām*), there is no judgment (*dîn*); and if you wish judgment, there is no world. You are grasping the rope at both ends by wishing to have both the world and judgment. If you do not give up a bit, the world will not stand. God replied: 'You love justice (*ṣedeq*) and hate wickedness (*reš'a*) (Ps 45:7/8): [this means]: you love to justify my creations, and you hate wickedness, namely you refuse to indict them [the word for wickedness, *reš'a*, can be understood as 'indictment'] . . .

This midrash encapsulates a notion that some 1,500 years later Isaiah Berlin would call the incompatibility of values. Our most important and basic values are often in tension, if not conflict, with each other. Berlin gave such examples as the pairs of liberty and equality; mercy and justice; knowledge

2 *Gen R.* 49.9 (see also *Gen R.* 39.6): אמר רבי לוי: הֲשֹׁפֵט כל הארץ לא יעשה משפט: אם עולם אתה מבקש אין דין ואם דין אתה מבקש לית עולם. את תפיס חבלא בתרין ראשין. בעי עלמא ובעי דינא, אם לית את מוותר ציבחר, לית עלמא יכיל קאים. א״ל הקדוש ברוך הוא אברהם (תהלים מה, ח): אהבת צדק ותשנא רשע—אהבת לצדק את בריותי ותשנא רשע, מאנת לחייבן. My transliterations of Hebrew follow the SBL academic standard; my transliterations of Arabic (below) follow the *Encyclopedia of Islam* system.

and happiness. The midrash constellates a different pair: judgment (*dîn*), namely, fairness, on the one hand, and 'the world,' in the sense of its very survival, on the other hand.

Yet, unlike Isaiah Berlin, who believed in the utter incommensurability of the value clashes, stating that "these collisions of values are of the essence of what they are and what we are,"[3] the midrash offers a resolution. It poses the higher value of justice (*ṣedeq*), which ultimately tips the scales in favor of survival, even at the expense of the infringement of judgment, of *dîn*. According to the midrashic reading, Abraham and God both agree that the utterly wicked dwellers of Sodom do not, according to judgment, deserve to live, but Abraham convinces God that the higher value of *justice* demands that they be spared.

I quote this midrash in support of the most basic tenet of Zionism, in its original Herzlian sense. The first, and, many would say, continuing, goal of Zionism is to ensure the survival of Jewish *bodies*. One can discuss whether the State of Israel succeeds in achieving that goal; whether Jews, in Israel and in the diaspora, are less endangered in our current reality than they would have been in the counterfactual scenario in which no Jewish state had been established. But on a spiritual level, beyond any practical test, it is in the midrash's understanding of Abraham's demand for divine justice that we find a prooftext for the premium that Zionism puts on sheer physical survival.

Herzl, and classic Zionist thought, sees the matter primarily from the perspective of Jewish bodies. In and of itself, I do not think there is anything wrong with that; but I also think there is potential for more. Marc Rastoin, following Daniel Boyarin, mentions the potential threat the "reality of the State of Israel" poses to "classical religious Talmudic Judaism." David Meyer attempts to recruit sources within that "classical religious Talmudic Judaism" to articulate a language of peace and compromise. Personally, I can identify with both projects. I also see the ways in which Talmudic culture is receding, or transforming, in the face of the reality of the State of Israel; I also sympathize with attempts to highlight strands within the rabbinic tradition that can speak to our present reality. But, at the same time, I think it is high season, given the radically different political reality ushered in by the very existence of the State of Israel, to think about the ways in which the mainstream of Talmudic culture is fundamentally ill-suited to our present situation, and to contemplate alternatives. After all, Talmudic culture was always a culture of the minority, of the powerless. Zionist culture, by its very definition, strives to be a majority culture that wields political power.

3 Isaiah Berlin, *The Crooked Timber of Humanity: Chapters in the History of Ideas* (Princeton University Press, 1990), 13.

My call to seek inspiration from other sources within our tradition besides the Talmudic ones is, of course, not new. From its earliest beginnings, central currents within Zionism sought to leapfrog over two thousand years of rabbinic tradition, back to the Hebrew Bible.[4] What Zionism found in the Bible is well-known: the Hebrew language; political and military independence; the connection to the land (often at the expense of its inhabitants); and the universal justice of the prophets.[5]

I think there is another highly important resource within the biblical tradition that is at the same time both very relevant to the meaning and message of Zionism and woefully untapped by Zionist thinkers, religious and non-religious (as far as I know). One way in which rabbinic language departs critically from its biblical inheritance concerns the word *gēr* (גר). As is well known, the biblical *gērîm* are minority "dwellers" in the land who do not belong to the majority population or culture.[6] The *gēr*'s status need not entail lesser rights or privileges, as the case of the patriarchs proves. For Genesis describes the latter as *gērîm*, both in the land of Canaan (e.g., Gn 20:1, 23:4, 26:3, 35:27) and in Egypt (e.g., Gn 12:11, 47:4). This is not because they were discriminated against by the local inhabitants; the narrative indicates that they were treated with respect. In Egypt they enjoyed privileges as the family of the viceroy Joseph. But they were *gērîm* because they were a minority group dwelling among a different population and culture.

Similarly, Pentateuchal law legislates equal rights for both the majority and the minority: "The community is to have the same rules for you and for the *gēr* residing among you. This is a lasting ordinance for the generations to come. You and the *gēr* should be the same before the Lord" (Nm 15:15). It should be emphasized that although the minority *gēr* may be a newcomer to the land and its majority culture, such as was the case with Abraham and

4 For this trend, and internal critiques of it, see Anita Shapira, "The Bible and Israeli Identity," *AJS Review* 28 (2004): 11–42, esp. 30–32.

5 This topic has been much studied. For two examples (written from different perspectives), see Yaacov Shavit and Mordechai Eran, *The Hebrew Bible Reborn: From Holy Scripture to the Book of Books: A History of Biblical Culture and the Battles over the Bible in Modern Judaism,* trans. Chaya Naor (De Gruyter, 2007), 475–520; Nur Masalha, *The Zionist Bible: Biblical Precedent, Colonialism and the Erasure of Memory* (Routledge, 2013). For a study of the Bible's shifting reception within more recent Israeli society, see Shapira, "The Bible and Israeli Identity."

6 I prefer this definition, more resonant with our current political structures, to alternative definitions. The classic English translation of the biblical *gēr* is "resident alien"; another translation is "protected stranger." For an analysis of the term in the various biblical documents, see Jacob Milgrom, *Leviticus 17–22: A New Translation with Introduction and Commentary* (Doubleday, 2000), 1416–28 and 1493–1501; Samuel E. Loewenstamm, "Ger," *Encyclopedia Biblica* [Hebrew] (Bialyk Institute, 1954), s.v. See also Adi Ophir and Ishay Rosen-Zvi, *Goy: Israel's Multiple Others and the Birth of the Gentile* (Oxford University Press, 2018), 23–56.

Sarah and their descendants, both in Canaan and in Egypt, the word *gēr* can also designate, and, according to some scholars, most often does, minorities whose presence in the land has predated that of the majority.[7]

Although the *gēr*'s status need not entail discrimination, the risk is always there. That is what soon happened to the descendants of the Israelite patriarchs, who were enslaved by the Egyptian majority. It is precisely for this reason that the Torah is obsessive about the fundamental importance of treating *gērîm* with love and respect, giving, according to one Talmudic counting, no fewer than thirty-six different forms of that injunction.[8] The Torah itself repeatedly makes the link: love the *gēr* in your midst because you yourselves were *gērîm* in Egypt.[9] Viewed within the context of the biblical documents' ancient Near Eastern surroundings, the concern expressed for the well-being and care of the *gēr* is both unprecedented and unparalleled.[10]

Yet a historical process that began in the Second Temple period, and culminated in the rabbinic period, led to a radical transformation of the biblical *gēr*.[11] The latter mostly ceased to be understood as a minority population, living among a majority, sovereign Jewish population—a reality that the rabbis, and many of their Second Temple predecessors, never experienced. Within the new conception, most appearances of *gēr* in the Bible came to be understood as references to converts to Judaism. Although Talmudic

7 See Loewenstamm, "Ger," 2.547: "It seems that most of the *gērîm* in Israel were those among the land's earlier inhabitants whom the Israelites did not succeed in expelling." Milgrom, *Leviticus 17–22*, 1416, viewed things differently: "The *gēr*, however, is a resident alien; he has uprooted himself (or has been uprooted) from his homeland and has taken permanent residence in the land of Israel."

8 *b. B. Metzia* 59b; according to another count there, the number is even higher, 46, and according to yet another source (*Midrash Tanhuma, Leviticus* 2), the number is 48.

9 This link is made four times in the Pentateuch: Ex 22:20 (21), Ex 23:9; Lv 19:34; Dt 10:19. See further below.

10 José E. Ramírez Kidd, *Alterity and Identity in Israel: The Ger in the Old Testament* (De Gruyter, 1999), 112–16.

11 The rabbinic evidence is clear. See, e.g., Moshe Samet, "Conversion in the First Centuries C.E.," in *Jews and Judaism in the Second Temple, Mishnaic and Talmudic Period: Studies in Honor of Shmuel Safrai*, ed. Aharon Oppenheimer, Isaiah Gafni, and Menahem Stern (Yad Yitzhak Ben-Zvi, 1993), 316–43; Ophir and Rosen-Zvi, *Goy*, 180–83. The Second Temple evidence is debatable. The Septuagint often uses προσήλυτος (the origin of our "proselyte") to translate *gēr*; the question is whether already in that context the word was intended to mean "convert." See, e.g., Loewenstamm, "Ger," 2.549, and Martin Goodman, *Mission and Conversion: Proselytizing in the Religious History of the Roman Empire* (Clarendon, 1994), 72–73, as opposed to Matthew Thiessen, "Revisiting the προσήλυτος in 'the LXX,'" *JBL* 132 (2013): 333–50 (followed by Ophir and Rosen-Zvi, *Goy*, 180n3). By the time of Philo, at any event, it is clear that the Septuagint's προσήλυτος was usually understood as a convert. See Samuel Belkin, *Philo and the Oral Law: The Philonic Interpretation of Biblical Law in Relation to the Palestinian Halakah* (Harvard University Press, 1940), 44–48. See also further below.

literature does distinguish between the *gēr šenitgayēr*, or, less commonly, the *gēr ṣedeq*—both designations for the convert—and the *gēr tôšaḇ*—the resident alien—it interprets almost all biblical references to the *gēr*, including, most importantly, the repeated injunctions to love and honor the *gēr* as referring not to the latter category, but to the former category, namely converts to Judaism.[12]

In some later sources we find a certain extension of the laws concerning the *gēr* from converts to yet a third category: the Jew who has moved from one community to another.[13] But the laws, and the whole moral outlook, concerning the *gēr*, in the original, biblical sense of the word, namely a member of a minority population living among a Jewish majority, were, with some precious exceptions, almost completely lost in rabbinic literature and subsequent halachic deliberation and codification.[14] I will later return to the "precious exceptions" signaled in the previous sentence, highlighting one major early medieval rabbinic voice that offers a more biblically-tinged outlook on the *gēr*, one that swims against the majority rabbinic consensus. But first I want to spell out what I sense is the hitherto woefully untapped potential of biblical gerism within the context of modern Zionism, for this is the heart of my essay.

Fulfillment of such biblical obligations as "you shall love the *gēr*, for you were *gērîm* in the land of Egypt" (Dt 10:19); and "you shall not wrong or oppress the *gēr*, for you were *gērîm* in the land of Egypt" (Ex 22:20[15]) is only possible in a political and demographic situation of majority and minority populations. If Jews—and any other nation, for that matter—are to fulfill this biblical vision they require precisely that political sovereignty that Zionism has sought, and succeeded, to accomplish. But no less importantly, of course, the minority population is also required. Understood through the lens of what may be called the Torah's gerist ideology, the Arab, and other non-Jewish, residents of the land and citizens of the state are not an obstacle or a cause of tension. Precisely the reverse. Their continued presence and flourishing in

12 See, e.g., *Mekhilta d'Rabbi Ishmael, Neziqin* 18; *Sifra Kedoshim* 4.4; *b. B. Metzia* 59b. For the relative infrequency of the term *gēr tôšaḇ* in the rabbinic corpus, see Samet, "Conversion in the First Centuries C.E.," 337–40; Ophir and Rosen-Zvi, *Goy*, 180–81.

13 Bahya ben Asher, *Kad ha-Kemah*, s.v. *gēr*; Israel Meir Ha-Cohen, *Sefer Mitzvot Katzar*, s.v. *ahavat ha-ger*.

14 See the succinct summaries of the halachic codification on all matters pertaining to the *gēr*, in the *Talmudic Encyclopedia* [Hebrew] (Talmudic Encyclopedia Institute, 1947–), s.v. *ahavat ha-ger, ger, ger toshav, gerut*.

15 Ex 22:21, according to other divisions.

the land define the very project of Jewish political independence.[16] Biblically speaking, the Jewish state depends on the Arabs. Only through the just and loving treatment of its minority populations can the State of Israel fulfill its biblical promise. At the moment, Israel remains very far off from achieving that goal; but without Zionism, just as without Israel's Arabs, there would be no way *at all* to fulfill it. Rather than giving up on Zionism, let us perfect it in light of the promise of its biblical roots. The moral luxury of Talmudic powerlessness may meet the nearsighted, individualistic demands of *dîn* (judgment) but it fails miserably at the bigger, and more critical, test of *ṣedeq* (justice). Pursuing that justice, by saving Jews and honoring Arabs, is the meaning of Zionism.

I stress that, unlike the original, pre-democratic biblical political context, the current situation in which political independence is embodied in a democratic context, differences between majority and minority must be reflected only in matters of demography and culture, and not in any way in civic, political, legal, religious, or economic rights. In a biblical "gerist" fulfillment of Zionism the Arabs of Israel would flourish no less, if not more, than Jews do, as a demographic and cultural minority in democratic states around the world (as well as in, one would hope, a future democratic State of Palestine). In contradistinction to the prevalent conception that sees a tension between the modern State of Israel's "Jewish" and "democratic" aspects, in the gerist vision these are not even two contradictory, or even completely independent, aspects. Rather than contradicting each other, these two aspects, in the alternative conception that I am proposing, mutually reinforce each other. Democracy is what enables the best fulfillment of the state's Jewishness, and the biblical demand from the majority not just to vouchsafe for the minority's rights, but to actively *love* the minority, offers a spiritual foundation for the state's democratic essence and identity.

I mentioned earlier that despite the overwhelming rabbinic consensus shifting the majority of the biblical injunctions about the *gēr* from the non-Jewish minority to the convert to Judaism, some whispers can be found of another voice within medieval rabbinic culture that harks back to the biblical categories. Although several instances of this alternate voice could be cited and developed at length, in the remaining space of this contribution

16 It is at this crucial point that my suggestion differs from the common treatments of the question of Israel's minorities within the context of Jewish law. Within those treatments the question of the status of the minority is dealt with on an *ex post facto* level, rather than as an a priori, desired ideal, as I am arguing here. For examples of the usual approach to the question, see Eliezer Hadad, *The Status of Minorities in the Jewish State: Halakhic Aspects* [Hebrew] (Israel Democracy Institute, 2010); David Novak, *Zionism and Judaism: A New Theory* (Cambridge University Press, 2015), 197–224.

I would like to focus on what I believe is the very first instance of this alternate viewpoint. It comes from the Egyptian-Iraqi rabbinite luminary Rabbi Saadia Gaon (882–942), who as academy head, prolific writer, and community leader, had a long-lasting effect on medieval Judaism.[17] Saadia's partial reorientation away from the rabbinic understanding of the *gēr* and back toward the biblical understanding is somewhat surprising given that he is known for his trenchant defense of rabbinic halachic tradition in the face of the challenges mounted against it by the contemporary Karaite movement.[18]

Saadia's biblical *gerism* emerges most clearly in his influential translation of the Pentateuch into Judeo-Arabic.[19] Saadia's translational approach to the biblical *gēr* significantly departs from the most famous rabbinic translation of the Pentateuch, namely Targum Onkelos, the traditional Aramaic version, which Saadia knew well and elsewhere usually followed.[20] In order to appreciate the full measure of Saadia's innovation, we must first present Targum Onkelos's approach to the word *gēr* and all its associated verbal forms.

Targum Onkelos, which may date from anywhere between the early second and the fifth centuries,[21] and, which, interestingly, is traditionally thought to be the work of a convert,[22] strongly reflects the rabbinic tendency

17 See, e.g., Robert Brody, *The Geonim of Babylonia and the Shaping of Medieval Jewish Culture* (Yale University Press, 2013), 235–335.

18 See, e.g., Robert Brody, *Sa'adyah Gaon*, trans. Betsy Rosenberg (The Littman Library of Jewish Civilization in association with Liverpool University Press, 2013), 147–54.

19 While not the very first translation of the Bible, or parts thereof, into Arabic, Saadia's had the longest and widest appeal. It was used by Jewish communities across the Arab world throughout the generations, and is still in use among some Jewish congregations today. For the impact of Saadia's translation within the Jewish community, see most of the studies collected in Yitzhak Avishur, *Studies in Judaeo-Arabic Translations of the Bible* (Archaeological Center Publications, 2001; in Hebrew and English). For the impact of Saadia's translation outside the Jewish world, see Berend Jan Dikken, "Some Remarks about Middle Arabic and Saʿadya Gaon's Arabic Translation of the Pentateuch in Manuscripts of Jewish, Samaritan, Coptic Christian, and Muslim Provenance," in *Middle Arabic and Mixed Arabic: Diachrony and Synchrony*, ed. Liesbeth Zack and Arie Schippers (Brill, 2012); Ronny Vollandt, "Sa'adia Gaon's Translation of the Torah and Its Coptic Readers," in *Jewish Biblical Exegesis from Islamic Lands: The Medieval Period*, ed. Meira Polliack and Athalya Brenner-Idan (SBL Press, 2019), esp. 81.

20 See, e.g., Haggai Ben-Shammai, *A Leader's Project: Studies in the Philosophical and Exegetical Works of Saadya Gaon* [Hebrew] (Bialik Institute, 2015), 12. See further Joshua Blau, *Notes on R. Saadya Gaon's Translation of the Torah: Part I: Genesis* [Hebrew] (Israel Academy of Sciences, 2019), *16-*17, citing Ex 21:11, 21:24, and 23:19 as examples of Saadia's translational changes made to accord with rabbinic halacha. The third example ("do not cook a kid in its mother's milk" translated as "do not cook meat in milk") follows Onkelos.

21 See Judah (Otto) Komlos, *Encyclopedia Biblica* [Hebrew] (Bialyk Institute, 1988), 8.743; Philip S. Alexander, "Targum, Targumim," in *Anchor Bible Dictionary*, ed. Meira Polliack and Athalya Brenner-Idan (Doubleday, 1992), 6:321.

22 *b. Megilah* 3a; *b. Gittin* 56b; *b. Avodah Zarah* 11a.

to convert (as it were) the biblical *gēr* into a convert to Judaism. Thus, when the Pentateuchal text employs the word and its derivatives to refer to *non*-Israelites in situations, following the conquest of the land of Canaan, where Israelites will be the majority corporate identity, Onkelos, will, as a rule, offer Aramaic cognates denoting conversion: *giyōrâ* (גיורא), *yitgayar* (יתגיר), etc.[23] The most common formulation of this type is: "When a *gēr* sojourns (*yāgûr*) with you" (Ex 12:48; Lv 19:33; Nm 9:14, 15:14), which Onkelos invariably translates as "When a convert (*giyōrâ*) converts (*yitgayar*) among you."[24]

When, by contrast, the text uses *gēr* words to speak of Abraham, Isaac, Jacob, or of Moses and the Israelites, Onkelos will only translate them with words denoting either temporary residence or permanent dwelling; never with words denoting conversion to a different corporate identity. This is for the simple reason that the Pentateuchal narrative is itself the story of the emergence of Israelite corporate identity, in the transition from family, to tribe, to nation. It would make no sense to interpret statements about the patriarchs' *gēr* status in Canaan and Egypt, or statements about the Israelites' *gēr* status in the land of Egypt (e.g., Ex 6:4, 22:2, 23:9; Lv 19:34) or Moses's phrase about being a *gēr* in Midian (Ex 2:22, 18:3), as indicating conversion to the corporate identity of the surrounding majority culture. In all those cases Onkelos understands the *gēr* words in their original, non-technical, sense of residence or dwelling, employing most frequently the Aramaic root *dwr* (דור: "to reside"), and, less often, the root *ytb* (יתב: "to dwell").[25]

Naturally, Onkelos first begins to employ "conversionist" vocabulary only in the last four books of the Pentateuch, once, according to the biblical narrative, an Israelite people has emerged, and a situation in which it will occupy majority status within its own land can begin to be imagined.[26] While Onkelos never refers to conversion in his translation of *gēr* words in

23 On Onkelos's unified translational policy regarding diverse derivative from the same root, as applied specifically in this context, see Rafael B. Posen, *Parshegen: Explanations, Commentaries, and Sources concerning Targum Onkelos: Exodus* [Hebrew] (Parshegen Institute, 2015), 434.

24 See further Ex 12:49, Lv 16:29, 17:8, 10, 12, 13; 18:26; 20:2, Nm 15:15, 26, 29; 19:10, for similar phrases, all translated in the conversionist sense by Onkelos.

25 See Rafael B. Posen, *The Consistency of Targum Onkelos' Translation* [Hebrew] (Magnes, 2004), 274–77.

26 Toward the end of Genesis, the family of Jacob is referred to as "Israelites" (בני ישראל), e.g., Gn 42:5 and 46:5; it is only in the Book of Exodus that the larger collective begins to be referred to as a people (עם), e.g., Ex 1:9 and 15:13 (although "Israelites" continues to be used, far more frequently, to refer to the collective).

Genesis,[27] his translation for those words in the rest of the Pentateuch, following rabbinic tradition, is, as noted just above, almost always "conversionist."[28]

Onkelos's translational policy leads to various difficulties. If, according to rabbinic halacha, the status of the convert to Judaism is no different from that of Jews from birth, the injunction in Leviticus 19:33: "when a *gēr* sojourns with you in your land, you shall not wrong (תונו—*tônû*) him" appears redundant. For there is another command not to "wrong (תונו—*tônû*) one another" (Lv 25:14, 17). It is due to this redundancy that later codifiers established that wronging a convert constitutes an additional transgression to wronging a native-born Jew, even if is the same exact act of wronging in both cases.[29]

Besides the difficulty of redundancy, Onkelos's translational policy leads to a serious exegetical difficulty in the following four verses that equate the situation of the *gēr* in "your land"' with that of the Israelites in Egypt:

27 I leave to the side the notion, attested in rabbinic sources of different periods, that Abraham and Sarah were the founders of conversion to Judaism, and are considered the Jewish parents of all future converts. On the rabbinic notion, see, e.g., *Sif. Deut* 32; *Gen R.* 84:4; and Chana Safrai, "Abraham und Sara: Spender des Lebens," *Evangelische Theologie* 62, no. 5 (2002): 348–61. Onkelos hints at this understanding in his translation of the segment in Gn 12:5 referring to the "souls" Abram and Sarai "had acquired" (presumably referring to the slaves they acquired) as the "souls they subordinated to the Torah."

28 I have pointed out this difference between Genesis and the rest of the Pentateuch, and given the reason for it, to counter an argument recently made with reference to the other, earlier, and even more famous, ancient Jewish translation of the Pentateuch, namely the Septuagint. Due to space constraints, I will not delve too deeply into the matter here, but only present the general contours of the question, which cannot be ignored in this context because it figures prominently in studies of the history of the transition from biblical to rabbinic conceptions of the *gēr*. Simply put, the Septuagint seems to display a similar pattern to that found in Onkelos. The Greek word the Septuagint translators often use for *gēr* is προσήλυτος (the origin of our "proselyte"). In his classic, oft-cited, article, "On the Meaning of ΠΡΟΣΗΛΥΤΟΣ in the Septuagint," *Expositor* IV, no. 10 (1894): 264–75, W. C. Allen showed that "in the great majority of cases where *ger* occurs in the Hebrew text, the Greek translators have not simply translated into the exact Greek equivalent, but have read into the word the later meaning which it has in the Mishna" (266). Allen shows how subsequent translations, primarily Onkelos, but also the Syriac and the Ethiopic versions, "seem to follow the LXX." Allen's conclusions had long been followed in scholarship, but they have recently been challenged by Thiessen, "Revisiting the προσήλυτος." Thiessen argues that different translational policies are evident for the different Jewish Greek translations of the different books of Bible that only later come to be grouped together as the Septuagint. He claims to have shown "that there is no firm evidence that any translator used προσήλυτος to mean a convert to Israelite or Jewish religion." I am not convinced, primarily due to the overarching similarities between the Septuagint's translational choices and Onkelos," which are, for example, identical in Genesis (for the reasons given above). Thiessen, unlike Allen, completely ignores this important comparative evidence.

29 Maimonides, *Mishneh Torah*, "Laws of Sale," 12:1 and 14:15–17 (on the basis of *b. B. Metzia* 59b; see further *Shulhan 'Arukh, Hoshen Mishpat* 228.2). For the universal injunction against wronging both Jews and non-Jews, see Maimonides, *Mishneh Torah*, "Laws of Sale," 18.1, and *Shulhan 'Arukh, Hoshen Mishpat* 228.6.

> You shall not wrong or oppress the *gēr*, for you were *gērîm* in the land of Egypt (Ex 22:20[21]).
>
> You shall not oppress the *gēr*; you know the soul of the *gēr*, for you were *gērîm* in the land of Egypt (Ex 23:9).
>
> The *gēr* who sojourns with you shall be to you as the native among you, and you shall love him as yourself; for you were *gērîm* in the land of Egypt: I am the Lord your God (Lv 19:34).
>
> You shall love the *gēr*, for you were *gērîm* in the land of Egypt (Dt 10:19).

In each of these four verses, which we may classify as the "equationist" verses, Onkelos, in keeping with his policy, translates the *gēr* whom you are to treat fairly and love, as a convert (*giyōrâ*), while he translates the *gērîm* which you once were in Egypt, as sojourners (דיירין: *dayārîn*). The exegetical problem with such an approach is obvious. The whole point of these four verses is to establish an equivalence between the Israelites' *gēr* status in Egypt with the status of the *gērîm* residing among them. The equivalence breaks down if two different words are used to denote the two elements of comparison, especially given that the sojourner and convert experience different kinds of otherness vis-à-vis the majority group. It may be said that the sojourner's otherness, felt at any moment in his given present, is synchronic, whereas the convert's, stemming from a change of status that occurred in the past, is diachronic.

Scholars have noted the exegetical difficulty with Onkelos's translation of these four verses.[30] Other ancient translations, namely the Septuagint,[31] the Samaritan Aramaic versions,[32] and Palestinian Aramaic Targum Neofiti,[33] all also apparently under the influence of the notion of *gēr* as convert, attempt to

30 See, e.g., Dov Rappel, *Targum Onkelos as a Commentary on the Torah* [Hebrew] (Hakibbutz Hameuchad, 1985), 98–99.

31 Thiessen, "Revisiting the προσήλυτος," 342–43, views this fact as proof that the LXX translators of the Pentateuchal books did not have a "conversionist" understanding of προσήλυτος.

32 The situation in the Samaritan Targum is complex, for it is extant in two main "branches" which differ on this question. One branch consistently offers "convert" words for both sides of the equation, while the other offers for Lv 19:34 the word תותב (*tôtāb*), meaning "dweller" for both sides of the equation. See Abraham Tal, *The Samaritan Targum of the Pentateuch* [Aramaic and Hebrew] (Tel-Aviv University, 1980–81), 1.314–17, 2.84–85, 337. On questions of dating, and similarities between the Samaritan Targum and Onkelos, see Alan D. Crown, *Samaritan Scribes and Manuscripts* (Mohr Siebeck, 2001), 17–18.

33 See Alejandro Díez Macho, *Neophyti 1: Targum palestinense, Ms de la Biblioteca Vaticana* (Consejo superior de investigaciones científicas, 1970), 2:145, 151. Although the Aramaic word used there is the same as Onkelos's גיורא (*giyōrâ*), the translators into the various European

solve the problem by making both sides of these verses refer to converts, but doing so only creates a new problem by having the text refer to the Israelites in Egypt as converts![34] Even the late ancient translations of the Bible that may be thought to be less beholden to the tradition culminating in the rabbinic period that makes the *gēr* a convert, offer versions of these verses that do not entirely skirt the problem. Thus, to cite one example,[35] while the Syriac Peshitta offers a clean solution for Exodus 22:20(21) and 23:9,[36] its translations of Leviticus 19:34 and Deuteronomy 10:19 use "conversionist" language in the first parts of the verses and "sojourning" language in the second parts of the verses, thus creating the same problems discussed above.[37] It is only when we reach Saadia Gaon, in the tenth century, it appears, that we find a clean solution to the problem. What is interesting is that this solution comes from a champion of rabbinic Judaism, whose approach to the question must come at the cost of sidelining the rabbinic tradition on the *gēr* in these cases, alongside many others.

Like Onkelos, and all other translators, ancient and other, Saadia's Arabic translation of the *gēr*'s appearances in Genesis employs a word meaning "stranger" or "foreigner": *gharīb* (غريب גריב).[38] There is nothing original in this, for, as we have seen, all agree that the patriarchs in Canaan and Egypt had the status of a minority population. What is original in Saadia's translation is that he uses the same word to translate most appearances of *ger* also when they are used in the later books of the Pentateuch to speak of the

languages provided in this edition opt, I think incorrectly, for "sojourner" words, rather than "conversionist" ones.

34 This embarrassment is often reflected in variants within the textual tradition that attempt to solve the problem. See, e.g., Díez Macho, *Neophyti 1*, 2.145.

35 The situation reflected in the Latin translations, both the Old Latin and Jerome's Vulgate, is interesting in this regard, but due to its complicated nature I will not get into it here.

36 Ex 22:20(21): "You shall not wrong or oppress sojourners (ܥܡܘܪ̈ܐ), for you were sojourners (ܥܡܘܪ̈ܐ) in the land of Egypt"; Ex 23:9: "You shall not oppress the sojourners (ܥܡܘܪ̈ܐ); you know the soul of the sojourners (ܥܡܘܪ̈ܐ), for you were sojourners (ܥܡܘܪ̈ܐ) in the land of Egypt."

37 Lv 19:34: "Those who turn to me (ܐܠܝܢ ܕܡܬܦܢܝܢ ܠܘܬܝ) who sojourn with you shall be like you and from among you; love them as yourselves, for you too were sojourners in the land of Egypt: I am the Lord your God"; Dt 10:19: "You shall love those who turn to him (ܐܠܝܢ ܕܡܬܦܢܝܢ ܠܘܬܗ), for you were dwellers (ܬܘ̈ܬܒܐ) in the land of Egypt."

38 E.g., Gn 15:13: "Your seed shall be *gharīban* (foreign) in a land that is not theirs"; Gn 23:9: "I am a *gharīb* (stranger) and a *ḍayf* (guest) among you." For more on the word *ḍayf*, here translating Hebrew *tôšaḇ* (תושב), see note 53 below. Saadia's "minority" understanding of *gēr*'s appearances in Genesis, as reflected in his translation of it with *gharīb*, emerges also in his commentary on Genesis. See, e.g., his comments on Gn 15:13 and 23:4, in Moshe Zucker, *Saadya's Commentary on Genesis* [Judeo-Arabic and Hebrew] (The Jewish Theological Seminary, 1984), 117, 144–45 (Arabic), 360, 404 (Hebrew).

local, non-Israelite minority dwelling among the Israelite majority. Unlike the Septuagint, Onkelos and the other ancient translators, who all followed, to one degree or another, the ancient "conversionist" tradition, Saadia, with few exceptions, retains their otherness. Thus, for the four "equationist" verses we discussed above, Saadia offers:

> You shall not wrong or oppress the *gharīb* (stranger; גריב غريب), for you were *ghurabā'* (strangers; גרבא غرباء) in the land of Egypt (Ex 22:20).
>
> You shall not oppress the *gharīb*; you know the soul of the *gharīb*, for you were *ghurabā'* in the land of Egypt (Ex 23:9).
>
> The *gharīb* who comes in among you[39] (*al-dakhīl fī mā baynakum*; אלדכיל פי מא בינכם; الدخيل في ما بينكم) shall be to you as the native among you, and you shall love him as yourself; for you were *ghurabā'* in the land of Egypt: I am the Lord your God (Lv 19:34).
>
> You shall love the *gharīb*, for you were *ghurabā'* in the land of Egypt (Dt 10:19).

With one slight exception, to be discussed soon, the injunctions to love and not to wrong the *gērîm*, according to the simple meaning of Saadia's translations, which themselves follow the simple meaning of these verses, refer not to converts to Judaism but to those minority populations who live among the Israelites in the land of Israel. Saadia offers the same translation for the injunctions in Deuteronomy commanding the Israelites to take care of the more vulnerable groups within society: the widows, the orphans, the Levites (who do not possess their own lands), and the *gērîm*.[40] Whereas Onkelos consistently offers *giyōrâ* ("convert") for those *gērîm*,[41] Saadia lets us know that the command refers to the strangers in our midst, consistently offering the Arabic word for "stranger," not the word for convert.

It is clear that Saadia uses the word *gharīb* in its general sense of "stranger," "minority," or "sojourner," and not as a synonym for "convert," because he also has another word he uses for *gēr*, in certain contexts, which does indeed have a "conversionist" meaning. The word is *dakhīl* (דכיל; دخيل),

39 This phrase will be explained shortly.

40 E.g., 14:29; 16:11, 14; 24:19, 20, 21; 26:12, 13. This category is not limited to Deuteronomy, but is most common there. See, e.g., Lv 19:10.

41 And, similarly, the Septuagint gives προσήλυτος in all these cases.

which literally means "he who enters," but came to denote the convert[42] (in a semantic process identical to Greek προσήλυτος, "he who has come over").[43] Thus, when the Torah includes the *gēr* in the framework of the laws of sacrifice,[44] of Yom Kippur,[45] and in dietary,[46] sexual,[47] and cultic and purity-related[48] prohibitions, Saadia uses the *dak̲hīl* root, either in conjunction with *g̲harīb*, such as *al-g̲harīb al-dak̲hīl fī mā baynakum* ("the sojourner who comes in among you"),[49] or on its own, such as *dak̲hala fīkum dak̲hīl* ("he who enters has entered"), or simply *al-dak̲hīl* ("he who enters").[50] In all those cases, which can be said to be of a more ritual, or cultic, context, Saadia follows Onkelos's usage of *giyōrâ*, and consistently employs *dak̲hīl* to indicate that these injunctions do not apply to all inhabitants of the land, but only to the Israelites, both native-born and those who have "entered," namely the converts. They are the ones who are required to fast on Yom Kippur, to bring sacrifices, to observe the sexual and dietary laws, and so forth. The latter demands are not made on the non-Israelite minorities living in the land.[51]

42 Saadia's contemporary, Jacob al-Qirqisānī, speaks explicitly of "he who has entered into the religion" *al-dak̲hīl fī al-dīn* (אלדכ'יל פי אלדין; الدخيل في الدين); see Joshua Blau, *A Dictionary of Mediaeval Judeo-Arabic* [Hebrew and Judeo-Arabic] (The Academy of the Hebrew Language / The Israel Academy of Sciences and Humanities, 2006), 207.

43 This is not the place to elaborate, but it is interesting to note that the post-biblical tradition give us two main words for conversion, one based on a notion of "turning," and the other based on a notion of "coming over," or "entering." Traditions such as the Greek and the Arabic, which use "entering" words, do not use "turning" words, and traditions such as Syriac and Latin, which use "turning" words, do not use "entering" words. Furthermore, Latin *advena*, meaning "he who has come over," is used in precisely non-conversionist contexts (see, e.g., 1 Pt 1:1). For interesting observations on this terminological question in the rabbinic corpus, see Samet, "Conversion in the First Centuries C.E.," 343.

44 Ex 12:48; Lv 17:8, 22:18; Nm 9:14, 15:14–16, 26, 29.

45 Lv 16:29.

46 Lv 17:10, 12, 13.

47 Lv 18:26.

48 Lv 20:2; Nm 19:10.

49 This is the most common phrase, found, e.g., in Lv 16:29; 17:8, 10, 12, 13; 18:26; 20:2; Nm 15:26, 29. There are also other variants, such as Ex 12:48: "*dak̲hala maa'kum g̲harīb*" ("a foreigner who has come in with you").

50 Both in Nm 9:14.

51 Two interesting exceptions to this rule are the prohibition against leaven on Passover (Ex 12:19) and work on Sabbath (Ex 23:12) where Saadia uses only *al-g̲harīb*. Saadia must have understood these prohibitions as a matter of public interest, not just private practice. It is interesting that it is precisely these two areas of Jewish observance that have the greatest impingement on the public square in Israel today, following the legislation of Israeli laws banning the display of leaven in public during Passover, and laws relating to the permissibility of commerce on the Sabbath. Another special case is the cities of refuge. Saadia sensitively translates Nm 35:15, which legislates the founding of six cities of refuge for those who kill inadvertently, as including everyone:

When it comes, however, to how the Israelites must treat the *gēr*, Saadia, as we saw above, uses "stranger," and not "convert," language. Departing from the rabbinic tradition, reflected in Onkelos's Aramaic translation, which had understood the verses commanding love for the *gēr* and prohibiting his mistreatment as referring to the convert, Saadia translates them as referring to the non-converted minorities living among the Israelites.

Nevertheless, there is a caveat. In three out of the four "equationist" verses commanding fair treatment of the *gēr* on the grounds that "you were *gērîm* in Egypt," Saadia uses only the word *gharīb*. Yet in one of those four cases—Leviticus 19:34—he synthesizes it with *dakhīl* language: "The *gharīb* who comes in (*dakhīl*) among you shall be to you as the native among you, and you shall love him as yourself; for you were *ghurabā'* in the land of Egypt . . ." It is unclear why Saadia chose to translate this one verse with an added "conversionist" tinge.[52] Perhaps he does so as a nod to the rabbinic tradition, which understands that there is a positive commandment to love the convert. Thus, Saadia cleverly leverages the Pentateuch's repetition of the command to love the *gēr* to extricate two injunctions from it: to love the non-Jewish minorities living in your midst, and to love the converts to Judaism.[53]

Alongside his influential translation of the Pentateuch, Saadia authored a detailed commentary on parts of the Pentateuch, explaining many of his translational choices. Unfortunately, most of the commentary has not survived directly, but parts of it can be reconstructed thanks to citations by subsequent authors. Abraham Ibn Ezra's commentary on Exodus 22:20, "You

"the children of Israel, the *gharīb, and the dakhīl*." Protection is equal to all, whether they be of the majority, of the minority, or of those who have converted from the minority to the majority.

52 One might think that this is due to the added verb: הגר הגר אתכם (*ha-gēr ha-gar itkem*)—"the *gēr* who dwells with you," unique among the four cases. Yet, Saadia translates the previous verse (Lv 19:33), which also has an added verb, without using "conversionist" language: "When a *gēr* resides [*gar*] with you in your land, you shall not wrong him." Saadia offers: "When a *gharīb* resides [*sakana*; סכן, سكن] with you in your land, you shall not wrong him." There is no hint of conversionist language in Saadia's version of that verse (although Saadia's version of the verse goes against the rabbinic tradition which predicates the command on the convert. See note 29 above).

53 Before moving on, it is worth noting that in four places Saadia uses one other word to translate *gēr*: it is the word *ḍayf* (ضيف, צ'יף), meaning "guest." Saadia uses it only in cases where *ger* appears with a possessive pronominal suffix: Ex 20:10 and Dt 1:16, 5:14, 24:14. In certain other cases where *gēr* appears with a possessive pronominal suffix he will use *gharīb*, but drop the suffix (Dt 29:10, 31:12). Saadia interestingly avoids applying possessive suffixes to the words *gharīb* and *dakhīl*. Both members of the non-Jewish minority populations and converts simply cannot be said to be "yours," in the way that your guest can. Within modern criticism these appearances of the *gēr* with possessive pronouns have been understood as a Deuteronomic conception of the *gēr* as someone who can only enter into the Israelite community as a client, who must depend on an Israelite patron. See Saul Olyan, *Rites and Rank: Hierarchy in Biblical Representations of Cult* (Princeton University Press, 2000), 74–81.

shall not wrong or oppress the *gēr*, for you were *gērîm* in the land of Egypt," offers us a precious glimpse into Saadia's thinking about the *gēr*.

Saadia's comment comes in the context of his attempt to relate this verse to the preceding one, which, at first sight, seems completely unrelated. Exodus 22:19 reads: "Whoever sacrifices to any god, other than the Lord alone, shall be devoted to destruction." Ibn Ezra offers the following to report about Saadia's exegesis of the connection between the two verses:[54]

> "You shall not wrong the *ger*:" The Gaon (= Saadia) explained how this is related to the preceding verse, "Whoever sacrifices to any God. . ." The judgment on such a person is restricted to Israelites, who may not do as the people of Kuth, who "worshipped God, but also served their own gods" (2 Kgs 17:33). This is why it then says "you shall not wrong the *gēr*," for that refers to the case of someone like Na'aman, who worshipped God, but would also bow to his gods (2 Kgs 17:18). Thus, "you shall not wrong the *gēr*" refers to a resident *gēr* (as opposed to a convert), who has no succor . . .

The *gēr* whom Israelites are here commanded to love and not to oppress cannot be a convert, for otherwise the juxtaposition with the preceding verse (which Saadia understands as an opposition) would make no sense. Unlike the Israelites (including converts, of course), who must only worship God, the minorities living in their midst may worship God alongside other gods.[55] It is precisely due to that religious distinction that the Torah comes along and reminds the majority not to oppress the minority. Every care must be taken not to allow theological differences to be translated into social harassment or exploitation.[56]

54 Ibn Ezra (1089–1164) wrote two commentaries on the Book of Exodus. This passage is from the so-called short commentary, written first, in Italy:

'וגר לא תונה'—פירש בו הגאון: בעבור שהוא סמוך עם 'זובח', שדין הזובח הוא על ישראלי. וטעם 'לה' לבדו'—שלא יעשה כמעשה הכותים—'את ה' היו יראים', וטעם 'וגר לא תונה' כמו נעמן שהיה משתחוה גם לאלהיו. וטעם 'וגר לא תונה'—הוא גר תושב, כי אין לו עוזר...

In his later commentary on Exodus, Ibn Ezra makes no mention of Saadia, and interprets the verse and its link to the previous verse quite differently: the prohibition still refers to non-Jewish minorities (in contradistinction to the rabbinic tradition, as reflected in *b. B. Metzia* 59b, which limits it to converts to Judaism), but they must worship God alone, and this is why monotheistic worship is demanded in the previous verse.

55 In halachic discourse this category is called *shittuf* ("sharing"), which is prohibited for Jews. The medieval authorities discuss whether non-Jews are also prohibited to engage in *shittuf*. It plays a prominent role in the discussions about the halachic status of Christianity, which, according to a prominent halachic perspective, belief in the Trinity and the incarnation renders a form of *shittuf*. See Jacob Katz, *Exclusiveness and Toleration* (Schocken, 1973), 163–64.

56 It should be noted that there are some open questions about Saadia's exegesis here, which I cannot get into. They arise both from a difference within the manuscripts, and from another,

We do not know what it was about the *gēr* that led Saadia to complicate the traditional rabbinic position and to offer a reading that is both closer to the simple meaning of the biblical text,[57] and in line with the reading offered by his Karaite opponents.[58] Saadia's stance is later followed, to some degree, by Ibn Ezra,[59] and hints of its logic can be found among other writers.[60] It is precisely thanks to our new political reality that our ears have once again become attuned to those minority voices within the rabbinic tradition.

Those voices are themselves only echoing the Torah's clear words on this matter. It is thanks to Zionism that Jews in Israel, just like, I would hope, the majority culture in any other country, can understand the delicate social relationship envisioned in the biblical text: "When a *gēr* sojourns with you in your land, you shall not wrong him" (Lv 19:33). Only when it is "your land," namely when you are in majority status, can you fully understand that the *gēr* is the minority who lives in your midst, for whom you are responsible, for whom you are held accountable.

---

later, work of Saadia's where he seems to express a slightly different opinion. For more details, see *Torat Haim* (Mossad Harav Kook, 1986–93), Exodus II.43; Moshe Zucker, *On R. Saadia Gaon's Translation of the Torah* [Hebrew] (Feldheim, 1959), 347–48.

57 Saadia's translation was far from literal. For two studies of his translational techniques, see Haggai Ben-Shammai, "The Tension between Literal Interpretation and Exegetical Freedom: Comparative Observations on Saadia's Method," in *With Reverence for the Word: Medieval Scriptural Exegesis in Judaism, Christianity, and Islam*, ed. Jane Dammen McAuliffe, Barry Walfish, and Joseph Ward Goering (Oxford University Press, 2003), 33–50; Ronny Vollandt, "Flawed Biblical Translations into Arabic and How to Correct Them: A Copt and a Jew Study Saadiah's *Tafsīr*," in *Studies on Arabic Christianity in Honor of Sidney H. Griffith*, ed. David Bertaina et al. (Brill, 2018), 56–90.

58 See Zucker, *On R. Saadia Gaon's Translation of the Torah*, 194–95, quoting from Daniel al-Kumisi, Saadia's older contemporary, who read the command not to oppress the *gēr* as applying precisely to the non-Israelite minorities, not to converts. For what it is worth, it is interesting to note that we find already in Philo an approach to the biblical *gēr* that is similar to Saadia's. Philo normally understands the Septuagint's προσήλυτος as a convert, but in his comments on Ex 22:20 (21) and 23:9, he argues, based on the comparison to the Israelites' προσήλυτος status in Egypt, that there the command must not refer to converts but rather to the non-Jewish believers in God, in other words, to those whom the rabbis would later refer to as the *gēr tôšaḇ*, just as Saadia explains here. See Belkin, *Philo*, 46–47.

59 Unlike the rabbinic tradition, Ibn Ezra understands the injunction not to oppress the *gēr* as referring to minorities living in the land, but the latter must, according to his understanding, worship only God. See note 54 above.

60 See, e.g., *Sefer Ha-Hinukh* (thirteenth-century Spain), Commandment 331: "We must learn from this valuable injunction to have mercy on every sojourner in one's town, who is not originally from that place." The possible ramifications of this statement are reflected in the super-commentary *Minhat Hinukh*, by Joseph Babad's (ninteenth-century Ukraine), *ad loc.*: "It is clear that the author's words 'to have mercy on every sojourner' is a matter of general ethics, but is not strictly part of the injunction which is limited to converts alone."

Having explained my idea, I immediately want to note a certain discomfort I have with it. Although shifting the focus from land to the peoples that dwell therein, my proposal still looks at the matter from the perspective of one side. The minorities who play a crucial role in my scheme may be said to be treated functionally, even if positively.

If there's one thing we can learn from Jewish-Christian dialogue, it is the importance of mutual agency. How can the "gerist" vision of Zionism benefit from Muslim and Christian perspectives, Palestinian and other?[61] I would need to hear, and learn, from my neighbors.

61 For a Muslim majority perspective on non-Muslim minorities, see Anver M. Emon, *Religious Pluralism and Islamic Law: Dhimmis and Others in the Empire of Law* (Oxford University Press, 2012); for a Muslim minority, specifically Palestinian, perspective on Muslim minorities among non-Muslim majorities, see Iyad Zahalka, *Shari'a in Modern Times: Muslim Minority Jurisprudence* [Hebrew] (Resling, 2014); for an influential Muslim perspective on Islam within different minority situations across the world, see Muhammad al-Ghazali, *How We Should Think about the Future of Islam outside of Its Land* [Arabic] (Dār al-shurūq, 1997). For an interesting Christian perspective on the question, see Clive Pearson, "The Quest for a Coalitional Praxis: Examining the Attraction of a Public Theology from the Perspective of Minorities," in *A Companion to Public Theology*, ed. Katie Day and Sebastian Kim, Brill's Companions to Modern Theology (Brill, 2017), 418–40.

17

BRIEF REFLECTIONS

UNIVERSALITY AND PARTICULARITY, SECULARITY AND THEOLOGY

Judith Wolfe

Both papers raise the question of what counts as a 'theological' explanation or course of action, what counts as a 'secular' explanation or course of action, and why it matters which of these we adopt when we seek to explain or take action vis-à-vis the land and State of Israel. I will argue that the Jewish and Christian understandings of what counts as theological differ significantly and raise significant challenges for each other. I will also argue that both papers propose a mediating term between the theological and the secular—natural law in Catholic thought, gerism in Jewish thought—that may be able to govern the complicated terrain of a land inhabited by both Jews and non-Jews. These mediating terms may be more compatible than the two religions' theological positions *per se* and may suggest a fruitful way forward for each individually and together.

Generally speaking, from a Jewish perspective, the central mark of a theological approach is the acknowledgment of the divine election of Israel. To give a theological explanation of the people, land, and State of Israel means, first and foremost, to explain them in terms of their special election by God. Conversely, the central mark of a secular approach (from a Jewish perspective) is universality. To give a secular explanation of the people, land, and State of Israel means to evaluate them using principles or criteria that are generalizable across people groups.

A significant and challenging consequence of this framing of the distinction between the theological and the secular is that from a Jewish perspective, Christian theology is, in effect, often coextensive with secularity, because the general tendency of Christian theology is universalizing. It is a basic tenet of Christianity that the people-specific revelation and calling that marked the BCE era was, through the work of Jesus and the early church, widened to a revelation and calling addressing *all* peoples. From a Jewish perspective, this is tantamount to a denial of the central importance of Israel's election and therefore of the heart of a theological approach to people, land, and state. Only recently has an acknowledgment of Israel's special standing entered Catholic discourse, opening a new space for a dialogue that both sides recognize as theological.

However, this recent Catholic acknowledgment of Israel's ongoing election remains a relatively tentative and marginal *spanios legomenon* in Christian theology as a whole. It may play an important role in theological conversations going forward; nevertheless, in an interfaith discussion of the relative significance of theological versus secular approaches, it is crucial to emphasize that Christian theologians do not align theology with election and secularity with universality but, rather, distinguish between forms of universality that are proper to theological thought and forms that are proper to secular thought.

From a Christian perspective, secular 'universality' refers to modes of explanation that rely on principles and criteria which are naturalistically grounded and therefore allow replicability. In other words, within a secular explanatory framework, human behavior follows patterns that are explicable in naturalistic terms and generalizable across domains of life (including the religious and the political). Thus, for example, within such an explanatory framework, religious institutions are social hierarchies whose roles and dogmas can be analysed functionally without remainder. By contrast, theological 'universality' affirms the universal love of God for creation. This universality relies on a personal relationship with God and others—which involves, in Etienne Vetö's words, asymmetry, equality, and mutual dependence—and is therefore not reducible to homogenizing secular explanations or modes of action.

Instead, from a Christian perspective, a key difference between theological and secular frameworks of explanation and action is that theological frameworks rely on God's ability to transform reality. Christian theology begins from the assumption that religious belief can transform people at the deepest level, because reality transcends the structures that are basic to naturalistic conceptions of human psyche and society: above all, the conditions of scarcity and therefore competition that animate evolutionary and social dynamics. If secular explanations assume that human needs and behavioral strategies are necessarily determined by scarcity and competition, theological explanations trust that through God's grace, life is or can be radically different than it appears through a naturalistic lens. Rather than being determined or constrained by self-interest, such a life draws its energy and orientation from a conviction in the boundless love and plenitude of the divine, extended as gifts to humanity and creation at large. For Christian theology, scarcity and competition are the secondary or belated conditions of a sinful humanity; they are not intrinsic to the created world, and in the restored and glorified creation of the messianic kingdom, they will be decisively left behind. For Christian theology, this messianic kingdom will be established fully at the second coming of the messiah and the resurrection (and judgment) of all people at the end of secular history.

However, this kingdom has already been announced and inaugurated by the messiah's first coming, in the form not of a king but of a servant, and especially in his atoning death, his resurrection from the dead, and his ascension to heaven until his return. By doing so, the messiah has already proleptically defeated sin and death (and with them, the ultimate barrier to communion and plenitude). Through grace and the help of the Holy Spirit, those who believe in his redemptive work can already participate in the new life he has wrought, even though they are still partially subject to the conditions of a fallen world. Until his Second Coming in glory, and the establishment of the messianic kingdom after the resurrection of all flesh, this participation is always fraught and subject to conflict and error. It is a matter of considerable theological debate how the new life in the messiah interacts with the sinful life of individuals and their communities, and whether or to what extent God's grace should be expected to transform primarily the *disposition* of believers (e.g., enabling them to bear adversity and rejoice even in hardship) or also their *conditions* (e.g., protecting them from physical harm and material deprivation).

Within both Judaism and Christianity, theological principles inform not only reflection but also action. Such action includes the creation of communal and institutional structures. In Judaism, communal structures that are built on theological principles are, first and foremost, those that structurally affirm and protect Israel's election. In Christianity, institutional structures that are built on theological principles are, first and foremost, those that structurally rely on God's power of transformation. The Catholic Church as a whole is intended to be such a theological institution; monastic orders and similar communities are theological institutions in a more intense and radical form. The monastic vows of poverty, chastity, and obedience, for example, actively declare: 'Even if you take away from me the natural conditions of human flourishing—property, offspring, sexual intimacy, and autonomous choice—I will flourish by God's free and transformative grace.' Such theological institutions carry a great deal of risk: If the inner transformation on which they rely does not come about (or only very partially comes about), they may lead to deprivation and inner deformation, and/or harbor misbehavior and abuse. On the other hand, if inner transformation flourishes, they can be radiant testimonies to a source of life, grace, love, and hope beyond ordinary human resources.

The Catholic concept of natural law, which Thomas Joseph White invokes, functions as a mediating term between the theological and the secular within Christian thought. It assumes that the entire created order is, in principle and by nature, the work of God and under his governance, even though in practice human life and communities are always inflected by grace and/or sin. The concept of natural law therefore asserts that it is in principle possible to discern the needs and purposes whose attainment comprises natural human flourishing; to formulate the goods, rights, and obligations required to enable and safeguard such flourishing; and to make individual and communal decisions in accordance with them. This mode of argument governs a realm of explanation and action that neither relies on divine transformation nor cedes to a purely immanent frame. Rather, the concept of natural law (in distinction from both divine and human positive law) assumes that people naturally discern certain conditions of individual and communal flourishing and have the capacity to act in accordance with them. Although these conditions will not enable the *ultimate* flourishing that consists in a personal relationship with God, they nevertheless form an adequate basis for communal life in the world, within which humans can pursue such ultimate flourishing. (How the idea of natural law interacts with the Christian assertion of human sinfulness is another matter of considerable theological debate, and Christian traditions with a very strong emphasis on humanity's depravity tend to deny the existence of a natural law, or its practical usefulness, altogether.)

These accounts of the terms 'theological,' 'secular,' and 'natural' provide a clearer lens on the question regarding what it would mean to explain or build the State of Israel on theological principles, from a Jewish and from a Christian perspective. They also make clear that the Christian perspective, though different from the Jewish, might be able to inform Jewish thinking constructively. From a Christian perspective, there are two options. The first, which Fr. White suggests, is that the State of Israel falls within the realm governed by natural law, which demands recognition of "the rights of states to self-determination in accord with universal ethical norms and international law," as well as the religious freedom of individuals and communities. This approach positions the State of Israel as an establishment that is not itself built or explained on specifically theological principles, but which should nevertheless be a space within which theological lives can be pursued. The second option, which other authors in this book suggest, is that the State of Israel is itself a theological institution, that is, is structurally reliant on God's transformative power.

Christian history will make Christian theologians hesitant to affirm the second option, not because of a lack of faith in the Jewish people or their divine election, but because of Christians' own disillusionment with the possibility of relying for the formation of political systems on a community's inner transformation. In the past several hundred years, attempts at doing so have repeatedly engendered abuse and oppression in the Christian West and its colonial reach. The Catholic Church's recent official documents have therefore focused increasingly on the Church as a minority (sometimes using the biblical language of 'remnant' or 'leaven') whose mission is within and vis-à-vis the wider world, rather than as a political structure that is imperial in tendency.

The recent shift in the Catholic Church's attitude to the Jewish people firmly affirms that people's theological significance in both a Christian and a Jewish sense: that is, the Jews' receipt of God's transformative calling and gift. But for just that reason, and informed by the Church's own experience, Christians are reluctant to identify that significance with a political entity. Rather, they understand the theological significance of people and land primarily against an eschatological horizon, in which the coming of the messiah will indeed transform individuals, communities, and creation more widely. To our Jewish interlocutors, this affirmation might seem to have little to no real-world value. However, it can, at least, raise constructive questions for joint discussion, including the following: To what extent is the need for (and promise of) inner transformation part of a Jewish understanding of divine election and covenant? To what extent is such a transformation integral to the conception of the State of Israel? To what extent is it necessary as a condition of living justly in the land?

To some extent, Yonatan Moss's paper proposes answers to these questions by suggesting precisely that the Pentateuch demands of a sovereign Jewish community that it be more tolerant, even protective, of non-Jewish minorities in its land than is common among the nations—in other words, that Israel's divine election and covenant demand higher norms of fairness and faithfulness even to outsiders, funded by God's own faithfulness to Israel. Moss argues that these norms concerning strangers (or non-Jewish minorities) were systematically reinterpreted by the rabbinic tradition of the diaspora to refer to Jewish converts, largely because injunctions concerning minorities in their sovereign lands were irrelevant to Jews who were themselves minorities. A sovereign State of Israel, however, makes such questions once more urgent. In effect, therefore, Moss suggests that it is a covenant responsibility of Israeli Jews to treat strangers (or non-Jewish minorities) in accordance with what White presents as natural law—just as for White it is a covenant responsibility of Christians to treat Israeli Jews in this manner. For both, then, universality and particularity, secularity and theology interact in complex ways, both within each religion and between the two.

Fruitful further questions for discussion would include what Israel can learn from Christianity's long and often painful experience with the attempt to build political structures on theological principles, and whether or how Israel might be able to model a different practice; and, intractably but vitally, what the role of eschatology should be in our joint theological thought about Israel.

SECTION 5

CRITIQUE OF THE THEOLOGICAL AFFIRMATION OF THE 'LAND,' 'PEOPLE,' AND 'ISRAEL'

18

THE LAND, THE STATE OF ISRAEL, AND THE CATHOLIC CHURCH

Fr. Marc Rastoin, SJ

The promise of the land is inseparable from the God of Israel. This is a land made of earth and rivers, cities and hills. How do we take biblical divine promises, about land in particular, into account in Catholic theology today? How do we take into account the existence of the State of Israel? Is it possible for theology to find a place for Israel, the modern political entity, in the Catholic landscape?

I will try to offer a few lines of reflection but I am deeply aware of the complexity and sensitivity of the question. I have lived with this question since my childhood and I do not have a purely intellectual relationship to it. When I was fifteen, I was a Zionist and wrote graffiti "vive Tsahal" and "vive Sharon" on the tables and benches of my high school during the "Shalom haGalil operation" (1982). In the two decades that followed, I slowly moved from having these visceral Zionist feelings to a more critical approach. I read the books of Yeshayahu Leibowitz and came to understand his critical stance on the occupation.[1] For Leibowitz, the occupation in itself was a poison in itself, something that would endanger Israel's ethical position.

I met Daniel Boyarin in 2001 when he came to teach in Rome for the first time. And I discovered his point of view and his fear that a Talmud-based

1 See, in particular, Yeshayahu Leibowitz, *Israël et Judaïsme: Ma part de vérité* (Desclee de Brouwer, 1993).

Judaism be substituted by a neo-Hasmonean power Judaism.[2] What was he fearing? That the Israeli would more and more rely mostly on power and military strength. For him the Zionist 'new Jew' was very different from the man of studies of traditional Judaism.[3] He writes:

> On the stairs of my synagogue, in Berkeley, on Rosh Hashanah this year, I was told that I should be praying in a mosque, and versions of this, less crude perhaps, are being hurled at Jews daily by other Jews. [. . .] More piercing to me is the pain of watching a tradition, my Judaism, to which I have dedicated my life, disintegrating before my eyes. It has been said by many Christians that Christianity died at Auschwitz, Treblinka, and Sobibor. I fear, God forbid, that my Judaism may be dying at Nablus, Deheishe, Betein (Bethel), and El-Khalil (Hebron). [. . .] If we are not for ourselves, other Jews say to me, who will be for us? And I answer, but if we are for ourselves alone, what are we?[4]

Boyarin choose to leave the State of Israel; Leibowitz stayed.

In 2003, I wrote a short paper for a Catholic periodical, "The State of Israel: A Question for Judaism?," in which I expressed my fears for the spiritual future of the Jewish faith.[5] Leibowitz and Boyarin were always in my mind. This paper gave rise to a meeting with a Parisian rabbi who became a great friend. As with many great friendships, the beginning was rough but, as we continued our discussions, we realized that we shared many things in common. My question has increasingly become: What is the reality of the State of Israel doing to classical religious Talmudic Judaism? Does not the political and social reality now take precedence over the spiritual reality of the Jewish faith? The State helps to preserve Hebrew language and Jewish communal identity, but what is the cost in terms of the spiritual content of the religion? I am sure that I am not the only one living with those questions. With the passing of the years they become more and more urgent, not less.

2 See Daniel Boyarin, *A Traveling Homeland: The Babylonian Talmud as Diaspora* (University of Pennsylvania Press, 2015), *Judaism: The Genealogy of a Modern Notion* (Rutgers University Press, 2019), and *The No-State Solution: A Jewish Manifesto* (Yale University Press, 2023).

3 See on this point Daniel Boyarin, *Unheroic Conduct: The Rise of Heterosexuality and the Invention of the Jewish Man* (University of California Press, 1997).

4 See Daniel Boyarin, *Border Lines: The Partition of Judaeo-Christianity* (University of Pennsylvania Press, 2006), xiv. The last sentence is a clear allusion to the famous maxim by Rabbi Hillel as reported in the Pirkei Avot 1:14.

5 See Marc Rastoin, "L'Etat d'Israël: Une question pour le Judaïsme," *Croire Aujourd'hui* 166 (2003): 12–14.

I begin with several important, preliminary considerations before trying to articulate a tentative Catholic theological position.

THE GREAT REVERSAL

Until the creation of the State of Israel, and even until 1967, the vast majority of Jews lived outside the State. Most committed religious Jews still upheld the three oaths (see Ketubot 110b–111a). This term means the way the Talmudic tradition interprets the return "as a political force" in the land of Israel. It considered that it should be the mission of the messiah. Therefore pacific returns in Israel are allowed for individual Jews but there should not be a desire to establish a political power in the land. Diaspora is read as an exile decided by God and God will not allow the nations of the world to persecute the Jews in a disproportionate manner. We can understand why some Orthodox rabbis considered, during and after the Shoah, that the three oaths were no longer valid.[6]

Relevant here is Franz Rosenzweig's *The Star of Redemption*, published in 1921. In this philosophical and spiritual masterpiece, Rosenzweig articulated a vision of a Jewish faith outside the flow of history, living in a sacred *time* rather than a sacred *space*. Christianity on the contrary was immersed in the flow of world history and trying to bring God's message to the world. Rosenzweig conceived a kind of philosophical, modern reformulation of the Talmudic vision, as expressed for instance in Boyarin's *A Traveling Homeland: The Babylonian Talmud as Diaspora*: "where there is Talmud, there is Judaism." Judaism was in exile but this exile was not an obstacle to a life lived in accordance to the Torah: the covenant was alive and well. In a Christian world obsessed with the march of history and prone to permanent infighting, Judaism incarnated transcendence and the sense of the eternal. This powerful vision was shattered by the Shoah.

In the meantime, Catholicism was expressing a strong desire to implement (sometimes even heretically expressed as "to build"!) the kingdom on Earth. In 1925, Pope Pius XI instituted the Feast of Christ the King. To expand the Catholic Church was to expand the kingdom for "the Catholic Church, which *is the kingdom* of Christ on earth, [is] destined to be spread among all men and all nations."[7] In Portugal and Spain, national Catholic regimes came to power where the laws of the state had to follow the rules of the Catholic

6 See on this question the book by Yakov M. Rabkin, *A Threat from Within: A Century of Jewish Opposition to Zionism* (Zed Books, 2006). Of course the content, validity, and meaning of this midrash is widely disputed even today.

7 *Quas Primas*, §12; available at vatican.va.

Church.[8] But then came Vatican II and the theological attitude changed. The Catholic Church now entered a new era in which she did not have to rule politically or even to hold a privileged position in society. Of course many Catholics resisted—and still resist!—this new political stance. However, the Church adopted a new attitude to the state and to societies, accepting the fact that she is now an intentional minority rather than a majority willing to impose its values and faith.[9]

This drastic change in Church thinking affects the relationship between Catholics and Jews. In Israel, Jews were rediscovering political sovereignty in a definite territory. They now had to deal with religious and national minorities themselves. This is something of which they have had no experience since the first century; they are in a position they have not been in since the time of the Hasmoneans (if we put aside the partially mythical Khazar Jewish state[10]). When Israel was wondering if the law of the new State of Israel should be the religious law, and to what degree, Catholics at this period were moving in a quite different direction. They were trying to come to terms with the fact that they were now a minority and that they could not, and should not, try to import their religious convictions into civil law. In fact, Catholics can learn—or could have learned—from the Jews, had they wished to do so. Diasporic Jews lived for centuries in hostile or indifferent environments and still managed to keep their unity, beliefs, and customs. As Jean-Pierre Denis, a contemporary French Catholic thinker, says: "Finally, Catholics have become Jews like the rest of them."[11] How do I understand this enigmatic statement? Many Catholics have assimilated into global society and its values. Gradually their identity has disappeared. Others tend to form neo-orthodox subcommunities which try to isolate themselves from 'worldly influences.' The fact that Catholics do not have, like Jews, the genealogical element to help them

8 This refers to the Franco regime in Spain (1939–75) and the Salazar regime in Portugal (1933–74). How ironic that in France (during the 2022 presidential elections), the neo-Maurassist political leader pleading for a national Catholicism is none other than a Jew: Eric Zemmour. Charles Maurras (1868–1952) was a key French political leader of the first half of the twentieth century. While personally agnostic, he thought that Catholicism should be the ideological force behind the new French monarchic state he envisioned.

9 Even if Vatican II inaugurated this new era, the Church renounced constitutional advantages and privileges only reluctantly. And the political landscape, in Poland for example, testifies to the fact that this new condition is not easily accepted.

10 The Khazar state was an independent kingdom between the Caspian and the Black Sea that became very powerful at the end of the sixth century. It seems that the king and the elite became Jews around the eighth century (even if the fact is still hotly disputed): it is the source of the famous book by Rabbi Juda Halevi (1075–1141) entitled *Kuzari*.

11 This was in a tweet published in 2013. I quoted it in Marc Rastoin, "Le sfide della Chiesa in Francia," *Civiltà Cattolica* 3999 (2017): 270–83.

maintain their collective identity is becoming evident. Christian identity is eminently fragile. But can becoming a self-marginalizing closed community really be an evangelical solution?[12]

During the half-century that followed Vatican II, the Church revised her teaching about the Jews (see *Nostra Aetate* 4) and gradually accepted the way Jews viewed themselves. This implied more and more a growing recognition of the State of Israel. The Vatican enacted this recognition in 1993; yet it was presented as a formal diplomatic matter and not as a theological declaration about the legitimacy of the State itself. Nevertheless could such a decision had been taken without the whole theological reevaluation of Judaism since Vatican II? I think not. What the Holy See, as a political entity, decides, cannot be entirely detached from the Catholic Church as a spiritual body. It certainly constitutes a de facto legitimation of the modern State of Israel[13] and this was well perceived at the time. There is no such thing as a 'purely diplomatic' recognition.

Catholics are more and more like the Jews of the Diaspora. And today Israeli Jews are conducting themselves as the Catholics used to, in the countries where they were dominant. This is a reversal of great magnitude. I believe we can learn from each other.

INCARNATION AND LAND

Being a Christian is to accept the incarnation of Christ and the fact that the eternal God enters human history. If Jesus is considered to be the Jewish messiah fulfilling the prophecies, that implies accepting that Israel was chosen

12 Sociologically speaking, each human group (religious or not) has to keep a balance between boundaries (and their markers) and openness. Some fundamentalist Catholic groups show that it is indeed possible to live in Catholic self-constructed "ghettos." My point is that this choice is not an evangelical spiritual legitimate option, even if one can understand why this is a seductive choice. Famous is Rod Dreher, *The Benedict Option* (Sentinel, 2017), in which he writes: "What is needed is the Benedict Option, a strategy that draws on the authority of Scripture and the wisdom of the ancient church. The goal: to embrace exile from the mainstream culture and construct a resilient counterculture." Significantly, he left the Catholic Church in 2006 to become Eastern Orthodox.

13 That is, it says at least that granting this recognition does not constitute something that would go against the Catholic faith. When we remember what Pope Pius X said to Herzl on January 25, 1904, "We cannot give approval to this movement. We cannot prevent the Jews from going to Jerusalem—but *we could never sanction it*. The earth of Jerusalem, if it was not always holy, has been made holy by the life of Jesus Christ. I as head of the Church cannot possibly say otherwise. The Jews have not recognized our Lord; we therefore *cannot recognize the Jewish people*," we see the road that has been travelled. See Sergio I. Minerbi, "Le Saint-Siège, les Juifs et l'État d'Israël," *Outre-Terre* 9 (2004): 341, author of *The Vatican and Zionism: Conflict in the Holy Land 1895–1925* (Oxford University Press, 1990).

by the Lord and that a land was given to Israel as a people. This was not a gift to a religion or a faith-based community as much late-nineteenth-century thought would have it.[14] But which land exactly? And what is the extent of this land?

I have always been struck by the fact that the borders of the promised land have never been clearly established. Borders vary, and different tribes are sometimes included: Jebusites or Gibeonites, for instance. Some of the twelve tribes are on the east side of the Jordan. Bashan, which is more or less the present-day Golan, has almost always had a Jewish population. The coastline has generally been populated and politically dominated by non-Jewish peoples. This vagueness has a purpose: it is a real obstacle to declaring the land and its borders to be sacred. This 'sacralizing' is very different from sanctifying. To sacralize is to attribute a quasi-divine aura to a created reality. To sanctify is to bring God's holiness to created realities. Family, nation, or work have to be sanctified, but not sacralized.

The most important figures in the history of Israel are the prophets, rather than the kings.[15] The beginning of the first Book of Samuel makes this very clear. The reader is expecting the birth of a *shaul* boy, the wanted son his mother is asking for. It is Samuel, the future prophet, who is given prominence and not the future king—Saul (see 1 Sm 1). When the people were without king, temple, or land, they kept their faith that God would bring them back to the land. Their faith showed them, also, that they were able to live outside the land. Later, the Babylonian exile from the land was read as God's judgment on the king and on the nation's infidelities.[16]

A special place in the land is Zion, or more precisely the Temple Mount. The second Temple was destroyed in 70 CE. Was this destruction a judgment of God? It turned out that Israel could live by faith and in synagogues without the sacrificial rituals of the Temple. Most halakhic authorities would say that the rebuilding of the third Temple will be accomplished by the messiah

14 It was common at the time for French or German Jews to describe themselves as "Français de confession mosaïque" or "deutsche Staatsbürger mosaischen Glaubens." The national, ethnic, and genealogical dimension of the Jewish people was played down to highlight the 'religious' and spiritual dimension.

15 Moses is above all a prophet. This is not to deny the importance of kings and priests. But it is usually assumed that in the Middle East of the time, Israel was characterized by the importance given to prophets.

16 Many texts express this conviction, e.g., "Isaiah said to Hezekiah, 'Hear the word of the Lord: The time will surely come when everything in your palace, and all that your predecessors have stored up until this day, will be carried off to Babylon. Nothing will be left, says the Lord. And some of your descendants, your own flesh and blood who will be born to you, will be taken away, and they will become eunuchs in the palace of the king of Babylon'" (2 Kgs 20:16–17). The post-exilic literature confirms this theological statement (see Zech 7:14).

and that, even if the possibility of rebuilding presented itself in historical or pre-Messianic times (after, say, an earthquake had cleared the Temple Mount of the shrines that are now there), it would probably be better not to rebuild for the sake of peace between the peoples and faiths.[17] These authorities commend this renunciation for the sake of peace, even though it makes it impossible to keep the commandments concerning the Temple. This signals that the possession of the land, including Mount Zion, is a good which can be renounced for the sake of peace. There is an order of priorities or, as Catholics might put it, a hierarchy of truths and commandments. The Temple is not an absolute. Nor is the land an absolute. The life of any single Jew, and the life of a single son of Adam, is more holy and more important than the Temple or than a square meter of land. *Pikuach nefesh* is not a marginal halakhic principle.[18] Many Jews, and many Israelis, are saddened by the deaths of Palestinian civilians not engaged in violent protests. The occupation has a moral cost, as Yeshayahu Leibowitz said so many times. An Israeli scholar and journalist, Carlo Strenger, wrote in 2015:

> Re-watching Dror Moreh's documentary "The Gatekeepers" you realize how right Leibowitz has been. The six former chiefs of the Shin Bet security service, who were interviewed at length by Moreh in the film, mostly talk about the moral cost of the occupation, and why Israel needs to end it for the country's own good and interest. They are not naïve pacifists. They did what had to be done to boost security and safeguard Israel, but in the course of doing that they never lost sight of morality. In fact, Israel's security services have been warning for years that the current wave of violence was unavoidable if Israel did not provide Palestinians with a political horizon. They know the daily reality of the occupation, and do not think for a minute that the so-called status quo of creeping annexation and constant humiliation is sustainable—and many of them, speaking off the record, admit to being appalled by the moral price of the occupation [. . .] I am writing this, even though there are daily attacks on Israeli lives, because Leibowitz never said that Israel had to end the occupation to achieve peace. He was a pessimist about human nature, and would probably not have been surprised about the violent chaos engulfing the Middle East. He said that we needed to end the occupation because it was immoral; because con-

17 This was the position of the Rav Abraham Kook (1865–1935). I confess the matter is highly disputed as some passages of the Rambam could be used to justify a rebuilding even before the coming of the messiah.

18 "To save a soul." Based on Lv 18:5 ("You shall keep My statutes and My laws, which a person shall do and shall *live by them*. I am the Lord"), it says that the Torah can be infringed (in most matters) for the sake of a human life.

> trolling millions of people without granting them political rights is morally untenable, and corrupts the society that perpetuates this state of affairs.[19]

I do believe that for the biblical authors the land of Israel was a loved reality, but not the greatest value.

WITH AHAVAT ISRAEL

What has the Catholic Church to say about the land of Israel? The position of the Church seeks to express an authentic sense of Ahavat Israel (true love of Israel). It is in the spirit of what Paul wrote in Romans 9:1–5: "For I could wish that I myself were accursed and separated from Christ for the sake of my brothers, my kin according to the flesh. They are Israelites; theirs the filiation, the glory, the covenants, the giving of the law, the worship, and the promises; theirs the patriarchs, and from them, according to the flesh, is the Messiah." Never again should a Catholic theological official statement be animated by a desire to humiliate or denigrate Israel. By 'Israel' here, I mean the community of Israel and the 'people,' the 'religion' and the 'nation.' Never again should Catholics (and all Christians) allow themselves to be carried away by those feelings of jealousy and scorn that they all too often expressed during the last two millennia. And if a critique of the politics of the State of Israel has to be made, the wording must be carefully chosen and not built on prejudices, old stereotypes, and generalizations.

If we believe that we cannot affirm too hastily that the present Zionist state exists by divine ordinance, or is the "first fruits of redemption," our hesitation should not be motivated by religious exclusivism or contempt for the Jewish people. It should be taken as expressing our way of showing our desire for the best for Israel, the "Israel of God," the Israel that will endure until the end of time (according to Rom 11). We respect God's mysterious ways. "'For my thoughts are not your thoughts, neither are your ways my ways,' declares the Lord. 'As the heavens are higher than the earth, so are my ways higher than your ways and my thoughts than your thoughts'" (Is 55:8–9). Catholics are impelled by Romans 11 to recognize that the covenanted reality of Israel should live—and shall live. We acknowledge also that God wants the people of Israel, his elect forever, to live until the end: "I do not want you to be ignorant of this mystery, brothers and sisters [. . .] in this way *all Israel will be saved*" (Rom 11:25a–26a). How will this great thing be achieved? We cannot say. We wish the Jewish people well. May they prosper all over the

19 See Carlo Strenger, "The Simple Truth about the Occupation," *Haaretz*, October 29, 2015.

world, including in the land of Israel. The Church loves believing as well as non-believing Jews, or, for that matter, believing and non-believing Israelis. Jews, whether they are Israelis or not, should be convinced, always and everywhere, that Catholics stand at their side when they are under threat or are in dire straits.[20] We have for them a special love and esteem that stems from our love for our Jewish messiah Jesus, who several times expressed his love for Israel and Jerusalem.

We cannot ignore, however, that not all religious Jews understand the State of Israel theologically. Many sincere Jews have reservations about the State. They resist the tendency to give too much religious value to the State itself and to the possession of the land. Yeshayahu Leibowitz is a good example of this attitude. We cannot and should not be more royalist than the king, or more Catholic than the pope. We must both affirm the special value of continued Jewish life "from Dan until Beersheba" (2 Sm 24:2), whatever the actual borders of that territory. However, we also believe that this presence cannot be affirmed as if there were not people of other nations living on that land, that is, the Palestinians. As Paul says: "Is he the God of the Jews only? Is he not also of the Gentiles? Yes, of the Gentiles also, for God is one" (Rom 3:29–30a). This is not a purely theoretical question. Hovering over the surface is a moral critique. A theological judgment about the promised land must consider the reality of the Palestinian population. The situation was already tense in the 1930s, and between 1948 and 1967, but it became even more acute after 1967.

Yeshayahu Leibowitz, who was not a religious anti-Zionist, recognized this. The words "Palestinian," "occupation," and "discrimination" cannot be avoided. June 1967 does create a difference. In the twentieth century, we have learned, at a very high cost, about nationalisms of all kinds and about putative religious justifications for them. There is every reason to be very cautious about attributing any kind of nationalism, or sacralization of a land, to divine intervention. The fact that the Palestinian national identity was not a given but constructed itself as a mirror image of nascent Israeli nationhood does not change the reality.[21] If Zionism had chosen a land where no one was living, would we not have an easier time accepting its

20 We have also to rejoice when they are rejoicing in the spirit of *Gaudium et Spes* 1. Of course, the judgment of whether they are in "dire straits" is a prudential one and different Catholics can have different views (in the same way as Israelis themselves can have a different opinion about a clear and present danger).

21 See, e.g., Rashid Khalidi, *Palestinian Identity: The Construction of Modern National Consciousness* (Columbia University Press, 1997).

claims? These questions are not only ours as Christians but run deep in the public conversation in Israel.

How can we take part in a debate that plumbs the depths of Israeli self-consciousness and divides the hearts and minds of a whole people? How can we, as Catholics, from the outside, affirm a theological stance that many Jews, on the land and outside it, cannot accept? The disagreement among Jews is profound. What value would there be in a Catholic statement which dared to affirm something so hotly disputed in Jewish communities, religious as well as secular?

Nevertheless, we must both respect the fact that there is a religious meaning to living on the land of the covenant and that this life is never entirely secured by human means. If the land was not made secure under Josiah, despite the promises made to David, it is surely much more precarious today. Maybe God wants a project born in a secular world and brought to completion by very secular Jews to be part of His will. This is possible because God acts unexpectedly. He surprises us. Could it be that God expects the project to change and grow in holiness and in order to be a light-giving example to the whole world? This may be what he has always wanted.

It could be the case that God is happy with the fact that some Jews prefer to live outside the land while understanding themselves to be fully Jewish. It reminds me of a dialogue between two Argentinian Jewish brothers in a film of 2008.[22] One brother is a *baal teshuva*, from the Diaspora, formerly secular, who has become Orthodox in New York. He says to his Israeli atheist brother, who refuses to give any religious value to his life on the land: "Aval ata Yehudi!" (But you are a Jew!), and the brother responds, provocatively: "lo, ani Israeli!" (No, I am an Israeli!). So the existence of the State does not necessarily help this Israeli to relate to his Jewish identity. However, it does enable him to live without reference to God or the Torah (while keeping a strong link to his traditional, historical, and genealogical identity that the Hebrew language helps him keep), which would be something more difficult in the diaspora. Forgetting Jewish identity outside the land favors assimilation in a much clearer way.

We cannot affirm as Catholics that God is not acting in Jewish political life in the land today. Likewise, we cannot affirm that he is not acting in the new minority status of Catholics in some countries where they used to dominate and where they enshrine their faith in the constitutions. Nor can we affirm with certainty that modern political Zionism comes from God. The end of the Pontifical State in Italy in 1870 or the end of the close association of church and state in France in 1905 may have been pleasing to God, but

22 See the film by Igaal Niddam (dir.), *Achim* ["Two Brothers"] (2008).

we cannot be certain. That God wills any particular state and the way that it is and acts, we are in no position to judge. We know by faith what relates to our Christian faith. We cannot know about the State of Israel by faith.[23] It is not part of what we need to know in that way; this is similarly the case for Vatican City. It is the Petrine office that is known and revered by faith, not the institutional forms it has taken in the course of its history. So Romans 11, as well as *Nostra Aetate* 4, affirm that the community of Israel will endure until the end of time. We affirm the same of the Catholic Church, but this says nothing about the historical and spatial conditions in which this existence will be maintained.

Was there a time in history when God was perfectly happy with his covenanted people? Was there a time when God was happy with what Christians were making of their vocation? God can be both eternally faithful and a severe judge: He can both be accepting of men's decisions and committed to rejecting them. For the biblical God 'repents' and 'changes his mind.'[24] This God can transform an evil reality into good. Jews and Christians believe what Joseph said to his brothers: "But as for you, you thought evil against me; but God meant it unto good, to bring to pass, as it is this day, to save many people who are alive" (Gn 50:20). God can just as readily deprive His people of good and bring evil to them.[25] For those who use the law coming from God and destined for the life of many, to do evil, shall reap evil. As Maimonides says:

> As it is written: "If a man obeys them he shall live by them" (Lv 18:5), but he must not die by them. From this you may infer that the laws of the Torah are not meant to wreak vengeance upon the world, but to bestow on it

23 This is not to deny that every people has a traditional right to its land; for Israel, even more so, as the special link between this people and this land has been expressed by God Himself. But it seems to me that to affirm that the modern State of Israel is from God would mean going further than this.

24 See the articles by Jean-Pierre Sonnet on this matter: "Between Poetic Justice and Poetic Mercy: God in the Flood Narrative (Genesis 6–7)," *Nova et Vetera* (English edition) 18 (2020): 1247–65; "God's Repentance and 'False Starts' in Biblical History (Genesis 6–9; Exodus 32–34; 1 Samuel 15 and 2 Samuel 7)," in *Congress Volume: Ljubljana 2007*, ed. André Lemaire (Brill, 2010), 469–94; "Les monologues divins dans le Pentateuque: Un Dieu shakespearien?" in *La Vita Benedetta*, ed. F. Ficco (GBP, 2018).

25 When the God of Israel is sending the people in exile out of the land of Israel (something that is a great evil for the people), He is not denying what he promised about the land before to the patriarchs and to the people at Sinai, but he is saying that goods are to be always thought as related to the giver and not possessed arrogantly. When the prophets Jeremiah (Jer 23) or Ezekiel (Ezek 13) are condemning the false assurances given by the false prophets about Zion and the Temple, they do not intend to deny the old promises and blessings. A land that has been given can still vomit out its inhabitants; see Lv 18:25 and 20:22: "You shall therefore keep all my statutes and all my rules and do them, that the land where I am bringing you to live may not vomit you out."

> mercy, kindliness, and peace. And it is written concerning those heretics who say that [the cure of a sick] is desecrating the Shabbat (Ezek 20:25), "I too have given them statutes that are not good and judgments that they will live with" (Mishneh Torah, Shabbat 2,3). It is life that God desires for His creatures.

A Catholic theological declaration about the State of Israel that would definitely affirm that *this is* a God given reality, whatever its misdeeds, creates problems. Such a statement would also be an affirmation that we can be sure of the 'signs of the times' and that we can discern with certainty what God wants here and now in our messy history. Would it not be an act of incredible arrogance and *hutzpah* to affirm such a thing? How could we know in respect of another community, what we do not even claim to know for sure about our own believing community?

Between 1870 and 1929, Catholics protested against the occupation of the Pontifical States by Italy and judged it an injustice. After 1929, they became more and more convinced that it had been, in the end, a good thing. When the Maccabees gained independence from Hellenistic rulers in the middle of the second century BCE, we, Christians and Jews, believe this liberation was from God. Nevertheless, two centuries later, the Temple was destroyed and Jewish political semi-independence in the land of Israel came to an end. This was also judged to be something that God at least tolerated, if not directly permitted. Is it not the Talmud itself that says: "Why was the Second Temple destroyed? Because of *sinat chinam*, senseless hatred of one Jew for another" (Yoma 9b)? Why do these debates continue? Because human agency and divine agency are intertwined. Human and divine freedom are also linked. What begins in the darkness can finish in salvation and what begins as salvation can finish in darkness. Discernment is difficult and it keeps having to be carried out again and again, according to the circumstances. However, the fact that we are not free to give a theological warrant to the State of Israel comes from our *Ahavat Israel* and our awe before God's mysterious ways, rather than for other reasons.

The rebirth of a Jewish state in the land of Israel was an improbable and, in some aspects, an incredible event brought by the most unlikely people. The ways of history are strange but God's ways are stranger still: "'For my thoughts are not your thoughts, neither are your ways my ways,' declares the Lord" (Is 55:8). The most important thing to remember and believe, for Catholics as well as for Jews, is that "the gifts and the call of God are irrevocable" (Rom 11:29). The *how* will remain a mystery.

19

ESCAPE FROM HOLINESS

NEGOTIATING THE HOLINESS OF THE LAND THROUGH THE HALAKHIC THOUGHT OF MEIR SIMKHA HACOHEN OF DVINSK

David Meyer

ON LANGUAGE, CHAOS, AND THE PROSPECT OF PEACE

The topic of the land, its holiness and the divine promise attached to it, is none other than a political and theological minefield. When approached through the lens of Jewish-Christian dialogue, it also becomes an "emotional minefield, [whereby] any serious discussion of the meaning of the Land is bound to be controversial."[1]

I wish to open this chapter by recalling what should truly be considered a prophetic teaching of Gershom Scholem, expressed in correspondence with Franz Rosenzweig dated from 1926, only discovered in 1985, in which Scholem foresaw the crucial role of the Hebrew language in shaping the future of this land:

> This country is a volcano, and language is lodged within it. [. . .] That sacred language on which we nurture our children, is it not an abyss that must one day open up? The people certainly don't know what they are doing. They think they have secularized the Hebrew language, have done away with its apocalyptic expression. But that, of course, is not true. [. . .] It is impossible to empty the words so bursting with meaning, unless one sacrifices the

1 David Klatzker, "The Holy Land in Jewish-Christian Dialogue," *Union Seminary Quarterly Review* 38, no. 2 (1983): 193.

> language itself. [. . .] But if we transmit the language to our children as it was transmitted to us, [. . .] shall not the religious power of that language explode one day? And when that explosion occurs, what kind of a generation will experience it?[2]

While Scholem's words resonate in our contemporary ears as we witness the devastating effects of a messianic/apocalyptic ideology of the land rooted in religious thoughts and terminology,[3] we aim at reversing the negative thrust of Scholem's words and envisioning how the creation of a theologically charged religious language of peace could be an important vector to offer some prospect of hope and negotiation in the region. Can a halakhic language of peace extinguish the volcano?

In the following pages, our aim will be to articulate a creative halakhic language of peace, based on the teachings of one of the great rabbinic thinkers of the first part of the twentieth century, Rabbi Meir Simkha HaCohen of Dvinsk. First, I will briefly introduce the figure of Meir Simkha HaCohen and evoke how his teachings have been used in the volatile Israeli context of war and violence. Second, turning my attention to the actual writings of Meir Simkha HaCohen, I will focus my analysis on one specific teaching developed by the author that I will creatively uproot from its original halakhic context, to suggest how it could, when applied to the question of the holiness of the land, become a pivotal idea to create a halakhic language of peace. Finally, in my concluding remarks, I will attempt to cast an overarching glance at the nature of the halakhic endeavor developed in this paper. I will posit that the path we uncover in this paper can serve the search for a peace that religious thought can adopt.

RABBI MEIR SIMKHA HACOHEN OF DVINSK, USED IN THE ISRAELI POLITICAL ARENA OF THE LATE TWENTIETH CENTURY

The late Yeshayahu Leibowitz (1903–94), an iconoclast Israeli Jewish thinker described by Isaiah Berlin as the "the conscience of Israel,"[4] is certainly the one who introduced the name and thought of Rabbi Meir Simkha HaCohen

2 Gershom Scholem, "On Our Language: A Confession," *History and Memory* 2, no. 2 (1990): 97.

3 We refer the readers to a succinct survey of the usage of messianic terminology and its potential human cost, from Rav Kook to the more recent authors of the *Torat Hamelekh*, in David Meyer, "Disruptive the Land Narrative: Forgotten Rabbinic Voices and Their Consequences on the Identitary Temptation in Contemporary Jewish Politics of Messianism," *Leuven Studies* 42, no. 3 (2019): 293–99.

4 Isaiah Berlin, "The Conscience of Israel," *Haaretz*, March 4, 1983 (18).

of Dvinsk to a wider non-rabbinic specialist readership. Leibowitz did not hesitate, on multiple occasions,[5] to call on him to support the idea that the land of Israel carried no holiness or sanctity of its own and that any "excessive attachment"[6] to it becomes idolatry.

While Meir Simkha HaCohen of Dvinsk (1843–1926), who served as the *mitnaged* rabbi of Dvinsk, did not live to face the creation of the State of Israel, let alone the political reality of occupation after the Six-Day War that Leibowitz so vehemently denounced, the Zionist ideal and the various endeavours toward the return of the Jewish people to their ancestral land, was a matter close to his heart.[7] Displaying astonishing human and theological insight, the author, commenting on Moses breaking the tablets on Mount Sinai, warned his readers about the idolatrous danger to see the land of Israel as an intrinsic recipient of holiness:

> The idea is that the Torah and the faith are the essentials of the Jewish nation, and all the holinesses, be it Eretz Israel, or Jerusalem, etc. . . ., they are only details and corollaries of the Torah, and they are sanctified by the holiness of the Torah. Therefore, there are no distinctions for any issue in the Torah between the place and the time that is all equal either in Eretz Israel or outside of it [except for the Mitzvot dependent on the land].[8] [. . .] And do not come to imagine that the Temple and the tabernacle are holy in themselves, heaven forbid. The Eternal, Blessed be His name, dwells amongst his children and if they are [behave] like someone who

5 Yeshayahu Leibowitz, *Accepting the Yoke of Heaven: Commentary on the Weekly Torah Portion* (Urim Publications, 2002), 88–89; see also his *Judaism, Human Values and the Jewish State*, ed. and trans. Eliezer Goldman (Harvard University Press, 1992), 132.

6 While the expression we are using, "excessive attachment," is purposely undefined and loose, it intends to recognize the existence of an historical, emotional, and religious relationship between the Jewish people and the land of Israel that is evident in many parts of the biblical canon, while simultaneously drawing attention to the danger inherent to the classical understanding of holiness, where "excess" is of the essence. We rely here on the commentary of Nahmanides (1194–1270) on Lv 19:2, based on the earlier teaching of the halakhic midrash known as the Torat Kohanim (or Sifra) where *Keddushah* (holiness) is defined as the ability to "self-restrain from what is permitted."

7 See for instance the two known letters of support to the Zionist movement that Simkha HaCohen penned, first to the *Hovevei Zion* (in 1891) and later in the columns of *Ha-Tor* in 1921 (vol. 3).

8 Yehuda Cooperman, ed., *Meshekh Hokhmah*, vol. 1 [Hebrew]. "One should not see a contradiction between these words of our rabbi and those of the classical commentators, known to us, through the words of the Ramban, on the importance of Eretz Israel as a place to keep Torah and the commandments. [. . .] The emphasis on Eretz Israel is what it is in the field of the thoughts and words of Kabbalah, this does not change the basic fact that, in the halakhic field, we cannot find a difference between Eretz Israel and outside of it, apart from the commandments' dependent on the land."

> transgresses the covenant, any holiness is removed from them and they are like a vulgar/profane tool.[9]

Unrelated to the current political question of the land, these words nevertheless resonate to our contemporary ears as a clear warning against the ideological perception that the land of Israel, because of its assumed holiness, is an "untouchable" cornerstone of Jewish/Israeli identity and, as such, cannot be negotiated or renounced even for the sake of possible peace.

Yet, these words of Meir Simkha HaCohen, taken from his commentary to the Torah—the *Meshekh Hokhmah*—even if pertaining to some legal conclusion, are coined in an exegetical and theological frame. If one is to attempt to root an authentic rabbinic argument capable of affirming the holiness of the land, while avoiding its pitfalls, and still being audible to the religious population today who cling to the holiness of the land and refuse to negotiate the land for peace, the words of Meir Simkha HaCohen will need to be articulated through innovative halakhic concepts.[10] It is this creative language of peace that we now aim at the discovering in the halakhic writings of the author.

A HALAKHIC NOVELLA (HIDUSH) ON RABBINIC LAND THEOLOGY AND THE CREATION OF LANGUAGE OF PEACE

Meir Simkha HaCohen of Dvinsk was not only a commentator of Maimonides's Mishneh Torah, but also a daring halakhist capable of discovering legal subtleties in the vast literature of the Talmud and the codes to respond to the needs of his time. One particular area of his halakhic innovation will be the focus of my attention: that of the relationship with the gentiles. As the leader of the Jewish community of Dvinsk, he was sensitive to the nature of Jewish/Christian relations and as such to the status of gentiles in Halakhah, as the Jews not only made up half of the population of the city but were also involved in the government of it.[11]

While resolutely unrelated to the topic of this book, I will attempt to look at this aspect of the author's rulings, to relate and apply the creative halakhic thinking of Meir Simkha HaCohen to the topic of land and peace.

9 Author's translation. *Meshekh Hokhmah*, on Ex 19:32.

10 We are relying primarily on Berkovits's definition and understanding of the role and function of Halakhah. See E. Berkovits, "The Role of Halakhah: Authentic Judaism and Halakhah," *Judaism* 19, no. 1 (1970): 72.

11 Yitshak Cohen, "Rabbi Meir Simcha of Dvinsk and His Attitude toward Gentiles," *The Review of Rabbinic Judaism* 17 (2014): 219.

My ambition is to discover a halakhic terminology that could root the principle of negotiating the promised and Holy Land into the thickest realm of rabbinic authenticity, the realm of "Halakhah that determines the authenticity of a Jewry."[12]

From Teaching Torah to Gentiles, to Defining the Promised Land as *Hefker*

As the rabbi of a Jewish community experiencing positive and enriching relations with its non-Jewish neighbors in the city of Dvinsk, Meir Simkha HaCohen was concerned by some aspects of the rabbinic attitude toward encounters with Christians, and in particular with the halakhic prohibition to teach Torah to gentiles. Indeed, in the words of the Rabbi Yohanan, a Talmudic sage, we learn that: "A gentile who engages in Torah study is liable to receive the death penalty, as it is stated: 'Moses commanded us a law [Torah], an inheritance [of the congregation of Jacob]' (Deuteronomy 33:4). An inheritance for us, and not for them. [. . .] A gentile who studies Torah robs [the Jewish people] of it."[13]

Widely accepted by most rabbinic legislators,[14] such a prohibition relies on two interconnected Torah prescriptions. As the last part of the verse from Deuteronomy 7:2—in the context of the promise of the conquest of the Land—enjoins the children of Israel to "show no mercy to them [the gentiles, inhabitants the Land]," the rabbis interpreted the commandment as a prohibition against offering an undeserved gift to gentiles, that is, to donate to a non-Jew a good belonging to a Jew.[15] Thus, Torah as an inheritance of the Jewish people could not be taught to gentiles.

Unsatisfied by this rather unfriendly posture and commenting on Maimonides's affirmation of a legal distinction present in the Torah between the "stranger that is in your gate"[16] to whom one can give an undeserved

12 E. Berkovits, "The Role of Halakhah," 67.

13 Talmud Bavli 59a. A slightly different formulation can also be found in Hagigah 13a.

14 For a comprehensive review of rabbinic literature on the subject, see J. David Bleich, "Survey of Recent Halakhic Periodical Literature: Teaching Torah to Non-Jews," *Tradition: A Journal of Orthodox Jewish Thought* 18, no. 2 (1980): 192–211.

15 Talmud Bavli, Avodah Zarah 20a; Eruvin 64b, Lev Rabbah 37:3; Tossefta Pessahim 2:15.

16 First part of Dt 14:21. As a legal category, the expression defines the *Ger Toshav*, that is, the resident alien, that lives in the land of Israel (under a theoretical Jewish political sovereignty) and who, while refusing to convert to Judaism, has nevertheless accepted to observe the Noachide laws (Mishnah Avodah Zarah 8:4 and Sanhedrin 56a–b).

present, and the "foreigner"[17] to whom one can only sell such an item,[18] Meir Simkha HaCohen developed a sophisticated argument that I will partially cite and deploy.[19] At its core stands a double reality. First, that the Christian gentiles belong to the legal category of *Nokhim* (and not of resident alien), foreigners equated with idolaters.[20] Consequently, and this accounts for the second reality, if one could in theory "sell" his teaching of Torah to such a gentile, the Torah would become a "a spade which to dig,"[21] transforming Torah into a tool of financial gain, thus desecrating its own essence.[22] Displaying innovative and audacious halakhic craftmanship, Simkha HaCohen attempted to overcome this ideological hurdle and to create a different halakhic perspective that would favor more peaceful relationships between Jews and gentiles. Hence, he wrote, commenting on Maimonides's ruling:[23]

> For Rabbi Yehuda we hold according to his opinion: But he taught us a new detail in Yerushalmi, on 'show no mercy on them,'[24] [and, following Maimonides on] 'do not give them an undeserved present': "It is taught: A story about Rabban Gamaliel who was walking on a road and he saw a

17 Second part of Dt 14:21. As a legal category, the "stranger" (*Nokhi*) is a worshipper of idols and does not benefit from any protection or consideration. See Hans-Georg Wuench, "The Stranger in God's Land—Foreigner, Stranger, Guest: What Can We Learn from Israel's Attitude Towards Strangers?," *Old Testament Essays* 27, no. 3 (2014): 1139–42.

18 "It is forbidden to give them a undeserved present, but it is permitted to give an undeserved present to an alien sojourner, even as it is said: '*Unto the stranger that is in your gates you can give it, that he may eat it; or you may sell it unto a foreigner*' (Deut 14:21)—to an alien by selling it to him, and not by presenting it to him." Maimonides: Mishneh Torah: Hilkhot Avodat Kokhavim Umazlot 10:4.

19 For a fuller citation and analysis of the ruling of Meir Simkha HaCohen, see Yitshak Cohen, "Rabbi Meir Simcha of Dvinsk and His Attitude toward Gentiles," *The Review of Rabbinic Judaism* 17 (2014): 230–32.

20 The Talmud itself defines Christianity as idolatry (Bavli, Avodah Zarah 6a–7b). And most classical rabbinic authorities have indeed considered Christians to be idol worshipers, mostly on account of the Trinity. See Edward Kessler, *An Introduction to Jewish-Christian Relations* (Cambridge University Press, 2010), 69.

21 Mishnah Avot 4:5.

22 The Talmudic tradition clearly forbids using Torah as a means of earning a livelihood. See Talmud Bavli, Nedarin 62a: "Rabbi Eliezer bar Rabbi Tzadok says: Do things for the sake of their performance, [not for any ulterior motive], and speak [words] of [Torah] for their own sake. Do not make them a crown with which to become glorified, and do not make them nor make them an axe with which to hoe [i.e., do not use Torah study as a means of earning a livelihood]."

23 "It is forbidden to give them a undeserved present, but it is permitted to give an undeserved present to an alien sojourner, even as it is said: 'Unto the stranger that is in thy gates canst thou give it, that he may eat it; or thou mayest sell it unto an alien' (Deut 14,21)—to an alien by selling it to him, and not by presenting it to him." Mishneh Torah, Hilkhot Avodat Kokhavim Umazlot 10:4.

24 Dt 7:2.

> cake [laying on the road] and he said to Tabi his servant to take this cake [and he saw a Gentile coming toward him] and he said to him [Tabi]: 'Give him this cake,' [and Rabbi Eilaï ran after him and said to him: 'What is your name?' and he answered: 'Mabgai,' and again: 'Where are you coming from?,' and he answered: 'From the cities of the station guards.' He said to him: 'Have you ever met Rabban Gamaliel in your life?,' and he answered: 'No']."[25] And since there was no [further] resolution [of the difficulty], it is clear that his intention is that something that is the financial property of a Jew, is forbidden to give to a non-Jew, but something that is *hefker* and that has not yet belonged to him, it is permitted to give to a worshipper of idols. And therefore, Tabi his slave does not have ownership for himself [as a slave] since what a slave owns should be considered as owned by his master. Who should have been the owner? Rabban Gamaliel. But he did not intend to own it and only lifted it so as [to respect the commandment of] 'do not pass by food [on the ground].'[26] Therefore, it is permitted to give to the gentile.[27]

Halakhic texts are notoriously difficult to understand and unpack, necessitating what Levinas described as the presence of an halakhic-intellectual muscle "which is not given to everyone."[28] Let us attempt to decipher the argument, to enter the dynamic of the halakhic reasoning and hermeneutics of the text, before creatively extrapolating the conclusions of Simkha HaCohen to the theological contemporary question of the Land.

Unpacking the Halakhic Hermeneutic

As a preamble, and as is often the case in legal rabbinic writings, the true topic addressed by the author is only treated in a concealed way. While teaching Torah to gentiles is truly what stands at the heart of Simkha HaCohen's agenda, it is through the lens of "undeserved gifts to gentiles" that the halakhic discussion will be shaped. The reader should be aware that the prohibition concerning Torah is, in itself, the result of the status of Torah as "inheritance," as the Talmudic text of Avodah Zarah 20a[29] quoted previously made clear.

25 Talmud Yerushalmi, Avodah Zarah Chapter 1, Halakhah 9.

26 Talmud Bavli, Eruvin 64b.

27 Or Sameakh, on Mishneh Torah Hilkhot Avodat Kokhavim Umazlot 10:4.

28 E. Levinas, *Nine Talmudic Readings*, trans. Annette Aronowicz (Indiana University Press, 1999), 32.

29 See also Eruvin 64b, Lev Rabbah 37:3; Tossefta Pessahim 2:15.

That being understood, the author first cites a narrative present in the Jerusalem Talmud. The story about a cake found on a road and that, through the agency of Tabi—Rabban Gamaliel's servant—is offered to a stranger (called Mabgai), as an "undeserved present." The narrative raises a halakhic difficulty. How can such a cake be offered to Mabgai? To be sure, the Talmudic story invites a secondary rabbinic figure, Rabbi Eilaï, who, questioning Mabgai, will undoubtedly establish an important fact and dispel a possible misunderstanding. Mabgai, as it soon appears, is from a different city, and has never met Rabban Gamliel. He is unacquainted with the rules and customs of Judaism. Mabgai-the-stranger is a *Nokhi*, and not a resident alien. The cake should not and cannot be given to him!

Having precisely defined the nature of the halakhic difficulty present in the Talmudic narrative, yet knowing that Rabban Gamaliel could not have shown contempt for the law, the author introduces a halakhic game-changer in the discussion, whose legal ground he will endeavour to demonstrate. The Talmudic ruling according to which an undeserved gift cannot be given to a stranger only applies if the gift/object is indeed the financial possession of the Jew. Could one argue that the cake—like any object found on a road or unspecified halakhic no-man's-land—should be considered *hefker*,[30] ownerless, not really belonging financially to the Jew who happened to pick it up, and could consequently be given to the *Nokhi*?

An objection may be raised. Asking his servant Tabi to perform the "lifting," should Rabban Gamaliel be considered as not "possessing" the cake that he, himself, has not touched? Meir Simkha HaCohen addresses the issue by reminding his readers that, as the servant possesses no legal entity of his own, what he acquires truly belongs to his master. Hence, Rabban Gamaliel should be considered the real owner and as such not permitted to gift the cake to Mabgai-the-stranger. To deepen the legal difficulty in which Rabban Gamliel could find himself, one can argue that if the cake on the road is *hefker*, the act of placing it in one's hand, by lifting, should be considered a proper method of legal acquisition,[31] thus reinforcing once more the actual status of ownership enjoyed by Rabban Gamliel. Our Talmudic hero looks indeed to be in halakhic murky waters! How could such a master transgress so blatantly the Halakhah?

30 Defined in the rabbinic codes as properties found in seas, rivers, or deserts that are supposed to be ownerless. Shulkhan Arukh, Hoshen Mishpat, 273:12.

31 According to Talmudic and later halakhic norms, an object is deemed acquired by different ways, amongst which is the *Hazakah*, the act of taking possession by holding with one's hand. See Mishnah Kiddushin 1:5.

To save the day, Meir Simkha HaCohen, displaying great Talmudic scholarship, alludes to a teaching from tractate Baba Batra 54a, expanded in the Tossafot[32] to the same page in which a distinction is made between the modality of acquisition of a regular object and that of *hefker*-like one. To acquire an item whose status is that of *hefker*, we learn that "lifting" alone is not sufficient and one must display an action and an intention to acquire "in the manner people normally take possession."[33] Consequently, quoting the Tossafot, the Simkha HaCohen concludes that placing the cake in one's hand and lifting it from the ground, if no intention to possess can be asserted, can never be considered a proper acquisition. Rabban Gamliel, acting to respect the commandment of "do not pass by food on the ground,"[34] did not intend to take possession of the hefker-cake and should not be seen as its "owner." Gifting it to the *Nokhi*-foreigner becomes permitted.

Decoding a Concealed Halakhic Dynamic

Meir Simkha HaCohen did not elaborate further regarding his halakhic commentary. The reader is left with a conclusive legal ruling: The permissibility to offer as an undeserved *hefker*-item to a gentile. But is that truly about permitting, as we have argued previously, teaching Torah to non-Jews? If so, how is the suggested analogy hermeneutically constructed?

On one level, the analogy seems to be relying on the idea that just as the cake was thought of as a possession of the Jew, the Torah and its wisdom are also "possessions" of the Jewish people. The verse from Deuteronomy 33:4 defining Torah as "the heritage/possession [*morashah*] of the congregation of Jacob" immediately comes to mind. Yet, for the halakhic analogy to properly function, one needs to assume that Torah, understood now as an item, is in its essence an *hefker*-object, a "heritage" of the Jewish people that nevertheless escapes its "possession."[35] Hence, one must wonder: In what way can the

32 Additional critical and explanatory glosses to the Talmudic text, written by the sages of the school of Rashi during the Middle Ages, and printed on the margin of the traditional Vilna edition of the Talmud.

33 The Talmud (Baba Batra 54a) here opposes the claim of possession of a woman cutting the branches of an ownerless tree to that of a person ploughing that same tree. According to the Talmudic ruling, the ploughing is, in the case of an *hefker* tree, an action indicating "intention to possess." In the words of the Tossafot to the page, "if it is known that he did not intend to acquire, he has not acquired."

34 Talmud Bavli, Eruvin 64b.

35 Certainly, the teaching from Pirkei Avot (Ethics of the Fathers) 2:12 comes to mind: "Perfect yourself for the study of Torah, for it is not an inheritance to you." This teaching, in the name of Rabbi Yosse, highlights a certain reluctance of parts of the rabbinic tradition to accept too

"congregation of Jacob" of the Deuteronomic verse, be considered as the legal heir of Torah, without claiming its ownership?

To establish the legal status of Torah as *hefker*, and not as "possession," to hermeneutically ground the analogy, is not without difficulties. Yet it is precisely as we attempt to do so that the true halakhic genius of Meir Simkha HaCohen is revealed. We will recall that two halakhic hurdles were addressed by the author, in his defense of the action of Rabban Gamaliel. First, that the servant (Tabi) acted as an intermediary agent; second, that Rabban Gamaliel clearly did not intend to claim possession of the object lying on the road. Surely not by chance, these two singularities also defined, in their own ways, the nature of the relationship between the children of Israel and the Torah. Was not Moses, certainly known on multiple occasions not only as the *Eved Adonai*,[36] "God's servant," but also as the intermediary agent serving the Jewish people![37]

Hence, while Moses by "taking in his hands" the tablets of the covenant on Mount Sinai,[38] in the wilderness (a place in itself defined as *hefker*[39]), displayed an act akin to a personal acquisition, it is truly for the benefit of Jewish people as a whole that the seemly act of acquisition is done. As a "servant" with no legal ownership of his own, we can paraphrase the words of Meir Simkha HaCohen and contribute to the building of a strong halakhic analogy: "Who should have been the owner of the Torah received by the hands of Moses? Israel." In addition, the question of the absence of intention to claim possession is also an important marker, for the rabbis, of the nature of the relationship between Torah and Israel. In this respect, the choice of the desert as the location of the giving of the Torah, just like the public pathway in the cake story, carries its own important exegetical and halakhic meanings. On multiple occasions, scattered throughout rabbinic literature, one easily discovers that the desert stands as a place where the absence of intention to possess is key.[40] Taken as a whole, the analogy between the cake found on the public path by the servant of Rabban Gamaliel, and the Torah received by

plainly the idea of an inheritance-possession that could define the relationship of the Jewish people to Torah.

36 Dt 34:5 and later in Jos 1:1.

37 While nowhere in the Torah is Moses referred to as the "servant of the people," passages such as Ex 32:30–33 where Moses intercedes to save the people from divine anger, contribute to such a perception.

38 Ex 34:4.

39 Shulkhan Arukh, Hoshen Mishpat, 273:12.

40 See for instance Numbers Rabbah 1:7, or Mekhilta de Rabbi Shimon Bar Yohai on Ex 19:2, Tractate BaHodesh.

Moses, the servant of God and of the children of Israel, in the *hefker* of the wilderness, becomes binding and ultimately enables Meir Simkha HaCohen to rule that the Torah, just like the cake of the Talmudic story, can be offered and taught to gentiles, shared between Israel and the non-Jews.

The true novelty introduced by the halakhic thinking of Meir Simkha HaCohen must now be stated in its full force. By making the Torah a *hefker*-object, no particular demands or conditions are placed on the non-Jews to whom the Torah can now be shared. The *hefker*-object is an absolute in itself. In that sense, Meir Simkha HaCohen radically departs from some of his predecessors who already ruled that under special conditions—such as the desire to practice its commandments—non-Jews could be taught Torah and partake in its wisdom.[41] As an *hefker*-object, no such limits apply, and the Torah becomes in itself a shared possession, whatever the context, the intentions or the ideology of the recipient.

It is precisely this very absence of conditionality placed on the recipient that should now capture our imagination, as we attempt to relate the halakhic dynamic of Meir Simkha HaCohen into the tumultuous question of Land to be shared with the Palestinians in the current Israeli context.[42]

WEAVING THE THREADS OF A NEW ANALOGY: THE LAND OF ISRAEL AS *HEFKER*

The halakhic dynamic used in the ruling of Meir Simkha HaCohen must now be thought of as a stepping-stone for our own contemporary concerns. As we aim at creating a halakhic language of peace in which the land of Israel could become an *hefker*-heritage of Israel, a place to be shared with the others and not just exclusively possessed by Israel, a new analogy, building on the first, must be carefully crafted.

Can the case of the land of Israel be compared to that of the Torah? Can one envisage that the nature of the relationship between Israel and land be thought off as identical to that of Israel and Torah? Objections will be raised

41 See for instance the commentary of the Meiri (1249–1315) to Sanhedrin 59a, as well as Rabbenu Gershom commentary to Baba Batra 21b.

42 In this respect, the core argument of this paper differs considerably from the political stance taken and argued by Eugene Korn who only envisages land negotiations if the Palestinians "accept the sovereign rights of Jews to live in peace and security in their covenantal homeland," thus imposing a Jewish theological/political vision upon the Palestinians as a condition for sharing part of the land. See Korn, 170.

and reluctance to do so will abound. Is not the land an irrevocable promise?[43] Is not the land so intrinsically linked to the covenant that any attempt to mitigate its absolute holiness is doomed to failure? And yet, since the land is only the "second most popular substantive in Jewish Scripture ([after] Torah),"[44] and given that Meir Simkha HaCohen qualified the Torah as an *hefker*-object, should we not be inspired and empowered by his audacity? Do not the ethical demands of the land covenant[45]—given the urgency of the political situation on the ground—beg for halakhic courage, creativity and audacity?

Hence, a first anchor to posit an analogy between Torah and land must be rooted in textual and halakhic ground, and recognize that the Torah and the land of Israel share the qualification of being an "inheritance" (*morashah*) offered to the children of Israel.[46] If the halakhic ruling of Simkha HaCohen could be applied to the Torah as being a *morashah*, could it not also be fitting to duplicate the halakhic reasoning to the land, understanding more loosely and with some ambiguity the very notion of inheritance, making room for an *hefker*-inheritance legal status?

To add weight to the suggestion, one may recall a fascinating short passage from the Jerusalem Talmud in which the ambiguity of the concept of inheritance, when applied to either the land or the Torah, comes to the fore:

> Rabbi Yohanan answered [quoting Ex 6:8]: "*And I will bring you in to the land, concerning which I swore to give it to Abraham, to Isaac, and to Jacob, and I will give it [wənāṯattî 'ōṯāh] to you as an inheritance [morashah]; I am the Lord.*" [Since the verse uses two different words, namely *matanah* and *morashah*] if it is a gift, *matanah*,[47] why the language of inheritance *yerushah*? And it is an inheritance, *yerushah*, why say that it is a gift, *matanah*? [Answered Rabbi Yohanan]: After God gave it to them as a *matanah*, He gave it to them as an inheritance, *yerushah*. Rabbi Oshayah said: In every place where it says *morashah* this must be considered as ambiguous/vague language (*lāšôn ḏêhā'*). Yet, it also says: "*morashah kehilat yaakov*—[Moshe commanded us the Torah], the inheritance of the community of Jacob" (Dt 33:4). Would you say that this inheritance as well

43 Indeed, out of the 250 biblical references to the covenant, 176 of them include a reference to the land.

44 See Korn, 161.

45 See, e.g., Lv 18:24–25. See as well the emphasis on this ethical dimension developed in Ahrens, 53–55.

46 For the Torah, see Dt 33:4. For the land of Israel, see Ex 6:8. The term is mostly used in its verbal form, on multiple occasions, to describe the act of inheriting the land.

47 Based on the same root as the expression *wənāṯattî* in Ex 6:8.

> is ambiguous/vague? Yes, no situation is more ambiguous than this, since without efforts one cannot receive and comprehend the Torah.[48]

The interest of this Talmudic discussion, for the purpose of our own exploration of a possible flexible halakhic meaning of the concept of *morashah*, is clear. The affirmation of a certain vagueness and ambiguity of the concept of inheritance, either when applied to Torah or to the land of Israel, opens an exegetical breach that a halakhic creative mind can exploit. Building on the halakhic construction of Meir Simkha HaCohen, we can now, unafraid of some remaining ambiguities, continue weaving the threads of a new halakhic analogy.

THINKING THE LAND AS A BOOK

If the land is to be compared to Torah, let us work out the details of the analogy. Both are, as we have already pointed out, God-given, a faint-*morashah*, sharing an identical legal status. In addition, both are fruits of revelation: the first born out at Sinai, the latter in the aftermath of the "revelation of Auschwitz,"[49] thus sharing a comparable historical and theological origin. Finally, both are tools by which Israel, as a people, can accomplish itself,[50] thus sharing a comparable religious function.[51]

The analogy is not only deeply grounded at multiple theological levels, but also shares commonalities with the nature of the halakhic arguments made by Meir Simkha HaCohen in constructing his own analogy between the cake found on the public path and the Torah given in the wilderness of Sinai. In particular, the two halakhic triggers, namely the legal status of "servant" defining the condition of the receiver, as well as the overt intentionality not to take possession of the object under scrutiny, are present in the land considered as an *hefker*-object, just as they were in the case of the Torah.

48 Talmud Yerushalmi, Baba Batra, Chapter 8:2 (23a).

49 The daring thought of comparing Auschwitz to a moment of revelation comparable to Sinai has been made by Elie Wiesel and later by Emil Fackenheim. H. J. Cargas, *Conversation with Elie Wiesel* (Paulist Press, 1976), 8. See also Emil Fackenheim, *God's Presence in History: Jewish Affirmations and Philosophical Reflections* (New York University Press, 1970), 84–85.

50 We are thinking in particular about *Pirkei Avot* 3:14 where the Torah is explicitly called a *kelī*, a tool. Similarly, the land, in particular in relation to the commandments dependent on it, can also be thought of as a physical "tool" for the accomplishment of the Torah legislation.

51 For a complete and detailed analysis of the analogy, see David Meyer, "Israël: Tout autre chose: Judaïsme, Israël et l'enjeu démographique," in *Europe et Israël: Deux destins inaccomplis*, ed. Bernard Philippe and David Meyer (Lessius, 2017), 71–114.

First, references to the children of Israel as "servants" of God, in the Torah[52] and even more so in the Book of Psalms, are multiple.[53] While the covenantal idea that the essence of faith would lie in a blind obedience akin to servitude is highly debatable in classical and contemporary rabbinic writings,[54] it remains true that the children of Israel are called God's servants and are, in their own relation to the land they are to inherit, no more than an intermediary agent. In this respect, their legal status resembles that of Moses receiving the Torah, or that of the servant Tabi lifting up the cake from the public path.

More difficult is the possibility of applying to the proposed land analogy the second halakhic condition advocated by Meir Simkha HaCohen. Could it be argued that the children of Israel displayed an intention not to claim ownership of the land? While intellectual honesty demands that one recognize an overwhelming affirmation, in the Bible, of the centrality of possession of the land of Israel by the Israelites,[55] the uncovering of some dissonant biblical and rabbinic passages will suffice to open a horizon in which an argument for the absence of intentionality to possess can be made.

Two meaningful passages from the Bible come to mind. Both relate to the narrative of the possession of the land, albeit in radically different contexts. The first appears in Numbers 14:31 as Moses and Aaron face the rebellion of the people and of the majority of the spies sent to tour the land. Particularly relevant are the words of Moses, admonishing the community for having "rejected the land." The expression does imply the perception of a certain distance, at least emotional, between the children of Israel and the land. Additionally, it is this same idea of a "distance" separating the people from the land that is key to the narrative of the conquest in the first verse of Joshua 3: "Early next morning, Joshua and all the Israelites set out from Shittim and marched to the Jordan. They did not cross immediately, but spent

52 Lv 25:55.

53 Pss 113:1, 134:1, 135:1. See also Is 41:8.

54 See, e.g., the very critical stand taken by the midrash in ironically comparing the children of Israel, former "slaves of Pharaoh" and now "slaves of God" (Midrash Tehilim 113:1). See also André Neher, *Regard sur une tradition* (Bibliophane, 1989), 164–65.

55 See for instance the introductory affirmation of Frankel on this very subject: "The theme of Israel's relationship to its land is clearly pivotal, holding a central place within the overall structure of the narrative of the Hebrew Bible. With the exception of just a few biblical books, noted the Israeli scholar S. D. Goiten, 'the entire Bible is one long story with one theme: how the people of Israel merited the land, how they lost it, and how they regained it.'" David Frankel, *The Land of Canaan and the Destiny of Israel: Theologies of Territory in the Hebrew Bible* (Eisenbrauns, 2011), 1.

the night there."[56] Is not the night spent on the east side of the Jordan, after so many years of anticipation, the sign of a demand for a temporal distancing between the people and the land? Is not the ark, suddenly brought into the picture of the conquest but from which the people were to "keep a distance of some two thousand cubits,"[57] also the marker of a physical distancing with the land, suggested to the children of Israel? Could it be argued that, with subtleties, the biblical text thus alluded to the reluctance of the children of Israel to take possession, too overtly and too poignantly, of the land?

If our proposed reading is correct, we can claim to have found some rigorous grounds to ascertain the two halakhic conditions set out by Meir Simkha HaCohen in his own defense of a *hefker* definition of Torah, that is now applicable to the land of Israel. Making the land a *hefker*-object, despite its holiness and the divine promise, not just as a fanciful proposition but as a tangible halakhic reality, opens the door to the possibility of offering part of the land as an "undeserved gift" to others, thus paving the way for a halakhic language of peace and negotiation.

CONCLUDING REMARKS

The explicit aim of this paper has been to create a halakhic language of peace, capable of rooting the idea of negotiating and thus renouncing part of the holy/sacred and promised land, in order to open up the possibility of peace in Israel between Israelis and Palestinians. To do so, we first relied and then extrapolated on the halakhic teachings of Meir Simkha HaCohen of Dvinsk, whose innovative thinking and ruling could shed some light on the path to follow. We have attempted to demonstrate that defining the land of Israel as a *hefker*-object was within the reach of halakhic possibilities. By so doing, one can certainly contribute to avert the volcanic explosion of the "religious power of language"[58] dreaded by Scholem. One can also hope that a positive dynamic of peace, carried by an innovative halakhic language, could find its place in the hearts and minds of Jewish populations currently opposed to any land compromise. Indeed, one may think of the potential benefits of mitigating the language of "holiness" with that of "*hefker*-ness" to avoid the pitfall of a radical sanctity of the land that would prevent any possibility of negotiation. Let us not be prisoners of holiness!

56 Jos 3:1.

57 Jos 3:4.

58 Gershom Scholem, "On Our Language: A Confession," *History and Memory* 2, no. 2 (1990): 97.

Yet a halakhic language of peace is not simply made of words. The hermeneutical dynamic, attempting to root the legal and theological creativity we claim in past halakhic wisdom, recognized by all, stands at the core of this paper. The hermeneutical endeavor is, in itself, a witness to the difficulty of the task at hand. It aims not only at sustaining refutations (that will no doubt abound), but above all at valuing the honest and substantiated arguments of those who will oppose such a theological vision. It has the ambition to engage a religious population that is currently a "prisoner of holiness," unable or unwilling to renounce total possession of the land, and to offer them a possible path to reconsider their legal and theological posture. It is indeed a narrow and uncertain path, for many doomed to failure. Yet one cannot continue to boast about peace if one is not ready to take the necessary religious steps to actually make peace possible. Lest we succumb to Jeremiah's warning, "saying 'peace,' 'peace' and yet there is no peace,"[59] the narrow path I have attempted to offer should be considered with care, not so much for its actual solution and conclusion, but for the process of thought that it displays.

Seeking hope, a Talmudic teaching may be recalled. The essence of holiness, said Rabbi Eliezer, lays in the ability to squeeze between two letters.[60] So perhaps is the essence of the Holy Land, found in this ability to invent a narrow path, standing "between two letters," between the demands of a halakhic language of peace and the demands of a broader ethical engagement, seeking justice and equity for all.

59 Jer 8:11.

60 Sanhedrin 92a.

20

BRIEF REFLECTIONS

JUDAISM, THE STATE OF ISRAEL, AND THE DONATIST-CATHOLIC SCHISM

Karma Ben-Johanan

The question of the theological meaning, or lack thereof, of the State of Israel is undoubtedly one of the most tormenting questions of our time, not only for interreligious (Jewish, Christian, and Muslim) relations but also for Judaism in and of itself. Meyer quotes Scholem's famous letter to Rosenzweig with regard to the volcanic nature of modern, secularized Hebrew language, renewed by Zionist Jews; there is no doubt that this explosive nature is also characteristic—in an even less metaphorical way—of the political innovation of Zionism, that is, the State of Israel. Modern Hebrew was built on the foundations of biblical Hebrew. The State of Israel was built on the biblical land. These complex mergers of old and new, especially under the conditions of an ongoing conflict, carry an explosive potential.

In my reflections on Meyer's and Rastoin's papers I intend to engage in a historical comparison, which I find helpful in thinking about current historical and political events, and the debates regarding their theological implications. In other words, instead of touching directly the volatile material involved, I will employ a Brechtian "distancing effect" (*Verfremdungseffekt*), and think about the implications of the State of Israel for Judaism—through the lens of a distant, yet most relevant chapter in Christian history: the story of the Donatist schism and the controversy regarding the nature of the true church in the fourth and early fifth centuries.[1] Beside the cooling effect which historical distance provides, an additional benefit to my chosen strategy is that it absorbs Rastoin's "great reversal" thesis and meets his challenge of "learning from each other" in a way that, so I hope, allows us to explore current tensions from a somewhat refreshing perspective.

Prior to Christianity becoming the preferred religion in the Roman Empire, indifference toward worldly matters, and especially worldly politics, were the central identifying markers of the Church. Unlike the Roman gods, Jesus did not promise any worldly benefit to his followers, and encouraged them to put their trust in the kingdom of heaven rather than in the emperors of the earth. This world, ruled by Roman pagans, was seen as a blatant contrast to the small and pure Christian community that awaited Christ's return. Indeed, Christ himself faced a humiliating approach in his earthly life. The world has betrayed him, tortured him, and finally executed him like a thief. The crucifixion has proven to the Christian community of the first centuries that this world is not theirs; that they are in the world, but not of it. When the Christian faced difficulties, she had to accept her fate with equanimity and testify to her faith. She had to prefer God over the world, even over her own life, if push came to shove. The Christians were members of a small and resilient sect, united in their expectation for the approaching redemption. While in this world, they were careful not to interact too much with their corrupted surroundings, in order to keep their purity intact.

From the middle of the third century to the first years of the fourth century, this self-perception was further strengthened, time and time again, by the Roman persecution of Christians, which reached its peak during the Diocletian persecution of 303–4.[2] The gradual hardening of anti-Christian measures during the Diocletian persecution shows that many Christians did not hurry to surrender to the imperial dictates. Some Christians cooperated with the rulers, to some degree, but the leadership, which filled the prisons, did not yield to imperial pressure. Many of the priests heroically accepted the death penalty which was bestowed on them and provided their communities with a rich martyrological tradition.[3]

Those Christians who lapsed and failed to resist the imperial edicts were at times judged severely by the community. Some Christians explained the

1 For the fullest historiographic account of the Donatist church, see W. H. C. Frend, *The Donatist Church: A Movement of Protest in Roman North Africa* (Oxford University Press, 2000).

2 Lucy Grig, *Making Martyrs in Late Antiquity* (Duckworth, 2004).

3 Michael Gaddis, *There Is No Crime for Those Who Have Christ* (University of California Press, 2005), 30. See also Maureen A. Tilley, ed., *Donatist Martyr Stories: The Church in Conflict in Roman North-Africa* (Liverpool University Press, 1996), 29–67.

persecution as an apocalyptic means to differentiate between the true and false Christians. The sinners, they argued—that is, those who conceded to the regime's demands—were the chaff, not the wheat. They were not truly part of the church. The persecution just exposed their true face. The true Christian community was composed of those who maintained their separation from the world, even onto death.

Soon, however, things changed. The strong differentiation between the Christian community and the Roman world was fundamentally challenged by the conversion of Constantine, the first Christian emperor. The challenge deepened in the next decades, when Christianity was not only tolerated, but became the official religion of the Roman Empire. Christians had power, Christian power, and they held it in this world, here and now.[4]

Many contemporaneous Christians saw the *tempora Christiana* as a blessing and an act of providence. Even those who did not hurry to declare Constantine's conversion as divinely willed and as a fulfillment of OT prophecies were mostly enthusiastic; the Church grew bigger and cosmopolitan, encompassing large territories and many peoples. It was a strong Church which did not hesitate to use the power of the emperor and the Roman institutions to promote the interests of the true religion everywhere. This Church did not turn its back on what was Caesar's, but rather eagerly participated in Caesar's plan to Christianize the entire empire.[5]

Others, however, were more skeptical with regard to the new developments. They saw the antagonism between the world and the Christian faith not as a political issue that could be solved with the Christianization of the emperor, but as an essential dichotomy between human kingship—whether Christian or pagan—and the kingdom of heaven. The very idea of masses who enter the church in the hope of a more comfortable life and powerful cultural position stood in sharp contrast to the idea of a pure and sinless community of martyrs. To them, the Christianization of the Roman emperor—and subsequently the empire—were simply an illusion, because a Christian *world* was, in essence, a *contradictio in adjecto*.

The most prominent representatives of this approach came to be known as Donatists, after the name of one of their leaders, Donatus. The Donatists were an African Christian sect which saw itself as the true heir of the martyr church of the great persecution. They looked with anxiety at the Catholic leniency toward sinners, its inclusive willingness to broaden its borders and

4 H. A. Drake, *Constantine and the Bishops: The Politics of Intolerance* (Johns Hopkins University Press, 2000).

5 Ramsay MacMullen, *Christianizing the Roman Empire A.D. 100–400* (Yale University Press, 1984), 52–58.

swallow the entire world into it; they saw how lifestyles which were not long ago irreconcilable with Christianity became part of the communal reality, when Christians were integrated into the empire's institutions as full citizens, at times as a hegemony; they witnessed masses of pagans converting to Christianity at a speed which did not allow for a systematic Christian indoctrination; they saw their Christian brothers and sisters implementing the message that even if they committed the worst of sins, the Church will let them return to the fold and live as Christians. They saw the gap between the Church and the world getting smaller by the day. This, to them, was an indication that the Catholic Church cannot be the true Church, as it betrayed everything that the pure and smaller church of previous decades—indeed just a blink of an eye ago—stood for.

The Donatists did not see themselves as a new or as an alternative church, but, rather, as the "true" Church: they were the heirs of the martyrs, who gave their lives in order not to compromise. The gap between the true Church and the world was, in their eyes, incommensurable. This Donatist perception was not new; on the contrary, they maintained the traditional Christian identity. They did not let the friendly gestures of Constantine and his heirs confuse them; being Christian is not an easy task, and it should not coincide with comfortable life. Their claim for a continuous identification with the early church, against the Catholic Church, which also declared itself to be the original church of the apostles, stood on solid ground.

Yet history, as we know, did not take the side of the Donatists. The Christian encounter with power changed Christianity profoundly. In the battle between Donatism and Catholicism over the nature of the true church, it was eventually the Catholic Church that prevailed. Today, no one would ever claim that the Donatists were the true Church while the Catholic Church was not.

The battle was won, as is well known, mostly by one man, St. Augustine, who theologically conceptualized the transition between the persecuted Christian sect and the Church of the empire, and also actively oppressed the Donatist community (which was mutually violent against the Catholic community), not seldom by appealing to secular authorities and applying them against his rivals. Augustine provided Christianity with a different perception of sin, with a different perception of history, and with a nuanced and extremely complex understanding of the relationship between the Church and the world. He developed the intellectual means that enabled the Church to preserve its identity notwithstanding the radically opposed, and rapidly changing, historical conditions, and enabled her, when needed, to flirt with, some would say even to marry, political power. The Church's spread "throughout the whole inhabited world," Augustine argued, was a fulfillment of OT prophecies,

> of which it has been predicted that it shall have dominion from sea to sea, and from the river onto the ends of the earth—a prediction which seems from actual proof to be in process of fulfillment; why is it that, in defense of this unity, [the Donatists] do not acknowledge the true and universal law that inheritance which rings forth from the books that are common to us all: "I shall give thee the heathen for thine inheritance, and the uttermost parts of the earth for thy possession."[6] (C. litt. Pet. I: 13)

The move from political weakness to political power, at times even from persecuted to persecutor, was in itself predicted, so Augustine argued, in Scripture. Indeed, Christ appears in the Gospels humiliated and persecuted. But he also appears, in certain places, precisely as a persecutor:

> The Lord Christ drove out the impious merchants from the temple with scourges; in which connection we also find advanced the testimony of Scripture, where it says, "The zeal of Your house has eaten me up." So . . . we do find the apostle delivering over to condemnation, and *Christ a persecutor*.[7]

Augustine theologically adjusted the church to the state of political power. On the one hand, he saw proofs that the situation is willed by God in Scripture. The time of the persecuted sect was gone—now it is the time of Christian emperors. Yet as is well known, when the Western empire collapsed in the beginning of the fifth century, Augustine was able to adjust to the new situation once more. The Church's relationship with power was fundamentally susceptible to change.

It is unfair to extract only these short excerpts from Augustine without explaining his position with more nuance, especially since his theological approach toward political power is not at all a simple and triumphalist one. Nevertheless, the above-mentioned theological arguments are the important ones for my comparative purposes.

Now, I would like to turn to Rastoin's and Meyer's papers. Naturally, the difference between contexts is greater than the similarity, and the entire

6 Augustine, *Against the Letters of Petilian* I:13, in "The Letters of Petilian, the Donatist," in *The Writings against the Manicheans and against the Donatists*, ed. Philip Schaff, trans. J. R. King (Kessinger Publishing, 1987). Augustine cites Ps 8:2.

7 Augustine, *Against the Letters of Petilian* II:10. Augustine cites Jn 2:17; emphasis added. See also *Against the Letters of Petilian* II:81: "Christ persecuted even with bodily chastisement those whom He drove with scourges from the temple."

comparison is anachronistic. And yet, the transformation of Judaism in light of the ingathering of masses of Jews in the land of Israel, the foundation of the State of Israel, and not least the Israeli-Palestinian conflict, poses significant challenges to Judaism which share some significant characteristics with the challenges which Rome's Christianization posed to Christianity. Could we look at these questions of Meyer and Rastoin as providing, *mutatis mutandis*, a Donatist critique of contemporary Judaism?

While Meyer, recalling Yeshayahu Leibovich's warnings against what he calls land idolatry, explores the possibility of "extinguish[ing] the volcano" through using a "halakhic language of peace," Rastion asks with Daniel Boyarin: What is the reality of the State of Israel doing to classical religious Talmudic Judaism? Does not the political and social reality now take precedence over the spiritual reality of the Jewish faith? Not unlike the Donatists who witnessed the implications of the empire's conversion for the small and persecuted Christian community, so Rastoin and Meyer watch with anxiety the implications of the State of Israel for Jewish tradition and identity, to the traditional (read: Diasporic) study of the Torah, as well as to the moral standards of Judaism which they perceive as deeply compromised in the context of the Israeli-Palestinian conflict.

While Zionism—at least its religious branches—often celebrates Jewish worldly power as part of God's plan for history and as a fulfillment of OT prophecies, Rastoin and Meyer rightly point out that the reality of the State of Israel changes some of the core precepts of the Jewish tradition, and reforms—even revolutionizes—Jewish identity, Jewish learning, and in certain contexts also legitimizes the lessening of Jewish observance. For centuries, so it seems, the Jewish faith remained essentially unidentified with modern perceptions of nationalism and sovereignty, and the Jews found a way to maintain their distinctiveness in an often-hostile world. Persecutions—with the Holocaust as an epitome that even compromising one's Jewish observance could not ease—threatened, at times, the community's very existence. Those bursts of hostility, of alienation, were forged into the Jews' self-understanding and identity, as a community in *galuth*, or, if you wish, as a people who is in the world but not of it. The merging of the Jewish tradition with the nation-state—let alone the burning question of the colonialization of Palestine—was not at all natural for this community, and to the tradition which it cultivated for long centuries.[8] And yet, with or without God's will, with or without God's consent (this is obviously the central question), the Jewish state was established, in the very land for which

8 See on this matter Aviezer Ravitzky's classic, *Messianism, Zionism, and Jewish Religious Radicalism* (University of Chicago Press, 1996).

Jews have been longing during their long *galuth*. All of this was foreign to Judaism until a short while ago.

Just as in the Constantinian case, here, too, the embrace of earthly power involves a much more lenient approach to the reality of sin, a reality which is tied to power in the umbilical cord. Who, then, is the true synagogue? The one who wishes to maintain continuity with the persecuted Diasporic community of previous decades? Or rather, the newly established community of Jewish power and sovereignty, who shoves its hands in to the dirty mud of "war and violence" (to paraphrase Meyer)? Indeed, arguing that the State of Israel was teleologically concealed in the Jewish tradition the whole time, merely waiting to appear, is as anachronistic as claiming that the separation between Church and state was always essential for the Catholic tradition. Certainly, both claims are true and false at the same time.

I agree with Rastoin that Israel changes the *Wesen* (essence) of Judaism profoundly. I agree with Meyer that it is wise to develop halakhic and theological languages that would challenge the Jews' "wedding" with the State of Israel, and open alternative Jewish worlds of meaning that would criticize each other, hopefully without clashing into each other like Donatists and Catholics. Sin, of course, lies in wait at power's door. Yet the reality of Jewish power necessitates a complex, ambivalent treatment, not simply rejection in the name of a powerless and pure Judaism which is no longer accessible, at least not in the form it used to have before the State of Israel was founded (since Diasporic Judaisms are also deeply influenced by the existence of the Israeli state and by the Israeli-Palestinian conflict). The theological adjustments are unavoidable.

Yet, keeping in mind the next historical great challenge that the Catholic Church had to face, that is, the collapse of the newly Christianized empire in the fifth century, I am also anxious about the twists and turns of history, and about the possibility that the Israeli project will not last forever. As a Jew, and especially as an Israeli, I can only hope that Judaism will be able to maintain its own version of Augustinian sobriety, and live as peacefully as possible with history's volcanic caprice.

BIBLIOGRAPHY

Agnon, Shay. *Only Yesterday*. Translated by B. Harshav. Princeton University Press, 2000.

Ahrens, Jehoschua. "Christen bleiben Christen: Zur Debatte um einen Aufsatz Benedikts XVI. über den christlich-jüdischen Dialog." *Herder Korrespondenz* 73, no. 5 (2019): 49–51.

Ahrens, Jehoschua. "Jüdisch-christlicher Dialog in Israel." *ZfBeg* 1 (2019). Available at zfbeg.org/ojs/index.php/cjbk/article/view/504/472.

al-Ghazali, Muhammad. *How We Should Think about the Future of Islam outside of Its Land.* Dār al-shurūq, 1997.

Allen, W. C. "On the Meaning of ΠΡΟΣΗΛΥΤΟΣ in the Septuagint." *Expositor* 4, no. 10 (1894): 264–75.

Angel, Hayyim. *Haggai, Zechariah, and Malachi: Prophecy in an Age of Uncertainty*. Maggid, 2016.

Angel, Marc D. "Religious Zionism Revisited: A Symposium." *Tradition* 28, no. 4 (1994): 6–7.

Ansorge, Dirk. "Does a Catholic Theology of Sacraments Help to Achieve an Affirmative Approach to the State of Israel?" in *Contemporary Catholic Approaches to the People, Land, and State of Israel*, edited by Gavin D'Costa and Faydra Shapiro. The Catholic University America Press, 2021.

Ateek, Naim. *A Palestinian Christian Cry for Reconciliation*. Orbis Books, 2008.

Ateek, Naim. *A Palestinian Theology of Liberation: The Bible, Justice and the Palestine-Israel Conflict*. Orbis Books, 2017.

Ateek, Naim Stifan. *Justice, and Only Justice: A Palestinian Theology of Liberation.* Orbis Books, 1989.

Ateek, Naim Stifan, Cedar Duaybis, and Maurine Tobin, eds. *Challenging Christian Zionism: Theology, Politics and the Israel-Palestine Conflict.* Melisende, 2005.

Augustine. *The Writings against the Manicheans and against the Donatists*. Edited by Philip Schaff, translated by J. R. King. Kessinger Publishing, 1987.

The Authorized Daily Prayer Book of the United Hebrew Congregations of the Commonwealth. 4th ed. Collins, 2007.

Avishur, Yitzhak. *Studies in Judaeo-Arabic Translations of the Bible.* Archaeological Center Publications, 2001. (Hebrew and English)

Ayres, Lewis, and Stephen E. Fowl. "(Mis)reading the Face of God: *The Interpretation of the Bible in the Church.*" *Theological Studies* 60 (1999): 513–28.

Balla, Zsolt. "Das Land Israel und der Staat Israel im interreligiösen Dialog." In *Rabbiner im Gespräch mit dem Vatikan: Jüdisch-katholische Beziehungen nach Nostra Aetate und Korrespondenzen mit Benedikt XVI.*, edited by Jehoschua Ahrens and Arie Folger. LIT-Verlag, 2021.

Barker, Kit. "Speech Act Theory, Dual Authorship and Canonical Hermeneutics: Making Sense of *Sensus Plenior.*" *Journal of Theological Interpretation* 3 (2009): 227–39.

Belkin, Samuel. *Philo and the Oral Law: The Philonic Interpretation of Biblical Law in Relation to the Palestinian Halakah.* Harvard University Press, 1940.

Benedict XVI. "Grace and Vocation without Remorse: Comments on the Treatise *De Iudaeis.*" Translated by Nicholas J. Healy. *Communio: International Catholic Review* 45 (2018): 164–84.

Benedict XVI. "Gnade und Berfung Ohne Reue: Ammerkungen zum Traktat 'De Judaeis.'" *Communio/IKaZ* 47 (2018): 387–406.

Benedict XVI. *The Word of the Lord: Verbum Domini.* Pauline Books and Media, 2010.

Ben-Johanan, Karma. *Jacob's Younger Brother: Christian-Jewish Relations after Vatican II.* Harvard University Press, 2022.

Ben-Johanan, Karma. *Reconciliation and Its Discontents: Christians and Jews after Vatican II.* Harvard University Press, 2021.

Ben-Moshe, Danny, and Zohar Segev, eds. *Israel, Diaspora and Jewish Identity*. Sussex Academic, 2007.

Ben-Shammai, Haggai. *A Leader's Project: Studies in the Philosophical and Exegetical Works of Saadya Gaon.* Bialik Institute, 2015. (Hebrew)

Ben-Shammai, Haggai. "The Tension between Literal Interpretation and Exegetical Freedom: Comparative Observations on Saadia's Method." In *With Reverence for the Word: Medieval Scriptural Exegesis in Judaism, Christianity, and Islam*, edited by Jane Dammen McAuliffe, Barry Walfish, and Joseph Ward Goering. Oxford University Press, 2003.

Beinart, Peter. *The Crisis of Zionism*. Times Books, 2012.

Berkovits, Eliezer. *Essential Essays on Judaism*. Edited by David Hazony. Shalem, 2002.

Berkovits, Eliezer. *Faith after the Holocaust*. KTAV Publishing, 1973.

Berkovits, Eliezer. "The Role of Halakhah: Authentic Judaism and Halakhah." *Judaism* 19, no. 1 (1970): 66–78.

Berlin, Isaiah. *The Crooked Timber of Humanity: Chapters in the History of Ideas.* Princeton University Press, 1990.

Berlin, Rabbi Naftali Zvi Yehuda. *Ha-emeq Davar*. M. Y. Kuperman, 2004. (Hebrew)

Betz, Hans Dieter. *The Sermon on the Mount*. Hermeneia. Fortress Press, 1995.

Blau, Joshua. *A Dictionary of Mediaeval Judeo-Arabic.* The Academy of the Hebrew Language, The Israel Academy of Sciences and Humanities, 2006. (Hebrew and Judeo-Arabic)

Blau, Joshua. *Notes on R. Saadya Gaon's Translation of the Torah: Part I: Genesis.* Israel Academy of Sciences, 2019. (Hebrew)

Bleich, J. David. "Survey of Recent Halakhic Periodical Literature: Teaching Torah to Non-Jews." *Tradition: A Journal of Orthodox Jewish Thought* 18, no. 2 (1980): 192–211.

Boyarin, Daniel. *Border Lines: The Partition of Judaeo-Christianity.* University of Pennsylvania Press, 2006.

Boyarin, Daniel. *Judaism: The Genealogy of a Modern Notion.* Rutgers University Press, 2019.

Boyarin, Daniel. *The No-State Solution: A Jewish Manifesto.* Yale University Press, 2023.

Boyarin, Daniel. *A Traveling Homeland: The Babylonian Talmud as Diaspora.* University of Pennsylvania Press, 2015.

Boyarin, Daniel. *Unheroic Conduct: The Rise of Heterosexuality and the Invention of the Jewish Man.* University of California Press, 1997.

Brandes, Yehuda. *Judaism and Citizens Rights.* Israel Democracy Institute, 2019. (Hebrew)

Breger, Marshall J., ed. *The Vatican-Israel Accords: Political, Legal, and Theological Contexts.* University of Notre Dame Press, 2004.

Brown, Raymond E. "The Problems of the *Sensus Plenior.*" *Ephemerides Theologicae Louvanienses* 43 (1967): 460–69.

Brown, Raymond E. *The Sensus Plenior of Sacred Scripture.* St. Mary Seminary, 1955.

Brody, Robert. *The Geonim of Babylonia and the Shaping of Medieval Jewish Culture.* Yale University Press, 2013.

Brody, Robert. *Sa'adyah Gaon.* Translated by Betsy Rosenberg. The Littman Library of Jewish Civilization, in association with Liverpool University Press, 2013.

Burge, Gary M. *Jesus and the Land: The New Testament Challenge to 'Holy Land' Theology.* Baker Academic, 2010.

Burge, Gary M. *Whose Land? Whose Promise?* Pilgrim Press, 2003.

Cargas, H. J. *Conversation with Elie Wiesel.* Paulist Press, 1976.

Catholic Church. *Catechism of the Catholic Church, English Updated Edition.* 2nd ed. Libreria Editrice Vaticana and Our Sunday Visitor, 2020.

Catholic Church. *Compendium on the Social Doctrine of the Catholic Church.* 2004. Available at vatican.va.

Chachour, Elias. "An Arab Christian Speaks Out." *Face to Face—an Interreligious Bulletin* 2 (1977): 9–10.

Charlesworth, James H., ed. *The Old Testament Pseudepigrapha.* 2 vols. Anchor Bible Reference Library. Doubleday, 1985.

Childs, Brevard S. "The *Sensus Literalis* of Scripture: An Ancient and Modern Problem." In *Beiträge zur Alttestamentlichen Theologie: Festschrift für Walther Zimmerli zum 70. Geburtstag*, edited by Herbert Donner, Robert Hanhard, and Rudolf Smend. Vandenhoeck and Ruprecht, 1977.

Christiansen, Drew. "Palestinian Christians: Recent Developments." In Breger, *The Vatican-Israel Accords*.

Clark, Victoria. *Allies for Armageddon: The Rise of Christian Zionism*. Yale University Press, 2007.

Clifford, Richard, SJ. "Changing Christian Interpretations of the Old Testament." *Theological Studies* 82 (2021): 509–30.

Cohen, Yitshak. "Rabbi Meir Simcha of Dvinsk and His Attitude toward Gentiles." *The Review of Rabbinic Judaism* 17 (2014): 218–51.

Commission for Religious Relations with the Jews. "'The Gifts and the Calling of God Are Irrevocable' (Rom 11:29): A Reflection on Theological Questions Pertaining to Catholic-Jewish Relations on the Occasion of the 50th Anniversary of *Nostra Aetate* (No. 4)." December 10, 2015. Available at christianunity.va.

Commission for Religious Relations with the Jews. *Guidelines and Suggestions for Implementing the Conciliar Declaration "Nostra Aetate."* December 1, 1974. Available at christianunity.va.

Commission for Religious Relations with the Jews. *Notes on the Correct Way to Present the Jews and Judaism in Preaching and Catechesis in the Roman Catholic Church*. 1985. Available at christianunity.va.

Commission for Religious Relations with the Jews. *We Remember: A Reflection on the Shoah*. March 16, 1998. Available at christianunity.va.

Comprehensive Agreement between the Palestine and the Holy See. 2015. Available at vatican.va.

"The Conscience of Israel." *Ha'aretz*. March 4, 1983.

Cooperman, Yehuda, ed. *Meshekh Hokhmah*. Vol. 1. Even Yisrael, 2002. (Hebrew)

Cover, Robert. "Obligation: A Jewish Jurisprudence of the Social Order." *Journal of Law and Religion* 5 (1987): 65–74.

Cragg, Kenneth. *Palestine: The Prize and Price of Zion*. Cassell, 1997.

Crown, Alan D. *Samaritan Scribes and Manuscripts*. Mohr Siebeck, 2001.

Cunningham, Philip A., and Adam Gregerman. "'Genuine Brotherhood' without Remorse: A Commentary on Joseph Ratzinger's 'Comments on "*De Iudaeis*."'" *SCJR* 14, no. 1 (2019): 1–29.

Dalin, David, and Matthew Levering, eds. *John Paul II and the Jewish People: A Christian-Jewish Dialogue*. Rowman and Littlefield, 2007.

Daniélou, Jean. Review of Joseph Coppens, *Les harmonies des deux Testaments*. *Dieu vivant: Perspectives religieuses et philosophiques* 16 (1950): 149–53.

Davies, W. D. *The Gospel and the Land: Early Christianity and Jewish Territorial Doctrine*. University of California Press, 1974.

Davies, W. D., and Dale C. Allison, Jr. *The Gospel According to Saint Matthew.* 3 vols. The International Critical Commentary. T&T Clark Ltd., 1988–97.

D'Costa, Gavin. *Catholic Doctrines on the Jewish People after Vatican II.* Oxford University Press, 2019.

D'Costa, Gavin. "Christian Orthodoxy and Religious Pluralism: A Response to Terrence W. Tilley." *Modern Theology* 23, no. 3 (July 2007): 437–42.

D'Costa, Gavin. *Vatican II: Catholic Doctrines on Jews and Muslims.* Oxford University Press, 2014.

D'Costa, Gavin, and Faydra Shapiro, eds. *Contemporary Catholic Approaches to the People, Land, and State of Israel.* The Catholic University America Press, 2021.

Del Sarto, Raffaella A. "Israel's Contested Identity and the Mediterranean." *Mediterranean Politics* 8, no. 1 (2003): 27–58.

Díez Macho, Alejandro. *Neophyti 1: Targum palestinense, Ms de la Biblioteca Vaticana.* Consejo superior de investigaciones científicas, 1970.

Dikken, Berend Jan. "Some Remarks about Middle Arabic and Sa'adya Gaon's Arabic Translation of the Pentateuch in Manuscripts of Jewish, Samaritan, Coptic Christian, and Muslim Provenance." In *Middle Arabic and Mixed Arabic: Diachrony and Synchrony*, edited by Liesbeth Zack and Arie Schippers. Brill, 2012.

Don-Yehia, Eliezer. "Ideology and Policy in Religious Zionism: Rabbi Yitzhak Yaacov Reines' Conception of Zionism and the Policies of the Mizrahi under his Leadership." *Zionism* 8 (1981): 103–46. (Hebrew)

Don-Yehia, Eliezer. "Jewish Orthodoxy, Zionism, and the State of Israel." *The Jewish Quarterly* 31 (1984): 10–30.

Drake, H. A. *Constantine and the Bishops: The Politics of Intolerance.* Johns Hopkins University Press, 2000.

Duffy, Kevin. "The *Sensus Plenior* of Scripture: A Debate and Its Aftermath." *Louvain Studies* 38 (2014): 228–45.

Dunn, James D. G. *Romans 1–8.* Word Biblical Commentary. Word Incorporated, 1988.

Emon, Anver M. *Religious Pluralism and Islamic Law: Dhimmis and Others in the Empire of Law.* Oxford University Press, 2012.

Encyclopedia Biblica. Bialyk Institute, 1954, 1988.

Eskenazi, Tamara C., and J. Cornelis de Vos. "The Land in the Hebrew Bible." In *Enabling Dialogue about the Land*, edited by Philip A. Cunningham, Ruth Langer, and Jesper Svartvik. Paulist Press, 2020.

Fackenheim, Emil. *God's Presence in History. Jewish Affirmations and Philosophical Reflections.* New York University Press, 1970.

Farkasfalvy, Denis. "The Pontifical Biblical Commission's Document on Jews and Christians and Their Scriptures: Attempt at an Evaluation." *Communio: International Catholic Review* 29 (2002): 715–37.

Frankel, David. *The Land of Canaan and the Destiny of Israel: Theologies of Territory in the Hebrew Bible.* Eisenbrauns, 2011.

Fredricksen, Paula. *Augustine and the Jews.* Doubleday, 2008.

Frend, W. H. C. *The Donatist Church: A Movement of Protest in Roman North Africa.* Oxford University Press, 2000.

Gaddis, Michael. *There Is No Crime for Those Who Have Christ.* University of California Press, 2005.

Gazit, Shlomo. *Trapped Fools: Thirty Years of Israeli Policy in the Territories.* Routledge, 2003.

Goldman, Samuel. *God's Country. Christian Zionism in America.* University of Pennsylvania Press, 2018.

Goodman, Martin. *Mission and Conversion: Proselytizing in the Religious History of the Roman Empire.* Clarendon, 1994.

Gregerman, Adam. "Is the Biblical Land Promise Irrevocable?: Post-*Nostra Aetate* Catholic Theologies of the Jewish Covenant and the Land of Israel." *Modern Theology* 34, no. 2 (2018): 137–58.

Grig, Lucy. *Making Martyrs in Late Antiquity.* Duckworth, 2004.

Hacohen, Aviad. "The Essence of Authority in Hebrew Law." In *Collection on Religious Zionism*, edited by Simcha Raz. World Center of Mizrachi and Poel Mizrachi, 2002. (Hebrew)

Hadad, Eliezer. *The Status of Minorities in the Jewish State: Halakhic Aspects.* Israel Democracy Institute, 2010.

Hagee, John. *Beginning of the End.* Thomas Nelson, 1996.

Hagee, John. *Jerusalem Countdown.* Frontline, 2006.

Haiduc-Dale, Noah. *Arab Christians in British Mandate Palestine.* Edinburgh University Press, 2015.

Hammer, Leonard. "Discerning Israel's Interpretation of the 1993 Holy See-Israel Fundamental Agreement." In Breger, *The Vatican-Israel Accords.*

Hammer, Leonard. "The Holy See-PLO Agreement and Its Significance for Israel." In Breger, *The Vatican-Israel Accords.*

Hartman, David. "Israel: The Rebirth of a People." Transcript of speech delivered at the Second Colloquium of Jesuits in Jewish-Christian Dialogue, June 27–July 2, 2000. Available at individual.utoronto.ca/mfkolarcik/texts/jesuit_jewish_dialogue_02.html.

Hazony, David. "Eliezer Berkovits, Theologian of Zionism." *Azure* 17 (2004): 88–119.

Hervert, T. W. *Faith-Based War from 9/11 to Catastrophic Success in Iraq.* Equinox Publishing, 2009.

Herzberg, Arthur, ed. *The Zionist Idea.* Jewish Publication Society of America, 1959.

Herzog, Isaac. "The Rights of Minorities according to Jewish Law." *Tehumim* 2 (1951). (Hebrew)

Herzog, Isaac Halevi. "The Rights of Minorities in Jewish Law." In *The Jewish Political Tradition*, vol. 2, edited by Menachem Lorberbaum et al. Yale University Press, 2006.

Heschel, A. J. *Israele eco di eternità.* Queriniana, 1977. English: *Israel: An Echo of Eternity.* Farrar, Straus and Giroux, 1967.

Heschel, A. J. *Moral Grandeur and Spiritual Audacity.* Farrar, Straus and Giroux, 1996.

Heschel, Susannah. "Nazifying Christian Theology: Walter Grundmann and the Institute for the Study and Eradication of Jewish Influence on German Church Life." *Church History* 63, no. 4 (1994): 587–605.

Hoffman, Lawrence A., ed. *The Land of Israel: Jewish Perspectives*. University of Notre Dame Press, 1986.

Hütter, Reinhard. "'In.' Some Incipient Reflections on *The Jewish People and Their Sacred Scriptures in the Christian Bible*." *Pro Ecclesia* 13 (2004): 13–24.

Isaac, Mundher, ed. *Madkhal ila al-lahut al-filastini* [An Introduction to Palestinian Theology]. Diyar Press, 2017.

Ingrams, Doreen, ed. *Palestine Papers 1917–1922: Seeds of Conflict*. John Murray, 1972.

International Theological Commission. *In Search of a Universal Ethic: A New Look at the Natural Law*. Catholic Truth Society, 2012.

Irani, George Emile. *The Papacy and the Middle East: The Role of the Holy in the Arab-Israeli Conflict, 1962–1984*. University of Notre Dame Press, 1986.

Isaac, Munther. *From Land to Lands, from Eden to the Renewed Earth: A Christ-Centered Biblical Theology of the Promised Land*. Langham Monographs, 2015.

Janzen, Waldemar. "Land." In *Anchor Bible Dictionary*, edited by David Noel Freedman. Doubleday, 1992.

John Paul II. "Address of His Holiness Pope John Paul II to a Symposium on the Roots of Anti-Judaism." October 31, 1997.

John Paul II. "Address to Representatives of the West German Jewish Community." November 17, 1980. Available at ccjr.us/dialogika-resources/documents-and-statements/roman-catholic/pope-john-paul-ii/jp2-80nov17.

John Paul II. *Redemptionis Anno*. Apostolic Letter. April 20, 1984.

John Paul II. *Veritatis Splendor*. Encyclical Letter. August 6, 1993.

John Paul II et al. *John Paul II in the Holy Land: In His Own Words. With Christian and Jewish Perspectives*. Paulist Press, 2005.

Johnson, Stephen D., Joseph B. Tamney, and Ronald Burton. "Pat Robertson: Who Supported His Candidacy for President?" *Journal for the Scientific Study of Religion* 28, no. 4 (1989): 387–99.

Journet, Charles. "Le Congrès de l'association internationale des chrétiens et des juifs à Fribourg." *L'Amitié judéo-chrétienne* 2 (1948): 12–13.

Kantorovich, Eugene. "A Comparative Constitutional Perspective on Israel's Nation-State Law." *Israel Studies* 25, no. 3, *Marking 70 Years of the 1950 Ben-Gurion-Blaustein 'Understanding'* (2020): 137–52.

Kaplan, Aryeh. *Handbook of Jewish Thought*. Moznaim Publishing, 1992.

Kaplan, Aryeh. *Inner Space: Introduction to Kabbalah, Meditation and Prophecy*. Moznaim Publishing, 1990.

Karsh, Efraim. *Palestine Betrayed*. Yale University Press, 2010.

Katz, Jacob. *Exclusiveness and Tolerance*. Oxford University Press, 1961.

Kereszty, Roch. "The Jewish-Christian Dialogue and the Pontifical Biblical Commission's Document on 'The Jewish People and Their Sacred Scriptures in the Christian Bible.'" *Communio: International Catholic Review* 29 (2002): 738–45.

Kessler, Edward. *An Introduction to Jewish-Christian Relations*. Cambridge University Press, 2010.

Kessler, Edward. "Reflections from a European Jewish Theologian." 2015. Available at ccjr.us/dialogika-resources/documents-and-statements/analyses/crrj-2015dec10/kessler-2015dec10.

Khader, Jamal. "Christian-Jewish Relations from a Christian Palestinian Perspective." In D'Costa and Shapiro, *Contemporary Catholic Approaches*.

Khader, Jamal. "'nahwa qira'atin masihiyya falastiniyya li-'l'ahd al-qadim." In *madkhal ila al-lahut al-falastini*, edited by Munther Isaac. Diyar Press, 2017.

Khader, Jamal. "Theology of the Land—A Christian Perspective." In Cunningham et al., *Enabling Dialogue about the Land*.

Khalidi, Rashid. *Palestinian Identity: The Construction of Modern National Consciousness*. Columbia University Press, 1997.

Kinzer, Mark. *Jerusalem Crucified: Jerusalem Risen*. Wipf and Stock, 2018.

Klatzker, David. "The Holy Land in Jewish-Christian Dialogue." *Union Seminary Quarterly Review* 38, no. 2 (1983): 193–202.

Korn, Eugene. "Israel as Blessing: Theological Horizons." In *Judaism's Challenge—Election, Divine Love and Human Enmity*, edited by Alon Goshen-Gottstein. Academic Studies Press, 2020.

Korn, Eugene. "Rethinking Christianity." In *Jewish Theology and World Religions*, edited by Alon Goshen-Gottstein and Eugene Korn. Littman Library of Jewish Civilization, 2012.

Kook, Abraham Isaac Hakohen. *Orot*. Maggid, 2015.

Kuruvilla, Samuel J. *Radical Christianity in Palestine and Israel: Liberation and Theology in the Middle East*. I. B. Tauris, 2013.

Langer, Ruth. "Israel in Jewish Theologies." In Cunningham et al., *Enabling Dialogue about the Land*.

Legge, Dominic. "Do Thomists Have Rights?" *Nova et Vetera* (English edition) 17, no. 1 (2019): 127–47.

Lefebvre, Marcel. *I Accuse the Council!* Translated by Jaime Pazat de Lys. 2nd ed. Angelus Press, 1998.

Leibowitz, Yeshayahu. *Accepting the Yoke of Heaven: Commentary on the Weekly Torah Portion*. Urim Publications, 2002.

Leibowitz, Yeshayahu. *Israël et Judaïsme: Ma part de vérité*. Desclee de Brouwer, 1993.

Leibowitz, Yeshayahu. *Judaism, Human Values and the Jewish State*. Edited and translated by Eliezer Goldman. Harvard University Press, 1992.

Lemaire, André, ed. *Congress Volume: Ljubljana 2007*. Brill, 2010.

Levenson, Jon D. "Can Roman Catholicism Validate Jewish Biblical Interpretation?" *Studies in Christian Jewish Relations* 1 (2005–06): 170–85.

Levenson, Jon D. *The Hebrew Bible, the Old Testament, and Historical Criticism: Jews and Christians in Biblical Studies*. Westminster John Knox Press, 1993.

Levenson, Jon D. *Resurrection and the Restoration of Israel: The Ultimate Victory of the God of Life*. Yale University Press, 2006.

Levering, Matthew. *Christ's Fulfillment of Torah and Temple: Salvation according to Thomas Aquinas*. University of Notre Dame Press, 2002.

Levering, Matthew. *Engaging the Doctrine of Israel: A Christian Israelology in Dialogue with Ongoing Judaism*. Cascade Books, 2021.

Levering, Matthew. "The Pontifical Biblical Commission and Aquinas' Exegesis." *Pro Ecclesia* 13 (2004): 25–28.

Levinas, Emmanuel. *Nine Talmudic Readings*. Translated by Annette Aronowicz. Indiana University Press, 1999.

Levine, Amy-Jill. *The Misunderstood Jew: The Church and the Scandal of the Jewish Jesus*. HarperOne, 2006.

Levine, Amy-Jill. "Roland Murphy, the Pontifical Commission, Jews, and the Bible." *Biblical Theology Bulletin* 33 (2003): 104–13.

Lewis, Donald M. *The Origins of Christian Zionism: Lord Shaftesbury and Evangelical Support for a Jewish Homeland*. Cambridge University Press, 2013.

Litvinoff, Barnet. *Road to Jerusalem: Zionism's Imprint on History*. Weidenfeld and Nicolson, 1965.

Luz, Ulrich. *Matthew 1–7: A Commentary*. Translated by Wilhelm C. Linss. Augsburg, 1989 [1985].

MacIntyre, Alasdair. *After Virtue: A Study in Moral Theory*. 2nd ed. University of Notre Dame Press, 1984.

MacMullen, Ramsay. *Christianizing the Roman Empire A.D. 100–400*. Yale University Press, 1984.

Marchadour, Alain, and David Neuhaus. *La Terra, la Bibbia e la storia*. Jaca Book, 2007.

Mareijn, Elizabeth S. "The Revival of Palestinian Christianity: Developments in Palestinian Theology." *Exchange* 49 (2020): 257–77.

Marsden, George. *Fundamentalism and American Culture*. Oxford University Press, 1980.

Masalha, Nur. *The Zionist Bible: Biblical Precedent, Colonialism and the Erasure of Memory*. Routledge, 2013.

McDermott, Gerald R. *Israel Matters*. Brazos, 2017.

McDermott, Gerald R., ed. *The New Christian Zionism: Fresh Perspectives on Israel and the Land*. IVP Academic, 2016.

McMichael, Stephen. "The Covenant in Patristic and Medieval Christian Theology." In *Two Faiths, One Covenant?*, edited by Eugene Korn and John Pawlikowski. Rowman and Littlefield, 2005.

Merkley, Paul Charles. *Christian Attitudes towards the State of Israel*. McGill-Queen's University Press, 2001.

Meyer, Barbara U. "Engrafted and Rooted Ways of Belonging—Alternatives to Abrogation in Post-Shoah and Palestinian Theologies." In Cunningham et al., *Enabling Dialogue about the Land.*

Meyer, David. "Disruptive the Land Narrative: Forgotten Rabbinic Voices and Their Consequences on the Identitary Temptation in Contemporary Jewish Politics of Messianism." *Leuven Studies* 42, no. 3 (2019): 293–99.

Meyer, David. "Israël: Tout autre chose: Judaïsme, Israël et l'enjeu démographique." In *Europe et Israël: Deux destins inaccomplis*, edited by Bernard Philippe and David Meyer. Lessius, 2017.

Miccoli, Giovanni. "Two Sensitive Issues: Religious Freedom and the Jews." In *History of Vatican II, vol. 4: Church as Communion: Third Period and Intersession, September 1964–September 1965*, edited by Giuseppe Alberigo and Joseph A. Komonchak. Orbis Books, 2003.

Milgrom, Jacob. *Leviticus 17–22: A New Translation with Introduction and Commentary.* Doubleday, 2000.

Miller, Charles H. "Translation Errors in the Pontifical Biblical Commission's *The Jewish People and Their Sacred Scriptures in the Christian Bible*." *Biblical Theology Bulletin* 35 (2005): 34–39.

Minerbi, Sergio I. "Le Saint-Siège, les Juifs et l'État d'Israël." *Outre-Terre* 9 (2004): 341–51.

Minerbi, Sergio I. *The Vatican and Zionism: Conflict in the Holy Land 1895–1925*. Oxford University Press, 1990.

Mirsky, Yehudah. *Rav Kook: Mystic in a Time of Revolution*. Yale University Press, 2014.

Munayer, Salim. "Reconciliation as a Christian Response to the Israel-Palestine Conflict." In *Christians and the Middle East Conflict*, edited by Paul S. Rowe, John H. A. Dyck, and Jens Zimmerman. Routledge, 2020.

Murphy, Roland E. "The Biblical Commission, the Jews, and Scriptures." *Biblical Theology Bulletin* 32 (2002): 145–49.

Murphy O'Connor, Jerome. *Keys to Jerusalem: Collected Essays*. Oxford University Press, 2012.

Neher, André. *Chiavi per l'ebraismo*. Marietti, 1988.

Neher, André. *Regard sur une tradition*. Bibliophane, 1989.

Nelson, Cary. "Introduction." In *Peace and Faith: Christian Churches and the Israeli-Palestinian Conflict*, edited by Cary Nelson and Michael C. Gizzi. Presbyterians for Middle East Peace, 2021.

Neuhaus, David M. "Where to from Here? Continuing Challenges in Jewish–Catholic Conversation." *Religions* 12, no. 929 (2021).

Neuhaus, David Mark. "A Catholic Perspective on the People, Land, and State of Israel." In D'Costa and Shapiro, *Contemporary Catholic Approaches*.

Nickelsburg, George W. E., and James C. VanderKam. *1 Enoch 1: A Commentary on the Book of 1 Enoch, Chapters 1–36, 81–108*. Hermeneia. Fortress Press, 2001.

Nietzsche, Friedrich. *On the Genealogy of Morality*. Translated by C. Diethe. Cambridge University Press, 2006.

Novak, David. "Supersessionism Hard and Soft." *First Things*. February 2019.

Novak, David. *Talking with Christians: Musings of a Jewish Theologian*. Eerdmans, 2005.

Novak, David. *Zionism and Judaism: A New Theory.* Cambridge University Press, 2015.

Oesterreicher, John M. "Declaration on the Relationship of the Church to Non-Christian Religions." In *Commentary on the Documents of Vatican II, vol. 3: Declaration on the Relationship of the Church to the Non-Christian Religions: Dogmatic Constitution on Divine Revelation: Decree on the Apostolate of the Laity*, edited by Herbert Vorgrimler. Burns and Oates, 1969.

Olyan, Saul. *Rites and Rank: Hierarchy in Biblical Representations of Cult*. Princeton University Press, 2000.

Ophir, Adi, and Ishay Rosen-Zvi. *Goy: Israel's Multiple Others and the Birth of the Gentile.* Oxford University Press, 2018.

Oz, Yoel A. *Abrahamic Confederation: A Solution to the Israeli-Palestinian Conflict*. Self-published, 2018.

Palmieri-Billig, Lisa. "Correspondence between Pope Emeritus Benedict XVI and Arie Folger, the Chief Rabbi of Vienna." 2018. Available at jcrelations.net/articles/article/the-pope-and-the-rabbi.html.

Paul VI. *Nobis in Animo*. Apostolic Exhortation. March 25, 1974.

Pearson, Clive. "The Quest for a Coalitional Praxis: Examining the Attraction of a Public Theology from the Perspective of Minorities." In *A Companion to Public Theology*, edited by Katie Day and Sebastian Kim. Brill's Companions to Modern Theology. Brill, 2017.

Pennington, Jonathan T. *Heaven and Earth in the Gospel of Matthew.* Brill, 2007.

Percy, Walker. *The Message in the Bottle*. Farrar, Straus and Giroux, 2000.

Playfair, Emma. *International Law and the Administration of Occupied Territories: Two Decades of Israeli Occupation of the West Bank and Gaza Strip*. Oxford University Press, 1992.

Polliack, Meira, and Athalya Brenner-Idan, eds. *Anchor Bible Dictionary*. Doubleday, 1992.

Pontifical Biblical Commission. *The Interpretation of the Bible in the Church.* St. Paul Books and Media, 1993. Available at vatican.va.

Pontifical Biblical Commission. *The Jewish People and Their Sacred Scriptures in the Christian Bible*. May 24, 2001. Available at vatican.va.

Posen, Rafael B. *The Consistency of Targum Onkelos' Translation.* Magnes, 2004. (Hebrew)

Posen, Rafael B. *Parshegen: Explanations, Commentaries, and Sources concerning Targum Onkelos: Exodus.* Parshegen Institute, 2015. (Hebrew)

Rabkin, Yakov M. *A Threat from Within: A Century of Jewish Opposition to Zionism*. Zed Books, 2006.

Ramírez Kidd, José E. *Alterity and Identity in Israel: The Ger in the Old Testament*. De Gruyter, 1999.

Rappel, Dov. *Targum Onkelos as a Commentary on the Torah.* Hakibbutz Hameuchad, 1985. (Hebrew)

Rastoin, Marc. "L'Etat d'Israël: Une question pour le Judaïsme." *Croire Aujourd'hui* 166 (2003): 12–14.

Rastoin, Marc. "Le sfide della Chiesa in Francia." *Civiltà Cattolica* 3999 (2017): 270–83.

Ratzinger, Joseph. *Many Religions, One Covenant: Israel, the Church and the World.* Ignatius, 1999.

Ratzinger, Joseph Cardinal. "Biblical Interpretation in Conflict: On the Foundations and Itinerary of Exegesis Today." Translated by Adrian Walker. In *Opening Up the Scriptures: Joseph Ratzinger and the Foundations of Biblical Interpretation*, edited by José Granados, Carlos Granados, and Luis Sánchez-Navarro. Eerdmans, 2008.

Ravid, Barak. *Trump's Peace: The Abraham Accords and the Shake-Up in the Middle East.* Yedioth Press, 2021. (Hebrew)

Ravitzky, Aviezer. *Freedom Inscribed: Diverse Voices of the Jewish Religious Thought*. Am Oved, 1999. (Hebrew)

Ravitzky, Aviezer. *Messianism, Zionism, and Jewish Religious Radicalism*. University of Chicago Press, 1996.

Ravitzky, Aviezer. "The Revealed End: Messianic Religious Zionism." Chapter 3 in *Messianism, Zionism, and Jewish Religious Radicalism*. Translated by Michael Swirsky and Jonathan Chipman. University of Chicago Press, 1996.

Riskin, Shlomo. "Religious Zionism Revisited: A Symposium." *Tradition* 28, no. 4 (1994): 30–33.

Rosen, David. "Israel-Vatican Relations since the Signing of the Fundamental Agreement." In Breger, *The Vatican-Israel Accords*.

Rosen, David. "Reflections on the Recent Orthodox Jewish Statements on Jewish-Catholic Relations." In *From Confrontation to Covenantal Partnership: Reflections on To Do the Will of Our Father in Heaven*, edited by Jehoschua Ahrens et al. Urim, 2020.

Rosenthal, Gilbert S. *What Can a Modern Jew Believe?* Wipf and Stock, 2007.

Rotberg, Robert I., ed. *Israeli and Palestinian Narratives of Conflict: History's Double Helix.* Indiana University Press, 2006.

Rutishauser, Christian M. "Land and State of Israel: Theological Reflections from a Roman Catholic Perspective." In D'Costa and Shapiro, *Contemporary Catholic Approaches*.

Ryrie, Charles C. *Dispensationalism*. Moody Publishers, 1995.

Safrai, Chana. "Abraham und Sara: Spender des Lebens." *Evangelische Theologie* 62, no. 5 (2002): 348–61.

Saks, Jeffrey. "Rabbi Soloveitchik Meets Rav Kook." *Tradition* 39, no. 3 (2006): 90–96.

Samet, Moshe. "Conversion in the First Centuries C.E." In *Jews and Judaism in the Second Temple, Mishnaic and Talmudic Period: Studies in Honor of Shmuel Safrai*, edited by Aharon Oppenheimer, Isaiah Gafni, and Menahem Stern. Yad Yitzhak Ben-Zvi, 1993.

Satlow, Michael L. *Creating Judaism: History, Tradition, Practice*. Columbia University Press, 2006.

Scholem, Gershom. "On Our Language: A Confession." *History and Memory* 2, no. 2 (1990): 97–99.

Schweid, Eliezer. *The Land of Israel: National Home or Land of Destiny*. Translated by Deborah Greniman. Fairleigh Dickinson University Press, 1985.

Second Vatican Council. *Dei Verbum*. Dogmatic Constitution on Divine Revelation. November 18, 1965.

Second Vatican Council. *Dignitatis Humanae*. Declaration on Religious Freedom. December 7, 1965.

Second Vatican Council. *Nostra Aetate*. Declaration on the Relation of the Church to Non-Christian Religions. October 28, 1965.

Shapira, Anita. "The Bible and Israeli Identity." *AJS Review* 28 (2004): 11–42.

Shavit, Yaacov, and Mordechai Eran. *The Hebrew Bible Reborn: From Holy Scripture to the Book of Books: A History of Biblical Culture and the Battles over the Bible in Modern Judaism*. Translated by Chaya Naor. De Gruyter, 2007.

Siegman, Rabbi Henry. "A Decade of Catholic-Jewish Relations—A Reassessment." *Journal of Ecumenical Studies* 15 (1978): 243–60.

Simon, Uriel. *Seek Peace and Pursue It*. Yediot Aharonot, 2002. (Hebrew)

Sokolowski, Robert. *Eucharistic Presence: A Study in the Theology of Disclosure*. The Catholic University of America Press, 1994.

Soloveitchik, Joseph B. "Confrontation." *Tradition* 6, no. 2 (1964): 5–28. Reprinted in *Bridges: Documents of the Christian-Jewish Dialogue. Vol.1, Road to Reconciliation (1945–85)*, edited by Franklin Sherman. Studies in Judaism and Christianity. Paulist Press, 2011.

Soloveitchik, Joseph B. *Kol Dodi Dofek: Listen—My Beloved Knocks*. Translated and annotated by David Z. Gordon, edited by Jeffrey R. Woolf. Yeshiva University, 2006.

Sonnet, Jean-Pierre. "Between Poetic Justice and Poetic Mercy: God in the Flood Narrative (Genesis 6–7)." *Nova et Vetera* (English edition) 18 (2020): 1247–65.

Sonnet, Jean-Pierre. "Les monologues divins dans le Pentateuque: Un Dieu shakespearien?" In *La Vita Benedetta*, edited by F. Ficco. GBP, 2018.

Soulen, R. Kendall. *The God of Israel and Christian Theology*. Fortress Press, 1996.

Strenger, Carlo. "The Simple Truth about the Occupation." *Haaretz*. October 29, 2015.

Taji-Farouki, Suha. "A Contemporary Construction of the Jews in the Qur'an: A review of Muhammad Sayyid Tantawi's *Banu Isra'il fi al-Qur'an wa al-Sunna* and Afif Abd al-Fattah *Tabbara's al-yahud fi al-Qur'an*." In *Muslim-Jewish Encounters: Intellectual Traditions and Modern Politics,* edited by Ronald L. Nettler and Suha Taji-Farouki. Harwood Academic Publishers, 1998.

Tal, Abraham. *The Samaritan Targum of the Pentateuch*. Tel-Aviv University, 1980–81. (Aramaic and Hebrew)

Talmudic Encyclopedia. Edited by Yosef Shlomo Zevin et al. 50+ vols. Talmudic Encyclopedia Institute, 1947–.

Taubes, Chaim Zwi. "Das Gemeinsame in Judentum, Christentum und Islam" [The common in Judaism, Christianity and Islam]. Religious Zionist Archives Jerusalem, Nachlass Taubes, 2–29–12, 1940.

Taubes, Chaim Zwi. *Lebendiges Judentum*. Midgal, 1946.

Thiessen, Matthew. "Revisiting the προσήλυτος in 'the LXX.'" *JBL* 132 (2013): 333–50.

Thomas Aquinas. *Summa Theologica*. Translated by Fathers of the English Dominican Province. 3 vols. Benziger, 1947–48.

Tilley, Maureen A., ed. *Donatist Martyr Stories: The Church in Conflict in Roman North-Africa*. Liverpool University Press, 1996.

Tobias, Norman C. *Jewish Conscience of the Church: Jules Isaac and the Second Vatican Council*. Palgrave, 2017.

Torat Haim. Edited by Mordechai Leib Katzenellenbogen. 7 vols. Mossad Harav Kook, 1986–93.

Trainor, Michael F., and J. Cornelis de Vos. "New Testament Perspectives on the Land." In Cunningham et al., *Enabling Dialogue about the Land*.

Vall, Gregory. "'Man is the Land': The Sacramentality of the Land of Israel." In *John Paul II and the Jewish People: A Jewish-Christian Dialogue*, edited by David G. Dalin and Matthew Levering. Rowman and Littlefield, 2008.

Venard, Olivier-Thomas, OP. "Les deux asymptotes de sense littéral des Écritures." In *Le sens littéral des Écritures*, edited by Olivier-Thomas Venard, OP. Éditions du Cerf, 2009.

Vetö, Etienne. "Land and Redemption: Why Does God Promise a Land?" In D'Costa and Shapiro, *Contemporary Catholic Approaches*.

Vollandt, Ronny. "Flawed Biblical Translations into Arabic and How to Correct Them: A Copt and a Jew Study Saadiah's *Tafsīr*." In *Studies on Arabic Christianity in Honor of Sidney H. Griffith*, edited by David Bertaina et al. Brill, 2018.

Vollandt, Ronny. "Sa'adia Gaon's Translation of the Torah and Its Coptic Readers." In *Jewish Biblical Exegesis from Islamic Lands: The Medieval Period*, edited by Meira Polliack and Athalya Brenner-Idan. SBL Press, 2019.

Waddell, Peter. Review of Naim Stifan Ateek, *A Palestinian Theology of Liberation: The Bible, Justice, and the Palestinian Conflict* in *Religion and Theology* 25, no. 4 (2018): 620–22.

Walatka, Todd. Review of Naim Stifan Ateek, *A Palestinian Theology of Liberation: The Bible, Justice, and the Palestinian Conflict*. *Studies in Christian-Jewish Relations* 14, no. 1 (2019): 1–3.

Walzer, Michael. *Exilpolitik in der Hebräischen Bibel*. Mohr Siebeck, 2001. (German-English)

Wansbrough, Henry, OSB. "'Can Catholicism Validate Jewish Biblical Interpretation?'– A Reply to Jon D. Levenson." *Studies in Christian-Jewish Relations* 2 (2007): 86–93.

Westcott, Brooke Foss. *The Gospel According to St. John*. John Murray, 1882.

White, Thomas Joseph. *Exodus*. Brazos, 2015.

White, Thomas Joseph. "The Right to Religious Freedom: Thomistic Principles of Nature and Grace." *Nova et Vetera* (English edition) 13, no. 4 (2015): 1149–85.

Wilken, Robert. *Liberty in the Things of God: The Christian Origins of Religious Freedom*. Yale University Press, 2019.

Williams, Rowan. *Faith in the Public Square*. Bloomsbury, 2015.

Williams, Rowan. "Holy Land and Holy People." In *Challenging Christian Zionism: Theology, Politics and the Israel-Palestine Conflict*, edited by Ateek Naim et al. Melisende, 2005.

Williams, Rowan. *On Christian Theology*. Wiley-Blackwell, 1999.

Williams, Rowan. *Open to Judgment*. Darton, Longman and Todd, 1996.

Winter, Tim. "America as a Jihad State: Middle Eastern Perceptions of Modern American Theopolitics." *The Muslim World* 101 (2011): 394–411.

Winter, Tim. "The Inception of *A Common Word*." *In The Future of Interfaith Dialogue: Muslim-Christian Encounters through A Common Word*, edited by Yazid Said and Lejla Demiri, 16–20. Cambridge University Press, 2018.

Wright, N. T. *The Resurrection of the Son of God*. Fortress Press, 2003.

Wright IV, William M. "*Dei Verbum*." In *The Reception of Vatican II*, edited by Matthew L. Lamb and Matthew Levering. Oxford University Press, 2017.

Wright IV, William M., and Francis Martin. *Encountering the Living God in Scripture: Theological and Philosophical Principles for Interpretation*. Baker Academic, 2019.

Wuench, Hans-Georg. "The Stranger in God's Land—Foreigner, Stranger, Guest: What Can We Learn from Israel's Attitude Towards Strangers?" *Old Testament Essays* 27, no. 3 (2014): 1129–54.

Würzburger, Walter, and R. J. Zvi Werblowsky. "Land, People and Nation in Jewish Perspective." In International Catholic-Jewish Liaison Committee, *Fifteen Years of Catholic-Jewish Dialogue 1970–1985: Selected Papers*, 3–8. Libreria Editrice Vaticana, 1988.

Wyschogrod, Michael. *Abraham's Promise: Judaism and Jewish-Christian Relations*. Edited by R. Kendall Soulen. SCM Press, 2006.

Wyschogrod, Michael. "Inkarnation aus jüdischer Sicht." *Evangelische Theologie* 55, no. 1 (1995): 13–28.

Yisraeli, Shaul. "The Gentile as Knesset Member and Municipal Member." *The Oral Torah* 16 (1974): 72–79. (Hebrew)

Yisraeli, Shaul. *The Right Pillar*. Moreshet, 1966. (Hebrew)

Zahalka, Iyad. *Shari'a in Modern Times: Muslim Minority Jurisprudence*. Resling, 2014. (Hebrew)

Zoldan, Yehuda. "The Appointment of Gentiles to Public Positions." *Tehumim* 21 (2003): 348–57. (Hebrew)

Zucker, Moshe. *On R. Saadia Gaon's Translation of the Torah*. Feldheim, 1959. (Hebrew)

Zucker, Moshe. *Saadya's Commentary on Genesis*. The Jewish Theological Seminary, 1984. (Judeo-Arabic and Hebrew)

SCRIPTURE INDEX

OLD TESTAMENT

NEW TESTAMENT

EXTRA-BIBLICAL REFERENCES

INDEX

A

O

P

R

S

CONTRIBUTORS

RABBI DR. JEHOSCHUA AHRENS

Rabbi Dr. Jehoschua Ahrens is Director Central Europe of the Center for Jewish-Christian Understanding in Jerusalem and a Research Fellow at the University of Salzburg. He studied for his BA at Bar-Ilan University, earned his Master's degree at Cambridge University and his PhD at the Institute of Jewish-Christian Research at the University of Lucerne. He is a federal board member of the German Coordinating-Council for Christian-Jewish cooperation organizations and of the Muslim Jewish Leadership Council of Europe. Rabbi Ahrens is one of the initiators and authors of the Orthodox Rabbinic Statement on Christianity "To Do the Will of Our Father in Heaven—Toward a Partnership between Jews and Christians".

PROF. GARY ANDERSON

Professor Gary Anderson is Hesburgh Professor of Catholic Thought, University of Notre Dame. He is interested in all dimensions of Biblical studies. His specialization is in the Hebrew Bible/Old Testament, but because of his interest in the history of interpretation, he also works in Second Temple Judaism and early Christian sources. Some notable publications: *Sin: A History.* New Haven, CT: Yale University Press, 2009. Best Book of the year in Biblical Studies, Christianity Today; *Charity: The Place of the Poor in the Biblical Tradition.* New Haven, CT: Yale University Press, 2013 - One of the best books in Religion of 2013, Religious News Service; Award of merit from Christianity Today; Finalist for the 2014 American Academy of Religion Awards for Excellence in the Study of Religion; *Christian Doctrine and the Old Testament: Theology in the Service of Biblical Exegesis.* Grand Rapids,

MI: Baker Academic, 2017 and *Creatio ex nihilo: Origins and Contemporary Significance*. Edited with Markus Bockmuehl. University of Notre Dame Press, 2017.

PROF. KARMA BEN-JOHANAN

Prof. Karma Ben-Johanan holds the chair in Jewish-Christian relations at the Faculty of Theology at Humboldt University Berlin. She studied history at Tel Aviv University, and held research and teaching positions at the University of California, Berkeley, The Gregorian University in Rome, and the Van Leer Jerusalem Institute. Her research focuses on institutionalized religions in the late-20th and early 21st century, Jewish-Christian polemic and dialogue, secularization, and political theology. Her book, *Jacob's Younger Brother: Christian-Jewish Relations After Vatican II*, was published in Hebrew in 2020 and won the Shazar Prize for Research in Jewish History. The English version was published in 2022 by Harvard University Press.

PROF. GAVIN D'COSTA

Prof. Gavin D'Costa is Emeritus Professor of Catholic Theology at the University of Bristol, UK and Invited Professor of Interreligious Dialogue at the Pontifical University of St. Thomas Aquinas, Rome. D'Costa was born in Kenya, and his parents are from India. He completed his doctorate at Cambridge University. He is author of eight books, most recently: *Vatican II: Catholic Doctrines on Jews and Muslims*, (OUP, 2014) and *Catholics and Jews After Vatican II* (OUP, 2019). His work has been translated into seven languages. D'Costa has also published a book of poetry. His interests are in dogmatics, theology of religions, specifically the relation of Catholicism to Jews and Muslims. He is an advisor to the Roman Catholic Bishops in England and Wales on matters related to other religions and has worked with the World Council of Churches and the PCID, Vatican City.

ARCHBISHOP BRUNO FORTE

Archbishop Bruno Forte was born in Naples. He studied at Tübingen University associated with Hans Küng, Joseph Ratzinger, and Walter Kasper. He also spent time in Paris, before gaining a Laurea degree in philosophy from Naples University. In 2000, he oversaw the preparation of the Vatican document, "Memory and Reconciliation: The Church and the Faults of the Past," which led to the famous liturgy in St Peter's Basilica in which John Paul II asked God's forgiveness for 2,000 years of sins. He was appointed as Archbishop of Chieti-Vasto by Pope John Paul II on 26 June 2004. Since 2019 he is consultor for the Commission for Religious Relations with the Jews. He teaches Dogmatic theology at the Pontificia Facoltà Teologica dell'Italia Meridionale (Papal Theological Seminary of Southern Italy).

RABBI DR. EUGENE KORN

Rabbi Dr. Eugene Korn is an ordained Orthodox rabbi who holds a doctorate in moral philosophy from Columbia University. He is the former Academic Director of The Center for Jewish-Christian Understanding and Cooperation in Israel, which he helped found, and National Director of Interfaith Affairs at the Anti-Defamation League. Dr. Korn's primary interests are Jewish ethics, theology, and Jewish-Christian relations. He has taught at Seton Hall, Yeshiva and Columbia Universities. Rabbi Korn's most recent books are *Israel and the Nations: The Bible, The Rabbis and Jewish-Gentile Relations* (2023) and *A Holy People: Jewish Tradition and Ethical Values* (2021). He has co-edited and contributed to seven books, including *From Confrontation to Covenantal Partnership; Jewish Theology and World Religions*; *Returning to Zion: Christian and Jewish Perspectives; Plowshares into Swords?*; *Covenant and Hope;* and *Two Faiths, One Covenant?* He is also the author of the popular volume, *The Jewish Connection to the Land of Israel—An Introduction for Christians*. Dr. Korn's writings have been translated into Hebrew, Italian, Spanish, and German. He lives in Jerusalem with his wife, Lila Magnus Korn. They are blessed with three children and seven grandchildren.

RABBI PROF. DAVID MEYER

Rabbi Prof. David Meyer was born in Paris in 1967. He is an ordained Rabbi from the Leo Baeck College, rabbinic seminary in London. After finishing his degree in Applied Mathematics at the University of Paris IX, he obtained a Master's degree from the École des Hautes Études en Sciences Sociales in Paris and later a Master's degree in Hebrew and Jewish Studies with Distinction. He holds a PhD in Religious Studies from Katholieke Universiteit Leuven (KUL) in Leuven, Belgium. Rabbi Meyer is currently a lecturer at the Cardinal Bea Centre for Judaic Studies at the Gregorian Pontifical University in Rome where he teaches Classical Rabbinic Literature and Contemporary

Jewish Thought. Rabbi Meyer teaches in various universities and countries around the world from Belgium to Peru to China. Over the years, he has published numerous books in French, English, and Portuguese, on rabbinic and interreligious topics, including *Lutter contre la violence monothéiste* (2018); *Europe et Israël, deux destins inaccomplis* (2017); *Painful Verses : Bible, Gospel and Quran Between Conflict and Dialogue* (2014); *La Vocation de la terre sainte* (2014); *A vida fora da lei* (2012); *Croyances rebelles* (2011); *Le Minimum humain* (2010); *La Vie hors la loi* (2008); *Les Versets douloureux* (2008).

DR. YONATAN MOSS

Dr. Yonatan Moss (Ph.D. Yale University, 2013), holds the Leeds Senior Lectureship in Comparative Religion and serves as the Director of the Center for the Study of Christianity at the Hebrew University of Jerusalem. He works on the histories and comparative study of the Abrahamic religions, and on the relations between them. He is the author of *Incorruptible Bodies: Christology, Society and Authority in Late Antiquity* (University of California Press, 2016), and a wide range of articles on the Abrahamic religions in the Mediterranean basin (and beyond) during the first millennium (and beyond).

RABBI PROF. DAVID NOVAK

Rabbi Professor David Novak is an ordained rabbi and holds the J. Richard and Dorothy Shiff Chair of Jewish Studies as Professor of the Study of Religion and Professor of Philosophy at the University of Toronto since 1997. His areas of interest are Jewish theology, Jewish ethics and biomedical ethics, political theory (with a special emphasis on natural law), and Jewish-Christian relations. Novak has authored 19 books and more than 200 articles in scholarly journals. His book *Covenantal Rights: A Study in Jewish Political Theory* (Princeton University Press, 2000) won the American Academy of Religion Award for "best book in constructive religious thought" in 2000. He is a regular contributor to the ABC News's *Religion and Ethics* portal. He frequently addresses interfaith conferences and contributes to books and journals published by Christian theologians.

FR. PROF. MARC RASTOIN, SJ

Fr. Prof. Marc Rastoin, SJ is a Jesuit, doctor of biblical Theology, member of the ACFEB, graduate of the Institut d'Études politique in Paris, Professor of Sacred Scripture at the Centre Sèvres-Facultés jésuites in Paris and at the Pontifical Biblical Institute in Rome (Biblicum). He is author of several books, including *Tarse et Jérusalem : La double culture de l'apôtre Paul en Ga 3,6-4,7* (GBP, 2003) and *Du même sang que Notre Seigneur: Juifs et jésuites aux débuts de la Compagnie* (Bayard, 2011). His interests are in Pauline studies, Historical Jesus, Luke's theology, History of Judaism and Jewish tradition. He is Advisor for Judaism for the Superior General of the Society of Jesus.

RABBI DAVID ROSEN KSG, CBE

Rabbi David Rosen KSG, CBE, former Chief Rabbi of Ireland, is the Jerusalem based International Director of Interreligious Affairs of the American Jewish Committee. He is a member of the Chief Rabbinate of Israel's Committee for Interreligious Dialogue and is an International President of the World Conference on Religion and Peace, Honorary President of the International Council of Christians and Jews, and the only Jewish member of the Board of Directors of the King Abdullah International Center for Interreligious and Intercultural Dialogue established in 2012 by the King of Saudi Arabia together with the governments of Austria and Spain and the Holy See. He served twice as chair of the International Jewish Committee for Interreligious Consultations (IJCIC, which represents world Jewry to other world religious bodies.) In 2005, Pope Benedict XVI bestowed upon Rabbi Rosen a Papal Knighthood in recognition of his contribution to promoting Catholic-Jewish reconciliation and in 2010 he was awarded a CBE (Commander of the British Empire) by Queen Elizabeth II for his interfaith work.

REV. DR. YAZID SAID

Rev. Dr. Yazid Said is Lecturer in Islam at Liverpool Hope University and a priest in the Church of England. He is a Palestinian-born Israeli citizen. He studied Classical Arabic and English Literature at the Hebrew University in Jerusalem, and Christian theology at the University of Cambridge. He completed his PhD at Cambridge on the medieval Muslim theologian Abu Hamid al-Ghazali in 2010. He is the author of *Ghazali's Politics in Context*

(Routledge 2012) and co-editor of *The Future of Interfaith Dialogue: Muslim-Christian Encounters Through A Common Word* (Cambridge, 2018).

JOSEPH SIEVERS

Joseph Sievers, born and raised in Germany, began his studies at the University of Vienna and the Hebrew University in Jerusalem. He holds a Ph.D. in Ancient History from Columbia University (1981) and a Lic. Theol. from the Pontifical Gregorian University (1997). He has taught at CUNY, Seton Hall Universiy, Fordham University, and other institutions in the U.S., Italy, and Israel. From 1991 until his retirement in 2023 he taught Jewish history and literature of the Hellenistic period at the Pontifical Biblical Institute in Rome, where he was a Full Professor. In addition, from 2003 to 2009 he served as Director of the Cardinal Bea Centre for Judaic Studies at the Pontifical Gregorian University. Since October 28, 1965, he is a member of the Focolare Movement, with whose Center for Interreligious Dialogue he collaborates since 2002. He has published several books and numerous articles, primarily in the areas of Second Temple History (especially Flavius Josephus) and Christian-Jewish relations. With Amy-Jill Levine, he edited The Pharisees (Grand Rapids, MI: Eerdmans, 2021; Italian translation Milan: San Paolo, 2021; German translation Freiburg i. Br.: Herder, 2024).

BISHOP ETIENNE VETÖ

Bishop Etienne Vetö is a Franco-American Catholic Priest of the Chemin Neuf Community. He is Professor of Theology at the Pontifical Gregorian University and Director of the "Cardinal Bea Centre for Judaic Studies" of the same university. He is consulter of the Vatican "Commission for Religious Relations with the Jews" (Dicastery for the Promotion of Christian Unity) and member of the International Theological Commission. His last book was *The Breath of God: An Essay on the Holy Spirit in the Trinity* (Cascade, 2019).

TEHILA WENGER

Tehila Wenger is the Deputy Director of the Geneva Initiative in Israel, an NGO that promotes a peace agreement between Israelis and Palestinians through diplomatic, educational, and public tools. She holds a BA in Politics from Princeton University and an MA in Diplomatic Studies from Tel Aviv

University. Originally from Ohio, Tehila moved to Tel Aviv in 2015 as a Dorot Fellow. During the fellowship program, she organized and participated in seminars about minority rights in Israel, the Israeli-Palestinian conflict, and Jewish history and identity. She also volunteered at the Arous Albaher women's empowerment center in Jaffa and with the Tag Meir Forum, which combats racism and hate in Israeli society. Her work at the Geneva Initiative includes organizing and facilitating joint dialogue forums for influencers, advocacy and outreach with Israeli decision-makers and international stakeholders, and coordinating research projects on the topics of reconciliation, Jerusalem, and the two-state solution.

FR. THOMAS JOSEPH WHITE, OP

Fr. Thomas Joseph White, OP is the *Rector Magnificus* of the Pontifical University of St. Thomas (Angelicum) in Rome. He is the author of various books and articles including *Wisdom in the Face of Modernity: A Study in Thomistic Natural Theology* (Sapientia Press, 2011), *The Incarnate Lord, A Thomistic Study in Christology* (The Catholic University of America Press, 2015) *Exodus* (Brazos Press, 2016), *The Light of Christ: An Introduction to Catholicism* (The Catholic University Press of America, 2017), and *The Trinity: On the Nature and Mystery of the One God* (The Catholic University Press of America, 2022). He is co-editor of the journal *Nova et Vetera*, a Distinguished Scholar of the McDonald Agape Foundation, and a member of the Pontifical Academy of St. Thomas Aquinas.

PROF. JUDITH WOLFE

Prof. Judith Wolfe is Professor of Philosophical Theology at the University of St Andrews, Scotland. Austrian and Israeli by birth, she has lived and worked in Vienna, Milwaukee, Jaffa, Jerusalem, Oxford, Berlin, and St Andrews. Her research is in systematic & philosophical theology and theology & the arts, with a special interest in eschatology and apocalyptic. She is also actively involved in discussions of questions surrounding Jewish Christianity.

DR. WILLIAM M. WRIGHT IV

Dr. William M. Wright IV is a Professor of Catholic Studies and Theology at Duquesne University and a specialist in New Testament studies. He is the author of several books, including *The Lord's Prayer: Matthew 6 and Luke 11 for the Life of the Church* (Baker Academic, 2023) and (with Francis Martin) *The Gospel of John* (Baker Academic, 2015) and *Encountering the Living God in Scripture: Theological and Philosophical Principles for Interpretation* (Baker Academic, 2019). He has been elected to the *Studiorum Novi Testamenti Societas* and the Academy of Catholic Theology.

ALSO IN
JUDAISM AND CATHOLIC THEOLOGY

The Mortara Case and Thomas Aquinas's Defense of Jewish Parental Authority
with Original Documents from the Mortara Case:
Pro-memoria, Syllabus, Brevi cenni
by Matthew Tapie

Contemporary Catholic Approaches to the People, Land, and State of Israel
Edited by Gavin D'Costa and Faydra L. Shapiro
Preface by H. B. Pierbattista Pizzaballa

The Challenge of Catholic-Jewish Theological Dialogue
Edited by Alan Brill, Matthew Levering, and Matthew Tapie